GERMAN ARCHITECTURE
AND THE CLASSICAL IDEAL

David Watkin · Tilman Mellinghoff

GERMAN ARCHITECTURE
AND THE CLASSICAL IDEAL

THE MIT PRESS
CAMBRIDGE, MASSACHUSETTS

1 *Frontispiece* Klenze's original design of 1818 for the Odeonsplatz, Munich, with a military memorial flanked by the Leuchtenberg Palais on the right and the Odeon on the left. See p. 148.

First MIT Press edition, 1987

Library of Congress Cataloging-in-Publication Data

Watkin, David, 1941-

German architecture and the classical ideal

  Bibliography: p.
  Includes index.
  1. Neoclassicism (Architecture)--Germany.
2. Architecture, Modern--17th-18th centuries--Germany.
3. Architecture, Modern--19th century--Germany.
4. Architecture--Germany. I. Mellinghoff, Tilman. II. Title.
NA1066.5.N46W38 1986 720'.943 86-2840
ISBN 0-262-23125-5

Printed and bound in Spain by Artes Graficas Toledo S.A.
D.L.: TO-1660-86

Contents

Prefatory note

THE territory covered in this book is that of modern Germany, both east and west, since the Second World War. Any choice must necessarily be arbitrary since Germany as a country did not exist in the period from 1740 to 1840. It at least seems logical to exclude Austria and the former Hapsburg territories since in some ways they formed even in the eighteenth century an architecturally and culturally separate unit. It is also not easy to be logical in the use of English and German names. The pattern adopted with towns and cities is to use the German name except in the following cases which all have established English names: Brunswick, Cologne, Hanover and Munich. Similarly, proper names have been left in German with the exception of Frederick the Great. However, king, prince, duke, count and their feminine counterparts have been rendered in English, while lesser nobility and official titles have been left in German with translations in brackets where necessary. Platz (square), Strasse (street), Schloss (castle), and Residenz (palace which is the seat of a court) are also left in German.

PART ONE

History, Patronage and Style

CHAPTER I

The German Reality:
the historical, political and cultural background

IT is important to realize that, despite the title of this book, there was no such country or nation as Germany in the period which it covers. Nationalism on the continent of Europe is essentially a doctrine invented at the start of the nineteenth century and, according to one view, has been responsible for untold harm during its spread to all parts of the world. The German-speaking parts of Europe in the eighteenth century enjoyed diverse political systems and the fact that Prussians, Bavarians, Bohemians and Silesians all spoke German did not seem sufficient justification for their regarding themselves as a single nation. Nonetheless, the evolution of classicism in the German-speaking countries coincided with one of the most decisive chapters in the history of those countries. This was a period of vital political change which led from the enlightened absolutism of the eighteenth century to the parliamentarianism and liberalism of the nineteenth. These twin poles are typified by the enlightened despot, Frederick the Great (1712–86), at the beginning of the period, and the burgher-king, Friedrich Wilhelm IV (1795–1861) at the end. The period witnessed the birth of nationalism in Prussia which gradually and painstakingly transformed a conglomeration of territories and principalities into a uniform nation and, from 1871, into the new German empire. German literature and music, accompanied by intense philosophical speculation, rose to a new height in what must be an unparalleled cultural achievement. The emphasis on personal self-determination in the philosophy of Immanuel Kant (1724–1804) encouraged the move to national self-determination in the work of philosophers such as Johann Gottlieb Fichte (1762–1815). However, in terms of establishing itself as a nation, Germany was, for better or worse, far behind Britain and France. It was also these two countries which, as we shall see, conditioned German Neo-classicism.

The story of French influence begins with the Huguenots who left France after the revocation of the Edict of Nantes in 1685. One such was the Baroque architect Jean de Bodt (1670–1745) who settled in Berlin in 1698 and in Dresden in 1728. The architect Robert de Cotte (1656–1735) became famous beyond France for his châteaux inspired by the work of J.H. Mansart and of Le Vau at Versailles and elsewhere. Though he never left France, he produced plans for palaces at Schleissheim, Bonn, Poppelsdorf, Frankfurt, and Strasbourg. Some of this architectural efflorescence was connected with the return from exile of German rulers who had fought on the French side in the War of the Spanish Succession (1701–13). Among the most important of these was Max Emanuel of Bavaria who from 1708 employed the brilliant designer François de Cuvilliés (1695–1768) to create a series of Late Rococo interiors in the Residenz at Munich, the Amalienburg Pavilion at Schloss Nymphenburg, and Schloss Brühl and Falkenlust near Cologne.

Germany in the mid-eighteenth century was a colourful assembly of over three hundred states or political units which were combined till 1806 in the Holy Roman Empire. Some of these were powerful European states, others little more than a Schloss and a few villages. About a third of these were ruled by imperial counts or knights; ninety-four by abbots, dukes, margraves or landgraves; fifty-one were self-governing free cities; forty were ruled by prince-bishops, archbishops or bishops; and eight by Electors. The force of a unifying centre was missing and travelling was a crippling experience. For German travellers in England, such as the Berlin pastor Carl Philipp Moritz in 1782, it came as a surprise that 'no stern examiner comes here to search and inspect us, or our luggage, no imperious guard demands a sight of our passport; perfectly free and unmolested we here walk'. German towns, by contrast, were encircled by walls and only entered through gates and toll-houses, guarded by sentries. Indeed, gates and toll-houses became a characteristic building type for the expression of Neo-classical ideals in Germany. The existence of Baroque ramparts was also an historically conditioning factor, for German Neo-classical town-planners responded imaginatively to the challenge of turning the zig-zag lines of the fortifications into picturesque Elysian fields surrounding the towns as a green belt. These green areas, mostly created from around 1800, still help define the original size of the eighteenth-century towns and thus indicate their vast expansion in the nineteenth century. Good examples survive at Brunswick, Bremen, Cologne, Düsseldorf, and Oldenburg. Most of these are in the north of Germany and were originally free towns belonging to that most famous medieval trading circle, the Hanse.

A more permanent north/south division was left by the Thirty Years War in the seventeenth century, with the north largely Protestant, and the south largely Catholic. The main Protestant states were Prussia, Saxony, the Thuringian duchies, Hesse-Darmstadt, Hanover, Mecklenburg and Brunswick. The principal Catholic states were Austria, Bavaria-Palatinate, two-thirds of Baden and half of Württemberg, while there were further Catholic states in Franconia and the Rhineland. Though in terms of the production of palace architecture these religious differences were not of great significance, they had considerable impact on the design of churches in the feudal eighteenth century. Thus Catholic churches in the Protestant north, for example at Oldenburg, Frankfurt and Kassel, lacked spires and were disguised as stately houses, while in the Catholic south Protestant churches, as at Mannheim and Stuttgart, were simply *Betsäle* (preaching halls).

Far more serious were the social and intellectual divisions caused by the religious split. With the striking exception of the liberal reforming rule of Joseph II in Austria from 1765 to 1790, the Catholic states were traditionalist and feudal in character, the Protestant states quick to adopt the reformist and progressivist ideals of the *Aufklärung* (Enlightenment). The best example of the latter is Prussia which rose from a provincial status to national leadership. Under Friedrich Wilhelm I (1688–1740), king of Prussia from 1713, strict absolutism went hand in hand with the pietism which had developed in the Lutheran church in the seventeenth century. The king, who wore nothing but uniform, is said to have declared of his subjects, 'Their soul is God's but everything else is mine'. Discipline, order and severity, tempered by piety, became the guiding principles of life in the Prussian state. The imposition of this authoritarian rule was helped by the extensive army of eighty thousand soldiers for two and a half million inhabitants, and by the newly founded civil service. It was Friedrich Wilhelm I, the soldier king, who did much to create an outlook which not only led to the rise to power of Prussia but also conditioned the severity of the Franco-Prussian style in late eighteenth-century Prussian architecture.

Different in character yet of the same stock, Friedrich Wilhelm's son Frederick the Great (1712–86), king of Prussia from 1740, continued his father's reforms and maintained the division of the social classes in which the army and the civil service were run by the aristocracy, while trade and industry remained the domain of the middle classes. However, Frederick the Great did not consider himself as an absolute monarch but the first civil servant of his state. Author of the *Anti-Machiavel* (1739), he was the archetype of the paternalistic ruler which survived well into the nineteenth century in Germany. An English visitor to Prussia in 1825 during the reign of Friedrich Wilhelm III wrote with surprise that

> the predominating influence of the aristocracy ... still exists as to its power of excluding all other classes which have gradually risen to be worthy of a more efficient voice. ... The system is bad in theory ... [yet] in practice it is not productive of real oppression because, from the personal character of the monarch, he is as anxious to promote the happiness of his kingdom as of his own family. ... But ... a king with a less estimable heart and no better a head ... could do infinite mischief.

Frederick the Great replaced military rule in Prussia by a process of law and order which was strictly controlled by a devoted civil service. He also widely expanded the realm, built up a network of roads and canals to improve transport, colonized provinces in the east, and created the first building department out of which grew Schinkel's Ober-Bau-Deputation. An English traveller entering Prussia in 1799 via Hanover and Brunswick immediately noted that 'The gradual improvement of the country is visible to the most careless observer. Roads, plantations, neat cottages, pleasant country estates, well built towns and good inns, take the place of the appearance of poverty and depopulation'.

Other states produced less coherent architectural results. Friedrich II of Kassel (reigned 1760–85), a great nephew of Frederick the Great, also saw himself as a 'prince philosophe', for example in his *Pensées diverses sur les princes* (1760). Together with his court architect Simon Louis du Ry (1726–99), he transformed Kassel and initiated what has been hailed as Germany's first Neo-classical building, the Museum Fridericianum. A founder of academies and a reformer, he also fostered the industries of his country. However, the impact of his idealistic aims was limited by a less dynamic personality than Frederick the Great's as well as lesser financial resources. His attempts to raise money by selling his soldiers to fight on the English side in the North American war revealed his continuing support for the old-fashioned system of mercenaries which is surprising in view of his commitment to Enlightenment ideals.

Karl Friedrich of Baden transformed his dominion into a *Musterländle* (a model little state), yet in terms of architecture little was achieved, and the projects for the market square of the 1760s and 70s were not realized till the 1820s. In fact most of these courts, for example those at Weimar, Mannheim and Darmstadt, were less important architecturally than as general cultural centres lending support to the arts and sciences. Taste at the court of Grand Duke Karl August of Saxe-Weimar (1757–1828) was directed by Goethe himself, while the Elector Karl Theodor (1743–99) founded an Academy of Science at Mannheim in 1763. His court became famous for its encouragement of music and for the establishment of a National Theatre in which Schiller's *Die Räuber* was first performed. At Darmstadt the charming Landgravine Karoline maintained close contacts with the major figures of her time, including Goethe, Herder, Wieland, Klopstock, and Frederick the Great. Even the despotic Duke Karl Eugen (1744–93) sometimes pursued enlightened ideals and founded the Karlsschule at Stuttgart. It was in this school that Schiller, a leading figure in the Enlightenment, was educated. However, his egalitarian ideals led him to despise it as the creation of an absolutist duke. Ironically, many of the new liberal thinkers were protected by the courts they affected to condemn. Just as Marie-Antoinette could perversely enjoy *The Marriage of Figaro* with its revolutionary social sentiments, so the German courts, though still modelled on Versailles, were capable of supporting revolutionary ideas. Sponsored by the ducal court at Brunswick, the writer Gotthold Lessing (1729–81) fought against the dominance of French drama in Germany and sought to establish a German literature. At the same time Justus Möser (1720–94), the writer, philosopher and politician, pointed towards the Germanic and Teutonic past, while Friedrich Gottlieb Klopstock (1724–1803) also fostered patriotism in his *Messiah*. German intellectuals discovered their own spiritual identity in the ideals of the Enlightenment and established a culture of their own. In doing so they prepared the intellectual ground for an avant-garde Neo-classical architecture at a time when Germany was still relying heavily on imported French architects working in a Louis XVI style, although French influence in north Germany was tempered by the impact of English Palladianism. An indigenous German Baroque coexisted with both these trends so as to create a disparate picture which has no equal in France or England. The rise of Prussian architects such as Gentz and Gilly in the 1790s must be seen as a reaction against this cultural background. Classicism was for them not the adoption of a style but a means to create a language of their own, a national style. Though Gilly noted 'Athens is the Model. Acropolis' on a preliminary sketch for his Monument to Frederick the Great of 1797, he considered 'dignity and utter simplicity' to be his real guiding principles. This approach remained valid for Klenze in his designs for the Walhalla (1814–42) when he insisted that 'nothing is more important, nothing more advisable than to capture the hellenistic idea and to continue in its noble notion, and nothing is more objectionable than rigid unconditional copying'.

While the search for national identity was one of the mainsprings of German Neo-classicism, the *Sturm und Drang* movement of 1760–80 and the establishment of the *jardin anglais* also played important parts. Both incorporated the validity of Greek architecture as the ideal of freedom, truth and humanity; both were based on the discovery of truth through sensibility. In the Picturesque landscaped garden Goethe saw the approach of a 'Golden Age', in which the humanist ideals of the Greeks would be symbolized in temples and classical structures. While paying tribute to the classical ideal, the *Sturm und Drang* movement as well as the ensuing Romantic movement, transformed nationalist sentiment into a political plea. Goethe's *Götz von Berlichingen*, Schiller's *Jungfrau von Orleans* and *Wilhelm Tell*, and later Kleist's *Hermannsschlacht*, were passionate calls for national liberation: 'To be one people is the religion of our time,' wrote Ernst Moritz Arndt (1769–1860). As early as the 1780s this mood had sparked off the project for a monument to Frederick the Great as a national manifesto. There was vehement debate as to whether Frederick should be dressed in a classical or Teutonic manner. The same nationalist Romanticism lay behind Schinkel's designs for a Neo-Gothic National Cathedral in 1815 and the completion of Cologne Cathedral from 1842.

The humiliating Napoleonic occupation of Berlin from 1806 to 1813 was another decisive influence on the development of German nationalism. In 1792 Austria and Prussia had declared war on France but by 1795 Prussia was exhausted and sued for a separate peace. Thus, as a result of the Treaty of Basel (1795), north Germany was neutralized and Prussia conceded the French occupation of Prussian territories on the west bank of the Rhine. This provided ten years of peace but, following the renewed outbreak of war between England and France, in 1803, Napoleon sent troops into Hanover. The Treaty of Paris, which Friedrich Wilhelm III of Prussia signed in February 1806, agreed to the French occupation of Hanover. The rupture between Prussia and England to which this led caused such damage to Prussia's maritime trade and commercial prosperity, that the king issued a manifesto on 9 October 1806 demanding the withdrawal of French troops from Prussian frontiers. This led to Prussia's shattering defeats at Jena and Auerstädt, to Napoleon's entry into Berlin on 27 October 1806, and to the flight of the Prussian royal family to Königsberg.

The impact of Napoleon varied in the different parts of Germany, again more or less following a north/south division. Among the most significant alterations Napoleon imposed on the Holy Roman Empire was his policy of mediatization. This removed the emperor as the immediate overlord of a number of small German states and subjected them directly to one of the princes in southern Germany whose power the French attempted to consolidate as a counterpoise to that of Prussia. In southern Germany Napoleon secured the active cooperation of Bavaria, Baden and Württemberg in 1805. Their Electors were all made completely sovereign though, of course, they were tied to Napoleon's throne and to military alliance with him. This led to the curious circumstance of Germans fighting on both sides in the Battle of Leipzig in October 1813: while Prussia was fighting with the allies against Napoleon, Bavaria, Baden, Württemberg and Hesse-Darmstadt provided contingents for the French side. Napoleon placed his relatives on thrones in Naples, Italy, Spain and Holland, and created the German Grand Duchy of Berg on the east bank of the Lower Rhine for his brother-in-law, Joachim Murat. Napoleon's step-son, Eugène de Beauharnais, viceroy of Italy, married the daughter of the new king of Bavaria; his cousin, Stéphanie de Beauharnais, married Karl of Baden, heir presumptive to the throne of Baden; his brother Jérôme married a Württemberg princess and was created king of Westphalia.

In 1806 Napoleon established the Rhenish Confederation of sixteen states in the west and south of Germany. In addition to Bavaria, Württemberg, Baden, Hesse-Darmstadt, Nassau and Berg, this included ten small non-mediatized counts or princes. Their secession from the Holy Roman Empire in 1806 spelt the death of that august institution. The members of the Rhenish Confederation were despised by the Prussian minister Stein as *Zaunkönige* (i.e. wrens, but translated literally, 'kings on the fence'). Their willing association with Napoleonic grandeur and with the idea of a new Roman empire resulted in a rich flowering of the Empire Style of Percier and Fontaine which was as extensive as anything in France. Fabulous examples survive, or have recently been restored, in the south of Germany, for example the Toskanazimmer in the Würzburg Residenz, rooms in the new corps de logis in the Schloss at Ludwigsburg near Stuttgart, interiors in the Munich Residenz and Schloss Fasanerie, near Fulda.

The reasons for the alliance of southern Germany with Napoleon included the weakness of German national sentiment in the south and the already existing sympathy for the reforming spirit of Joseph II of Austria. Moreover, the 'middle states' which Napoleon created in 1803–6 cleverly corresponded to existing territories with legitimate dynasties. The desire to embellish the capitals of the newly created kingdoms and duchies resulted in extensive town-planning schemes, for example by Weinbrenner in Karlsruhe, Moller in Darmstadt, Thouret in Stuttgart and, above all, Fischer, Klenze and Gärtner in Munich. In terms of administration the reorganization of the old systems of the Holy Roman Empire was the most important impact of Napoleon in southern Germany. Thus in Baden the *code civil* was adopted and peasants were freed, though the separation of education from the church led to the confiscation by statesmen of monastic property. In Munich the Bavarian minister Maximilian von Montgelas, who governed from 1799 to 1818, was a child of the French Enlightenment and the son of a French aristocrat from Savoy. He believed that his reforms must be carried out by north Germans and so brought Hegel to the Gymnasium at Nuremberg in 1806, Jacoby and Thiersch to the Academy in Munich, and Schelling to Würzburg. He thus ended the traditional cultural isolation of Bavaria and the bishoprics on the Main.

It was in the Rhineland that the Napoleonic experiment enjoyed its greatest degree of success and of long-term influence. For almost twenty years the west bank of the Rhine, including Cologne, Bonn, Speyer and Trier, was ruled directly by France in seven departments in which the *code civil* was introduced and feudal privileges abolished. Elsewhere, especially further north, the tale was a different one. The Napoleonic kingdom of Westphalia was clumsily carved out of Hanover, Brunswick, electoral Hesse and the Prussian territories west of the Elbe. With its centralized political administration and its egalitarian social order, Westphalia was a piece of Napoleonic France transported to north-west Germany. The administrative reforms failed to find much local support and the monarch, Jérôme, was not much loved. He retreated to Wilhelmshöhe, now renamed Napoleonshöhe, where he commissioned Klenze to design a court theatre, which had rather dull exteriors. More attractive were the Empire Style interiors he created at Wilhelmshöhe and nearby Kassel, extremely rare examples of this style in north Germany. The French occupation successively interrupted major town expansions, first in Koblenz and then in Brunswick, which had just been started, ironically from designs by the same architect, Peter Joseph Krahe (1758–1840). In Berlin, too, architects were put out of work so that Schinkel, for example, turned to painting in 1806.

Although she paid dearly for her opposition to Napoleon in the short run, Prussia eventually benefited by the French occupation for it helped to stir up nationalist pride more completely than elsewhere in Germany. This gave her, for better or worse, the impetus to turn herself from a humiliated state into a leading nation. Concentrating their attention on building Prussia up as a coherent and independent state, the politicians Stein, Hardenberg, Scharnhorst and Gneisenau started a reform movement with the motto 'the Revolution has to come from the top'. The leading figure was Heinrich Friedrich Karl Freiherr von und zum Stein. Born in 1757 in Nassau, not as a Prussian but a knight of the Holy Roman Empire, Stein therefore felt responsible only to the emperor. Although a devout Prussian civil servant, he declared, 'I only have one fatherland and that is Germany.' After a short period of disfavour with Friedrich Wilhelm III of Prussia during which he drew up his plans for change, he put his reforms into practice in 1807–08. He first freed the peasants and then abolished the restrictions of the classes so as to enable everyone to have a free choice of profession as well as the right to acquire land. Towns were given autonomous powers to levy taxes and to maintain law and order. The country itself was divided into three provinces with administrative subdivisions and rural districts, while government offices were also reorganized. The existing Ober-Bau-Department was also reformed and renamed as the Technische Ober-Bau-Deputation. The Berlin department was now divided into five divisions with one Baudirektor in each province who controlled the Landbaumeister (responsible for works in the country), and the Bauinspektor (responsible for town works). While four of the Berlin divisions were mainly concerned with technical works, the fifth division was responsible for the aesthetic supervision of plans for new public buildings and for a variety of functional buildings, as well as for the care of historic buildings. From 1810 this important division was run by Schinkel to whom every project costing over 500 Thaler had to be submitted for planning permission. Although the Ober-Bau-Deputation had considerable power, the system was a democratic one. Thus some of his suggestions for improvements, for example to buildings in Bonn, Aachen and Düsseldorf, were successfully resisted.

Not only was the administrative system of Prussia made more efficient, but education was also reorganized. The political writer and statesman Wilhelm von Humboldt (1767–1835), a supporter of Schinkel, played a leading role in the development of the new education system and thus in the creation of the new Prussia. Deeply rooted in the neo-humanism of late-eighteenth-century German thought, Humboldt was a Brandenburg Junker who had lived, as a close friend of Schiller and Goethe, in Jena and Rome, devoting his time to the cultivation of his personality. From March 1809 to June 1810 he directed the education policies of Prussia, creating the forms which were to survive in Germany until 1933. He made the state the sole authority for education, which was available to all classes. The Gymnasium was founded on the ideals of Winckelmann, Rousseau, Pestalozzi and Humboldt's own humanism. In it a pupil followed a ten-year programme from the age of about nine, covering Greek, Latin, German and mathematics. Religion was not emphasized. Instead attention was concentrated on the cultural significance of Greece and of the German past, which was interpreted by Romantics as an inspiring synthesis of Germanic and Christian elements symbolizing the Teutonic contribution to world history. This philosophical idealism – which was taught from *c*.1800 at the University of Saxony-Weimar in Jena by Hegel, Schelling, Schiller and Fichte – was brought to Berlin by Humboldt, who founded the university there in July 1809. Hegel himself came to Berlin from Heidelberg in 1817. His philosophical aim was mastery of the universe through speculative reason. In this process history was for him what nature had been for Goethe – the manifestation of the reality of the spirit. The rights of the individual were of lesser consequence than the sovereignty of the state and it can be argued that his rejection of the concept of natural law had as much impact as the French Revolution itself.

Prussia's rise to dominance began after the final defeat of Napoleon. Castlereagh wanted Prussia to assume sentry duties along the Rhine, an idea which went back to the younger Pitt. This involved giving her the left bank of the Rhine in addition to her restored Westphalian possessions on the right bank. Although Prussia did not want mastery over the major part of the Rhineland and the direct contact with the French that this would involve, she was nevertheless transplanted against her will to the Rhineland in a move which separated her from her eastern provinces by Hanover and Hesse-Kassel. Simultaneously ceding most of her Polish provinces to Russia, she became a fundamentally German state to a greater extent than if she had been allowed to annexe all of Saxony instead of merely the northern half. Her extensive stake in widely separated parts of north Germany created problems in the field of defence and economics, the solution of which encouraged her to take an ever more active part in pan-German affairs.

After the Congress of Vienna of 1815 which restored traditional order to post-revolutionary Europe, the reforms introduced under Napoleon were forgotten and Prussia returned to something like her former absolutism. No serious electoral reforms were carried out after 1815, even though Friedrich Wilhelm III had at first promised a new electoral system with a second chamber of representatives of districts. However, in 1823 the cautious monarch returned to the old system of *Provinzialstände*. Stein's reforms were curtailed and he, Gneisenau and Schleiermacher were regarded as traitors. The so-called Biedermeier style in furniture and interior design from *c.*1815 to 1848, which is like the Napoleonic Empire Style stripped of its glittering ornament, seems to reflect the supremacy of bourgeois values in early-nineteenth-century Germany. This unpretentious *gemütlich* tone also characterizes certain aspects of the life and setting of the Prussian kings Friedrich Wilhelm II and III, who reigned from 1786 to 1840. They now lived like burghers and tended to build themselves town houses and country houses rather than royal palaces. The country house which David Gilly built in 1796–1800 at Paretz for Friedrich Wilhelm III was one of the first of these modest royal seats which were soon echoed all over Germany, for example at Wiesbaden, Darmstadt, Stuttgart, Kassel and Karlsruhe.

In south Germany, where acquiescence in Napoleonic domination had been greater, liberalism survived the Congress of Vienna. The most Napoleonic constitution was, as we have already noted, that of Baden in 1818 in which the second chamber was composed, like the French Charte Constitutionnelle of 1814, of representatives of districts not corporations. The southern part of Baden, formerly the Austrian Breisgau, had been influenced by the ideals of the Enlightenment promoted under Joseph II. Nineteenth-century Baden thus became the home of German liberalism, while the constitution of Württemberg, proclaimed in September 1819 under King Wilhelm I (1816–64), was similar to that of Baden.

Of the three south German constitutions the Bavarian one of 1818 was the most traditionalist. Crown Prince Ludwig (1786–1868), together with a group of noblemen, succeeded in overthrowing the rule of Count Maximilian von Montgelas though many of his administrative reforms were retained in post-Napoleonic Bavaria. The ideals of Ludwig, who reigned from 1825 to 1848, were cultural and religious rather than political. His aim was first of all to turn Munich into a centre of German culture with the help, especially, of the north German architect, Leo von Klenze (1784–1864). Although the political system in Bavaria was more liberal than in Prussia, the authoritarian tone of Ludwig I was similar to that of his brother-in-law, Schinkel's principal patron, Friedrich Wilhelm IV of Prussia (reigned 1840–58). Both monarchs were keenly interested in architecture, imposed their will on their architects, and personally supervised the buildings they commissioned, while Friedrich Wilhelm was undoubtedly an architect manqué. They represented the twin poles of German Neo-classicism: Friedrich Wilhelm with his wish to fuse Greek, Gothic and Teutonic elements into a vision of a united Germany; Ludwig with his aspirations for a monumental Munich inspired by both ancient Greek and early Italian Renaissance architecture, which he regarded as symbols of a common ideal. The complex ambitions of Friedrich Wilhelm and Ludwig, of Schinkel and Klenze, came as the climax of a century during which, as we shall see, Germany had been increasingly devoted to the re-creation of a classical ideal.

CHAPTER II

The Impact of France and England from 1740–90

THE German-speaking countries in the eighteenth century are known above all for the incomparable magnificence of their Late Baroque and Rococo architecture. The Baroque tradition established around 1700 by Schlüter in Berlin, Pöppelmann and Longuelune in Dresden, and Fischer von Erlach and Hildebrandt in Vienna, was developed into the mid-century and beyond in a series of breathtaking masterpieces in central and southern Germany by Neumann, Fischer, the Asam brothers and Zimmermann. In such a rich soil it was difficult for the austere doctrines of Neo-classicism to take root. They thus arrive sporadically as importations from France and England, two countries where Baroque architecture had never been adopted so enthusiastically as in Germany. Characteristic examples of this influence are the short-lived Palladian revival under Frederick the Great, and the Louis XVI elegance of Pigage's garden buildings at Schwetzingen and of Guêpière's Monrepos at Ludwigsburg, which are unequalled in Europe as enchanting expressions of the *douceur de vivre* of pre-Revolutionary France.

The employment by German rulers of French architects such as Pigage and Guêpière was often seen as a mark not only of fashionable elegance but also of a progressive approach in line with the ideals of the Enlightenment. French architects were imported directly into west and south-west Germany, while in the north the impact of French theory on German architects was more important, as in the cases of Krubsacius, Gontard, Langhans, Fleischer and Du Ry. Another difference between the Protestant north and the Catholic south was that the former was more inclined to Palladianism and the latter to French classicism. We should, of course, remind ourselves that Neo-classicism was not a static force between 1740 and 1790 but included a number of contrasting themes such as the Franco-Italian classicism established at the French Academy in Rome around 1750; the impact of Piranesi's romantic vision of antiquity; the fundamentalist doctrines of Laugier; the development of a belief, fostered by Winckelmann, in the moral force of Greek culture; the archaeological investigation of Greek and Roman sites; the emphasis on the expression of sensation in architecture by writers like Le Camus de Mézières, and the parallel growth of the Picturesque tradition in England.

Palladianism was promoted with especial vigour by King Friedrich II of Prussia (1712–86), known as Frederick the Great, who was no less outstanding as a patron of the arts than as a military leader and statesman. Frederick was first and foremost a Francophile. Even when fighting against the French in the Seven Years War, he invited French officers to dine with him on the eve of the battle of Rossbach in 1757, explaining that he could not accustom himself to regarding the French as enemies. It was at Rossbach, where Frederick, a Protestant prince, defeated Catholic Austria and France, that, according to Voltaire, German nationalism was born. Frederick's artistic tastes, however, were not only Francophile but Anglophile and Italophile. This led to his promotion of a

2 Ferdinand Wilhelm Lipper: staircase hall of the Schloss, Münster, c.1775.

3 Georg Wenzeslaus von Knobelsdorff: Berlin Opera House, designed 1740, with the dome of St Hedwig's church in the background.

confusing range of architectural styles from Neo-Palladianism via Rococo to the Franco-Italian classicism of the 1740s. He was fortunate in having at his service architects of high distinction such as his friend Georg Wenzeslaus von Knobelsdorff (1699–1753), Jean-Laurent Legeay (c.1710–86), and Karl von Gontard (1731–91). Knobelsdorff was a Prussian aristocrat who began his career in the army but resigned in 1729 after an illness in order to study painting and architecture at the Berlin Academy. He became a close friend of Frederick, then crown prince, whom he accompanied in 1732 to the garrison town of Neuruppin, Brandenburg, where he built a circular Temple of Apollo in the Tuscan order in the prince's Amalthea Garden in 1735. He was sent by the prince on a study tour of Rome, Venice and Florence in 1736–7, and on his return took up residence at the prince's court at Schloss Rheinsberg, Brandenburg, where he remodelled the river front with an elegantly French open screen of coupled Ionic columns. On ascending the Prussian throne in 1740 Frederick appointed him Oberintendant of Palaces and Gardens and sent him on a further tour to Dresden and Paris.

In 1740 Frederick gave Knobelsdorff the commission for designing the Berlin Opera House, the first important monument of Neo-Palladianism in Germany. Conceived as a temple dedicated to Apollo, it was also intended to unite opera with the festivities and ceremonies of the court in a way that had been anticipated at Dresden. Thus the Hall of Apollo served as vestibule and dining room, while the floor of the auditorium could be raised to make a ballroom. It was a perfect representation of Frederick's own taste: the seats were not for sale, the audience being invited by the king. Moreover, it was to form part of a new Forum Fridericianum, a kind of cultural *place royale*, with a palace for the king facing it on the other side of Unter den Linden and an Academy of Science and Letters further to the west. This forum was eventually realized, though in a rather different way, with the church of St Hedwig playing a dominant role.

3 With its temple portico on the short street front, perhaps inspired by Palladio's Villa Rotonda, and the monotonous horizontality of its side elevations, nineteen bays long, Knobelsdorff's Opera House was a conscious echo of houses like Colen Campbell's Wanstead (*c.*1714–20), which represented English Palladianism at its most daunting. Wanstead had been illustrated in Campbell's *Vitruvius Britannicus*, vol. I (1715) and vol. III (1725). Frederick owned *Vitruvius Britannicus* as well as Burlington's *Fabbriche Antiche disegnate da Andrea Palladio Vicentino* (1730) and the editions of Palladio's *I Quattro Libri* by Leoni and by Algarotti. Count Francesco Algarotti (1712–64), a Venetian of great personal charm with whom Frederick had a romantic friendship, was influential in popularizing the ideals of the Enlightenment in Italy, France and Germany. His *Saggio sopra l'architettura* (1757) was translated into German by R.E. Raspe in 1769 and dedicated to the engraver Tischbein, the sculptor Nahl and the architect S.L. du Ry. Algarotti was also in touch with Lord Burlington to whom he wrote from Potsdam in 1751 asking him to send drawings of his buildings to Frederick. Algarotti described Burlington as 'the restorer of true architecture in this century', a role which Frederick doubtless wished to play in Germany. In his writings on architecture Algarotti gave expression to the ideals of Carlo Lodoli (1690–1761) who proposed a radically new architecture consisting of load-bearing elements with all unnecessary ornament eliminated. This anti-Baroque version of classicism was supposedly in harmony with the purest antique ideals. It was further believed that Palladio had come close to realizing those ideals: hence the Neo-Palladianism of Knobelsdorff's Berlin opera house.

Frederick's life-long love affair with France meant that he was equally attracted to Rococo as to the emerging ideals of Neo-classicism. Thus in the 1740s Knobelsdorff provided for him the enchantingly Rococo interiors at Schloss Charlottenburg near Berlin, and at Potsdam the Stadtschloss and Sanssouci. Despite the Rococo gaiety of the pink and white palace of Sanssouci, it has at its

4 core an oval domed hall, the Marmorsaal, surrounded by coupled Corinthian columns and remotely inspired by an antique source, the Pantheon in Rome. In 1746 Frederick the Great quarrelled with Knobelsdorff over the design of Schloss Sanssouci, and his former subordinate Johann Boumann the younger took over from him. However, Frederick made amends on Knobelsdorff's death in 1753 by composing the celebrated 'éloge funèbre' in which he declared that Knobelsdorff 'aimait la noble simplicité grecque et sa finesse réprouvait toute ornementation déplacée ... l'architecture des Anciens lui semblait revêtir plus de majesté que celle des Modernes'.

After Knobelsdorff's death, Frederick, encouraged by Algarotti, indulged in the curious experiment in Potsdam of recreating a number of Palladio's designs for town palaces, thus making what had previously been a garrison town into a kind of architectural museum. It was a process akin to that by which Ludwig I of Bavaria and his architect, Leo von Klenze, were to turn Munich into a museum of styles in the early nineteenth century. Buildings erected under Frederick's command from 1753 to 1755 included the version of Sanmicheli's Palazzo Pompei, Verona, at no. 3, Humboldtstrasse, by C.L. Hildebrandt; of Burlington's house for General Wade at 2, Blücherplatz, by A.L. Krüger; and of the following versions of Palladio's projects for palaces in Vicenza: the Palazzo Barbarano at 1, Schwertfegerstrasse, by Hildebrandt; the Palazzo Capra at 12, Am Alten Markt, also by Hildebrandt: the Palazzo Angarano at 2, Am Alten Markt (the Town Hall), by J. Boumann; the Palazzo Valmarana at 7, 5 Schlossstrasse, by Hildebrandt; and the Palazzo Thiene at 5, Am Neuen Markt, by J.G. Büring. These were followed in 1769 by 26–7, Breiterstrasse, designed by G.C. Unger in imitation of Inigo Jones's designs for the Palace of Whitehall as published in *Vitruvius Britannicus*. These buildings resembled stage scenery in that they did not recreate Palladio's internal planning and were occupied not by noblemen but by members of the professional classes who scarcely needed the large entertaining rooms envisaged by Palladio.

4 Georg Wenzeslaus von Knobelsdorff: the Marmorsaal at Sanssouci, Potsdam, 1740–6.

5 J.G. Büring: No.5, Am Neuen Markt, Potsdam, 1753–5.

Frederick's uncertainty of aim is further suggested by the third and last of the palaces with which he is associated at Potsdam, the Neues Palais. This was built 6,7 in the park at Sanssouci in the 1760s from designs by J.G. Büring which were based on the south front of Castle Howard, designed by Vanbrugh and Hawksmoor and illustrated in *Vitruvius Britannicus* in 1715 and 1725. Fronting the Baroque Neues Palais is an extensive pile, itself a miniature palace, known as the Communs. Far more arresting than the Neues Palais itself, to which it acts as a 8 service wing, this was designed in 1763 by the talented and enigmatic French architect, Jean-Laurent Legeay (*c*.1710–86). Frederick's imaginative appointment of Legeay as Premier Architecte du Roi on 1 January 1756 confirmed the position of Berlin as a centre of advanced Neo-classical design. Legeay had been one of a group of brilliant French designers such as Le Lorrain, Challe, Dumont, Jardin and Petitot who, as *pensionnaires* of the French Academy in Rome in the 1740s, had developed a heady style for large-scale public buildings which combined the columnar grandeur of both antique and Baroque architecture. Monumental visionary projects of this kind, which owed something to Piranesi's seductive etchings of ancient and modern Rome, were presented to the world in a simplified and codified form by M.-J. Peyre in *Oeuvres d'architecture* (1765), a book which exercised considerable influence on the development of eighteenth-century European architecture.

6 Air view of the Neues Palais, Potsdam, facing the monumental service wing known as the Communs.

7 J.G. Büring: the Neues Palais, Potsdam, 1760s.

8 (Below) Jean-Laurent Legeay: the Communs, Potsdam, designed 1763

Having studied at the French Academy in Rome from 1737 to 1742, Legeay
returned to Paris but in 1747–8 he and Knobelsdorff prepared designs for the
Catholic church of St Hedwig in Berlin. This church is a monument to the 9
religious toleration of Frederick the Great, who may have suggested its Pantheon
form, though it is also indebted to Serlio's restoration of the Pantheon; to the
Mausoleum of Augustus in Rome; and to Bernini's church at Ariccia. It is
arguably the first Neo-classical building in Germany, though Boumann built a
reduced version of it as the French Reformed church in Potsdam from designs by
Knobelsdorff of 1752–3. It was Boumann and Büring who eventually executed St
Hedwig's in 1772–3. Having been remodelled in 1894 in a form closer to the
original project of Knobelsdorff and Legeay, it was destroyed by bombing in
1943 but was rebuilt in 1952–3.

Legeay's patronage by Frederick the Great led to his appointment as architect
to Christian Ludwig II, Duke of Mecklenburg-Schwerin, in 1748. At Schwerin
in flat and unpromising territory Legeay created a grand water garden in the
style of Le Nôtre's Versailles in 1749–55. For Christian's successor, Duke
Friedrich, he prepared a monumental Utopian project in 1766 for the palace,
park and garden of Ludwigslust. In front of the palace was to be a vast circular
area surrounded by double rows of trees arranged like the columns in Bernini's

Piazza S. Pietro. Opening on to this was a free-standing circular church. In its visionary geometrical character, its enormous scale, and its powerful combination of antique and Baroque effects, the scheme anticipated the work of Boullée and Ledoux.

The duke was unable to carry out Legeay's project but in Potsdam, once the Seven Years War was over, Frederick the Great found the means to execute Legeay's fantastic stylophilistic scheme for the Communs. The building consists of a grandiose semi-circular colonnade flanked by a pair of domed and porticoed side pavilions, of an ultimately Anglo-Palladian derivation, approached up curved double staircases. With its triumphal arch in the centre of the colonnade, its carved trophies, garlands and obelisks, the Communs, executed by Gontard after Legeay's departure from Germany in 1763, is an imaginative synthesis of the Baroque ideals of Bernini and Juvarra, the gravity of English Palladianism, and the columnar sweep of the Franco-Italian classicism of the 1740s. Recognition should also be paid to Knobelsdorff who as early as 1747 had erected a semicircular colonnade in front of the palace of Sanssouci at Potsdam.

In 1763, the year that Legeay left Germany, Karl von Gontard (1731–91) arrived in Berlin from Bayreuth. In 1750 he had imbibed the ideals of French classicism in J.-F. Blondel's school of architecture in Paris. His first patron was

11 Karl von Gontard and G.C. Unger: the Brandenburg Gate, Potsdam, 1770.

12 (Opposite above). Karl von Gontard: the Königskolonnaden, in their original position on the Royal Bridge, Berlin, 1777–80.

13 (Opposite below). The Gendarmenmarkt, Berlin, showing the two early eighteenth-century churches with the drums and domes added by Gontard in 1780–5.

the Margrave Friedrich of Bayreuth whose wife, Wilhelmine, was a sister of Frederick the Great and deeply interested in the arts. In 1754 Gontard travelled to southern France, Rome and Naples with the margrave and margravine, and on his return became teacher of perspective and building design in the newly founded Academy of Art in Bayreuth where tuition was given free. The margrave and his wife rebuilt their capital as a centre of the arts, with a celebrated theatre containing an elaborately Baroque auditorium of 1746–8 designed by Giuseppe and Carlo Galli-Bibiena. In his more classicizing style Gontard built the Palais Reitzenstein, Haus Spindler, and Haus Athenaris for 10 himself. On the death of the margrave in 1763, Gontard and G.C. Unger (1743–c.1808) came to Prussia to work for Frederick the Great, who took over many of the artists employed by his brother-in-law. In 1768 Gontard built the Antique Temple in the Tuscan order and the Temple of Friendship in the Corinthian order in a crisp Louis XVI style in the park of Sanssouci. In 1770 he and Unger built the imposing Brandenburg Gate in Potsdam based on a sketch by Frederick 11 the Great. With its coupled Corinthian columns and emphatic military trophies, it recalls monuments of French classicism such as Perrault's triumphal arch of 1668 at the Porte St Antoine in Paris.

In 1777–80 came the Königskolonnaden, an extensive assembly of Ionic 12 colonnades built as part of the now destroyed Royal Bridge in the Alexanderplatz in Berlin, but moved in 1910 to their present site in the Kleistpark in the Schöneberg district of Berlin. Here Gontard was inspired by Knobelsdorff's colonnades at Sanssouci and, more particularly, by Legeay's at the Communs of the Neues Palais. Gontard's most striking urban contribution to Berlin was his additions to the two Baroque churches which flank the

14 Karl von Gontard: overdoor of a dressing room in the Marmor Palais, Potsdam, 1787–91.

Gendarmenmarkt (now Platz der Akademie). The French Protestant church on 13 the north side was built in 1701–5 by Louis Cayart for the Huguenot community in Berlin, while the balancing German or New Church on the south was executed in 1701–8 by Giovanni Simonetti from designs by Martin Grünberg. In 1780–5 both churches were boldly remodelled by Gontard and provided, at Frederick's request, with tall drums and domes. It has been suggested that the idea of the twin domes owes something to those by Wren at Greenwich Hospital, though Gontard's lack Wren's Baroque detailing. In 1787–91 Gontard built the Marmor Palais at Potsdam for Frederick the Great's successor, King Friedrich 14 Wilhelm II of Prussia. A Palladian cube surmounted by a belvedere overlooking the Heiligensee, this contains austerely Neo-classical interiors by C.G. Langhans. It is set in a Picturesque park designed by J.F. Eyserbeck in the style of that at Schloss Wörlitz.

As a final example of the fluctuating tastes of Frederick the Great we should note the royal library which he built on the west side of the Forum Fridericianum in Berlin in 1774–80. With its curved façade designed by Unger and Boumann on the basis of engravings which Frederick gave them of the Baroque range of the Hofburg in Vienna, this unexpected souvenir of Baroque Vienna was not only stylistically retardataire for its time but also contrasted oddly with the Palladian restraint of the adjacent Opera House and church of St Hedwig.

The most distinguished example of Anglo-Palladianism in Germany is in Saxony, where Prince Franz of Anhalt-Dessau (1740–1817) together with his friend and architect, Friedrich Wilhelm von Erdmannsdorff (1736–1800), created the park and Schloss of Wörlitz from 1766 to 1799. The prince was typical of those German patrons whose sympathies with the ideals of the French Enlightenment led them to create the kind of English landscaped park which was admired on the continent as an expression of a modern and progressive spirit. This point is underlined by the monument to Rousseau which, as we shall see, the prince chose to set up in his English garden at Wörlitz.

In 1761 the prince sent Erdmannsdorff on a study tour to Italy, while in 1763 the two men travelled together in England and in 1765–6 in Italy. In Rome they met Clérisseau, the French painter who taught the art of Picturesque draughtsmanship to Chambers and Adam. They also met Winckelmann who had recently published his *Gedanken über die Nachahmung der griechischen Werke in der Malerei und Bildhauerkunst*, 1755 (Reflections on the Imitation of Greek Art in Painting and Sculpture) and his *Geschichte der Kunst des Alterthums*, 1764 (History of Ancient Art). Erdmannsdorff wrote in his diary:

> During the six months that I spent in Rome with our prince in 1766, I saw Winckelmann every day. He used to come to us at about nine o'clock in the morning to accompany the prince on the tours which we made of the art collections in Rome. We would do this until three or four of the afternoon when Winckelmann would dine with us or the three of us would dine with the Prince of Mecklenbourg where the conversation would often be a repetition of the lessons of the morning. Winckelmann's energy was indefatigable. We went out with him to stay in the villas of his intimate friend Cardinal Albani at Castelgandolfo and Nettuno. On these occasions Winckelmann would act as host.

In February and March 1766 Erdmannsdorff travelled south to Naples and Sicily. Here he met Sir William Hamilton who was forming his important collection of Greek vases, at that time believed to be Etruscan. He also saw the Greek temples at Paestum, an advantage shared by few of his contemporaries. Later in the same year he and the prince returned to Germany via France, England and, more surprisingly, Scotland and Ireland.

Following the prince's marriage in 1767, Erdmannsdorff designed interiors at his town palace in Dessau where a new wing had been begun in 1747 from designs by Knobelsdorff. Interiors such as the princess's circular study with its neo-antique stucco-work and painted medallions show his ability to work in the style of Chambers and Adam. The same is true of the superb interiors at Schloss Wörlitz which he built as a summer residence for the prince, about twelve miles from Dessau, in 1769–73. This is no longer in the form of a Baroque Schloss with a *cour d'honneur* but is a free-standing villa leaning heavily on English Palladian precedent. Indeed its façades are curiously close to Claremont, Surrey, designed by Capability Brown and Henry Holland in the same year, 1769, and executed in 1771–6. Chambers's Duddingston, Edinburgh, of 1763–4, published in *Vitruvius*

15 Friedrich Wilhelm von
Erdmannsdorff: Schloss
Wörlitz, near Dessau,
1769–73.

Britannicus, vol. IV, 1767, has sometimes been suggested as a source, but Wörlitz lacks the most stylistically advanced feature of Duddingston which was its omission of a basement storey. This meant that the portico at Duddingston, unencumbered by flights of steps, rises from a low stylobate like that of a Greek temple.

The unusual plan of Schloss Wörlitz is remote from contemporary practice in 15 England or France but closer to Palladio's own designs. There is a staircase on either side of the small Pantheon-like entrance hall; there are numerous rooms of 16 roughly the same size but virtually no smaller ante-rooms; and in the centre of the house is an open court with screens of columns. Decorative details are drawn from Robert Wood's *The Ruins of Palmyra* (1753) and from the frescoes in the ruins of the Roman house in the grounds of the Villa Negroni in Rome; while the chimney pieces were inspired by designs by Piranesi and much of the furniture was sent from England.

The park, with its numerous exotic garden buildings, is a combination of influences from English gardens such as Kew, Stowe, and, especially, the lake-landscape at Stourhead. It was laid out gradually from 1764 by J.F. Eyserbeck (1734–1818), J.L. Schoch the elder (1728–93) and Neumark (1714–1811). One of its most surprising features is the Rousseau Island of 1782, an imitation of the poplar-planted island in the lake in the landscaped park at Ermenonville near Paris, which contained Rousseau's tomb. The prince had met Rousseau in 1775

on his way back from his third visit to England. In the 1790s Erdmannsdorff
added four new garden buildings: the Pantheon; the Temple of Flora; the
circular Temple of Venus which, like Arens's Roman House at Weimar (1791–
7), was remarkable as an early instance of the Greek Doric; and the Stein
Pavilion or Villa Hamilton, inspired by Sir William Hamilton's villa near
Naples. This contains three exquisite interiors enriched with stucco-work by
Friedemann Hunold, wall and ceiling paintings by Johann Fischer, and
furniture by Johann Andreas Irmer (1720–98). The decorative treatment was
inspired by engravings of the recently excavated interiors at Herculaneum and

16 Friedrich Wilhelm von
Erdmannsdorff: the dining
room, Schloss Wörlitz,
near Dessau, 1769–73.

17,18

19

31

17, 18, 19 Three of the garden buildings added by Erdmannsdorff to the park at Schloss Wörlitz in the 1790s. Above left: the Pantheon. Above right: Temple of Flora. Opposite: interior of the Villa Hamilton.

featured ruin paintings by Clérisseau, copies of Raphael's frescoes at the Villa Farnesina, busts, classical reliefs made at the Wedgwood manufactory, and Neo-Greek klismos chairs of pearwood with gilt bronze mounts supplied by Irmer in 1794. These remarkable chairs, which are perhaps the earliest of their type in Europe, should be compared with those possibly made *c.*1785–8 from designs by Joseph Bonomi for the Pompeian Gallery at Packington Hall, Warwickshire. Indeed Bonomi's gallery has much in common with the Villa Hamilton, though the latter is superior in artistic imagination. Erdmannsdorff's elegant, brittle and self-conscious interiors, in a building inspired by the villa of an English connoisseur settled in Italy, are like a gem or miniature encapsulating the Neo-classical spirit with its refined allusions to the classical, whether antique, Renaissance or modern, whether Greek, Roman or English.

Adjacent to the Villa Hamilton, somewhat grotesquely, is a miniature Vesuvius, originally issuing real smoke! This is the Stein (rock), constructed *c.*1788–90 on the Stein Island in a branch off the main lake. This bizarre man-made cone of rocks, about eighty feet high, containing red glass windows and belching fire and smoke, may have been influenced by Sir William Chambers's description of similar effects in Chinese gardens in his *Dissertation on Oriental Gardening* (1772). The prince knew Chambers and owned a copy of his *Dissertation* as well as of Sir William Hamilton's book on volcanoes (Naples 1776). The park at Wörlitz also contained a model farm run along English lines and a cast-iron bridge built in 1791 as the first of its kind on the continent, a miniature version of that at Coalbrookdale by Abraham Darby of 1778. Erdmannsdorff's gift for

20, 21, 22 Friedrich Wilhelm von Erdmannsdorff: Schloss Luisium, near Dessau, *c*.1775. Above: the villa in its setting. Opposite above: ceiling of the library. Opposite below: room in the north-east corner.

small-scale design and for brittle but richly ornamented Neo-classical interiors was nowhere better expressed than at the pretty little villa known as Schloss Luisium which he built *c*.1775 near Dessau for the prince.

Wörlitz was widely known and admired for its novelty in the eighteenth century: for example, Goethe made drawings of it in 1778. Garden buildings were, of course, a building type in which architects frequently experimented with new ideas. This was particularly so in England in the work of architects like Kent and Stuart. Apart from Wörlitz, other early English gardens in Germany, laid out as an expression of sympathy with the Enlightenment, include those in and around Hanover: Marienwerder near Hanover; Schwöbbern near Hameln; and Harbse near Helmstedt. The lovely garden of the electoral palace of Schwetzingen near Mannheim was laid out in the formal Baroque taste in 1753–8 by J.L. Petri but was adorned with Neo-classical garden buildings between 1761 and 1795 by Nicolas de Pigage and developed with belts of trees in the manner of Capability Brown by F.L. Sckell between 1771 and 1804.

Nicolas de Pigage (1723–96), born in Lunéville, Lorraine, was trained by J.-F. Blondel in Paris, and subsequently visited Italy and probably also England, for it is known that he considered writing a book on English landscaped gardens. From 1749 he worked in various Palatinate possessions up and down the Rhine where he introduced an up-to-date French classicism. His extravagant patron, who consciously modelled himself on Louis XIV, was Karl Theodor, Elector Palatine from 1742 and Elector of Bavaria from 1778 until his death in 1799.

20–22

At Schwetzingen Pigage's most important buildings for the Elector, all
surviving, were the sumptuous Court Theatre (1752); the Temple of Apollo
(1761), an Ionic monopteros perched high up on an elaborate grotto; the Bath
House (1766–73); the Mosque (1778–95); and a ruined aqueduct. The Bath
House, though modest enough from the outside, consists of seven interlocking
rooms of contrasting shapes decorated in the most exquisite Louis XVI style
conceivable. It is one of the most perfect buildings of its kind in Europe and
establishes Pigage as perhaps the most talented of the many French architects
working in eighteenth-century Germany. From the Bath House a corridor of
treillage leads through the garden to a circular aviary surrounded by fountains. At
the end of this axis is a grotto painted with a convincing trompe l'œil landscape
on its back wall. No less extravagant in its different way is the Mosque, which 23
visitors accustomed to the comparatively small scale of most English garden
buildings will find astonishingly large. With its central domed pavilion flanked
by two tall minarets, it is probably inspired by the now demolished mosque
which Chambers built at Kew in 1761 and illustrated in his *Plans . . . of the Gardens
and Buildings at Kew in Surrey* (1763). A similar mosque had already been erected

in 1782–5 in the park at Schloss Wilhelmshöhe, probably from designs by S.L. du Ry.

For the Elector Pigage also built Schloss Benrath (1755–65), a ravishingly beautiful French *pavillon* near Düsseldorf. Benrath is hard to classify stylistically: a French Baroque *pavillon* with a plan derived ultimately from Le Vau's Vaux-le-Vicomte (1657) and with Rococo interior decoration, it has one room, the circular dome room or Kuppelsaal in the centre of the garden front, in a style verging on the classicism of Louis XVI.

In Württemberg the leading architect was the Frenchman Philippe de la Guêpière (*c.*1715–73), who succeeded the Italian Baroque architect Leopoldo Retti in 1752 as court architect to Duke Karl Eugen (ruled 1744–93). Guêpière, who was a pupil of J.-F. Blondel in Paris, completed the monumental Neues Schloss at Stuttgart which Retti had begun for the Duke in 1746. His work here from 1752 to 1756 included the decoration of the interiors – none of which were completed on Retti's death in 1751 – and the construction of the town wing. His interiors are important as an early example of French classicism in Germany but he was hampered by the need to work within Retti's framework. Purer examples

24 Philippe de la Guêpière: Monrepos, near Ludwigsburg, 1760–64.

37

25 Pierre-Michel
d'Ixnard: Benedictine
monastery of St Blasien
in the Black Forest,
1768–83.

of his style can be seen in his two principal buildings, both for the duke of
Württemberg. These are elaborate pavilions with French names – Solitude
(1763–*c.* 1769) crowning a hill near Stuttgart, and Monrepos (1760–64) near the
palace of Ludwigsburg. The exteriors of Solitude are attractive early examples of
French classicism, while the decoration of the interiors follows an interesting
division between restrained Rococo for the private rooms and classical for the
public rooms: for example, the Marmorsalon in the French *goût grec* manner and
the central oval saloon which, with its coupled Corinthian columns and stucco
figure sculpture, recalls Knobelsdorff's saloon of 1747 at Sanssouci. Monrepos, 24
influenced by Bélanger's Bagatelle, is another important example of early
classicism in Germany. Its garden front rises enchantingly from a lake while its
plan is similar to that of Pigage's Benrath of a decade earlier. The central oval
saloon, like that at Benrath, has the stamp of Neo-classical severity, but this is
partly due to a remodelling in 1804 by Thouret.

    The architect who introduced French Neo-classicism into south-west Ger-
many was the Frenchman Pierre-Michel d'Ixnard (1723–95). His real name was
Pierre Michel but, like Pigage who added 'de' to his name, Lerouge who changed
his name to Louis-Rémy de la Fosse, and Salins who added 'de Montfort' to his
name, he found that it helped to appear as a French aristocrat in seeking a
German princeling as a patron. Born in Nîmes, D'Ixnard came to Paris in 1750
where he acted as a craftsman builder for Servandoni and Contant d'Ivry and
met J.-F. Blondel. From 1764 he worked in Germany where his principal works,

25 both much altered, were the Benedictine monastery of St Blasien in the Black Forest (1768–83), and the Residenz Schloss at Koblenz (designed 1777–9). His patron at St Blasien was Martin Gerbert von Hornau (1720–93), a scholar, musician and, in his capacity as Abbot of St Blasien, a Prince of the Holy Roman Empire. Following the destruction by fire of the old abbey in July 1768, D'Ixnard provided a large domed church inspired remotely by the Pantheon and more particularly by the Catholic church of St. Hedwig in Berlin. The relation of the church to the monastic buildings perhaps echoed the disposition of the Invalides in Paris, but the monastic choir formed a long rectangular projection to the south of the church, an arrangement which was criticized by Nicolas de Pigage who condemned the whole building as 'un véritable colifichet galli-germanique'. Pigage intervened to give the dome a flatter more antique profile than D'Ixnard had intended, but the north entrance front with its Doric colonnade is D'Ixnard's own design. The impressive interior is encircled with a row of giant mainly freestanding Corinthian columns, but rebuilding after a disastrous fire in 1874 has left the whole building with a colder and more sober air than either D'Ixnard or Pigage intended. Nonetheless, St Blasien is a monumental building which is one of the most important statements of classical ideals anywhere in Germany in the eighteenth century.

In 1776 Clemens Wenzeslaus, the last Elector of Trier and an uncle of Louis XVI of France, decided to abandon the old castle of Ehrenbreitstein near Koblenz and build a palace in Koblenz on the banks of the Rhine. D'Ixnard

26 proposed a vast scheme in 1777 and another in 1779 which he published in his *Recueil d'architecture* (Strasbourg 1791). In front of the palace was a huge rectangular courtyard approached through a screen of columns and flanked by a

26 D'Ixnard's original design for the palace of Koblenz, 1777.

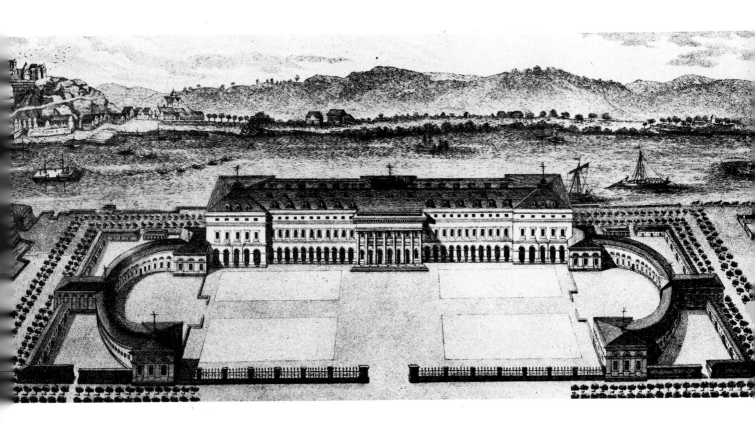

pair of semicircular courtyards. This was a somewhat uneasy combination of traditional elements and features inspired by the work of Gabriel and M.-J. Peyre. On the recommendation of the French Academy, the Elector replaced D'Ixnard in 1779 with Antoine-François Peyre (1739–1823). A pupil of his brother M.-J. Peyre, in Paris, he had won the Prix de Rome and spent 1763–7 at the French Academy in Rome. Between 1780 and 1792 he executed a simplified version of D'Ixnard's scheme, retaining the hemicycles and the octastyle unpedimented portico on the entrance front, though changing the order from exuberant Corinthian to restrained Ionic. The 39-bay front with its lack of ornamental incident and its unbroken horizontal skyline is a somewhat chilling statement of Franco-German Neo-classicism. It was not quite completed when it was turned into a hospital by the invading armies of Republican France. In 1842–5 it was restored by Stüler and Lassaulx for King Friedrich Wilhelm IV of Prussia. Following its virtual destruction in 1944 it was rebuilt in 1950–1; a few original interiors survive but the ground-floor arcade, formerly open, is now closed.

A.-F. Peyre helped excavate the Roman antiquities at Trier for the Elector, publishing these in 1785. Amongst his varied executed designs in Germany, some of which he published in 1818 as *Oeuvres d'architecture*, one of the finest was his Akademiesaal of 1786–7 in the seventeenth-century Electoral Schloss at Mainz, a noble two-storeyed hall surrounded by Corinthian columns supporting a gallery.

Among the architects involved in work on the interiors of the Schloss at Koblenz in the 1780s was the emigré French architect François-Xavier Mangin, who introduced a version of the *goût grec* classicism of mid-eighteenth-century France to the neighbourhood of Trier and Mainz. Born at Pont-à-Mousson in 1742 and probably trained in Paris by Gabriel, he was brought to Germany by Guiolet, chancellor to the Archbishop-Elector of Mainz. Mangin's first German work was the substantial villa called Mon Aise (1779–86) which he built near 27 Trier for Count Philipp-Nikolaus von Walderdorff, canon of Trier Cathedral. With its unpedimented Ionic portico in antis rising through the first and second storeys, it is an echo of Palladio and Gabriel but is handled with a stern angularity emphasized by the prominent Greek key pattern in the frieze. Mangin's principal work was the Grande Prévôté built in 1786 as the town mansion in Mainz of Count Damian-Friedrich von der Leyen, grand provost of the cathedral. The noble courtyard elevation with its Corinthian peristyle seems to be inspired by Ledoux's Hôtel d'Uzès in Paris of 1769, but the building was best known for its magnificent colonnaded gallery. With its coffered barrel vault and its top-lit apsed ends, recalling those of George Dance's gallery at Lansdowne House, London, of 1788–91, this was one of the most important early Neo-classical interiors in Germany. Not for nothing did Goethe describe the Grande Prévôté as an 'architectural paradise'.

Mangin also built two houses for Guiolet, one of which, dating from 1786, was characterized by massive horizontally channelled rustication. This has more than a touch of Ledoux, as also does the substantial house which he built for himself at Gartenfeld near Mainz *c.* 1790, following his application in 1789 for the full rights as a citizen of Mainz. As an example of the application of a Roman Doric temple for the purposes of a modern dwelling, this can be paralleled in the eighteenth century only by the design of 1788 by the visionary architect Jean-Jacques Lequeu for a house which was later partially executed as the 'Temple du Silence'. Mangin's house was square in plan with hexastyle Doric porticoes running the full height and width of the entrance front and garden front. The

27 François-Xavier
Mangin: Mon Aise, near
Trier, 1779–86.

unusual plan was dominated by two large rooms down the centre of the house,
flanked on each side by suites of smaller rooms. The career which Mangin had
established under his princely patrons was ended with the invasion of Mainz by
the armies of Republican France in 1792. Ironically for one who had only just
become a German citizen, he was forced to flee a city which was to belong to
France from 1792 until 1814. Tragically both Gartenfeld and the Grande
Prévôté were destroyed in the siege of Mainz by the Prussians and Austrians in
1793.

In Strasbourg and Frankfurt we should look at the architect Nicolas-
Alexandre Salins (1753–1839) who added the aristocratic suffix 'de Montfort' to
his name when in Germany. Little is known of his early youth and training but in
1779 he was invited by Cardinal Rohan, Prince Bishop of Strasbourg, to build a
new palace at Saverne (Zabern), near Strasbourg, to replace that by Robert de
Cotte which had been destroyed by fire. The extreme length, thirty-five bays, of
the façades of Saverne recalls the palace at Koblenz for which Salins had in fact
submitted designs in 1777. However, Saverne lacks the monotony of Koblenz
since it is adorned with giant pilasters after the manner of Ledoux's château de
Benouville (1768). In 1785–90 Salins made unexecuted plans for Schloss
Wilhemshöhe near Kassel. Unfortunately, the completion of the palace at
Saverne in 1789 coincided with the French Revolution whereupon the Cardinal
retired permanently to Baden Baden. After a difficult few years in Strasbourg,

Salins had settled in Frankfurt by 1797 where he established an extensive practice, working no longer for princes but for the increasingly prosperous professional classes. He now adopted a subdued Empire style inspired by Bélanger and, after a visit to Paris in 1802, by the decorative style of Percier and Fontaine, in buildings such as the Villa Gontard (1799), Mühlens house (1802–28 3) and Koester house (1816–17). Perhaps the most elegant building of his career was his bath house of 1798 for the banker Metzler at Offenbach near Frankfurt. A semicircular portico rising from artificial rockwork led into an oval saloon and thence to a columned rotunda containing the bath. Ledoux's celebrated Hôtel de Thélusson (1778–81) with a rotunda rising above a grotto may have influenced the design of the bath house, as it undoubtedly did that of the Obermain Tor which Salins designed in 1807 for Karl Theodor von Dalberg (1744–1817) who had become Primate of the Confederation of the Rhine with his seat at Frankfurt. It should be noted that Salins was once more working for a prince. The Obermain Tor contrived to have a completely circular entrance which recalled not only the gateway of the Hôtel de Thélusson but more particularly Ledoux's astonishing design for a circular house in the Champs-Elysées.

In 1807 Salins became court architect to the short-lived Napoleonic Grand Duchy of Würzburg. In this capacity he redecorated a suite of state apartments on the first floor of the fabulous Residenz at Würzburg, built by Balthasar Neumann between 1719 and about 1744. Known as the Toskanazimmer, after 29 Grand Duke Ferdinand of Tuscany, these were the finest Empire Style interiors in Germany and contained sumptuous furniture, bronzework and mirrors supplied from Paris. After their destruction in the Second World War the principal apartments are gradually being carefully recreated. Otherwise, the only surviving work by Salins is the palace of Saverne. His varied career makes him a classic instance of a French architect imported into Germany who worked in different parts of the country and for widely differing patrons, without any particular geographical ties.

The last important architect who need detain us in this section on central and southern Germany is the Portuguese-born but Paris-trained Emanuel Joseph von Herigoyen (1746–1817). He introduced the latest French and English Neo-classicism to central and southern Germany in the course of a long and varied career. His principal patron was the dynamic Archbishop Elector of Mainz, Friedrich Karl Joseph von Erthal (1774–1802), for whom he remodelled the interiors of the early-seventeenth-century Schloss Johannisburg at 158 Aschaffenburg between 1774 and 1784. These were destroyed in the war but his charming Schloss Schönbusch (1778–82), near Aschaffenburg, survives in a Picturesque park partly laid out in 1785 by F.L. Sckell as one of the earliest in Germany, though following those at Wörlitz, Schwetzingen (from 1771), and Landshut (1782–4). Schönbusch was created for the Elector as a Trianon, a romantic pastoral retreat from the formality of life in the immense Schloss Johannisburg. Its façade derives from plates in Neufforge's *Recueil élémentaire d'architecture* (9 vols., 1757–72), a masterly and influential synthesis of the Louis XVI style. However, the influence of Adam can be seen in interiors such as the Festsaal where the ceiling is based on George Richardson's *A Book of Ceilings, composed in the Stile of the Antique Grotesque*, 1776, pl. XXIX. Plate XXXVI of the same book was the model for the ceiling in the circular Breakfast Pavilion which Herigoyen built in 1782 in one corner of the grounds of Schloss Johannisburg. Following the secularization of Aschaffenburg under Napoleon in 1803 it became a principality in the control of Karl Theodor von Dalberg for whom Herigoyen also worked. Another secular principality under Karl Theodor von Dalberg from 1803 was Regensburg. Herigoyen's numerous buildings there include the palace of 1805 for the French Legation (now the police headquarters) in the Bismarckplatz. With its hexastyle Corinthian portico this is evidently derived from plates in Neufforge. His Dörnberg Palais, begun in the same year, is in a Franco-Palladian style similar to that of David Gilly, while his little circular Kepler Memorial of 1808 is a Greek monopteros surrounded by columns of the 30 Delian Doric order with fluting confined to the top and bottom of the shafts. Regensburg was incorporated into Bavaria in 1810, in which year Herigoyen was appointed Ober Bau Kommissar in Munich. Here in 1811–13 he built the town mansion of the Francophile Count Maximilian von Montgelas, chief minister to Maximilian I of Bavaria. This was derived from Neufforge while his project of 1811 for a National Theatre in Munich incorporated a façade based on a design by Neufforge for a barracks. He reverted to the Greek Revival in his striking entrance gateway of 1811 to the botanical gardens in Munich. Its Greek Doric columns and painted polychromatic decoration already belong to the world of Klenze not to that of Adam or Neufforge.

Perhaps the most outstanding contribution made by architects of French origin to eighteenth-century Germany was that of the Du Ry family who were court architects to the landgraves of Hesse-Kassel between 1685 and 1799. Paul du Ry (1640–1714), who was forced to leave France as a Huguenot, and his son Charles (1692–1757) developed the town of Kassel by adding the Oberneustadt (upper new town) with numerous public and private buildings in a subdued Baroque style. The most talented member of the dynasty was Charles's son Simon Louis du Ry (1726–99) who introduced the most up-to-date Neo-classical ideals. His importance in our story is considerable for he marks the breakthrough of the new style in the north. His principal work, the museum in Kassel, takes its place with Erdmannsdorff's Wörlitz and D'Ixnard's St Blasien as one of the three leading Neo-classical monuments of eighteenth-century Germany: typically, they are palace, museum, and church.

30 Emmanuel Joseph von Herigoyen: Kepler Memorial, Regensburg, 1808.

Trained first by his father, then in Stockholm by the Swedish court architect, Karl Hårleman, and finally at Blondel's school in Paris, he later studied antique and Renaissance architecture on a tour of Italy in 1753–6 which included a visit to Pompeii and Herculaneum. An architect with an ideal Neo-classical training, he then found the ideal patron in Landgrave Friedrich II (reigned 1760–85), who appointed him court architect in 1767 and travelled with him to Italy in 1776–7. An Anglophile who married a daughter of George II of England and whose brother-in-law was the Prince de Soubise, Friedrich was a man of wide cultural attainment and also a Roman Catholic convert. In 1769 he commissioned Simon Louis du Ry to build what has sometimes been claimed as the earliest independent museum building, the Museum Fridericianum. Built in 1769–79, the museum was also an important contribution to the town planning of Kassel since it formed part of one side of a large new square, the Friedrichsplatz, which, as a result of the removal of the old town ramparts in 1767, was able to serve as a link between the old town and the Oberneustadt. It is characteristic of the landgrave's sympathy with Enlightenment ideals that the principal building in this square should no longer be a palace but a museum. The short southern side of the square was left open to command a view of the countryside, while the Upper Königsstrasse led from the north side to the circular Königsplatz, another significant contribution by Du Ry to eighteenth-century German town-planning. The name of this square commemorated the fact that Landgrave Friedrich I was also king of Sweden.

31 View of the Friedrichsplatz, Kassel, showing (from left to right) part of the Rotes Palais (Bromeis, 1821–31), the Museum Fridericianum (Du Ry, 1769–76), the Hofverwaltungsgebaüde (Bromeis, 1826–9) and the Elisabethkirche (Du Ry, 1770–6).

The articulation with giant pilasters of the façade of the Museum Fridericianum may be relatively old-fashioned, but the flatness of surfaces, the horizontal skyline, and the severe portico are transitional from Palladianism to Neo-classicism. These features are derived from Colen Campbell's Wanstead and from a plate in Neufforge's *Recueil*, vol. VII, 1767. The plan of the U-shaped building echoes that of the Istituto delle Scienze in Bologna. Antique statuary was displayed on the ground floor in large galleries divided by columns. There were also smaller rooms for natural science collections, minerals, plants and butterflies, as well as for coins, prints, clocks, mathematical instruments, arms, and waxworks. The whole of the first floor of the front block was devoted to a library with reading desks for visitors, while the upper floor housed mechanical and musical instruments as well as a private study for Friedrich, even though his town palace was next door. Du Ry wrote his own description of this building, while Durand also recognized its importance by publishing it in his *Recueil et parallèle des édifices de tous genres* (Paris 1801), pl. 18. The interior was remodelled by Grandjean de Montigny in 1808–10 to serve as a Palais des Etats under the short-lived reign of Napoleon's brother, Jérôme, as King of Westphalia. The relationship of the building to the square has been destroyed by later buildings to left and right while, following its partial destruction in the Second World War, only the façades were rebuilt to Du Ry's design.

Landgrave Friedrich II was in close touch with Ledoux and De Wailly, the most original French architects of their day. Having met the landgrave in Paris in the summer of 1775, Ledoux visited Kassel at his invitation in the following November. Ledoux now designed for him an elaborate triumphal arch flanked by Ionic colonnades to close the Friedrichsplatz on the south. He also prepared a 214 'corrected' design of Du Ry's Museum Fridericianum so as to exhibit greater Neo-classical severity, as well as a fantastic town palace for the landgrave dominated by a megalomaniac decastyle Corinthian portico, four storeys high. Du Ry, who described him in an amusing letter to his sister as 'an architect of great vision who speaks of an outlay of 3 or 4 million Thalers as we would of 3 or 4 thousand', must have been relieved that, despite being fêted by the landgrave and his court, Ledoux did not in the end supplant him as court architect.

In the last year of his life, 1785, the landgrave turned his attention from the town of Kassel to improving his country seat, Schloss Weissenstein (known from 1798 as Schloss Wilhelmshöhe), six miles away. Here was, and is, one of the most fabulous Baroque parks in Europe. An impressive hill was crowned in 1701–18 by the Italian architect Giovanni Guerniero with a colossal octagonal structure which must be one of the largest garden buildings in existence. This great arcuated pile, surmounted by a tall obelisk capped with a copy of the Farnese Hercules, towers over one like some Baroque skyscraper. The impression of breathtaking verticality is complemented dramatically by the no less breathtaking horizontal vista which the octagon commands down the straight axis of the park, through the central dome of Schloss Wilhelmshöhe and beyond it along the straight road which leads to the town of Kassel. The upper part of the hill on which the octagon stands is laid out as a terraced water garden, for which the octagon serves as a reservoir, with crashing cascades, grottos and steps. Yet despite all this magnificence, the Schloss in axis with this cascade was in 1785 a modest building dating from 1606, known as Schloss Weissenstein. In 1785 Landgrave Friedrich invited Charles de Wailly to submit designs for replacing it with a monumental Neo-classical palace worthy of its setting. Thirty-three beautiful drawings by De Wailly, rediscovered in 1977 in the archives of Sanssouci at Potsdam, relate to three separate projects with richly inventive combinations of terraces and curved wings. Fortunately, the new landgrave, Wilhelm IX, shared his predecessor's enthusiasm for the project and, though he rejected De Wailly's proposals, commissioned plans from Du Ry and his pupil Heinrich Christoph Jussow (1754–1825) which were executed between 1786 and 1792.

What is astonishing about Schloss Wilhelmshöhe is the far-flung wings
32–34 reaching out into the landscape at angles of roughly forty-five degrees. Hugging the sloping site, these relate the house to its setting in a way more characteristic of the English Picturesque than of French or German Neo-classicism. The seventeenth-century Schloss was left intact initially and the first part of Du Ry's project to be executed was the south wing, followed by the north wing which was ready by 1790. When the time came to replace the old Schloss, stylistic difficulties began to emerge. Du Ry and Jussow, who had been a pupil of De Wailly while in Paris, produced a variety of schemes in one of which the wings were linked by a triumphal arch and in another by a kind of ruined Roman forum. What was eventually selected was Jussow's plans for a vast and austere Palladian pile, fifteen bays long and three storeys high plus attics and basement. It is a design which recalls that of John Wood's Prior Park, near Bath, of 1735–48. Crowned with a shallow Pantheon dome and fronted with a giant Ionic portico, it was linked to Du Ry's wings by one-storeyed quadrants. Unfortunately, these quadrant wings were raised to almost the full height of the main body of the Schloss in 1821, thus destroying the delicate and lively balance between the various parts of the whole complex as originally conceived. The principal interiors were handsomely remodelled in the Empire Style for King Jérôme but, apart from those in Du Ry's south wing, the interiors throughout the palace were

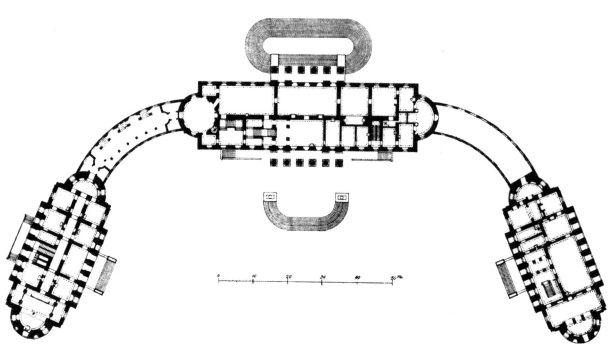

48

gutted and modernized after the Second World War. This treatment was unfortunately typical of many palaces in West Germany which were ruthlessly converted for museum or administrative purposes at this time.

Wilhelmshöhe has not yet yielded up all its delights, for the park contains one of the most fanciful and elaborate mock-Gothic castles in Europe, known as Löwenburg. This Picturesque extravaganza was designed in 1790 by Jussow for Landgrave Wilhelm IX and executed between 1793 and 1802. Jussow, who succeeded S.L. du Ry as court architect in 1799, had been sent by the landgrave in c.1787 to England where he probably saw designs by Robert Adam for Scottish castles such as Culzean (1779–92) in a similar style to the Löwenburg. As an extensive and romantic reflection of an English fourteenth-century castle, Löwenburg reflects not only the imaginative genius of Adam but also the chivalrous tastes of Wilhelm IX for whom Du Ry had submitted as early as 1786 a remarkable drawing in the manner of Clérisseau, showing one wing of the proposed Schloss Wilhelmshöhe in a ruinous state. In fact Löwenburg was built as a mausoleum for Wilhelm who had also built a 'ruin' for himself as a lodging in Wilhelmstal in 1779–81. He lived here with his mistress who used to wear 'period dress'. A romantic 'Burg' had already been built at Wörlitz for Prince Franz of Anhalt-Dessau.

The survival intact of the great park at Wilhelmshöhe with its Baroque octagon and cascade, landscaped lake, Gothic Löwenburg and Neo-classical Schloss, makes all the more poignant the destruction in the Second World War of the adjacent town of Kassel which had been one of the most charming if least known of the middle-German court residence cities. The attempts at restoration after the war must be amongst the most inadequate anywhere in Germany.

32, 33, 34 (Opposite) Simon Louis du Ry and Heinrich Jussow: Schloss Wilhelmshöhe, near Kassel, 1786–1792. Top: entrance front, with the quadrant wings later raised to full height. Centre: plan. Bottom: Jussow's fantasy of the building with the central block in ruins.

35 Heinrich Jussow: Löwenburg, in the grounds of Wilhelmshöhe, 1790.

Kassel became the seat of the Napoleonic Kingdom of Westphalia until its collapse in 1814, while following the victory of Prussia in the Austro-Prussian War of 1866, Electoral Hesse was incorporated into Prussia.

The spare elegance of Du Ry's Neo-Palladian style can be appreciated at the little Schloss Mont-Chéri which he built in 1787–8 near Hofgeismar, a small spa town in Hesse not far from Wilhelmshöhe. Its portico is in the same Ionic order he chose for the monopteros which he built in 1792 over the mineral spring at Hofgeismar. Apart from his extensive activities as court architect Du Ry was also professor of architecture from 1766 at the Collegium Karolinum in Kassel which had been founded by Landgrave Karl.

With Berlin and Kassel one of the leading centres of classicism in the north was Dresden, the capital of Saxony. At Dresden, as at Kassel, French Baroque classicism was introduced by Huguenot architects: Jean de Bodt (1670–1745) and Zacharias Longuelune (1669–1748). Appointed Superintendent of the Royal Works at Dresden in 1728 by the Elector Augustus the Strong (1694–1733), De Bodt assisted Pöppelmann and Longuelune in the design of the Japanische Palais at Dresden. He added the central pavilion to the north, in a style inspired by Perrault's east front of the Louvre. Thus, although Dresden is rightly famous for its rich Rococo tradition, the sympathy of architects like De Bodt and Longuelune for the more restrained French Baroque classicism of the years round 1700 made Dresden a natural setting for the adoption of Neo-classical ideals.

36 Friedrich August Krubsacius: stair-hall of the Landhaus (Chamber of Deputies), Dresden, 1770–6.

In 1754 Johann Joachim Winckelmann (1716–68) moved to Dresden where, as we have seen, he wrote one of the most influential books of eighteenth-century Europe, *Gedanken über die Nachahmung der griechischen Werke in der Malerei und Bildhauerkunst*, 1755 (Reflections on the Imitation of Greek Art in Painting and Sculpture). With his *Geschichte der Kunst des Alterthums*, 1764 (History of Ancient Art), this helped establish one of the most powerful myths of modern Europe, that the style of Greek art was noble because it was produced by noble people. Winckelmann's message was echoed in the work of prominent Neo-classical painters such as A.F. Oeser (1717–99), a friend of Winckelmann and Goethe, who was resident in Dresden from 1739 to 1756, and Anton Raphael Mengs (1728–79), who spent part of the years 1752–65 in Dresden.

No buildings were erected in Dresden as radical as Winckelmann's theories, but his contemporary, the architect Friedrich August Krubsacius (1718–89), led a move towards Palladian and Italian models, recommending Knobelsdorff's Berlin Opera House in his *Betrachtungen über den Geschmack der Alten in der Baukunst*, 1745 (Observations on the Taste of the Ancients in Architecture). A pupil of Longuelune, Krubsacius was an influential professor at the Academy in Dresden and was probably the author of a translation of Laugier's *Observations sur l'architecture* published at Leipzig in 1771. His principal work, the Landhaus (Chamber of Deputies) at Dresden (1770–6), is in the main transitional from Baroque to Palladian: its façade, inspired by Soufflot, boasts a powerful Tuscan portico and inside is a splendid stair-hall. Similarly transitional buildings in Dresden include the Gewandhaus or Drapers' Hall (1768–70) by Johann Friedrich Knöbel (1724–92), and two churches by Johann Georg Schmid (1707–74), the Kreuzkirche (begun 1764) and the Annenkirche (1764–9).

184

36

37 74

37 Johann Georg Schmid: Annenkirche, Dresden, 1764–9. The top of the spire was added by G.F. Thormeyer in 1823.

We arrive at something more truly Neo-classical with the intriguing architect Christian Traugott Weinlig (1739–99). Born in Dresden, he was a pupil of J.-F. Blondel and Le Roy in Paris in 1766–7 and then studied until 1770 in Rome where his belief in classicism was strengthened. From Rome he wrote a series of letters on architectural topics, subsequently published as *Briefe über Rom*, 3 vols., Dresden 1782–7 (Letters on Rome), from which we learn that the architect he most admired was Palladio. In Rome he met Winckelmann and sent back a design to the Dresden Academy entitled 'Idée d'une Maison de Plaisance au milieu d'un Jardin Anglais'. He published designs in Hirschfeld's *Theorie der Gartenkunst*, 5 vols, Leipzig 1779–85 (Theory of the Art of Gardening), but his principal works were the interiors in the palace for Prince Max in Dresden (1783) and the sober wings he added in 1788–91 to the Berg Palais range at Schloss Pillnitz, near Dresden, for the Elector Friedrich August III (1763–1827; created King of Saxony, 1806). This delectable palace complex on the banks of the Elbe at Pillnitz had been begun in the 1720s with the Wasser Palais and Berg Palais ranges built by Pöppelmann for the Elector Augustus the Strong as an orientalizing fantasy. Even Weinlig was influenced by its style as can be seen in his unexecuted project of 1782 for a *chinoiserie* palace at Pillnitz.

Saxony was also important as the setting for some of the earliest English gardens in Germany, for example the park of the Chevalier de Saxe at the Prinz Georg Palais (later Sekundogenitur) in the Lange Gasse, Dresden (1781), and especially that laid out from 1782 for Countess Christina Brühl at Seifersdorfer Tal, which was much admired by German Romantics such as Goethe, Schiller, Herder and Wieland. Mention of Goethe reminds us of the civilized court established by his patron, Grand Duke Karl August of Saxe-Weimar (1757–1828) at Weimar not far from Dresden. The buildings carried out here for the grand duke by Arens and Gentz from 1790 to 1803 are more appropriately discussed in the next chapter.

Having surveyed the principal centres of classicism in Germany we should end by glancing at some of the numerous minor provincial architects who worked in transitional and regionally influenced styles. One of the most distinguished was Johann Joachim Busch who was employed by Duke Friedrich of Mecklenburg-Schwerin at Ludwigslust, near Schwerin, to build the parish church (1765–70) and, facing it, the Schloss (1772–6). In a style transitional from French Baroque classicism, this work is similar to the work of Krubsacius. However, the interior of the church may reflect the Neo-classical ideals of Laugier, with its colonnades of Tuscan columns supporting a coffered tunnel vault. In 1766 the art-loving Duke Friedrich employed Legeay to design a vast palace complex at Ludwigslust but instead he gave the commission for the Schloss to Busch whose massive building has a Tuscan portico similar to that at Krubsacius's Landhaus at Dresden, and a sumptuous Goldener Saal, a Baroque room lined with Corinthian columns yet with hints of the Louis XVI style.

A more sophisticated building wholly in the Louis XVI style is Schloss 38,39 Richmond (1769) by Karl Fleischer (1727–97), court architect at Brunswick. 166 This was built near Brunswick for the English Princess Augusta, daughter of Frederick, Prince of Wales, and sister of George III. She married Carl Wilhelm Ferdinand, Duke of Brunswick, in 1764 and commissioned from Fleischer this delectable triangular *pavillon* of the kind which Gabriel himself might have erected on the outskirts of Paris. There are further English connections at Osnabrück, a former bishop's seat held from 1761 by George III in charge for his second son, Frederick, Duke of York, then a minor. The leading architect in Osnabrück was Georg Heinrich Hollenberg (1752–1831), whose most impres-

38, 39 Karl Fleischer: Schloss Richmond, near Brunswick, 1768; the exterior and main saloon.

sive buildings in the city are the Hirschapotheke and Haus Tenge, both of the 40
1790s. These are old-fashioned for their date since, with their façades adorned
with broad fluted pilasters and swags, they probably derive from plates in
Neufforge.

In Münster, the capital of Westphalia and another episcopal seat, the
architect Wilhelm Ferdinand Lipper (1733–1800) was responsible for introducing classicism following his travels in Italy and France. On the death of the
architect Johann Konrad Schlaun (1695–1773), Lipper took over the completion of the Baroque Schloss at Münster which had been begun in 1767 for the 2
Prince Bishop from Schlaun's designs. Lipper's classical interiors culminate in
the central oval saloon surrounded by engaged Corinthian columns in a heavy 42
Louis XVI style. His most important independent work is the Romberger Hof at 41
Münster, built in 1777–82 for Freiherr Friedrich Wilhelm von Heereman and
sold in 1798 to Freiherr von Romberg. The seventeen-bay street façade of this
imposing palace is in a weighty Palladian style but the garden front is in an
elegant up-to-date French manner. Its first floor, with round-headed windows
surmounted by swags set in unmoulded rectangular reveals, recalls Jean
Rousseau's theatre at Amiens of 1778. The rich interiors are similarly in a variety
of styles though the oval saloon is decorated in a delicate neo-antique style
reminiscent of Bélanger.

41 Ferdinand Wilhelm
Lipper: Romberger Hof,
Münster, 1777–82.

42 Ferdinand Wilhelm
Lipper: oval banqueting
saloon in the Schloss at
Münster, *c*.1775.

A parallel combination of heavy Italianate or Palladian forms with elegant French classicism occurs in the later work of Peter Anton von Verschaffelt (1710–93), better known as a Rococo sculptor. Born in Ghent where he was trained as a sculptor, he worked in Brussels and Paris in the 1730s as a pupil of Verbeckt and Bouchardon. He subsequently worked in Rome for fourteen years before visiting England in 1751 with a letter of introduction from Cardinal Albani. He was called to Mannheim in 1752 by that great patron, the Elector Palatine Karl Theodor, with whose brilliant court Mozart, Voltaire, Lessing, Goethe and Schiller were all associated. Verschaffelt worked as a sculptor with Pigage at Schwetzingen and Benrath but also designed Palais Bretzenheim, Mannheim 43 (1782–8), for the illegitimate children of the Elector by the dancer Josepha Seyffert. Both this building and his Mannheim Arsenal (1777–9) incorporate elements borrowed from the Louis XVI style of contemporary France.

Similar work was carried out in Stuttgart by Reinhard Ferdinand Fischer (1746–1813), the best of the many talented pupils of Philippe de la Guêpière whom he succeeded as court architect at Stuttgart in 1773. Fischer's most interesting work is Schloss Hohenheim, near Stuttgart, built for Duke Karl Eugen in 1785–96 in a style transitional from Baroque to Neo-classicism and surrounded by one of the most famous Picturesque parks in Germany. Less happy is his Schloss Scharnhausen (1784), near Esslingen about nine miles from Stuttgart, a modest Palladian villa with a somewhat ungainly Ionic portico. His church of St Eberhard, Stuttgart, has a rather gaunt façade which also recalls Palladian sources, notably Palladio's Venetian churches. Designed *c.*1770, this was originally built near Karl Eugen's palace of Solitude but was re-erected in Stuttgart in 1808 by Karl von Uber. Fischer also projected an Academy of Arts at Solitude with a circular dining hall which was in the end built in Stuttgart in 1774–5 as the Akademiesaal. This lively interior, now destroyed 44 by bombing, contained a circular arcade of free-standing columns, a device he

was to adopt in his Temple of Cybele (1785) in the grounds of Schloss Hohenheim. This feature is perhaps inspired by the late-antique mausoleum of Sta Costanza in Rome though it is used by Fischer with an almost Baroque vigour.

It cannot be pretended that the story unfolded in this chapter, complicated by geographical and regional differences, is a very coherent one. There is no unity because there is no cultural or political centre, no central guidance or national identification with a particular style. A figure like Verschaffelt has no fixed nationality or style. Pioneer buildings like the museum at Kassel, the Schloss and garden buildings at Wörlitz, the church of St Blasien and the villas of Solitude and Monrepos, formed part of no general pattern and exercised little influence. The next chapter will be devoted to the attempts made after 1790 to end this situation and to create 'a style for a nation'.

44 Ferdinand Heinrich Fischer: Akademiesaal, Stuttgart, 1774–5.

CHAPTER III

A Style for a Nation

I T is the purpose of this chapter to investigate the Franco-Prussian school to which Karl Friedrich Schinkel (1781–1841), the greatest architect of nineteenth-century Germany, was the heir. This will involve considering what happened to German architecture and architectural thinking in the years between 1780 and 1800. How far was a new style developed and how is it to be related to contemporary European architecture? The architects at whom we shall be looking, born in the years between 1733 and 1772, in marked contrast to those in the last chapter, were all German. It is proposed to call this style Franco-Prussian since it would have been unthinkable without the impact of Ledoux and was centred on Berlin, which Frederick the Great's successor as King of Prussia, Friedrich Wilhelm II (reigned 1787–97), was determined to make not only a cultural centre but one dominated by German artists. Accordingly he summoned to work for him in 1788 Erdmannsdorff from Dessau, Langhans from Breslau, David Gilly from Stettin, and the sculptor Schadow from Berlin.

This has always been considered one of Germany's most important periods of architectural innovation and self-recognition. Schinkel's belief in the cultural significance of architecture, his sincerity and sense of mission, can be fully understood only in the context of the intellectual achievement of this generation in assessing architectural values and developing new aesthetic theories. The triangle of Berlin, Paris and Rome was the setting in which the new Franco-Prussian architectural style was born. It is personified in one man, David Gilly's son Friedrich Gilly, who died tragically of consumption, like the romantic artist that he was, at the age of twenty-eight in 1800. For an architect who built so little, his impact was astonishing. Schinkel and Klenze were both fired to become architects as young men by seeing his youthful projects, which must have encapsulated for them the bolder and more imaginative aspects of eighteenth-century Neo-classicism. It was to be their task to carry his fire into the new century with its problems and its building types more varied than Gilly could ever have imagined. Schinkel always regarded him as his sole master. The project which captivated them, as it did the whole artistic circle of Berlin, was his stunning entry for the competition announced in 1796 for a monument to Frederick the Great. Following his death in 1786 numerous competitions were held until well into the nineteenth century for a monument to commemorate his glory. Nothing seemed really adequate except, perhaps, for the founding of the German Empire in 1871. This confirmed the dominance of Prussia which, though he would not necessarily have welcomed it in this form, Frederick had done much to promote. It gives us another reason for suggesting that the style typified by Gilly might not unreasonably be described as Franco-Prussian.

It is significant that as early as 1786 Hans Christian Genelli (1763–1823) had submitted designs for a monument to Frederick the Great in the form of a prostyle Greek Doric temple. This was a design of greater intellectual

45 David Gilly: Vieweg House, Brunswick, 1800–7.

significance than Stuart's temple at Hagley of thirty years earlier, though it was based on literary knowledge rather than on first-hand acquaintance with Greek architecture. Winckelmann's doctrine of ideal beauty had by now been replaced by a more specific belief in Greek architecture as a perfected system. Germans were in the front line of the Greek Revival as can be seen, for example, in Weinbrenner's projects made in Berlin in the 1790s for redesigning the Pantheon in the elemental forms of the Doric style. These years were noted for discussion of the canonic baseless Doric order which now became synonymous with modernity. Architects like Weinbrenner were eager to realize a new architectural language with which they could identify themselves completely. In this process they became keen students of the latest French architectural theories, in particular Le Camus de Mézières' influential book, *Le génie de l'architecture, ou l'analogie de cet art avec nos sensations* (Paris 1780). A German translation of this appeared in 1789 in Gottfried Huth's *Allgemeines Magazin für die bürgerliche Baukunst* (General Magazine for Civic Architecture). Le Camus's emphasis on the expressive use of form to evoke sentiments appropriate to the function and character of a building, of which the visionary designs of Ledoux and Boullée are a classic example, was keenly adopted in Germany by architects and theorists such as Gentz and Hirt. Similar arguments also appeared in Humbert's *Ouvrages divers sur les belles lettres, l'architecture civile et militaire*, which was also partially translated in Huth's *Allgemeines Magazin*, 1797, vol. II, part 2, pp. 147ff.

Le Camus de Mézières and Humbert helped provide the artistic freedom, based on classical imagery, which conditioned the Franco-Prussian classicism of the 1790s. The art historian Alois Hirt (1759–1834), friend of Goethe and teacher of Schinkel, developed from Le Camus the notion of the 'characteristic', which he defined as 'that certain individuality by which forms, rhythms, thought and expression are distinguished, and specifically in the way demanded by the given object' (*Versuch über das Kunstschöne*, Essay on Aesthetics, published in 1797 in Schiller's *Horen*). In his *Die Baukunst nach den Grundsätzen der Alten*, Berlin 1809 (Architecture according to the Principles of the Ancients), Hirt hailed the Greek Doric order for its elevated expression of stability and permanence which it derived from its tectonic completeness. With such a theoretical backing the creators of the Franco-Prussian style had gained an independence with which they could work in the spirit of antique architecture with a new artistic freedom. We shall see this exemplified in the Berlin Mint, designed by Gentz in 1798, and in the description which he published of its architectural meaning.

The other formative influence on German Neo-classicism in these crucial years was Rome, which exercised an impact described by Goethe as 'a rebirth which changes one from within'. The German colony in Rome from the 1780s played a role in the development of the new architecture similar to that which the French Academy in Rome had in that of French Neo-classicism in the 1740s and 50s. German architects and scholars in Rome in the 1780s included Krahe, Jussow, Hansen, Arens, Genelli, Goethe and Hirt; and in the 1790s, Gentz and Weinbrenner. Here they absorbed the ideals of French Revolutionary architecture against a background of archaeological investigation not only into Roman but now also into Greek remains. A visit to Paestum now became a virtual necessity. Not surprisingly it was in Rome that Hirt wrote his *Die Baukunst nach den Grundsätzen der Alten* and that Weinbrenner illustrated it. When these architects left Rome they came home with a changed view of architecture which resulted in an imaginative revolutionary style defined by a reductionist vocabulary of sheerly modelled stereometric solids and sparse Greek Doric forms. This we shall see in the work of Gilly, Krahe, Gentz, Weinbrenner and Arens.

46 Carl Gotthard
Langhans: Brandenburg
Gate, Berlin, 1789–94;
lithograph of about 1840.

Yet another determining factor in these years was the rise of German nationalism and patriotism. In 1782 a National Theatre, the first, opened in Mannheim with a performance of Schiller's *Die Räuber*. Fourteen years later the terms of the competition for a national monument to Frederick the Great stipulated that it would have to foster morality and patriotism. The heroic associations which the Greek Doric style had acquired in the German Romantic imagination made it specially appropriate for such a monument. *Die Bestimmung des Menschen* (The Vocation of Man), published in 1800 by the philosopher J.G. Fichte, lent further support to this sense of high moral mission, while the occupation of Berlin by Napoleon's troops in 1806–08 served only, as we have seen, to strengthen Prussian nationalism. Fichte's 'Addresses to the German Nation' delivered in Berlin in 1807–8 played an important role in stimulating this patriotic fervour. In the meantime German Romantic writers such as Wackenroder and his friend Tieck had been responsible in the 1790s for the rise of an appreciation of medieval architecture which also bolstered the growing national pride. Wackenroder's essays, *Herzensergiessungen eines kunstliebenden Klosterbruders*, 1797, (Confidences of an Art-loving Monk), its posthumous sequel, *Phantasien über die Kunst für Freunde der Kunst* (Fantasies on Art for Friends of Art), and Tieck's novel, *Franz Sternbalds Wanderungen. Eine altdeutsche Geschichte*, 1798 (The Travels of Franz Sternbald. An Old German Tale), emphasized a German past which earlier writers, with the exception of Goethe, had largely ignored or despised.

The gateway to Franco-Prussian classicism is, appropriately, the gateway to
46 Berlin itself, the Brandenburg Gate, built in 1789–94 at the west entrance to the city from designs by Carl Gotthard Langhans (1733–1808). Born in Landshut,

Silesia, Langhans worked in Breslau from 1764 where his most important work was the new wing he added to the Palais Hatzfeld (1766–86), still in an old-fashioned style. He travelled in Italy in 1768–9, and in France, Holland and England in 1775. He moved to Berlin in 1788 to act as Oberhofbaurat (Director of the Royal Office of Buildings). Here his dissecting theatre of the Veterinary School (1789–90) was the first building to show an awareness of the new trends in French architecture typified in the work of Brongniart and Gondoin. It is memorable for its massive form, bare Doric order and impressive dome with a timber frame inspired by that of the Halle au Blé in Paris by Legrand and Molinos of 1782–3. The dome of the Halle au Blé was subsequently to be described in David Gilly's architectural periodical (see below, p. 65).

It was at the king's suggestion that Langhans adopted the Greek propylaea as the basis for the design of the Brandenburg Gate in 1789. It was to be the first monument of the Greek Revival, which played a vital role in German and English architecture, though not in French. Widely admired at the time as an essentially honest building, it played an important part in the emerging interpretation of Neo-classicism in Germany. The Greek Revival in Germany was, moreover, coloured with vague associations with the struggles of an emerging state for independence and liberty. James 'Athenian' Stuart, after all, had written in his *Antiquities of Athens* (vol. II, 1789) that the buildings on the Acropolis had been erected 'while the Athenians were a free people'.

It was, however, from a French publication, J.-D. Le Roy's *Ruines des plus beaux monuments de la Grèce* (Paris 1758), that Langhans must have derived his knowledge of the Athenian Propylaea, the source of the Brandenburg Gate. He never visited Greece, and the volume of Stuart and Revett's *Antiquities of Athens* illustrating the Propylaea did not appear till 1789. The Brandenburg Gate is, of course, by no means a copy of the Greek original. It has a lighter, *Dixhuitième* flavour, for Langhans was not quite bold enough to adopt the baseless Greek Doric of the fifth century BC which would have seemed shockingly bare to his contemporaries. He thus gives the columns bases and also introduces demi-metopes at the ends of the frieze, an entirely Roman practice; he runs columns all the way round the side pavilions instead of leaving their end walls blank as at the Propylaea; and he replaces the pediment of the Greek original with a raised attic fronted with an unusual tiered platform supporting an enormous quadriga. This great winged figure of Victory driving her chariot is by Johann Gottfried Schadow (1764–1850), the greatest Neo-classical sculptor of Germany, a disciple of Canova and a friend of Friedrich Gilly. Schadow also designed the sculptured metopes depicting the battle of the Lapiths and Centaurs, as on the Parthenon, while the prominent relief in the attic is by Christian Bernhard Rode.

The Brandenburg Gate was an eye-catching monument which attracted much attention and was seen as a fulfilment of the ambitions of Winckelmann concerning the imitation of Greek art. Nevertheless, its replacement of the unadorned Greek pediment of the Athenian Propylaea with the proud quadriga of a Roman triumphal arch was fraught with political implications in a military capital such as Berlin. Thus it was natural that in 1807 Napoleon, following his triumphal entry into Berlin, should have transported the quadriga to Paris where it remained for seven years. The Brandenburg Gate provided a natural backdrop for military parades until the end of the Nazi period, and even today forms what is visually the most arresting moment in the tragic wall which divides the city with blood and iron.

It was the first of a number of Doric gateways of which the most distinguished was Klenze's Propylaea in the Königsplatz in Munich, constructed as late as

DEM VERGNÜGEN DER EINWOHNER

47 Carl Gotthard
Langhans: State Theatre,
Potsdam, 1795.

1846–60. On a visit to Berlin in December 1794, the influential collector, patron and designer, Thomas Hope, was so struck with Langhans's masterpiece that when ten years later he wrote a polemical pamphlet on the style to be adopted for Downing College, Cambridge, he recommended the Brandenburg Gate as a model for the entrance to the new college. In 1806 the architect William Wilkins, who had been recommended by Hope for the commission, provided a striking Porters' Lodge in the style of a propylaea. This was never executed but in 1810 Thomas Harrison gave Chester Castle a similar entrance gate on the basis of designs which he had been cogitating since 1788.

Langhans himself, though he erected numerous buildings in Berlin and Potsdam in the last thirteen years of the eighteenth century, never produced a formula as arresting as that of his Brandenburg Gate. His handsome interiors in the Niederländischen Palais in Potsdam of 1787 are exercises in the manner of Erdmannsdorff at Wörlitz, while his Belvedere in the park of Schloss Charlottenburg is an unaccountable reversion to a Baroque mode. More severe are the interiors which he designed from 1790 at Gontard's Marmor Palais at Potsdam, including the entrance vestibule with a coffered ceiling inspired by Wood's *Ruins of Palmyra* (1753). He built a theatre for Friedrich Wilhelm II in 1788–9 next to Schloss Charlottenburg which became a centre of cultural enlightenment in these years, attracting talents such as Goethe and Lessing. The façades of the theatre, which still survive, are in an unadventurous Palladian style. His State Theatre at Potsdam of 1795 was more original with a tall somewhat templar façade crowned with a prominent relief in the antique style. In a second period of activity in Breslau, 1794–5, he remodelled the Royal Palace for Friedrich Wilhelm II. In 1800–2 he built the Theatre in the Gendarmenmarkt in Berlin.

With its old-fashioned mansard roof, this was striking only for its Ionic portico which Schinkel subsequently echoed when he replaced Langhans's theatre after its destruction by fire in 1817. The ultimate victor in the competition for a monument to Frederick the Great, his project of 1797, markedly less adventurous than Gilly's, was for an Ionic monopteros containing a statue of the king bathed in a mysterious light. It was never executed, though the intention of erecting a great monument to Frederick was not abandoned until the death of Friedrich Wilhelm III in 1840.

The Greek Doric temple, as we have noted, had made its first appearance in German architecture with the design of 1786 by Hans Christian Genelli (1763–1823) for a mausoleum for Frederick the Great. Produced when Genelli was studying in Rome with his brothers from 1785 to 1787, this was a small temple with a portico of fluted, baseless Greek Doric columns supporting a richly sculptured frieze and pediment. A figured frieze ran round the four walls of the sepulchral chamber within, which was dominated by a semi-recumbent effigy of Frederick for which a drawing survives by Schadow. Genelli, whose archaeological interests were not exclusively Greek, published a reconstruction of the Mausoleum at Halicarnassus in an edition of Vitruvius (Berlin 1801), illustrated by Augustus Rode; a commentary on Vitruvius in the form of letters from him to Rode (vol. I, Brunswick 1801; vol. II, Berlin 1804); and a study of the theatre in Athens (1818). A philosopher and theorist rather than a practising architect, he built Haus Ziebingen near Frankfurt an der Oder in about 1800, a Neo-classical villa with a circular Ionic hall in the chastest of tastes.

David Gilly (1748–1808) was one of the principal leaders of taste in a neo-antique direction in late-eighteenth-century Berlin. He came from a line of Huguenots exiled from France in the seventeenth century, so that the 'G' in his name is pronounced soft, not hard as it would be if it were a German name. Nonetheless, he and his son, Friedrich, regarded themselves as German and, unlike the Du Ry dynasty in Kassel, habitually wrote in German not French. Born in Schwedt, Pomerania, David Gilly was the first to pass the newly established state architectural examination in 1770, thus enabling him to occupy the position in the Prussian civil service of Landbaumeister for Pomerania and, from 1779, of Baudirektor. The attempt to create a German, indeed a specifically Prussian, style was bolstered by the creation of a civil service which included posts for architects. Gilly founded a private architectural school at Stettin in 1783 where his teaching combined the theories of French rationalism with the realities of rural building construction. Following his move to Berlin in 1788 to take up the post of Geheimer Oberbaurat, he founded a Bauschule in 1793 which he re-established in 1799 as a Bauakademie. This was destined to be one of the most important architectural schools in Europe, with Schinkel, Klenze, Weinbrenner, Engel and Haller von Hallerstein amongst its pupils. Though it owed much to J.-F. Blondel's celebrated academy in Paris, it also took up the ideals of Gilly's school at Stettin and thus emphasized construction and materials as the basis of design. As part of his plan of educating taste, Gilly founded one of the first architectural periodicals in German, *Sammlung nützlicher Aufsätze und Nachrichten, die Baukunst betreffend*, Berlin 1797–1806 (Collection of Useful Essays and Reports concerning Architecture). His experience in Pomerania gave him an understanding of vernacular technique and of the importance of solving practical problems economically, which was to give both his school of architecture and his journal their characteristic stamp of realism.

It is rare to turn over the pages of an architectural journal charged with such dynamism, clarity and confidence as David Gilly's *Sammlung*. The most ambitious architectural magazine of its day, it is full of the sense of mission and the hard-headedness of the men who wanted to turn provincial Berlin into a capital city which could vie in cultural importance with London and Paris. In tone and impact it can be compared with the publications of movements like the Bauhaus, de Stijl and l'Esprit Nouveau. Moreover, poetry and fire were breathed into the venture in the contributions of the young Friedrich Gilly (1772–1800) whose powerful sketches, whether of blast furnaces or of a crazily Picturesque garden house for the King of Prussia at Schloss Paretz, are the quintessence of the radicalism and the Romanticism of Prussian culture in the 1790s.

The coloured frontispiece to the first issue in 1797 sets the tone of the whole enterprise: a reduction by W.L. Riedel of an English engraving of the celebrated iron bridge at Coalbrookdale. In their search for a new Prussian style Gilly and his followers were the reverse of insular, looking for inspiration to the architecture of Revolutionary and Napoleonic France, and to that of the Industrial Revolution in England. The journal thus contains articles on iron bridges, street lighting, road and canal construction and agricultural buildings in England, and on the timber dome of the Halle au Blé in Paris by Legrand and Molinos of 1782–3, on Bélanger's Bagatelle of 1777, and on the Picturesque garden at Le Raincy, as well as reviews of books such R. Fulton's *Treatise on the Improvement of Canal Navigation* (1796) and Krafft's *Plans, coupes et élévations de diverses productions de l'art de charpenterie* (1805).

In its combination of articles on historical topics and on technical problems, its book reviews and its illustrations, Gilly's journal is indeed the forerunner of all subsequent architectural periodicals. We have compared it with the manifestos of the architectural and artistic groups of the 1920s, but its roots in the antique gave it a wider perspective and a more authoritative tone. Archaeologists and art historians such as Hirt, Augustus Rode and Genelli regularly contributed papers on antique architecture, of which one of the most interesting for English readers is the account in the volume for 1805, part 1, of Robert Smirke's study tour in Greece and Sicily.

Gilly was much patronized by the Prussian royal family, building Schloss Paretz near Potsdam in 1796–1800 for the Crown Prince who succeeded as Friedrich Wilhelm III in 1797, and Schloss Freienwalde (1798–9) as a summer residence for the Queen Mother. Paretz is a long low house, giving the impression of a simple country building in a rustic classical style. Here the king could play at being a Prussian farmer, though Gilly also provided a model village with a Gothic church and a Romantic landscaped park with a Gothic Belvedere and a Japanese pavilion perched on a grotto. Schloss Freienwalde is an elegant classical box with charming painted interiors.

45
168 David Gilly's most important building is the Vieweg House in Brunswick of 1800–7. This was built as the publishing house and private residence of the distinguished publisher, Friedrich Vieweg. Its portico in a stripped Greek Doric order, its eccentric rustication, its unmoulded window surrounds, and the Mannerist recession of the centre bays on its longest façade, give it the taut, geometrical and aggressive quality which characterizes the Franco-Prussian style. This makes it untypical of David Gilly's work as a whole, which is more relaxed, so that it is hard not to believe that Friedrich Gilly, Krahe or Gentz did not have a hand in its design. However, despite its uncompromisingly Neo-classical appearance in photographs, in reality it blends surprisingly unobtrusively into the historic heart of old Brunswick, adapting itself to a medieval street pattern in the Burgplatz near the cathedral.

48, 49, 50 Friedrich Gilly:
design for the Monument
to Frederick the Great,
1797. Opposite: two
details showing the
triumphal arch on the left
and the right-hand side
with sphinxes and
obelisks.

The leaders of the Franco-Prussian school developed in Berlin were Friedrich Gilly and Heinrich Gentz, to whom we should now turn, having looked at their forerunners, Langhans and David Gilly. Born in 1772 in Altdamm, near Stettin, Friedrich Gilly was introduced to architecture at an early age by his father. Moving to Berlin in 1788 he was appointed inspector in the Königliche Baubehörde, despite his extreme youth, and was trained at the Akademie der Bildenden Künste (Academy of Fine Arts) by architects and artists of the distinction of Erdmannsdorff, Langhans, Schadow, Becherer and Chodowiecki. His feeling for the purity and nobility of antique forms was influenced not only by this training but by his reading of Winckelmann and Goethe. All this led him to adopt an architecture of elemental geometric forms represented in an abstract, linear drawing technique. At the same time, he was also influenced by the group of Romantics round the poets Tieck and Wackenroder into seeing himself as a romantic artist in lonely pursuit of eternal truths. The competition announced by the Academy in 1796 for a monument to Frederick the Great came at an ideal moment for this gifted twenty-four-year-old· who, after years of rigorous intellectual and architectural training, had formed an individual classical style and an heroic and exalted conception of his role as an architect. Here was a chance to express all this in a project which would symbolize the cultural achievement and national stability which had been achieved under the unifying influence of Frederick the Great.

Gilly's ravishing scheme of 1797 created a sacred temple precinct dominated 48– by a Doric temple raised high on a massive substructure containing Frederick the 50 Great's sarcophagus. The great empty space surrounding this royal shrine is populated not with people but with solemn obelisks. It is entered through a daunting gateway, flanked by Doric colonnades, which combines the Greek propylaea with the Roman triumphal arch. Gilly has taken Langhans's Brandenburg Gate and remodelled it in the abstract geometrical language of Boullée and Ledoux, though how far he was acquainted with their Revolutionary style is unclear.

Six architects entered the competition for the monument: apart from Gilly

they were Langhans, Gentz, Erdmannsdorff, Hirt and Haun. Having selected the most modest, by Langhans, the king promptly died and the project was more or less buried with him. The most extravagant project, by Gilly, had a long and influential life in the intellectual and visual imagination of architects like Schinkel, Klenze, Stüler and Johann Heinrich Strack. Gilly was extravagant not only in the scale of his building but in his choice of site. Seeking a grandiose and self-contained setting for his visionary scheme, Gilly hit on the Leipziger Platz immediately south of the Brandenburg Gate. In some notes accompanying his designs he argued that this was appropriate since the Leipziger Platz led south through the Potsdam Gate to Potsdam which Frederick had made especially his own, while the road from Unter den Linden through the Brandenburg Gate to the west led to Schloss Charlottenburg, which Frederick had abandoned fairly early as a main residence. The following extracts from Gilly's notes demonstrate clearly the exalted frame of mind in which he approached his task:

> Let this external enclosure show, even in its simple form as well as in its fixed and indestructible scale, that it is supposed to contain a unique, unforgettable object for posterity; it will thus appear as a unique honourable monument to mankind. A covered, enclosed room must be very large in order to make a large effect. The use of glass for covering is improper. I know of no more beautiful effect than to be enclosed on all sides, to be cut off from the bustle of the world, so to speak, and to see above one the open, the quite open, heaven ... Also large in scale. Easily the largest in the whole city. The Temple of Jupiter at Agrigentum. The ancients have obeyed this rule on the whole ... It is architecture alone whose works can become colossal without disadvantage. Only reduction in scale makes their effect as a whole a plaything.

Despite the originality of his design, Gilly had no wish to disregard the Renaissance interpretation of the antique as represented by Palladio. Thus in his notes he quotes from Fréart de Chambray's edition of Palladio's *Quattro Libri* of 1650 in which Palladio suggests that where the ancients were guided by superstition in choosing locations for their temples,

> we, who are by the special grace of God freed from that darkness ... shall choose those sites for temples that shall be in the most noble and most celebrated part of the city, far from dishonoured places, and on beautiful and ornamented piazzas, in which many streets finish, whereby every part of the temple may be seen with its dignity, and afford devotion and admiration to whomever sees and beholds it ... the floor of the temple is to be raised as much as is convenient above the rest of the city. One is besides to ascend to the temple by steps; since the ascent alone to a temple is what affords greater devotion and majesty.

Gilly goes on to describe how the substructure of the temple would be of a darker coloured stone than the surmounting temple which would be 'of a lighter material in order to make striking the noble effect of its gleam against the sky'. Vaulted arcades penetrating the substructure would allow views right through it from the Potsdam Gate to the Leipzigerstrasse. The vault above the sarcophagus, which would be placed above human reach, would be crowned with a wreath of stars. The temple itself, covered with a bronze roof, would contain a kind of cult statue of Frederick the Great placed on a large base in a niche opposite the entrance and dramatically lit from above. 'This,' Gilly explained, 'is the most beautiful kind of illumination, especially for a statue which is never well illuminated in the open or in a sidelight.'

This concern with lighting effects, with vaults and stars, and with gleaming stones set against dark ones, recalls the attempts of Le Camus de Mézières in his *Le génie de l'architecture* (1780), of Boullée in his spherical monument to Newton (*c.* 1784), and of Soane, to achieve an architecture which would grip one emotionally by its deployment of 'lumière mystérieuse'. However, one of the aspects that was so compelling about Gilly's project was that he was able to combine the sentimental rhetoric of Boullée with a practical concern for the relation of a building to its actual environment. Thus Gilly describes how

> coming out of the temple one has from the top steps a view over a large part of the royal city, Frederick's creation. A unique panorama of its kind! Around the monument there runs a street for carriages and riders. Somewhat elevated and next to the houses there is a tree-lined path or rather a promenade for pedestrians.

Here are the seeds of so much of what was to be central to Schinkel's approach. Schinkel was concerned not only with the individual monument as aesthetic statement but with its relation to its setting, whether rural or urban, and to its users. An environmental concern had been familiar in England as an aspect of the Picturesque sensibility which began with Vanbrugh in the early years of the eighteenth century. However, it had rarely been applied, even in England, to public monuments or urban architecture, though it was to be influential in the siting of Wilkins's National Gallery in London in the 1830s. In accounting for the quite extraordinary impact of Gilly's design one should not, moreover, forget its quality as a Romantic architectural drawing. Though garden buildings and monuments were occasionally represented in perspective and in natural settings, it was extremely unusual, if not unique, for a major public building to be represented in this pictorial fashion. Gilly's large watercolour, showing a monumental building in its setting, viewed from an angle and bathed in light and shadow, must have come as a revelation.

In fact Gilly's powers as a draughtsman had been publicly recognized as early as 1795, when his drawings of the fourteenth-century Marienburg Castle had been exhibited at the Berlin Academy. Made on a tour of inspection of East Prussia with his father in 1794, these sepia drawings, which were subsequently published as lithographs, were exceptional in their dramatic representation of medieval architecture. The uncompromising rectangularity in mass and detailing of much of the late medieval brick architecture of North Germany and Poland was not without affinities with the Franco-Prussian style of Gilly's own day. The renewed interest in this brick tradition was given eloquent expression in some of the late works of Schinkel. Gilly's persuasive drawings led directly to the restoration under royal direction of the castle at Marienburg, which had been the seat of the Grand Master of the Teutonic Order.

Friedrich Wilhelm II bought one of Gilly's drawings of Marienburg and awarded him a travel bursary. He subsequently travelled in France, England, South Germany, Vienna and Prague from 1797 to 1799. His reactions to Paris, which had dominated German architecture for so long, are naturally of considerable interest. From the drawings and notes he made on this tour it is clear that he was especially impressed by the originality of the work of Legrand and Molinos, for example their Théâtre Feydeau (1789) and the giant glazed dome which they added to the Halle au Blé in 1782–3. He also drew the rue des Colonnes which led up to the Théâtre Feydeau, a remarkable street designed by Bernard Poyet and lined with Doric colonnades with primitivist piers at the angles. Gilly was, of course, impressed with the work of Ledoux and made

51, 52 Friedrich Gilly: design for a National Theatre, Berlin, 1798; exterior and auditorium.

drawings of his *barrières* and Hôtel de Thélusson, but the two places of which he chose to publish accounts in his father's architectural journal were both surprisingly un-Revolutionary in character. These were Bélanger's Bagatelle, the charming *pavillon* erected for the Comte d'Artois in 1777, and the Picturesque park of Le Raincy near Paris, laid out from 1786 to 1793 for the Duc d'Orléans, later Philippe-Egalité. Gilly was struck by the elegant planning and decoration of Bagatelle, praising as 'very picturesque' the principal bedroom which Bélanger had designed in the manner of a military tent. With its blue and white striped silk hangings supported on bundles of spears, its chimney piece ornamented with cannons, and its stoves resembling cannons and grenades, this was a room which, like much of Bélanger's decorative style, was destined to be a profound influence on the Directoire style and hence on the Empire Style of Percier and Fontaine. Gilly, incidentally, notes that whereas before the Revolution Bagatelle was open to the public by tickets which were easily obtainable, now that it had become national property it was let to a restaurant proprietor who used it for banquets and extravagant parties.

Gilly gave a somewhat ambiguous welcome to the 'jardin anglais' at Bagatelle which had been designed by the Scotch gardener Thomas Blaikie in 1778. He considered that French gardening had lost a great deal when it abandoned what he described as the 'sublime' effects of Le Nôtre. However, his fancy was taken by Le Raincy (which he refers to as Rincy), where there was a Russian village and a a Swiss cow-barn, though he singles out for special praise the elegant classical dairy.

Back in Berlin in 1799 Gilly erected a small number of now demolished buildings in a style inspired by what he had seen in Paris: the Villa Mölter in the Tiergarten, based directly on Bagatelle; the Palais Lottum in the Behrenstrasse, inspired by buildings like Bruneau's proto-Empire-Style Hôtel Chenot (1790), no. 50, rue de Provence (not rue de Montmartre as Gilly's drawing records); and garden buildings in the park at Schloss Bellevue, including a Tahitian hut, a dairy and a farm. At Dyhernfurth near Breslau, a noble Greek Doric mausoleum with a bare arched interior was erected from his designs in 1800–2 for Countess Maltzan. Today a poignant ruin, it is his only surviving building. The most
51 important project of his last two years was his unexecuted design for the National
52 Theatre in Berlin. This had been founded in 1786 by Friedrich Wilhelm II as an institution dedicated to German drama, to take the place of the French Comedy Theatre in the Gendarmenmarkt. As we saw on p. 63, it was built by Langhans in 1800–2.

It seems that even before the announcement in 1798 of the competition for the new theatre in the Gendarmenmarkt, Gilly had been considering the ideal form for a theatre. In one of his projects the theatre has a circular plan, described as 'in the manner of Greek and Roman theatres', one half of which reflects the semicircular shape of the auditorium, while the other is an entirely ornamental encumbrance. The expression of a curved auditorium on the front façade of a theatre had been anticipated in the first designs for the Théâtre de l'Odéon in Paris by Peyre and De Wailly of 1769, though not in the building as executed in 1779–82, and also in the Théâtre Feydeau (1789) by Legrand and Molinos. The feature recurs with great power in Gilly's design for the Berlin theatre, made after he had drawn and studied both the Odéon and the Théâtre Feydeau. However, he also repeats the great hemicycle as an entirely non-functional feature round the back of the stage building, so that it is not quite right to hail the design, as some modern architectural historians do, as a pioneer of functionalism. Another model which Gilly had studied was Ledoux's revolutionary theatre at Besançon

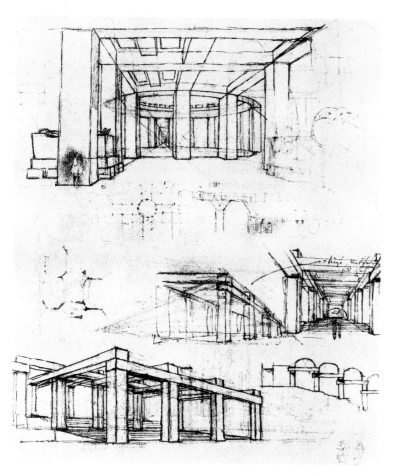

of 1775. Its virtually semicircular plan and absence of tiers of boxes were intended to recall the spirit of the antique amphitheatre: both features are echoed in Gilly's design.

It is the exterior which remains in the mind more than the interior, which is cluttered with rather mechanical Empire Style ornament. The largely unadorned masses of the exterior volumes – half-cylinders and cube – clash uncompromisingly with each other in a manner recalling the elemental geometry of Boullée and Ledoux. Also memorable are the imaginary monumental buildings with which Gilly supplies the Gendarmenmarkt. One of these represents one of the two already existing churches flanking the square, but Gilly had cavalierly replaced its tall drum and cupola by Gontard with a flattened Pantheon-type dome.

On his return to Berlin in 1799 Gilly had taken up an appointment as professor of optics and perspective at his father's Bauakademie which had been established under royal patronage in April that year. His concern with the pictorial representation of architecture made him akin to the painter J.M.W. Turner who was appointed professor of perspective at the Royal Academy in London in 1807, following Soane's appointment as professor of architecture in the previous year. A drawing Gilly produced at about this time for a square-piered mausoleum, in 53 which the conventional trappings of the orders have been pared away, is well known as one of the most advanced statements of the reductionist style which appeared in various European centres around 1800. Associated with the Greek Revival at its most imaginatively austere, this is represented by the outline engraving style of Carstens, Flaxman, Percier and Fontaine, and Hope; by the sans-serif lettering adopted, for example, by Soane; and by the linear disembodied architecture of the younger Dance and his pupil Soane.

54 Heinrich Gentz: the
Mint, Berlin, 1798.

Gilly built nothing as revolutionary as his square-piered mausoleum but the last building with which he was associated, the new Royal Mint in Berlin of 1798–1800, was perhaps the most striking executed monument of the Franco-Prussian school. The Mint was designed in 1798 by Gilly's brother-in-law, Heinrich Gentz (1766–1811), Gilly's contribution being the design of the broad figured frieze on the exterior. Gentz was born in Breslau where his father was Master of the Mint. He subsequently became General-Münzdirektor in Berlin and hence, doubtless, his son's commission for the Berlin Mint. Trained in Berlin by Gontard, Gentz travelled with a royal bursary from 1790 to 1795, spending three and a half years in Rome where he formed his blunt personal style in contact with the leading figures in the German artistic colony such as Weinbrenner, Tischbein, Hackert, Carstens and Hirt. His search for the origins of architecture led him to Paestum and Sicily to study the Greek temples. His journey home included visits to Holland, Paris and London, and on his return in the autumn of 1795 he was appointed Oberhofbauinspektor. His entry in the 1791 competition for a monument to Frederick the Great was an equestrian statue of the king wearing a toga, but for the competition of 1796 he produced an elaborate architectural scheme with Frederick's sarcophagus in a Corinthian monopteros flanked by Doric pavilions inspired by buildings such as Ledoux's Barrière des Bonshommes (1784–7). Gentz's third project of 1806 involved the replanning of central Berlin. He taught architecture from 1796 at the Academy of Fine Arts in Berlin, transferring two years later to the Bauakademie, where he taught the art of town-planning and cooperated closely as an architect with Friedrich Gilly.

54 Appropriately enough, the Berlin Mint, which is the fruit of that architectural association, housed the new Bauakademie on its upper floor from 1799 to 1806. It

also provided a home for the royal collection of minerals, as the inscription over its door, 'Friedericus Guilielmus III Rex, Rei Monetariae, Mineralogicae, Architectionicae', recorded. An uncompromisingly stark statement of the combined neo-antique and modernist ideals of Gilly and Gentz, it eschewed comfortable details such as mouldings and relied for its effect on bold cubic massing and on Gilly's emphatic figured frieze, 116 feet long and nearly six feet high. Executed by Schadow, this was carved with scenes symbolizing the various functions of the building, especially coining and mining. The Mint, which stood in the Werdersche Markt, was demolished in 1886 but the frieze survives on an apartment building in Charlottenburg.

In his account of the Mint in David Gilly's journal in 1800 Gentz wrote: 'In designing I had no Roman, or Greek, or Egyptian ideal; rather after I had let my spirit be actively absorbed in the purpose of the building, I designed a façade, which was not simply suited to the whole, but was necessarily derived from it and indeed which could not have developed in any other way'. He explained also that the 'thinking architect should develop the character of his building from his own self and from his vocation.' In his journal of his tour to Paestum and southern Italy he had recorded that 'I have in general noticed that I admired the appropriate design and the appropriate decorations and thought that this is the object of Greek architecture'.

Though emphasizing that the Mint was not a copy of any Greek building, he was not ashamed to point out that the capitals of the massive Greek Doric columns guarding the entrance were based on drawings in Stuart and Revett's *Antiquities of Athens*. Nor should it be forgotten that the Mint owed much to the studies which Gentz and Gilly had made of the most original monuments of Paris erected on the eve of the Revolution, such as Ledoux's barrières and the private houses of Bélanger in the rue Pigalle, rue des Capucins de la Chaussée d'Antin, and elsewhere. The plan of the Mint was no less striking than its exterior. The entrance door opened directly into an octagonal hall containing in the centre a circular staircase surrounded by eight columns. This hall led into a circular room which rose through the body of the building and was lit by a glazed dome. Fortunately, the interiors at Gentz's next commission, for remodelling the Schloss at Weimar in 1801–3, survive to enable one to appreciate his skill as a Greek Revivalist.

Gentz's work at Weimar included remodelling in 1803–4 the early-eighteenth-century Riding School with a smart Franco-Prussian façade punctu- 246 ated with prominent Greek key friezes. However, his achievement here cannot be discussed in isolation from the remarkable flowering of Romantic classicism in the modest grand-ducal capital of Weimar, under the guidance of Grand Duke Karl August of Saxe-Weimar (1757–1828) and his mentor, Goethe. In this remote town lived Wieland from 1772 to 1813, Goethe from 1775 to 1832, Herder from 1776 to 1803 and Schiller from 1799 to 1805, while architects summoned to work on the Schloss between 1789 and 1840 included Arens, Thouret, Gentz, Coudray and Schinkel. Goethe's eyes were opened to the power of architecture to move the soul by a visit to Strasbourg Cathedral in 1772. He became a champion of the then neglected Gothic style which he saw as a force akin to nature yet, at the same time, essentially German. He thus wrote of Strasbourg Cathedral in his *Von deutscher Baukunst*, 1772/3 (On German Architecture): 'this is German architecture, our architecture. For the Italian has none he can call his own, still less the Frenchman. . . . Come up and acknowledge the deepest feeling for truth and beauty of proportion, quickening out of the strong, rugged German soul.' He was also attracted in the 1770s and 80s by the

naturalistic and romantic effects aimed at the English Picturesque garden. He was in touch with Erdmannsdorff and the Prince of Anhalt-Dessau during the laying out of the park at Wörlitz and was also familiar with C.C.L. Hirschfeld's exhaustive five-volume study, *Theorie der Gartenkunst*, 1779–85 (Theory of the Art of Gardens). Following his move to Weimar, where he became one of the three ministers of state in 1776, Goethe laid out the Schloss park along the banks of the river Ilm with a series of Picturesque garden buildings from 1777. Apart from the usual grottoes, ruined columns and Gothic summer houses, there was the Altar of Good Fortune which Goethe built in 1777 in the form of an un-adorned sphere resting on an equally unadorned cube. The symbolism of timeless geometry in harmony with the forces of nature was one being exploited at about that moment by Boullée in his spherical monument to Newton.

Goethe's decisively important visit to Italy in 1786–7 helped transfer his artistic enthusiasms to classical ideals and especially, following his visits to Segesta, Agrigento and Paestum in 1787, to Greek architecture, to which he reacted as romantically as he had earlier to Gothic. This poetic interpretation of both Greek and Gothic as quintessential expressions of the German soul is something we shall recognize when discussing the early career of Schinkel. Goethe's enthusiasm for Greece found early expression in the interiors of the Schloss at Weimar which were remodelled under his guidance from 1789 onwards, having been gutted by fire in 1774. In 1801–3 Gentz provided a bold new staircase in the east wing which is one of the most thoroughgoing statements of the Greek Revival in Europe, and is especially remarkable for its early date.

55 Heinrich Gentz: staircase in the east wing of the Schloss at Weimar, 1800–3.

57 Johann August Arens:
crypto-porticus of the
Roman House, Weimar,
1791–7.

With its screen of impeccably detailed Greek Doric columns, its coffered ceilings and large reliefs on the walls, the staircase hall influenced that in the City Hall in Helsinki built in 1827–33 by C.L. Engel, who had been a pupil of Friedrich Gilly and Gentz at the Berlin Bauakademie.

56
243
To the north of the staircase lay the Festsaal, the principal reception room of the Schloss until the fire of 1774. In 1794 the seventy-three-year-old Clérisseau was approached for a design for rebuilding this room but his proposals for an interior in the then outdated style of Chambers and Adam did not find favour with Goethe. Instead, Gentz provided a new Festsaal, known as the Weisser Saal, in 1802–3, a rectangle defined by twenty free-standing columns with beautiful Greek capitals of the Erechtheum Ionic order. The running frieze round the outer walls was based on a Roman source from the Temple of Antoninus and Faustina in Rome. For the ceiling Gentz relied on a design made by Thouret, of whom more later. Interiors by Gentz in the north wing included the Cedar Room and the Falcon Gallery, while other chastely Neo-classical interiors in the east wing, dating from the 1790s, were by Thouret.

Johann August Arens (1757–1806), a native of Hamburg and a pupil of C.F. Harsdorff at the Academy in Copenhagen, worked under De Wailly in Paris before studying garden architecture in England and touring Italy in 1786–8. In Italy he met Goethe who brought him to Weimar in 1789 to remodel the Schloss. In 1790–4 he rebuilt the central range of the burnt-out east wing, providing an elegant Tuscan colonnade along the first floor of the east façade facing the bridge over the river Ilm. The interiors, as we have seen, were provided later by Thouret and Gentz. Arens, in the meantime, was building the so-called Roman House (1791–7) for Grand Duke Karl August near the southern end of the Schloss park.

This is a long rectangular pavilion on a sloping site with a Roman Ionic portico on the west entrance front and a remarkable crypto-porticus at the opposite end on the lower ground beneath the east front. The internal planning of this building, which became a favourite residence of the grand duke in his old age, was complex and asymmetrical, with three principal reception rooms, three smaller rooms and a staircase hall, all on the main floor. With their marbled walls punctuated with antique reliefs, these crisply decorated interiors, of which the finest is the domed Blue Room, were designed by C.F. Schuricht in 1794.

It is the design of the basement entrance or crypto-porticus which makes the 57 Roman House so fascinating, for one of its three shallow segmental arches is supported on two pairs of stumpy Greek Doric columns. These create a singularly archaic effect because, like the columns of some unexcavated temple, they seem half buried in the earth. Ledoux had achieved a similar impression in his entrance archway at the Hôtel de Thélusson, while Greek Doric columns supporting segmental arches featured in Bélanger's house in the rue des Capucins de la Chaussée d'Antin and in Bruneau's Hôtel Chenot in the rue de Provence. This primitivist note is untypical of Arens's work as a whole and is probably due to Goethe's studies in Paestum and Sicily. Indeed, a drawing which Arens made in Rome in 1788 for a building with a colonnade of six Greek Doric columns may well be a preliminary project for the Roman House, made under Goethe's influence. The drawing is inscribed 'Projet d'une Maison de Campagne', and we know that as early as 1787 Goethe had promised Grand Duke Karl August to bring back a design for a garden house from Rome.

When Friedrich Gilly visited Weimar in August 1798 to imbibe the atmosphere of this paradise of Romantic classicism, it is not surprising that he should have made a drawing of the Greek Doric basement entrance of the Roman House, for it must have seemed like a realization of a remarkable sketch for a Doric interior he had made in 1794. On the same page of his Weimar sketchbook he recorded the interior of the Court Theatre which had been built in the centre of the town from designs by J.F.R. Steiner in 1779–80 and had been remodelled internally by Thouret in 1798. Inspired by Ledoux's theatre at Besançon, Thouret's striking interior boasted a continuous colonnade of Greek Doric columns round the first-floor gallery. From 1791 to 1817 Goethe was director and was responsible for the first productions of *Egmont* and *William Tell*. Burnt in 1825, the theatre was rebuilt to a design by Coudray which in turn was replaced in 1905 with the stylish classical building by Heilmann and Littmann of Munich which survives today.

Nicolaus Friedrich von Thouret (1767–1845), born at Ludwigsburg near Stuttgart, was trained in Paris between 1789 and 1791 where he worked for a time under the Neo-classical painter J.-B. Regnault (1754–1829), and studied in Rome from 1793 to 1796 where he was much influenced by Weinbrenner. After working for Goethe and the grand duke at Weimar from 1798 to 1800, he returned to Stuttgart where he was extensively employed from 1803 to 1815 by Duke Friedrich of Württemberg (reigned 1797–1816) on the interiors of the palaces at Stuttgart, Ludwigsburg and Hohenheim, and the *pavillion* of 58 Monrepos. His interiors (now destroyed) at Stuttgart and surviving interiors at 60 Ludwigsburg were fine examples of the Empire Style which appropriately reflected the fact that Duke Friedrich had been made a king by Napoleon in 1806. One of Thouret's most attractive works is his Kursaal (Pump Room) of 59 *c.* 1825 at Bad Canstatt, Stuttgart. This is a late echo of Ledoux with its monumental, semicircular, glazed entrance-arch protected by a semicircular colonnade of Greek Doric columns, unfluted save for a band below the capital.

58 Nicolaus Friedrich von Thouret: staircase hall of Schloss Hohenheim, Stuttgart, 1806–15.

After Gilly and Gentz the most important architect who designed in what we have called the Franco-Prussian style was Friedrich Weinbrenner (1766–1826), although he was unable or unwilling to translate into built form his bold sketches of the 1790s with their reductionist vocabulary of stereometric solids and strong contrasts of light and shade. Thus it may be more appropriate to consider his architectural contribution to Karlsruhe in a later chapter which will investigate the post-Napoleonic creation of sober modern cities out of medieval and Baroque court seats.

It was on a visit to Berlin in *c.* 1791, where he met Langhans, Genelli and Gilly, that Weinbrenner was introduced to the new classicism. Soon he travelled to Italy in company with the painter Asmus Jacob Carstens where he remained for five years as part of the lively German artistic colony in Rome. He studied the Greek remains at Paestum and Sicily; he prepared the plates for Alois Hirt's theoretical work, *Die Baukunst nach den Grundsätzen der Alten*, Berlin 1809 (Architecture according to the Principles of the Ancients); and he made numerous sketches and designs for public buildings, tombs, prisons and monuments in a chilling antique style inspired by the visionary projects of Boullée and Ledoux and by the dramatic representational techniques of Piranesi. Most of his executed work in Karlsruhe, whither he returned in 1797, was in a more conventional manner, his pyramidal monument of 1825 to the margrave in the Marktplatz and his Mint of 1826 reflecting something of his earlier style. His most startling project never left the drawing board. This was for the remodelling of the Lange Strasse in 1808 with, on each side, a continuous colonnade of unmoulded round-headed arches rising through all three storeys, and crowned by an unbroken horizontal cornice. The stark relentless quality of the Franco-Prussian style is expressed in this shrill and hypnotic repetition of verticals and horizontals forming a street from which, like one in a nightmare, there is no escape.

Peter Joseph Krahe (1758–1840) is memorable as the architect of the Villa Salve Hospes at Brunswick in 1805–8, one of a considerable number of buildings, including Weinbrenner's Mint, which are dependent on Gentz's Berlin Mint. Krahe was trained as a painter but turned to architecture as a result of the powerful influence of the monuments of Rome where he stayed from 1782 until 1786. His designs at this time are in the megalomaniac style of the French Grand Prix winners, such as Vaudoyer with whom he may have been in contact. His career, first in Koblenz and then in Brunswick, was hindered by the political 61 upheavals of the Napoleonic Wars, so that the Villa Salve Hospes, a small country house for a merchant, is probably his major executed work. Its simple geometrical masses are unadorned save for occasional trophies pinned on like the 62 braid on a military uniform, while the garden front has an unexpected touch of 176 drama in the form of a shadowy coffered arch in the centre. It is worth noting that Gilly had designed an exactly similar façade in a project for a country house dated 1796.

Peter Speeth (1772–1831) is also known largely for the design of a single 63 building, the Prison at Würzburg (1811, 1826–27), built as guards barracks for the prince bishop of Würzburg, later used as a women's prison and today a YMCA hostel (with no original interior). As possibly the most extreme executed statement of the whole Franco-Prussian school, it is not inappropriate to end this chapter by considering it. Born in Mannheim, Speeth studied architecture from 1784 under Georg Weber in Frankfurt where he worked as an assistant to Nicolas de Pigage from 1788 to 1794. From 1807 to 1815 he was architectural director at the short-lived Hapsburg court at Würzburg of the Grand Duke Ferdinand of

59 Nicolaus Friedrich von Thouret: Kursaal at Bad Canstatt, Stuttgart, 1825.

60 Nicolaus Friedrich von Thouret: interior of Schloss Ludwigsburg, Stuttgart – ceremonial hall (1810).

81

61, 62 Peter Joseph
Krahe: front and back
elevations of the Villa
Salve Hospes, Brunswick,
1805–8.

Tuscany. The barracks which Speeth built below the Marienberg fortress are a gripping exercise in the *architecture parlante* of French Revolutionary classicism. We are meant to be impressed by the forbidding areas of rustication, alarmed by the daunting windowless masses, unnerved by the apparent dislocation of scale, and frightened by the impression that the tremendous weight of the upper part of the building is pushing the semi-circular entrance arch into the ground: again a device paralleled in the 'architecture ensevelie' of Boullée. While echoing the wilful distortion which characterizes Bélanger's late domestic architecture, the building was, to some extent, a freak both in function and design. The real heir to the Franco-Prussian style propagated by the Berlin Bauakademie was Schinkel. It is time we considered how far he was able to adapt the ideals of the eighteenth-century Bauakademie in which he was trained to the increasingly urban climate of the nineteenth century.

63 Peter Speeth: guards barracks at Würzburg, later used as a prison, 1811, 1826–7.

CHAPTER IV

Karl Friedrich Schinkel

THE creative genius of Karl Friedrich Schinkel (1781–1841) was so protean and his output so huge that, like most great artists, he defies neat stylistic classification. He is Greek yet Gothic; classical yet modern; rationalistic yet poetic; a sober civil servant with a commitment to architecture as a public service, yet the friend of princes and the designer of dream palaces. Profoundly influenced by philosophers like Fichte and Hegel with their essentially post-Christian understanding of man's place in history and in the moral order, he played an important role in the accompanying process by which Prussia achieved self-realization and eventual dominance over Germany. However, his search for architectural fundamentals gives him a permanent significance in European architecture which is independent of the particular historical circumstances of his day. For an indication of this we have only to consider the quite extraordinary amount of literary attention which has been paid to him. He must be the most written-about architect in history. Apart from the *Lebenswerk* series, begun in 1939 and now in its fourteenth folio volume, there are at least a dozen monographs, numerous exhibition catalogues and countless articles devoted to him. Moreover, as the anti-historical experiment of the Modern Movement comes to an end, practising architects are returning for inspiration to an architect whose classicism seems neither old nor new but timeless.

Schinkel was born in Neuruppin, a garrison town about seventeen miles from Berlin in the Mark Brandenburg province, where his father was a local inspector of churches and schools. In August 1787 a fire destroyed nearly two thirds of the town, including the Schinkel home, and precipitated his father's death in October from injuries sustained in rescue work. Schinkel's early years were spent in a town in the process of complete reconstruction under royal sponsorship. This was a formative start to his career and may also have encouraged his later concern with fire-proof construction. In 1794 he moved with his widowed mother and five brothers and sisters to Berlin where three years later the sight of Gilly's design for a monument to Frederick the Great at the Academy of Fine Arts filled him with the desire to follow Gilly's example by creating architecture of ennobling quality. Accordingly in March 1798 he presented himself as a pupil of David Gilly, Friedrich being on his foreign study tour at that moment. By 1799 he was living in the Gilly house in Berlin and attending the Bauakademie which opened that year in the new Mint building. The teaching at the Bauakademie, as we have seen, combined elements inspired by French schools such as Blondel's academy and the Ecole Polytechnique, with the emphasis on sound construction, simplicity and economy, which Gilly had acquired as director of country buildings in Pomerania. To this practical basis, provided by the teaching of David Gilly and Langhans, it added instruction in classical theory by the art historian Alois Hirt, as well as a strong dose of the forcefully romantic imagination of Friedrich Gilly and Heinrich Gentz. Gentz's *Elementarbuch* (1803) coloured Schinkel's attitude to the significance and the handling of the orders throughout his career.

64 Karl Friedrich Schinkel: staircase of the Altes Museum, Berlin, 1823.

Friedrich Gilly regarded Schinkel as his heir. On his death in August 1800 he left him his drawings which he and Klenze treated like precious icons, making copies of them and, in Schinkel's case, drawing on them for inspiration throughout his career. Schinkel began his professional life as an architect by winding up Gilly's practice and working on buildings in 1802–5 in Gilly's style, such as the Steinmayer House in the Friedrichstrasse and Schloss Buckow, near Berlin. These, as well as unexecuted designs for four villas on the water and for the colossal Schloss Köstritz with its Egyptian overtones, echo the blocky stereometric quality of the Franco-Prussian style and Gilly's concern for showing buildings in their setting.

In 1803 Schinkel left Berlin for the tour of Italy which Gilly was never able to undertake. With his Prussian outlook Schinkel did not respond to the warmth and charm of Italy but was certainly struck by the richness and variety of Italian medieval and vernacular architecture. He was more interested in constructional problems, for example those of Neapolitan domestic architecture, than of actual monuments. What he admired at Milan Cathedral was its sound building and he wrote to David Gilly that his highest principle was honesty and quality in building construction. He especially admired brick building and determined to develop this type in his own architecture, an ambition he eventually realized in his Bauakademie. Unlike Gentz, he did not measure and study actual buildings but immediately transformed everything he saw into a creative expression of his own. He wrote to Gilly in 1804 that 'For the most part, the monuments of antiquity do not offer anything new for an architect, because one has been acquainted with them since one's youth. But the sight of these works in their natural setting holds a surprise which comes not only from their size, but also from their picturesque grouping.' He also argued at this time that 'Gothic has everything in common, except for style, with the Greek'.

In Sicily in the winter of 1803–4 he fell in love with the extraordinary cultural mélange of Greek temples and Norman Romanesque with its Islamic overtones. In his numerous topographical drawings and paintings he specialized in panoramic views of towns and landscapes which emphasized the relation of individual buildings to their settings, whether natural or urban. No less captivating were his drawings of imaginary buildings in landscapes such as 'City Square by the Sea', 'Cathedral on a Height overlooking the Sea', and 'Basilica on a Hill'. His precise panoramic views, drawn from remote and detached positions, helped distance him from the varied styles of the individual monuments. He was later to employ this detachment from accidentals in the evolutionary account of architectural development in his unfinished *Architektonisches Lehrbuch* (Architectural Textbook), and in the views of his own works which he published in his *Sammlung Architektonischer Entwürfe*, 1819–40 (Collection of Architectural Designs). The engravings in the *Sammlung* depicted his buildings in relation to the surrounding buildings of all periods, watched by animated and intelligent male observers in the elegant dress of the day.

In Rome he moved in the long-established colony of German artists and writers which now included the philologist and diplomat, Wilhelm von Humboldt, and the painters Joseph Anton Koch, Gottlieb Schick and Karl Ludwig Kaaz, who gave him a helpful training in painting. This enabled him to translate into powerful oil paintings his sketches like 'Cathedral on a Height overlooking the Sea', which was inspired by Milan Cathedral. This skill was to prove especially valuable to him during the occupation of Berlin by the French following Prussia's defeat at Jena in 1806 when there were naturally few architectural commissions. One of the best known of these paintings is his

65

65 Schinkel: fantasy drawing showing Milan Cathedral on a height overlooking Trieste, 1809.

'Medieval Cathedral by the Sea' (1813), a tour de force which rivals the work of Caspar David Friedrich. This panoramic vision, combining heady romance with meticulous attention to detail, is not simply a piece of nostalgia for the lost Middle Ages, because the medieval town has been modernized with the addition of Neo-classical buildings such as a palace, a viaduct and a small Greek Doric portico on the waterfront.

In 1806 Schinkel began a career as a diorama and panorama painter for the theatrical impresario Wilhelm Gropius, sharing lodgings with two of Gropius's sons, Carl Wilhelm and Ferdinand, who were both painters. The technique of the panorama was an English invention which had recently been imported to Germany. With its illusionistic scene painting, artificial lighting and appropriate music, it was an early version of the modern *son et lumière* and could also be used to recreate not merely existing towns and scenery but historical and contemporary events such as the burning of Moscow and the defeat of Leipzig, both of which Schinkel presented with great dramatic effect in 1813. None of Schinkel's panoramas and dioramas, of which he painted about forty-five, has survived, though we have a small etching of his panorama of Palermo of 1808, a poor substitute for the original which was fifteen feet high and ninety feet long. After 1815, when he was made responsible for stage scenery at the royal Opera House, Schinkel switched from panorama painting to scenery, executing over a hundred sets for about forty productions from 1815 to 1828, including Gluck's *Alceste*, Spontini's *Olympia*, Weber's *Der Freischütz* and Hoffmann's *Undine*. The best known are the twenty-six spectacular scenes he painted in 1815 for *The Magic Flute*, which must represent one of the highest points in the history of stage design. Having studied the recent publications on Egyptian architecture of Denon, Belzoni and Gau, he presented this information with a pictorial genius

66 Schinkel: design for the bedroom of Queen Luise at Schloss Charlottenburg, 1810.

akin to that of Piranesi in ravishingly romantic scenes which do more than justice to the vapid rhetoric of the libretto. The scenes caused a tremendous stir in Berlin and were published by Thiele in 1823.

The Prussian royal family had returned from exile in 1809 in which year the much-loved Queen Luise, having been entranced by an exhibition of Schinkel's pictures, commissioned him to design some interiors in the palaces at Berlin and Charlottenburg. In the following year, with the support of Wilhelm von Humboldt, Minister of Education from 1809 to 1810, she acquired for Schinkel the post of Oberbauassessor in the Department of Public Works. He was thus responsible for reviewing the aesthetic element in all buildings erected by the state. Not that there were any in 1810, but at least this gave him time to consider the architectural image which it would be appropriate for Prussia to adopt once the war was over.

In the bedroom which Schinkel created for Queen Luise at Schloss 66 Charlottenburg in 1810 he attempted to simulate the roseate hue of dawn by hanging pink wallpaper with white muslin from floor to ceiling. The simple pear-wood furniture which Schinkel designed for the room, including an Empire Style bed of the 'lit-bateau' type, still survives, though the muslin-draped walls were re-hung in 1974 with considerably less panache than in Schinkel's original scheme.

The poor queen did not live long to enjoy her rosy bedroom and her death in July 1810 at the age of thirty-four heightened the already intense patriotic fervour of a country in the grip of Napoleon. Her husband, Friedrich Wilhelm III, had clear ideas as to the form her mausoleum should take. Only sixteen days after her death, Schinkel had drawn a stern Greek Doric façade which, resembling Friedrich Gilly's mausoleum at Dyhernfurth, was based on a sketch supplied by the king. With the assistance of Gentz he erected this modest but 67 impressive Doric mausoleum in the gardens of Schloss Charlottenburg in 1810. It houses a noble recumbent effigy of the queen by Christian Daniel Rauch. In the meantime Schinkel had prepared his own tribute to the memory of the queen in 68 the form of proposals for a striking Gothic mausoleum which he exhibited at the Berlin Academy in 1810. Caspar David Friedrich exhibited two paintings in the same exhibition and Schinkel's designs can be seen as his own independent contribution to the Romantic movement. However, unlike Friedrich, Schinkel did not generally paint ruins but intact Gothic structures such as this mausoleum.

The literary commentary which Schinkel found it necessary to submit with his design is one of the key documents of the Gothic Revival and shows how much he had been influenced by followers of Goethe such as Friedrich Schlegel and Clemens Brentano, for whom Gothic was an expression of the infinite. Just as

68 Schinkel: design for a Gothic mausoleum of Queen Luise, 1810.

69 Schinkel: design for the classical interior of the mausoleum of Queen Luise, 1810.

Gilly had seen his Doric monument to Frederick the Great as a symbol of Prussian order, so Schinkel now saw Gothic as embodying the national spirit, and as 'the outward and visible sign of that which united Man to God and the transcendental world'. Gothic was supposed to be 'higher in its principles than antiquity', since it expressed an idea, whereas classical architecture was supposedly dictated by materials and construction. He describes how

> Light falls through the windows which surround the sarcophagus on three sides; the stained glass suffuses the whole mausoleum, which is built of white marble, with a soft rosy glow. In front of this hall is a portico, surrounded by trees of the darkest hue; you ascend the steps and enter with a gentle thrill of awe into the darkness of the vestibule, from which through three high openings you look into the hall of palms, where the deceased surrounded by angels rests peacefully in the clear rose of dawn.

The roseate hue of this mausoleum must be seen as a reflection of Schlegel's colour theory whereby red or rosy colours are understood as a symbol of communication between heaven and earth. From Schlegel, too, Schinkel derived his ideal of Antiquity and Gothic as twin ideals and hence his ambition of synthesizing both in a new style whereby one would be improved by the other. Schinkel hints at this in his description of the mausoleum but the design itself is far more expressive since it is in effect a small temple with a portico of pointed arches. The smooth plain wall surface above the arches contradicts anything Gothic, while the steps similarly reflect the temple theme.

This synthesis of Gothic and classic forms recurred in the domed Gothic church which appears in his painting of 1811 called *Abend* (Evening) and in the National Cathedral which he designed in 1815 to commemorate the wars of liberation of 1813–15. This great Gothic building with a domed choir was to stand in the Leipziger Platz in Berlin which, significantly, Gilly had earlier envisaged as the setting for his monument to Frederick the Great. Like Gilly's monument, Schinkel's cathedral was to rise above the life of the city on a high platform. As a true expression of Romanticism the building was to be completed by future generations. Schinkel was urged in the Romantic nationalism of this project by the Crown Prince Friedrich Wilhelm (1795–1861), to whom he had given drawing lessons as a child and with whom, as we shall see, he was to work closely throughout his career. The sculptural programme of the cathedral included depiction of the Order of the Iron Cross, the highest honour awarded by the Prussian state. Schinkel's design of 1813 for the Iron Cross was in use till 1945. Though his national cathedral was never executed, a remarkable Gothic memorial in the form of a huge cast-iron pinnacle was erected from his designs in 1818 on the Templower Berg (now Kreuzberg) where it still survives.

It has been necessary, even in a book on Neo-classical architecture, to outline the early history of Schinkel's devotion to Gothic. Though he later dropped the intense Romanticism of his youth, he retained from his Gothic days a belief in architecture as an expression of high ideals and, in particular, of the cultural and political aspirations of Prussia. The contemporary philosopher J.G. Fichte, whose writings were the only book Schinkel took with him on his travels of 1803–5, had published *Die Bestimmung des Menschen* (The Vocation of Man) in 1800. It was Fichte's concept of moral vocation which helped form Schinkel's vision of architecture as a public responsibility, and it was Fichte's 'Reden an die Deutsche Nation' (Addresses to the German Nation), delivered in 1807–8, which stimulated patriotic fervour in Berlin and a sense of Prussian cultural identity. Fichte was first Rector of Berlin University, which had been founded in 1809 under the aegis of Wilhelm von Humboldt as Minister of Education. We have already seen in the first chapter how Humboldt created a total system of state education in which stress was put on the cultural development of German citizens under a powerful monarch by means of the study of Greek history and the German past – the twin poles of Schinkel's own architectural world. Moreover, when Friedrich Wilhelm III opened the university he made a speech emphasizing that the military defeat of Prussia must be compensated for by intellectual and cultural achievement.

It is against this remarkable background of self-conscious improvement, both national and personal, that we must see Schinkel's architectural contributions to the city of Berlin. In 1815 he was promoted within the Prussian civil service to the position of Geheimer Oberbaurat with special responsibility for the development of the city for which he produced a comprehensive plan in 1817, the first of many. The range of functions, from military to cultural, of the earliest and most important of his executed buildings in the city is significant: they are the Neue Wache (New Guard House) of 1816–18; the Schauspielhaus (Theatre and concert hall) of 1818–26; and the Altes Museum of 1823–33. These were all designed in a stern neo-antique style which contrasts strangely with the romantic effusions of 1810 in connection with the mausoleum for Queen Luise. However, Schinkel came to feel that the severer style was historically appropriate for post-1815 Berlin which, though now victorious in arms, was spartan in tone and economically depressed yet stirred by high reforming ideals. Like the Brandenburg Gate of 1789 at the west end of Unter den Linden, the Neue Wache near the east end marks the beginning of a new era in German Neo-classicism. The Greek Doric order was chosen in accordance with Gentz's recommendation of it for military buildings as a symbol of severity (*Ernst*), dignity (*Hoheit*), and strength (*Kraft*).

70 Schinkel: Neue Wache (Royal Guard House), Berlin, 1816–18.

Schinkel's first designs for the Neue Wache were for a building with round 70 arches in a kind of composed style between classic and Gothic. He carefully considered its relation to its setting, siting it romantically as a *point de vue* at the end of a proposed grove of chestnut trees which subtly insulates it from the adjacent Zeughaus (Arsenal), a vast Baroque building of 1695–1717. However, the king, who did not live in the royal Schloss facing the Lustgarten but in the much smaller Kronprinzenpalais in Unter den Linden, wanted to be able to see his soldiers changing guard from his windows. Schinkel was thus forced to bring the Guard House close to the road. He also changed the style to Greek Doric though the massive corner pylons, which help to separate the building from its neighbours, have a faintly Egyptian flavour. For Schinkel, however, the building resembled a Roman *castrum*. It has two features which were to be especially characteristic of Schinkel: it contrives to have an asymmetrical interior plan, despite its symmetrical Gillyesque exterior, and it is also beautifully related to its setting by trees and statuary. Though it is tiny in comparison with its enormous neighbours, the Baroque Arsenal and Palladian University, the little building has a quite extraordinary air of authority. It remains to this day a monument of programmatic significance for visitors to Berlin who watch the goose-stepping East German soldiers changing guard in front of it.

Schinkel's Schauspielhaus in the Gendarmenmarkt (now Platz der 71 Akademie), designed in 1818 and executed in 1819–21, is the first statement of a theme which was to become one of his hallmarks: the reduction of the classical language to a trabeated grid which, though generally independent of structure, is a poetic or visual expression of it. These square unmoulded mullions and horizontal entablatures form a kind of elegant scaffolding round this large building. In his account of the theatre in his *Sammlung* in 1821, Schinkel cited an antique source for these mullions in order to justify what he may have regarded as a revolutionary system of articulation. The source is the Choragic Monument of Thrasyllus, a Hellenistic monument formerly existing on the side of the Acropolis

71 Schinkel: Schauspielhaus, Berlin, 1818–26.

in Athens and probably known to Schinkel from Stuart and Revett's *Antiquities of Athens*, vol. II, 1789. However, he immediately justifies the system on functional grounds, since it allows window openings of the maximum size, and claims that he 'tried to emulate Greek forms and methods of construction insofar as this is possible in such a complex work'. This light trabeated framework also relieves the massiveness of the design as a whole, introducing the kind of almost Gothic openwork flavour which had appealed to Neo-classical theorists and designers in France such as Laugier and Soufflot. Indeed, the critic E. Guhl writing in 1859 regarded the building as a synthesis of Greek and Gothic forms. Schinkel had essayed this trabeated construction in a military building designed in 1817, though not executed until eight years later, the barracks and detention centre of the Lehreskadron in the Lindenstrasse. This was the kind of building which was to influence the architect Behrens a hundred years later.

The forceful impact of the Schauspielhaus derives partly from the novel way in which Schinkel gave poetic expression to its function by combining the auditorium building and the stage block behind into a single pedimented building, towering over the lower flanking wings. The great portico pushes forward into the square so as to relate directly to the porticos of the adjacent churches by Gontard, a point Schinkel romantically emphasized in the stage backdrop designed for the opening night which was a panoramic view of the whole Gendarmenmarkt painted by Gropius. It must be confessed that the portico has no real function since the entrances are at ground-floor level. Its role is symbolic and representational as the entrance to a temple of Apollo, a temple of the muses. The actual entrance foyer is, by contrast, somewhat small since Schinkel was obliged to re-use the foundations of the Langhans theatre and to comply with the king's demand for the incorporation of a concert hall. The body of the theatre is thus flanked by a magnificent galleried concert hall in the south wing, and rehearsal and storage space in the north. This tripartite plan is clearly expressed externally.

72, 73 Schinkel: Altes
Museum, Berlin, 1823;
exterior and central
rotunda.

94

In the third of this first group of public buildings in Berlin, the Altes Museum, Schinkel could indulge even more freely his belief that architecture should educate and improve the public by awakening its members to their own identity and to that of the historical culture to which they belonged. It was in Berlin around 1800 that there emerged the novel concept of a public museum to provide uplift for the middle classes by exposing them to the kind of paintings which had previously been confined to the interiors of royal palaces. Among those who promoted this idea was Schinkel's old master at the Bauakademie, Alois Hirt. He gave a clear definition of what a museum should be like in its combination of sculpture and painting, its architecture, its historical arrangement for educational purposes, and its lighting. In a public lecture in 1797 he outlined his proposals for bringing under one roof and arranging by their different schools the finest art treasures in Prussia. Following the acceptance of the idea by Friedrich Wilhelm III, Hirt submitted detailed proposals in 1798 for a rectangular Neo-Palladian building round a courtyard occupying roughly the site of Schinkel's later Neue Wache. However, after Prussia's defeat at Jena, Vivant Denon came to Berlin in 1806 to select works of art for removal to the Imperial Museum in the Louvre. While recognizing the illegality of the process of plunder by which Napoleon had accumulated paintings from countries which he had conquered, few visitors to the Louvre could fail to be impressed by the merits of a well-organized public museum on this scale. Thus an exhibition attended by the king in the Berlin Academy of repatriated works of art, arranged by Schinkel and Hirt in 1815, was all that was needed to put into execution Hirt's scheme for a public museum in Berlin. Indeed work began in 1816 on converting the old Academy building in Unter den Linden into a museum, but progress was interrupted after a slow start.

In 1822 Schinkel was invited by the king to prepare a comprehensive scheme for improving the appearance of the Lustgarten in front of the Schloss. Schinkel's proposals for this area, which he had first drawn up in 1817, involved filling in the mean canal which divided the island in two and, eventually, reorganizing the

74 Schinkel: view from the landing of the Altes Museum looking out through the portico; engraving from Schinkel's *Sammlung.*

facilities for river traffic and customs warehouses along the Kupfergraben. Schinkel's elegantly functional buildings to house some of these activities in the northern part of the island, the Packhofgebäude (1829–32), were demolished in the 1890s to make way for the Kaiser Friedrich Museum and the Pergamon Museum. Schinkel had toyed as early as 1822 with the idea of building an entirely new museum in the Lustgarten instead of adapting the Academy buildings. This juxtaposition of public museum and royal palace in a single square was a concrete embodiment of Humboldt's cultural and social programme and it is appropriate that he should subsequently have become the chairman of the commission for the establishment of the museum.

In the face of much misunderstanding between the king and the commission, Schinkel fought with vigour and diplomatic skill for his proposal which, with the support of the crown prince, the king accepted in 1823. The decorative programme of the building was, of course, planned to pay special homage to the king with the inscription on the frieze, the surmounting Prussian eagle, and the proposed equestrian statue. Schinkel rightly considered the museum as his finest work so far, the logical consequence of his improvements at the eastern end of Unter den Linden, the Neue Wache and the Schlossbrücke leading over the Kupfergraben to the Lustgarten where he had also remodelled the cathedral in 1820–1. For the façade of his museum Schinkel chose a long colonnade of eighteen Ionic columns which resembles a civic building like a Hellenistic stoa. In designing one of the first public buildings of the modern world which lacks a central emphasis, Schinkel was guided by his ambition to create a harmonious ensemble of individual parts, Schloss, church, museum, none of which would dominate or destroy the other. Thus even the dome of the museum is discreetly concealed behind a rectangular attic.

The museum was conceived by Schinkel to be as monumental as the far larger 73 Schloss which it faces. The majestic row of 40-foot-high Ionic columns along the 266-foot-long front seals the building off from the outside world yet at the same time compels the visitor to ascend the steps and enter. He is immediately rewarded for this act of faith by the double staircase which, leading up 64 picturesquely from within the colonnade, destroys the barrier between internal and external space. Schinkel captures the effect of this spatial interpenetration in one of the most beautiful architectural perspectives of all time. Published as an engraving in his *Sammlung*, this shows the panoramic view of the Lustgarten and 74 beyond, which the visitor has from between the upper portions of the columns when he finally reaches the landing of the staircase. This incorporation of an open staircase into a portico had already been achieved in a Baroque idiom at the abbey of St Florian, Austria, where the double staircase of 1706–14 by Carlo Antonio Carlone and Jakob Prandtauer is set behind an open arcade along the front of the building. Schinkel's colonnade is of stone but the rest of the building is rendered brick, the traditional technique in a city poor in building materials. Because the site was little more than a peat bog intersected by water-courses, construction was delayed during the formation of a complicated wooden pilotage to act as a foundation.

The plan of the building, including its Pantheon hall and reticent skyline, strongly recalls a design published by Durand in his *Précis des leçons d'architecture données à l'école polytechnique* (Paris, 1802–5). However, Schinkel was far from sharing Durand's drably functional view of the ends of architecture. Like a church, his museum was to 'exalt' the visitor, the Pantheon hall was to be 'the 72 sanctuary wherein the most precious is stored', and the staircase and back wall of the colonnade were richly painted with vast murals representing a highly-

1 Schinkel: design for the wall decoration of the palace for Prince Albrecht, Berlin, 1830–2.

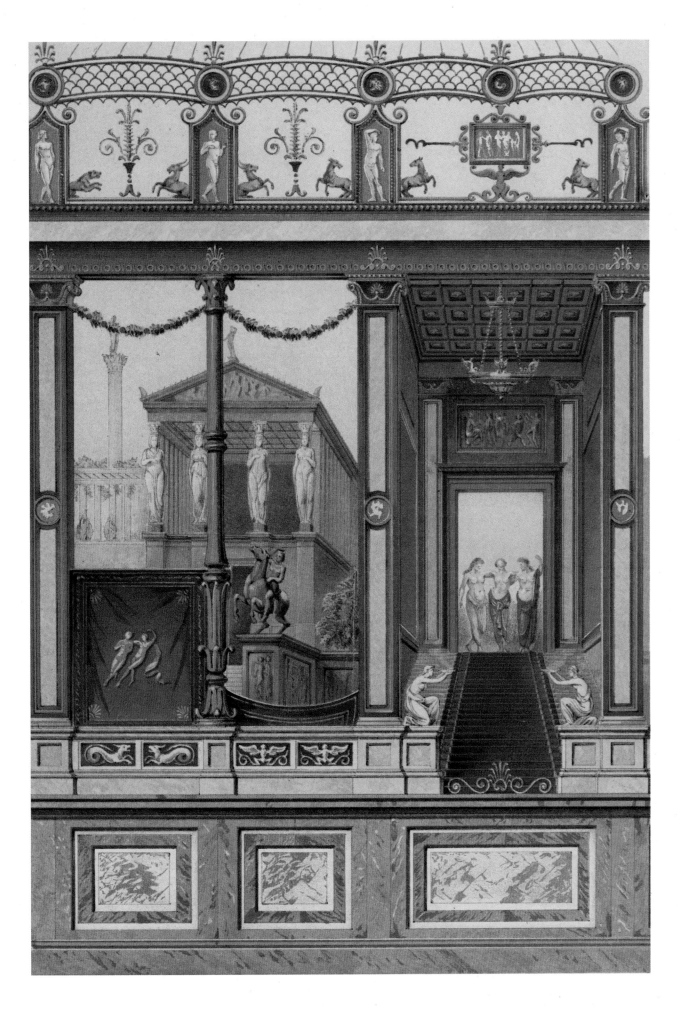

charged vision of the place of the arts in the development of mankind. A Pantheon-like hall or octagon as a sanctuary for the best work is a Renaissance idea realized by Buontalenti in 1581 in the Tribuna at the Uffizi in Florence, and taken up in the eighteenth century by Simonetti in the Museo Pio-Clementino at the Vatican and also by Frederick the Great who used the domed centre of his gallery at Sanssouci for the same purpose.

Inside the museum the ground floor contained the collection of antiquities, and the upper floor the picture galleries. The walls were hung with dark red tapestry and the ceilings painted yellow, white and red. Schinkel hung many of the pictures on low wooden screen walls projecting at right angles from the outer walls. This not only provided more space but took advantage of side lighting. It was not an idea of Schinkel's but had been proposed by Hirt in 1797 and was adopted by Schinkel partly because it fitted his design for the side façades of the museum. The lighting was not in fact satisfactory, for Schinkel had not given the kind of serious consideration to the question of lighting and exhibiting pictures that Klenze did at the Munich Pinakothek (designed 1822–4, executed 1826–36). The numerous bays formed by the screen walls facilitated the hanging of the pictures by schools in accordance with the ideas of Hirt. However, Schinkel, who wanted the public to be overwhelmed by beauty rather than instructed by facts, did not arrange the pictures sufficiently didactically for Hirt who resigned in 1829 and was replaced by a committee chaired by Wilhelm von Humboldt. Schinkel was supported by the great connoisseur, Dr Waagen, who became director of the museum in 1830. The memorandum which they published jointly in 1828, *Über die Aufgaben der Berliner Galerie* (On the Purpose of the Berlin Gallery), contains the memorable slogan, *Erst erfreuen dann belehren* (First delight, then instruct), which was as serious as Hirt's approach and no less influential.

For his friend and patron, Wilhelm von Humboldt, Schinkel built Schloss Tegel in 1820–4 in a wooded park in the northern part of what is now West Berlin. The Humboldt family had owned a modest country house of sixteenth-century origin on this site since 1765. In remodelling and enlarging this, Humboldt's principal aim was to provide a private museum or sculpture gallery. Schinkel did not greatly alter the old entrance front with its rounded oriel windows, but added startling classical towers at the four corners and a 75 completely new garden front and side façades, all in the trabeated system he had just adopted for the Schauspielhaus. The idea for the corner towers came from one which already existed at the house. They emphasize the role of the building as a Schloss but also echo a Palladian precedent, the Villa Trissino near Vicenza, which had been adopted in many English country houses of the seventeenth and eighteenth centuries such as Wilton, Hagley and Croome. The tops of Schinkel's towers, which are aligned on the four points of the compass, are strikingly adorned with figures of the four winds carved by C.D. Rauch in imitation of those 76 on the Tower of the Winds in Athens. The sculpture gallery, for the collection of antique sculpture and casts which Humboldt had begun accumulating in Rome in 1803, is not tucked away to one side of the house, as in English country houses such as Holkham and Newby, but forms a Greek Doric entrance vestibule on the ground floor. Needless to say Humboldt opened it to the public. With its richly painted and marbled hall, Schloss Tegel has been miraculously well preserved and is still open to the public today.

A delectable Neo-classical villa such as Schloss Tegel in a picturesque park on the edge of Berlin proved a popular idea. Thus, in 1824, Schinkel began work at Schloss Glienicke for Prince Karl, twenty-five-year-old son of Friedrich Wilhelm III, and in 1826 at Schloss Charlottenhof at Sanssouci, Potsdam, for Karl's

II Schinkel: Bauakademie, Berlin, 1831, with the Friedrich Werdersche Kirche in the background. Painting by Eduard Gärtner, 1868.

75, 76 Schinkel: exterior
and sculpture gallery of
Schloss Tegel, near Berlin,
begun 1824.

brother, the crown prince. Glienicke can be seen as an outcome of an extensive tour in Italy which Prince Karl had taken in 1822–3 with his father and older brother, Prince Wilhelm. Travelling to Naples and Pompeii via Verona, Venice and Rome, they returned via Florence, Pisa, Genoa, Milan and Trieste. Prince Karl began to collect antiquities and, on his return, wanted a summer residence to house them which would be a souvenir of his travels. The first building which
77 Schinkel provided in the park at Klein Glienicke was the Kasino perched above the river Havel with charming views towards Potsdam. As in many of his buildings for the royal family, he was far from having a free hand in the design of the Kasino: it was an existing building which, following preliminary sketches by the crown prince, Schinkel transformed into a miniature Italian villa by adding a storey, new windows and pergolas. It is a characteristic example of the tension provided in Schinkel's best work by a combination of tautly rectilinear detailing and picturesquely or environmentally dictated layout. Thus the Kasino is flanked by austerely detailed but vine-clad loggias beneath whose shade the prince could sit and imagine himself by the shores of an Italian lake. The interiors are richly ornamented in the Pompeian style and the central saloon, opening into a garden loggia, has a large mirrored wall so as to reflect the garden.

77 Schinkel: the Kasino at Schloss Glienicke, near Potsdam, 1826.

78 Schinkel: Schloss Glienicke, a lithograph of *c*.1840.

78

79 Schinkel: the Grosse Neugierde, added to the park of Glienicke in 1835.

The Schloss itself was a small eighteenth-century country house which, in a kind of architectural conjuring trick, Schinkel tranformed into a fashionably Italianate Neo-classical villa, the most striking feature of which was the replacement of the former mansard roof with a flat roof. To the irregular U-shaped court formed by the house Schinkel added in 1832 the detached Kavalier wing with an Italianate tower, first projected in 1826, thus making the whole composition emphatically asymmetrical in the manner of English Picturesque buildings such as Thomas Hope's Deepdene of c.1818–23. The Italianate top storey of the tower was added by Petzholtz in 1865, while the flanking wing was also heightened with a mezzanine storey by Schinkel's pupil, Ludwig Persius. The courtyard walls are studded with Prince Karl's antique fragments and casts recalling another English source, Sir John Soane's Museum, which Schinkel visited without enthusiasm in 1826. On the same English tour he inspected Lansdowne House in Berkeley Square with its magnificent sculpture gallery formed by Smirke in 1816–19 out of a core by Adam and Dance. Schinkel noted in his journal that the house provided him with numerous hints for the fitting up of the interiors of Schloss Glienicke.

The picturesque little park at Glienicke, begun by Peter Joseph Lenné (1789–1866) in 1816 for a previous owner, is crowded with garden buildings by Schinkel, Ludwig Persius and Ferdinand von Arnim. The most substantial of these, added by Schinkel in 1835, is the Grosse Neugierde in the south-west corner near the Glienicke Bridge to Potsdam. As with the Kasino, both the site and the form of this building were settled in sketches by the crown prince. It consists of a tholos of eighteen Corinthian columns from which sprouts a version of the Choragic Monument of Lysicrates in Athens, an unexpected addition by Schinkel of 1837. It commands a panoramic view of the surrounding landscape but has been moved since Schinkel's day and is no longer quite in its original

79

position. Elsewhere in the park is Schinkel's little Tudor Gothic hunting lodge of 1827–8 inspired by plates in books like J.B. Papworth's *Rural Residences* (1818) which were probably provided by the crown prince.

In 1824, the year following his journey to Italy, the king celebrated his morganatic marriage to Augusta, Princess von Liegnitz, by commissioning Schinkel to build a little pavilion in the garden of Schloss Charlottenburg. The king was usually extremely cautious about spending money on building but now, bitten by the Italianate bug, nothing would satisfy him but a house based on the Villa Reale Chiatamone near Naples in which he had stayed in 1822. He was particularly anxious to repeat the feature he had enjoyed in Italy of a continuous external balcony connecting all the rooms on the first floor. Schinkel provided this in a finely proportioned classical building which, though small, is a dominating object along the whole of the long terrace before the front of the Schloss itself. Inside the pavilion the axially placed garden room which commands this view has recently been restored with its blue velvet hangings. The existence of contemporary interior views and a complete inventory of 1826 has made possible a full restoration after serious bomb damage of a building for which Schinkel designed all the decoration and furniture.

A third commission which can be connected with the visits to Italy of Schinkel and members of the royal family in the 1820s is Schloss Charlottenhof and its 80 garden buildings, built at Potsdam for the crown prince from 1826 onwards. A modest country house on the southern edge of the royal park at Sanssouci was given by the king to the crown prince at Christmas 1825 on the occasion of his marriage to Princess Elisabeth of Bavaria, sister of Ludwig I of Bavaria. With apparently effortless skill Schinkel remodelled the existing house, most of whose walls he retained, into one of his most perfect small buildings: an elegant Trianon with a portico which helps create the impression of a one-storeyed building. It was the first occasion on which the crown prince was able to express his own architectural ideals: we know, for example, that he was responsible for the general layout and for the emphatic portico.

Schloss Charlottenhof is related with great delicacy and imagination to its site which Schinkel enlivened with a canal and a terraced garden flanked on one side by a long pergola leading to a semicircular arbour modelled on the tomb of the priestess Mamia in the Via delle Tombe at Pompeii. This gaily canopied arbour with its semicircular stone bench at the far end of the garden is in axis with the sterner Greek Doric portico of the Schloss itself. The walls within the portico are richly painted in the Pompeian style which Schinkel used with increasing frequency after his visit to Pompeii in 1824. The interiors of the Schloss were painted in vibrant colours, strong blues and Pompeian reds, setting off the crisply sumptuous neo-antique furniture designed by Schinkel.

The garden at Schloss Charlottenhof, gently elevated above the canal and characterized by an ingenious play with different levels, is like a private stage with a panoramic backdrop of park scenery, so that if it were not all so rooted in nature and construction, one would be tempted to call it theatrical. Certainly Schinkel here put to brilliant use the lessons he had learned as a stage designer. He prepared several panoramic engravings for his *Sammlung* to show how the little Schloss interlocked with the adjacent garden, pergolas, water, fountains, flights of steps, trees, park, and views through the park of other buildings such as the Neues Palais. There could be no more captivating expression of Schinkel's belief that 'architecture is the continuation of nature in her constructive activity'. Some of the credit for Charlottenhof should go to the court gardener, Peter Joseph Lenné, who provided the landscape gardening, and, as we have seen, to

80 Schinkel: Schloss
Charlottenhof, Potsdam,
1826.

the crown prince who furnished Schinkel with sketches outlining the disposition
of the building and its setting. The prince, who described his own architectural
compositions as 'malerisch' (picturesque), had studied Percier and Fontaine's
Choix des plus célèbres maisons de plaisance de Rome et de ses environs (Paris 1809), in
connection with the design of Charlottenhof, and had met Fontaine in Paris in
1815. At the same time we should recognize that Schinkel had been designing
and recording buildings of this kind since his Italian tour of 1803–4. From this
time dates his painting of an imaginary villa near Palermo, inspired by the actual
house of an Englishman resident in Italy. Also in 1804 he made a drawing of the
villa of Prince Valguarnera at Bagheria, Sicily, a Neo-classical building not
unlike Schloss Charlottenhof, and noted for the extensive views it commands. It
was Schinkel's achievement to bring key members of the royal family to share his
enthusiasm for this kind of architecture.

Under the aegis of the crown prince and his wife, Charlottenhof became the
scene of a glittering social and intellectual life. The house and its setting were as
idyllic as the prince had intended them to be. Indeed, his name for Charlottenhof
was 'Siam', a country known romantically at the time as the 'Land of the Free'.
He wanted to create a natural paradise of friendship, brotherhood and freedom,
in which he blended the sentimental rhetoric of Bernardin de St-Pierre's *Paul et
Virginie*, reminiscences of the military knights of medieval Germany, and the
exotic themes of a romance he had written in 1817 called *The Queen of Borneo*. He
signed his own architectural drawings with fanciful names like 'Fritz Siam' or
'Federigo Siamese'.

The merging of architecture and nature which had been achieved at Glienicke
and Charlottenhof was carried a stage further in the group of buildings, now
known as the Roman Bath, built in the grounds of Schloss Charlottenhof in
1829–37. Designed by the crown prince, Schinkel and his pupil Persius, who was
81 the executant architect, these began with the court gardener's house, an existing
cottage remodelled in 1829 as an Italianate vernacular villa along lines probably

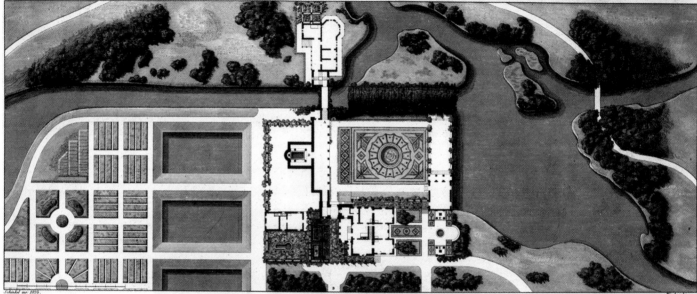

81 Schinkel: elevation
and plan of the court
gardener's house,
Charlottenhof, 1829 (from
Schinkel's *Sammlung*).

82 Schinkel:
Thermenhalle, Roman
Bath, Potsdam, 1829–37.

inspired by the 'Villa, designed as the residence of an artist' in Papworth's *Rural Residences* (1818, pl. XVII). Despite this English source, the design is deeply rooted in Schinkel's reminiscences of his Italian tour of 1803–4, when he prepared a long theoretical discourse on the relation of asymmetrical buildings to picturesque settings which was intended to serve as a chapter in his proposed *Lehrbuch*. The court gardener's house was followed by the tea pavilion in the form of a temple (1830), the assistant's house (1831–2), the arcaded hall (1833) and the Roman bath house (1834–40). The subtle grouping of a roughly L-shaped complex of buildings, linked with steps, loggias, passages, canals and an irregular sheet of water, the interpenetration of spaces, the contrast of void and mass, light and shade, the asymmetrical plan and elevation pivoting on a central tower, the total absence of a main façade or of any suggestion of a front or a rear, make this one of the most brilliant conceptions of its kind in the history of Western architecture. It has been compared with Frank Lloyd Wright but far surpasses him in subtlety of allusion and delicacy of detail: for example, Schinkel's intermingling of vine-covered trellis and Doric columns suggests the evolution of the Doric order as hinted at by Vitruvius and romantically developed by Laugier. Schinkel believed that he had created at Charlottenhof a 'never-finished architecture' in a setting to which new buildings could always be added.

The 1820s saw numerous elegant villas by Schinkel though he never developed a specific villa style. Several of them were brilliant conversions of existing buildings and, though he drew on a range of sources including Palladio and *Vitruvius Britannicus*, his own distinctive hand is recognizable throughout. Especially chaste were the low classical villa he built at Berlin-Charlottenburg for the banker Behrend in 1823 (demolished 1905), and the Jenisch House at Flottbeck, Hamburg (1828–34), where he co-operated with the local architect Franz Forsmann (1795–1878). In total contrast is one of his best preserved country buildings, the astonishing Château Antonin near Ostrovo in the province of Posen (now Ostrów, Poznań, Poland), built of wood in 1822–4 as a

hunting lodge for Prince Anton Heinrich von Radziwill, a musician and
composer. This has a three-storeyed central octagonal hall surrounded by two
tiers of galleries and dominated by an extraordinary centrally placed chimney-
stack in the form of a huge column. Though an interior of exceptional novelty,
this has sometimes been compared to William Jones's rotunda at Ranelagh
Gardens, Chelsea (1742, demolished 1805).

Contemporary with the garden buildings at Charlottenhof is Schloss
Babelsberg which Schinkel built for the king's second son, Prince Wilhelm 84
(1797–1888), King of Prussia from 1861 and first German Emperor from 1871.
On a wooded hill above the Havel about three miles from Potsdam, its Gothic
pinnacles can just be glimpsed from the Grosse Neugierde at Schloss Glienicke.
In its design the ever tactful Schinkel incorporated suggestions from the crown
prince, from Ludwig Persius, and from Prince Wilhelm's wife, Princess Augusta,
an enthusiastic anglophile. The crown prince's suggestion in 1826 was for an
Italianate villa; Persius's in 1831 for a Neo-Norman castle; and Princess
Augusta's two years later for an English cottage orné inspired by her study of
Lugar's *Architectural Sketches for Cottages, Rural Dwellings, and Villas* (London 1805;
reprinted 1815 and 1823). All the proposals were essays in the English
Picturesque, and the pattern eventually selected for construction in 1834–5, the

Castle Style of Nash and Wyatville, resulted in the most English building of Schinkel's career. Its irregular plan, pivoting on an octagonal vaulted dining room, is close to characteristic Nash plans like that of his own house on the Isle of Wight, East Cowes Castle (1798–*c.*1820). The external appearance of Babelsberg is somewhat heavier than Schinkel had intended, for it was altered in completion after his death by Persius and J.H. Strack in 1844–9. The landscaped park was begun by Lenné in 1833 and completed by Prince Hermann von Pückler-Muskau a decade later.

Schinkel's role as architectural conjuror to the royal family was further developed in the palaces which he remodelled for the king's sons in Berlin. The first was the palace for Prince Karl in the Wilhelmplatz in 1827–8 where Schinkel 85 smoothed over a town mansion of the 1750s, providing it with a sumptuous Pompeian gallery and an unexpected cast-iron staircase, the first of its kind in Berlin, with steps of Silesian marble. He also designed bold neo-antique furniture for the palace, for example a pair of giltwood armchairs which survive in the collection of the Staatliche Schlösser und Gärten, Berlin. With their sphinx armrests, they are modelled on a Roman chair engraved in *Le Antichità di Ercolano esposte* (9 vols, Naples 1755–92, vol IV, 1765, pl. 44).

The palace in the Wilhelmstrasse for Prince Albrecht of 1830–2, a remodelling

85 Schinkel: Blue Gallery of the palace for Prince Karl, Berlin, 1827–8.

86 Schinkel: staircase hall of the palace for Prince Albrecht, Berlin, 1830–2.

109

of the Baroque Anspachisches Palais, contained a yet more striking iron staircase. 86
Entirely of cast iron, this was designed on a grandiose scale so as to fill a whole
vestibule. The staircases were inspired by those Schinkel had seen in English
industrial buildings and it is remarkable to find them in a domestic interior,
especially that of a royal palace. Along the entrance to the palace courtyard from
the street Schinkel placed a columnar screen of the type employed by Adam at
the Admiralty and by Holland at Carlton House. Interiors such as the marble 1
oval saloon and Princess Marianne's boudoir, opening into a conservatory, were
exquisite statements of Schinkel's ability as an interior designer. In the Nazi
period the palaces for Princes Karl and Albrecht became respectively the
headquarters of the Ministry of Propaganda and of the Gestapo, a circumstance
which hastened their demolition after the war, though they could otherwise have
been restored.

Schinkel's visit to England in 1826, to which we have alluded more than once,
was a mission on which he was sent by the Prussian government in connection
with the Altes Museum. His ostensible purpose was to gather information on new
museums and their techniques of display, but what most fascinated him were the
architectural and social consequences of the Industrial Revolution. He travelled
with the head of the newly created Prussian Gewerbe-Institut (Technical
Institute), Peter C.W. Beuth, with whom he published *Vorbilder für Fabrikanten
und Handwerker*, 1821–37 (Models for Manufacturers and Craftsmen), an official
pattern book of designs for architectural ornament and household objects such as
ceramics, glassware, textiles and metalwork. Anxious to bring the Industrial
Revolution to Prussia, Beuth made numerous visits to England to learn
industrial techniques and to encourage English manufacturers to set up factories
in Prussia.

We know from Schinkel's diary of his tour, which ought to be available in an
English translation, that he was not on the whole impressed with the work of Neo-
classical architects like the Woods of Bath, Adam, Nash, Soane, Smirke, or the
Inwoods, but was overwhelmed by the technical ingenuity and the scale of the
new factories, warehouses, dock buildings, bridges, roads, canals, steam engines
and gas holders. He exclaimed of the cotton mills of Manchester: 'Here are
buildings seven to eight storeys high and big as the Royal Palace in Berlin. They
are vaulted and fireproof.' Buildings of this kind, supported by an internal
framework of iron columns and beams, threaded with iron staircases, and
wrapped round with a brick skin, gave him a thrilling sense of how his own
architecture might develop. He wanted to take these techniques and then to
civilize them, for he was appalled by what he described as 'factories which are
nothing but monstrous masses of red brick, built by a mere foreman, without any
trace of architecture and for the sole purpose of crude necessity, making a most
frightening impression.'

On his return to Berlin, Schinkel designed a number of buildings in brick,
terracotta, iron and glass which undoubtedly reflect his reactions to English
industrial architecture: these are the Kaufhaus or bazaar in Unter den Linden
(1827), the church for the Oranienburg suburb in North Berlin (1828), the
Feilner House (1828–9) in the Hasenhagerstrasse, the Packhof buildings (1829– 87
32), the Bauakademie (1831–6), and the State Library in Unter den Linden
(1835). Of these the only ones executed, all now demolished, were the Packhof
buildings, Bauakademie and the Feilner House, built for Tobias Christoph
Feilner, a manufacturer of terracotta ornament, bricks and stoves. The first
designs for the Feilner House, made by Hahnemann in 1828, proposed a
conventional façade of stucco scored to imitate masonry joints, but this was

87 Schinkel:
Salzsteuergebäude, part of
the Neue Packhof, Berlin,
1829–32.

transformed by Schinkel into a remarkable essay in constructional polychromy, incorporating beige unpainted terracotta and bricks of two colours, red and violet. This was not only a revolutionary attempt to re-introduce brick into Berlin domestic architecture but anticipated the experiments with constructional polychromy of Hittorff and his circle in Paris in the 1830s and 40s. Though he did not have a free hand in the planning, Schinkel also designed the two elegant canted rooms in the angles at the back of the house. These are related to a tradition known as the 'Berliner Zimmer' which allowed owners to extend their houses at the rear while adhering to byelaws governing the size of the front elevations.

In December 1830 Schinkel became Geheimer Oberbaudirektor. This involved examination of all state building schemes throughout Prussia, which helped to spread a consistent style for the public buildings of Germany in the early and mid-nineteenth century. The creation of the Allgemeine Bauschule, for which he designed a new building in 1831 following his appointment, was not promoted by the Crown but by Schinkel and by Peter Beuth who became first director of the school. It was the nerve centre of the Prussian architectural machine since it contained not only the school of architecture on the first floor but the offices of the Ober-Bau-Deputation on the floor above, and even Schinkel's private flat where he lived with his family from 1836 until his death in 1841. His presence here must have been a forceful symbol of his utter dedication to architecture and of his identification with the new Prussia.

Until its unwarranted destruction by the East German authorities in 1961, the 11 Bauakademie, as the Allgemeine Bauschule was known after 1848, formed the east side of the Werdersche Markt which also contained Gentz's Mint on the west side and Schinkel's austere brick Gothic Friedrich-Werder church of 1824–31 on the north. Being a large building, incorporating shops on the ground floor, it also ran right down to the river Kupfergraben where it played an important part in views from the Schlossbrücke leading to the Lustgarten. Schinkel's plans and drawings show his awareness of the relation of the building to its setting, whereas Durand characteristically illustrated it only in plan and elevation in his *Recueil et parallèle des édifices de tous genres* (3 vols., Venice 1833, vol. II, pl. 114c). The large site to some extent dictated the form of the building as a cube with four equal fronts. It is thus an early example of a monumental building which lacks an obvious main façade.

The demand for fireproof interiors and good lighting similarly influenced the construction and disposition of the building. Brick was the traditional building material of Prussia but recently it had been fashionable, as in England, to cover it with stucco. Schinkel exposed the naked brick in a square four-storeyed building with four façades each eight bays long, separated by piers corresponding to the internal vertical divisions which, inspired by English industrial precedent, were segmental brick arches supporting brick cap vaults and linked horizontally by iron beams. In fact the exterior was not always faithful to the interior for, as the section shows, the vaulting did not extend throughout the interior. The façades were in some sense an artistic symbol of a constructional principle and might almost be seen as prefiguring twentieth-century curtain-wall architecture. With its red and violet brickwork, glazed violet tiles on the buttresses, and window frames of unpainted terracotta, the building develops the constructional polychromy which he had introduced at the Feilner House.

The Bauakademie also represented the fusion of Greek and Gothic which had interested Schinkel at the start of his career: it is Gothic in its system of piers and buttresses, Greek in its horizontality and its decorative scheme. With its library and its model collection, it was an instructive celebration of the historical significance of architecture and of the constructional and decorative possibilities of brick and terracotta. Thus the panels under the first-floor windows and the surrounds of the two principal doorways, adjacent to each other in the centre of the north front, were handsomely enriched with delicate terracotta carvings, executed by C.F. Tieck and C. Gormann, depicting the origin and development of antique, Gothic, and Renaissance art and architecture. The frame of the door leading to the Allgemeine Bauschule was ornamented with carvings celebrating architecture as an art, while that of the flanking door, leading to the offices of the Ober-Bau-Deputation, emphasized the scientific and technological basis of architecture. The elaborately didactic iconographical programme, which has its roots in the writings of K.W. Solgers, Goethe and C.G. Carus, makes the building a fitting development from the Brandenburg Gate, Mint, Schauspielhaus and Altes Museum, all of which featured similarly symbolic ornament. Indeed the Bauakademie is the fulfilment of the programme Schinkel devised for the murals in the portico of the Altes Museum.

The Bauakademie was Schinkel's favourite among his buildings. Flaming red in colour, it shone forth as a commanding symbol of his high-minded architectural, constructional and educational ideals. Its function is related to the ambition he had cherished throughout his career of producing a monumental architectural textbook, *Architektonisches Lehrbuch*, which would provide a solution to every architectural problem. Here we find the only element of failure in Schinkel's career. He neither completed the book nor left a coherent statement of his architectural theory, lamenting that he had lost himself 'in a labyrinth'. His thoughts take the form of aphorisms on architecture which are sometimes contradictory. His guiding principle was to practise architecture as art and to combine function and beauty in accordance with the emphasis of Vitruvius on *utilitas*, *firmitas* and *venustas*. He was totally opposed to naked functionalism and to the equation by Durand of *utilitas* with *venustas*.

88 Schinkel: staircase of the Bauakademie, Berlin, 1831.

Though the orders were as important to Schinkel as they had been to Gentz as a fundamental historic link, he did not want to give the budding architect comparative drawings of the classical orders to copy, or illustrations of monuments of the past showing the history of styles, but rather to promote understanding of first principles in architecture which, he believed, rested on proper attention to three points: construction, custom, and nature. His study of the unfolding development of the materials, styles and constructional methods of architecture, from the trabeated buildings of the Greeks through the Roman arch to the Gothic vault, was an exercise in evolution akin to those of Alexander von Humboldt in natural history. Architectural construction, combinations and ornament are exemplified in five different building types in draft chapters which emphasize that 'all the important structural elements must be visible', but at the same time insist that the fulfilment of function is not enough. The demands of history, poetry and beauty must never be forgotten: thus, 'The principle of Greek architecture is to render construction beautiful, and this must remain the principle in its continuation.' This was clearly demonstrated in sumptuous designs for palaces in Athens (1834) and the Crimea (1838) which were subsequently published as *Werke der höheren Baukunst für die Ausführung entworfen*, 2 vols., Potsdam 1840–8 (Works of Higher Architecture designed for Execution). These were products of Schinkel's lifelong conviction that buildings should not just represent their mere function (*trivialer Zweck*) but should be ennobled by showing their higher purpose (*höherer Zweck*).

It was at the suggestion of the Prussian crown prince that Schinkel submitted designs in 1834 for a palace in Athens for Prince Otto von Wittelsbach, second son of King Ludwig I of Bavaria, who had been elected first king of Greece two years earlier at the age of seventeen. In a stroke of outrageously imaginative genius Schinkel boldly placed his palace on the Acropolis itself. The poetic symbolism of thus identifying the glories of fifth-century Athens with a liberal monarchy of the nineteenth century made a special appeal to the crown prince of Prussia. Schinkel did not, however, make the mistake of dominating the Parthenon with new buildings. He crowded his palace into the empty space at the eastern end of the Acropolis behind the Parthenon and Erechtheum. The asymmetry of his layout was not dictated by the awkward site but by a real understanding of antique practice which he had already deployed in the enchantingly Picturesque court gardener's house at Schloss Charlottenhof. He complained to Prince Maximilian of Bavaria, brother of the new king of Greece, of 'the long worn-out neo-Italian and neo-French maxims in which a misunderstanding of the concept of symmetry especially has produced so much hypocrisy and boredom and achieved such deadly dominion'.

The buildings of Schinkel's Acropolis palace are mostly one-storeyed like Schloss Charlottenhof, but the most spectacular is the richly coloured Great Hall. This combines memories of the cella of the Greek temple with the Corinthian splendour of the Romans beneath a timber-truss roof construction which is inspired by English examples, both medieval ecclesiastical and modern industrial. The rich colouring of this interior reflects the current researches into the polychromy of ancient Greek temples, a topic which became needlessly controversial in the 1830s.

These plans by Schinkel, as well as others by Klenze, were rejected in 1836 in favour of less ambitious proposals by Gärtner for the building which survives today in Syndagma Square. Just as the liberation of Greece from Turkish rule had been championed by the Romantics of Neo-classical England, so did the capital of the newly established kingdom become the model of what German Neo-classical architects and, with the change of dynasty, Danish, thought a cultured capital ought to look like.

Schinkel's Athenian palace, which Klenze dismissed as 'a charming Midsummer Night's Dream of a great architect', was followed by his no less visionary palace at Orianda near Yalta in the Crimea for the Empress of Russia, daughter of King Friedrich Wilhelm III of Prussia. Having purchased a hillside site called Orianda near the Black Sea, the Empress wrote to her brother, Crown Prince Friedrich Wilhelm, with whom she often corresponded on artistic matters, inviting him to design her a villa 'in der Art von Siam' (in the Siamese manner). She also enclosed a watercolour showing the site. The crown prince sent a set of drawings in response to St Petersburg, then Schinkel submitted a Gothic project and finally, early in 1838, a fantastic Neo-classical dream palace hugging the rocky promontory above the Black Sea like the monasteries of Meteora. Miraculously floating above its long low façades was an Ionic temple of whiter hue, a disposition and a colour contrast borrowed from Gilly's monument to Frederick the Great of over forty years before. Schinkel's temple rested on a high podium in the centre of an inner garden court, approached through a Pompeian atrium with frescoed walls and colonnades surrounding a pool open to the sky. Separating the atrium from the garden court with its canals, ponds, trees, and gilt winged lions, was a screen of octagonal columns clad with mosaics in floral and geometric patterns. These struck a Babylonian note which was heightened by the long flights of terraced steps on either side of the temple podium. The high walls of the podium were a striking demonstration of constructional polychromy with stripes of pink and yellow masonry. The same theme was repeated in the cavernous sculpture museum inside the podium, roofed with a curious stepped vault of oriental flavour. This shadowy and mysterious space was destined to receive works of art from the provinces between the Caucasus and Asia Minor.

III Schinkel: design for the garden court of Schloss Orianda, 1838.

III The garden court was surrounded on all four sides by an open colonnade, from which access might be had at the far end to the state apartments opening onto the terrace overlooking the sea. One of the most ravishing of Schinkel's watercolours
IV shows this terrace in perspective with the caryatid porch in the centre flanked by semicircular porticos with columns of the Erechtheum Ionic order. The spaces between the columns are filled entirely with glass in an ironically Picturesque fulfilment of Laugier's vision of an architecture consisting solely of load-bearing vertical members with no inert wall masses between. The dazzling scheme for Schloss Orianda, which Schinkel intended would symbolize the power of the Russian Empire, was one of the most ambitious contributions to the polychromy movement of the 1830s and 40s in France and Germany. Not surprisingly it was found too grandiose by the Empress who in the end built a very modest house on this splendid site.

Related to these designs for palaces in Greece and Russia are ambitious reconstructions which Schinkel made for the Prussian crown prince in 1833–5, of Pliny's villas at Tuscum and Laurentinum. Such is the consistency of Schinkel's architectural development that even these could be connected to his scheme for an ideal villa at Syracuse made during his Italian tour of 1803–4. Close to the reconstructions of Pliny's villas is his Ideal Residence for a Prince, designed for the crown prince in 1835. This is envisaged as the ceremonial centre of an ideal town and, as such, features in the final versions of the *Architektonisches Lehrbuch*. It seems that the crown prince had encouraged Schinkel to think that inclusion of such a scheme as the culmination of the lessons might facilitate the publication of the whole textbook.

The monumental scheme for the princely residence scatters buildings in different styles asymmetrically across a vast hilly terrain, each recognizable as a detached and self-fulfilled entity while merging into a coherently organized but astonishingly Picturesque architectural panorama. On the extreme left of the group is a Greek Doric temple, conceived as a shrine for national monuments, which is balanced on the far right by a theatre with an adjacent campanile. Towering over both of these is a Gothic church, a circular fantasy which is a late echo of his mausoleum of 1810 for Queen Luise. In the centre is a great porticoed building containing the throne room whence the all-seeing eye of the paternalist monarch could watch the comings and goings of ministers, civil servants and private subjects in the various administrative and cultural buildings which were to be an essential part of the working of the whole complex. The buildings interlock in the characteristic Schinkel way with luxuriant trees, secluded gardens and bright fountains, while, equally characteristically, Schinkel's drawings show the view of the surrounding landscape from the buildings as well as the buildings themselves. The whole is a vision which shows at its best the Prussian experiment of which Schinkel was so deeply a part. That it never came into being, either architecturally or politically, is hardly Schinkel's fault.

Schinkel was lionized both in his lifetime and immediately after his death as few architects can ever have been. His funeral in 1841 was a cross between that of a saint and a national leader. In 1842 King Friedrich Wilhelm IV ordered that his architectural drawings, paintings and models should be bought by the state and exhibited in the Bauakademie, and, from that year, an annual Schinkelfest has been held in Berlin. His work inspired the development of Berlin and other north German centres between his death and 1871 when the newly founded Empire encouraged the adoption of Neo-Baroque modes. Whatever his relevance today, and this is not the place to discuss that, there is no denying that he towers over all the other architects in the present book.

IV Schinkel: design for the terrace elevation of Schloss Orianda, 1838.

117

CHAPTER V

Neo-classicism in North Germany: 1818–45

W E shall be looking in the present chapter at the post-Napoleonic expansion of German towns by architects such as Cremer in Aachen and Elberfeld; Vagedes in Düsseldorf; Strack in Oldenburg; Ottmer in Brunswick; Bromeis in Kassel; Laves in Hanover; Coudray in Weimar; and Wimmel, Forsmann and Châteauneuf in Hamburg. The influence of Schinkel is paramount. It is felt to an astonishing degree in all north German centres and even in some southern ones, such as Stuttgart where Salucci, Knapp and Leins maintained his language till the mid-century. Whereas Laves upheld superbly Schinkel's classicism, other architects sought a solution to the tensions between Greek and Gothic by developing the hints contained in his Italianate designs and brick buildings into a full *Rundbogenstil*, an arched and vaulted architecture of brick or small stones combining elements from Byzantine, Romanesque, Lombardic and early Italian Renaissance buildings. In this search for a new public architecture applicable to the varied building types of the nineteenth-century city and to contemporary constructional requirements, attention was paid to the lessons of Durand and to the analysis of historical styles in terms of economy and function.

Schinkel's influence is understandably strongest in cities under Prussian rule such as Bonn, Aachen, Elberfeld, Cologne and Düsseldorf. Here his function as Oberbaudirektor obliged him to comment on designs proposed for public buildings. We shall begin this chapter by briefly investigating these centres, and will then turn to towns not under Prussian rule where his influence was less direct, for example Brunswick, Kassel, Hanover, Oldenburg, Dresden, Weimar and Hamburg. These, which include royal, electoral and grand-ducal capitals, are far richer for our purposes since most of them had strong indigenous classical traditions as well as leading architects of their own.

Cologne, which had always prided itself on its independent position, successfully resisted Schinkel's interference with a number of projects. Schinkel 90 objected to the original plan for the Appeal Court by the town architect Johann Peter Weyer (1794–1864), replacing it with a design of his own. However, Weyer's designs for a D-shaped building enclosing a semicircular arcaded courtyard were eventually executed in 1824–6. The design owed something to the remodelling in the mid 1790s of the Palais Bourbon in Paris for the Revolutionary assembly by Gisors and Leconte. It should be remembered that Cologne was under French occupation from 1794 to 1814. Another major public building erected in Cologne without interference from Schinkel, though in a simplified Schinkelesque style, was the Regional Government Offices (1830–2) 178 by Matthäus Biercher (1797–1869). The Kasino (1831–2; demolished 1938) was designed by the Berlin architect Johann Heinrich Strack, a pupil of Schinkel, and executed by Biercher. It contained an impressive staircase and two-storeyed galleried banqueting hall but the design as a whole would probably have benefited from attention by Schinkel. The Anatomy Theatre at Bonn is a good

89 Konrad Bromeis: Hortensiensaal, Schloss Wilhelmshöhe, near Kassel.

example of this process. The original designs by Schinkel's pupil, Friedrich Waesemann, were inspired by Langhans's Veterinary School at Berlin of 1787–90. As altered by Schinkel, the Anatomy Theatre, built in 1824–5, was dominated by a centrally placed circular lantern, elegantly side-lit. A similar building organized round a circular core is the Observatory at Bonn (1840–45), 163 designed by Peter Joseph Leydel in 1836–7 but considerably altered by Schinkel.

Schinkel also improved the designs for the Theatre and the Elisenbrunnen at Aachen by Joseph Peter Cremer (1785–1863). The entrance front of the theatre, 91 executed between 1822 and 1825, consists of a giant octastyle portico of Greek Ionic columns, whereas in Cremer's original design the portico was simply an attached feature. The Elisenbrunnen (1825–7) became, effectively, Schinkel's 92 own design: a Greek Doric tour de force far removed from Cremer's first design of 157 1819. Certainly Schinkel's most sparkling building in the Rhineland, it boasts a central tholos flanked by open colonnades. Cremer's Reginal Government Offices (1828–31) at Aachen were less altered by Schinkel whose proposals for an internal courtyard were rejected on financial grounds. More interesting was Cremer's design of 1827 for the Town Hall at Elberfeld, executed between 1829 190 and 1842 as one of the most powerful statements of the *Rundbogenstil* with a strong Neo-Renaissance flavour. For an English parallel to this robust arcuated composition one would have to point to a later building such as E.W. Godwin's warehouse at Stokes Croft, Bristol, of 1862. It is no surprise that Schinkel much approved Cremer's building when he visited it.

One of the leading Prussian architects in Schinkel's lifetime was Adolf von Vagedes (1777–1842). Though best known for his public building and town planning in and around Düsseldorf, one of his earliest works is a classical country house with an elegantly *Dixhuitième* flavour, Schloss von Korff (1805–6) at Harkotten not far from Münster. His visionary neo-antique scheme for a town

90 Johann Peter Weyer: Appeal Court, Cologne, 1824–6.

91 (Opposite above). Joseph Peter Cremer: Theatre, Aachen, 1822–5.

92 (Opposite below). Cremer and Schinkel: Elisenbrunnen, Aachen, 1825–7.

93 Adolf von Vagedes:
Ratinger Tor, Düsseldorf,
*c.*1810.

hall and exchange at Elberfeld, facing each other across a vast circular *place* with
a central obelisk, was not executed. However, the twin Greek Doric temples of his
Ratinger Tor (*c.*1810) provided Düsseldorf, then under French occupation, with 93
a convincing echo of Ledoux's *barrières*. Thus when Düsseldorf came under
Prussian rule after 1813 Vagedes was already an established architect, though he
was subjected to much interference from Schinkel when designing his government offices (1825) and school (1828–31). Both are dull buildings in which
Vagedes's contribution was largely confined to the interiors. Happier is his St
Laurence's church at Elberfeld, designed in *c.*1820 and executed, following some 94
assistance from Schinkel, in 1825–35. Well placed as the dominating feature of a
small square, it is a characteristic Schinkelesque composition with a tall classical
entrance arch on the façade beneath a pair of simple Gothic spirelets.

One of the most striking examples of the adoption of Schinkelesque urban
ideals by a town not under Prussian rule can be seen at Oldenburg, capital of the
Grand Duchy of Oldenburg until 1918. The town was completely transformed
under Duke Peter Friedrich Ludwig of Holstein-Gottorp (1785–1829) and his
son, Grand Duke Paul Friedrich August (1829–53), by the architects Carl
Heinrich Slevogt (*c.*1784–1832) and Heinrich Strack (1801–80). Slevogt, born
in Eutin, was stylistically orientated towards Berlin, as is evident in his
Prinzenpalais (1821–6), with its classical Schinkelesque façades, impressive
staircase and Pompeian Room. It was built by Grand Duke Peter for his Russian

grandchildren, Alexander and Peter, but its harmony was spoilt by additions in the 1860s by Karl Boos and Heinrich Strack. Slevogt also participated in the erection of military buildings around the Pferdemarkt, but Strack made a greater contribution to Neo-classical Oldenburg. In 1818–22 he was a pupil of C.F. Hansen whose influence can be detected in the Palladian features of his grand scheme for extending the Schlossplatz in the 1830s. Here Strack built an elegant crescent of ducal and public buildings screening the Schloss from the old town and including the Kavaliershaus (1839), a small palace for the grand duke with a splendid circular staircase; the Reithalle and Mews, both of 1835; and, most strikingly, the Hauptwache (1839), dominated by its Greek Doric portico. Nearby government offices were erected from 1830 to 1850, while in 1838–41 came the Peter Friedrich Ludwig Hospital designed by Strack in a style which, at the grand duke's request, was more monumental and important than that of the offices. Its long two-storeyed façade is dominated by a hexastyle Tuscan portico as in countless public buildings of around this date in England. Another set of public buildings was created along the Damm, a long street cutting through the ramparts. Planned in the late eighteenth century but not fully built up till later, this incorporates on one side the Museum, the Library and Archive Building, and Kastellanei (administrative offices), and, on the other, three private houses. Attractive villas in Palladian and Schinkelesque styles were built in the 1830s in streets such as the Hauptstrasse and Gartenstrasse.

The development of Brunswick as a Neo-classical centre had been begun, as we have already noted, at the turn of the century by the architect Peter Joseph Krahe. He was still at work in the 1820s, as can be seen in his villa for August Phillip von Amsberg which survives today as a bank. With the appointment as court architect in 1829 of the Brunswick-born Carl Theodor Ottmer (1800–43), the authentic stamp of Schinkelesque classicism was brought to the city, for he had been trained in the Berlin Bauakademie in 1822 and had collaborated with Schinkel in the design of the Singakademie in Berlin five years later. The impact of this association can be seen in striking villas by Ottmer such as the Villa Bülow (1839) in the Cellerstrasse, and no. 29 in the Wilhelmtorwall (1841). His 177 development of the ramparts with Neo-classical villas influenced other designers, such as those of no. 2 Theaterwall, and no. 16 Hohetorwall. His Brunswick Railway Station (1843–5), an ambitious Italianate building which is today a 171 bank, boasts the arresting feature of a tall open tholos of giant Corinthian 3–5 columns, but his magnum opus was sadly demolished following bomb damage in the Second World War. This was his Residenz Schloss, the destruction of which 95 has deprived Brunswick of a ceremonial centre. Built in 1831–8 after a fire, it was 169 the last great palace of its kind in a chain which goes back at least to the seventeenth century. Articulated with a giant Corinthian order, the twenty-five-bay-long entrance front of the U-shaped Residenz was preceded by quadrant

95 Carl Theodor Ottmer: Residenz Schloss, Brunswick, 1831–8.

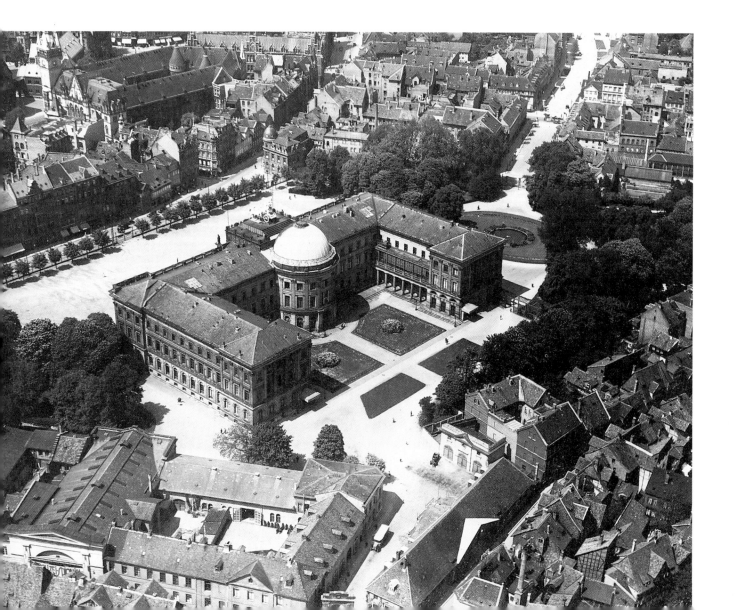

colonnades and crowned over the central portico by a high imperial attic. At the back, the circular staircase hall projected as a huge domed demi-rotunda rising the full height of the building. Ottmer's meticulous attention to detail was 96 everywhere evident, not least in the stern but arresting staircase hall with its squat Greek Doric columns and bold coffering.

96 Carl Theodor Ottmer: staircase hall of the Residenz Schloss, Brunswick, 1831–8.

The pattern at Brunswick was repeated at Kassel where a more modest electoral palace was built in 1821–31 by Johann Konrad Bromeis (1788–1854) who succeeded Heinrich Jussow as court architect to Wilhelm II, Elector of 217– Hesse-Kassel. The new palace, the Rotes Palais, was built in the Friedrichsplatz 219 as an extension to Du Ry's Palais Jungken which Bromeis had already remodelled in 1816–19. With the heavy but inventive detailing of its Greek Doric entrance colonnade, the Rotes Palais formed an aggressive contrast to Du Ry's Neo-Palladian Museum Fridericianum (1769–79), next to which it stood until it was largely destroyed in the Second World War. Its most important feature was its magnificent interiors, including the Throne Room, ballroom and Blue Room, which, somewhat belatedly, were in the First Empire Style of Percier and Fontaine. He created similar interiors, for example the barrel-vaulted Hortensiensaal, at Schloss Wilhelmshöhe near Kassel.

97 Georg Ludwig Friedrich Laves: the Leineschloss, Hanover, 1817–35.

One of the most able of those who worked in a style parallel to Schinkel was the architect Georg Ludwig Friedrich Laves (1788–1864). His principal works are in Hanover which, as court architect for half a century from 1814, he transformed into a Neo-classical capital rivalling Berlin. He was trained by his uncle, Jussow, in Kassel where he was also briefly employed until the fall of King Jérôme of Westphalia in 1813 when he became court building administrator in Hanover. After a study tour in France and England from 1814 to 1817 he returned to Hanover where he remodelled the Residenz, the Leineschloss, in 1817–35 and 97 1831–45 in a somewhat cold but crisply detailed monumental manner akin to that of Bromeis. The grandiose Corinthian portico, originally a porte-cochère but subsequently altered with a flight of steps, recalls that of the 1780s at Henry Holland's Carlton House, London. Laves revisited England in 1826, when he met Nash and drew his East Cowes Castle, in 1830, 1834 and finally in 1851. The interiors of the Leineschloss, like those of Bromeis's Rotes Palais, were richly decorated in the French First Empire Style and, like those at Kassel, were destroyed in the Second World War.

192

In the Berggarten at Herrenhausen near Hanover, Laves provided the Bibliothek-Pavillon and the Mausoleum. The former, built in 1818–19, is a composition organized round a circular glazed core, anticipating Schinkel's Anatomy Theatre and Observatory at Bonn. The Mausoleum (1842–7), fronted with a stern Greek Doric portico, recalls Schinkel's mausoleum of 1810 at Schloss Charlottenburg, though its interior is articulated with a Roman Corinthian order. Laves's first design was in a full Egyptian style. A Greek Doric portico is again the keynote of the villa known as Haus Bella Vista which Laves built in Hanover in the Franco-Prussian style. More Schinkelesque is his Wangenheim Palais (1829–33) in Hanover with its elegant but undemonstrative thirteen-bay entrance front adorned with a modest unpedimented portico of Roman Doric columns. More arresting is the side elevation, remodelled by Laves in 1844 with a projecting semicircular bay containing a winter garden on the first floor entirely surrounded by glass.

98

196
195

194

98 Georg Ludwig Friedrich Laves: Bibliothek-Pavillon, Herrenhausen, near Hanover, 1818–9.

99 Georg Ludwig Friedrich Laves: Royal Opera House, Hanover, 1845–52.

Laves's masterpiece is the Royal Opera House in Hanover of 1845–52, a brilliantly composed building in which a powerfully plastic effect is built up from three receding masses: the ground-floor entrance portico in which the Doric order is used; the first floor articulated with Ionic columns; and finally the pedimented attic storey with its round-headed windows set in unmoulded rectangular reveals. These windows are repeated on the side elevations which are astylar save for the columned doorways. The rhythm of these arcuated façades is doubtless derived from Schinkel's designs for the theatre at Hamburg of 1825–7. Laves was interested in the technical aspects of construction and invented the 'Laves beam' for wide spans. He also submitted a remarkable design of iron and glass for the Crystal Palace in London in 1850, the closest to Paxton's of the many designs entered in the competition held in that year.

Dresden was another royal capital with a vibrant classical tradition of its own. The leading architects at this time were Christian Friedrich Schuricht (1753–1832), Gottlob Friedrich Thormeyer (1757–1842) and Joseph Thürmer (1789–1833). Schuricht, a pupil of Krubsacius, had visited Rome and England and had collaborated with the garden theorist, Hirschfeld. Appointed court architect at Dresden in 1812, his most important work in that capacity was the Neues Palais (1818–26) which he added to Schloss Pillnitz for Elector Friedrich August III of Saxony. Here he cleverly managed to pay tribute in his skyline to the oriental spirit of the original range of Pillnitz by Pöppelmann in the 1720s, but in the main his building is Schinkelesque and even boasts entrances flanked by Greek Doric columns. Schuricht's designs for the Belvedere on the Brühlsche Terrasse at Dresden were an even bolder essay in the Greek Doric taste, but as executed in 1814 the building was less ambitious.

100 Christian Friedrich
Schuricht: the Neues
Palais, added to Schloss
Pillnitz in 1818–26.

101 Gottlob Friedrich
Thormeyer: gatehouse at
the Leipziger Tor,
Dresden, 1827–9.

Thormeyer, a pupil of G.A. Hölzer who had himself been taught by Krubsacius, was a prolific architect in Dresden where his commissions included the Trinitatis Cemetery chapel (1815–16); shopping arcades in the Antonsplatz (1826 onwards); and the gatehouse at the Leipziger Tor (1827–9). With their 101 dumpy Tuscan porticoes, these were much less distinguished than Schinkel's superb surviving Hauptwache in the same town, where a Greek Ionic portico in 185 antis is flanked by lower side wings which are articulated with the grid-like pilaster strips of the Berlin Schauspielhaus. The executant architect of the Hauptwache from 1830 to 1832 was Joseph Thürmer, who had been a pupil of Karl von Fischer in Munich but who became even more strongly influenced by Schinkel than either Schuricht or Thormeyer had been. This is evident in his Palais Lüttichau (*c.* 1830) in Dresden, a modest building but conceived in 186 severest Prussian style. A friend of Goethe, Thürmer was a man of varied talents including painting and engraving.

Turning to the little grand-ducal capital of Weimar means investigating the career of Clemens Wenzeslaus Coudray (1775–1845) who did much to modernize it in the post-Napoleonic period. He was named after Clemens Wenzeslaus, the last Elector of Trier, who employed his father as court interior decorator. Coudray thus worked as a young man for his father on the interiors of the Schloss at Koblenz which, as we saw in Chapter II, the Elector built chiefly from designs by A.-F. Peyre and left unfinished in the early 1790s. In the mid-1790s Coudray worked under Schuricht and J.A. Heyne in Dresden and from 1800 to 1804 received a thorough training in French classicism under Durand at the Ecole Polytechnique in Paris. He then travelled extensively in Italy, visiting Paestum and Sicily and meeting the German circle in Rome, including the Humboldt brothers, Madame de Staël, Schlegel, Hackert, Thorvaldsen, Rauch and Johann Martin von Wagner. On his return he was appointed architect to the Prince of Orange at Fulda and in 1816 became Oberbaudirektor to Grand Duke Karl August of Saxe-Weimar. He built extensively in Weimar in a chaste arcuated style derived from Durand, but did not move on from this to the full *Rundbogenstil* as Wimmel did in Hamburg.

Characteristic examples of Coudray's dignified but uneventful work are the Bürgerschüle (municipal school) of 1822–5, the west range of the Schloss (1830–45), the Wagenremise (coach house) of 1823, and the Hauptwache (main guard house) of 1834–8. The west range of the Schloss, with its round-arched ground floor, is mainly a two-storeyed link building between older ranges. However, at the south-west corner a three-storeyed pavilion contains a staircase leading to a large if somewhat plain chapel rising through the first and second storeys. This was carried out in 1829 for Grand Duke Karl Friedrich, who succeeded Karl August, Goethe's friend, in the previous year. Its Durandesque sobriety contrasts with the Neo-Greek dynamism of Gentz's staircase in the east range, and with the richer polychromy of the Goethe Gallery in Coudray's west range. With its dark wall paintings and sculptural reliefs over the doors, this was provided in 1840 with help from Schinkel.

Coudray was happy working on a small scale in buildings such as the Erfurter Tor of 1822–4, an elegant Doric pavilion recalling Speeth's Zeller Tor Guard House of *c.* 1813–24 at Würzburg. Coudray's Grand Ducal Mausoleum (1822– 247 4), in which Schiller and Goethe were eventually buried, is a square domed building preceded by a portico of unfluted Greek columns. The mausoleum is memorable for its interior with the austere almost abstract design of the twin tombs. One of Coudray's most interesting contributions to the urban pattern of Weimar was the dwelling houses combined behind a single palatial façade in the

manner of Nash's Regent's Park terraces. Good examples are in the Heinrich Heine Strasse (1817 and 1821), Heinrich Hess Strasse and, even more handsome, nos. 2–8 Steubenstrasse (1827).

We end this chapter at Hamburg which, after Berlin, was the largest and most important city in the north. As a free imperial city from 1618 it had no need of royal buildings and therefore lacks the kind of ceremonial centre which gives charm and interest to so many German towns. The tone of its architectural development as a bourgeois commercial centre in the first half of the nineteenth century was already hinted at in the work of Christian Frederick Hansen (1756–1845). Born in Copenhagen where he was trained by N.-H. Jardin and C.F. Harsdorff from 1770 to 1779, he studied in Rome from 1782 till 1784 when he was appointed Royal Inspector of Buildings for Holstein, a post he held for twenty
102 years. In the street known as Palmaille in Altona on the edge of Hamburg he built in 1801–5 a number of elegant stuccoed mansions in a Palladian style with hints of Ledoux. He had deployed the same style in the 1790s in a series of charming
103 villas in Picturesque grounds for rich Hamburg merchants on the banks of the
104 Elbe west of the city at Ottense, Othmarschen, Nienstedten and Blankenese. A later example of these waterside villas, by Christian Friedrich Lange (1768–1833), was Landhaus Prösch (1818; destroyed by fire 1842), a Palladian villa built for Senator Anton Prösch with a Corinthian portico overlooking the river.

Hansen was succeeded by Carl Ludwig Wimmel (1786–1845) and by his own pupil and rival, Alexis de Châteauneuf. They made Hamburg a centre of the brick *Rundbogenstil* architecture which emerged in the 1830s out of the influence of Schinkel and Durand. Wimmel was born in Berlin, the son of the master-mason who worked on the Brandenburg Gate, Neue Wache and Altes Museum. He studied carpentry under Steinmayer from 1802 to 1805 and architecture under C.G. Langhans in 1806. Following the French occupation of Berlin in 1806 he

102 Christian Friedrich Hansen: the architect's own house, No. 116, Palmaille, Altona, near Hamburg, 1803–4.

103, 104 Christian Friedrich Hansen: front and back elevations of Hirschparkhaus, Hamburg.

moved to Hamburg where he studied at the Bauschule under Christian Friedrich Lange from 1807 to 1809. He was a pupil of Weinbrenner at Karlsruhe from 1809 to 1810 and subsequently spent four years in Italy where, like so many others of his generation, he met the German colony in Rome and travelled to Paestum to study the Greek temples.

105 Carl Ludwig Wimmel: houses in the Esplanade, Hamburg, 1827–30.

Returning to Hamburg in 1814 Wimmel joined the city Buildings Department and two years later was appointed Stadtbaumeisteradjunkt and made his first city plan. His earliest buildings included two Greek Doric city gates, the Steintor (1818) and the Millerntor (1819). The modest St Paul's church (1819–20) and English Reformed church (1825–6) were also comparatively minor works, but the extensive general hospital (1821–3) affords the first hints of the kind of rigid arcuated style he was to adopt for major public buildings such as the Heilig-Geist-Hospital (1833–5), St Johannis Kloster (1834–7), and Maria-Magdalena-Kloster (1838–9). His Municipal Theatre (1826–7) and terraced houses in the Esplanade (1827–30) were in a simpler late classical style, but his best building,

106 Carl Ludwig Wimmel and Franz Forsmann: the Johanneum, Hamburg, 1837–40.

the Johanneum (1837–40), was in the Gärtner style, the rusticated Florentine manner that Friedrich von Gärtner, following Klenze's example, had made his own in Munich. The Johanneum was an enormous building containing a library 106 and two schools grouped round three sides of a courtyard with an open round-arched colonnade closing it on the fourth side. Designed in collaboration with his partner, Franz Forsmann (1795–1878), it was a remarkable realization of the ideals of educational public buildings which had been fostered in late-eighteenth and early-nineteenth-century France.

Wimmel's other major contribution to Hamburg was the Exchange, for which he first submitted designs in 1829 in collaboration with H.A.C. Koch. In 1834 he prepared further designs in a trabeated style close to Schinkel's Kaufhaus project of 1827 but the Exchange, as executed in 1837–41 from designs by Wimmel and 107 Forsmann, was in a totally different Neo-Cinquecento style influenced by a project for the building by Châteauneuf of 1835–6. In 1841 Wimmel was appointed first director of the Hamburg Buildings Department and made an extensive tour of Great Britain, following in the footsteps of Schinkel in 1826, Châteauneuf in 1828, Laves and Moller in 1840.

Wimmel's partner Forsmann was born in Hamburg, studied in Eutin under Wilhelm Tischbein and then travelled in France, England and Italy. Most of the major buildings by both Wimmel and Forsmann have been destroyed, except for the rebuilt Exchange, but Forsmann's best work, the Jenisch House at Flottbeck near Hamburg (1828–34), fortunately survives. It is one of the group of similar villas near the wooded banks of the Elbe west of Hamburg built by Hansen and others from *c.*1790 onwards. An elegantly stuccoed villa in a modest park for the Hamburg senator and merchant, Martin Johann Jenisch the younger, its tautly moulded façades are an admirable statement of Schinkel's ideals as expressed, for example, in his Schloss Tegel. This is not surprising for Schinkel himself supervised the designs of the Jenisch House. Buildings such as Schloss Tegel also lie behind the design of Landhaus Baur (1829–36), a villa built at Hamburg-Blankenese for the merchant C.F. Baur by Johann Matthis Hansen and Ole Jörgen Schmidt. Nearby at Hamburg-Othmarschen is the Landhaus Brandt (1817) with its stunning double curved portico, Greek Doric on the ground floor, Ionic on the first. This was built for Wilhelm Brandt, a merchant who traded with Russia, probably from designs by Axel Bundsen. He also designed Landhaus Rücker (1828–31) and the Friedhofskapelle at Flensburg, Schleswig-Holstein (1810–13), a little building of much originality in both plan and elevation. It is a domed funerary chapel designed in a sparse almost abstract manner.

107 Carl Ludwig Wimmel and Franz Forsmann: the Exchange, Hamburg, 1837–41.

More important than Forsmann was Alexis de Châteauneuf (1799–1853), the
son of a French nobleman and former ambassador at Geneva who took refuge in
Hamburg from the French Revolution in 1794. In 1816 Alexis became a pupil in
Hamburg of Wimmel and in 1817 in Paris of Achille Leclère (1785–1853), a
pupil of Percier. From 1818 to 1821 he studied under Weinbrenner in Karlsruhe
and after a tour of Italy returned to Hamburg in 1822. His first significant work
was the Post Office (1830–1), one of the earliest Italianate buildings in
nineteenth-century Hamburg. Following a visit to Italy and Greece in 1831 he
designed what was probably the most attractive building of his career, the
Abendroth house, which, like his Post Office, is now destroyed. Built in 1832–6
for Dr Abendroth, the former mayor of Hamburg, this exquisite monument
combined elements from Schinkel and Percier in a composition which had
already begun to return to an Italian Renaissance mode. It thus takes its part in a
development which had been started by Klenze in the Leuchtenberg Palais in
Munich (1816–21) and continued by Barry in the Travellers' Club in London
(1829–32). Its neo-antique interiors included a Carrara marble staircase with
unfluted Greek Doric columns on the ground floor supporting an Ionic
colonnade, and the semicircular saloon flanked by a curved Schinkelesque bench
below a mural depicting a hemicycle of Corinthian columns.

Following the loss of the competition for the Hamburg Exchange to Wimmel
in 1837, Châteauneuf moved to London which he had first visited in 1828. Here
he collaborated with Arthur Patrick Mee (1802–68), an obscure pupil of Soane,
in a competition entry for the new Royal Exchange in 1838–9. Mee had built a
villa for Richard Goddefroy at Nienstedten near Hamburg in 1838, a very
English-looking building which still survives. Their Neo-Renaissance design for

the Exchange, with a portico borrowed from the Loggia dei Lanzi in Florence, was awarded the second premium though the commission was eventually given to Sir William Tite.

In 1839 Châteauneuf entered the competition for the Nelson monument in Trafalgar Square with a design for a series of massive sculptural groups set against clipped trees of the kind with which Schinkel flanked the Cathedral in the Lustgarten in Berlin. In the same year he published *Architectura domestica* (London, Hamburg and Paris, 1839). A striking statement of faith in the Italianate Revival which appeared in the same year as W.H. Leeds's monograph on the Travellers' Club, this contained engravings of his house for Dr Abendroth and other minor works. In 1843 he followed this with an unusual and today little-known publication undertaken in collaboration with Lady Mary Fox, wife of the 4th Lord Holland. Entitled *The Country House*, the book consists of correspondence between Alexis de Châteauneuf and a patron who wishes to build a country house on a site near Foots Cray in Kent. The patron inclines towards the

109 Franz Forsmann: staircase of the Jenisch House, Hamburg, 1828–34.

Elizabethan style while Châteauneuf, on the other hand, explains, 'I propose to make a design in the "Greek style"', and 'If a determinate name must be given to the style, I propose I should call it, "the Renaissance style of the nineteenth century"'. This synthesis of trabeated and arcuated architecture, which we will find again in Klenze, was justified by Châteauneuf as part of his search for a unity between painting, sculpture and architecture: 'It is only,' he argued, 'in the genuine architecture of ancient Greece itself, and in the Italian style of the fifteenth century, that we meet with all three arts growing up to completeness together.' He was thus anxious for the interiors to be appropriately ornamented and recommended his patron to seek advice from Charles Eastlake, R.A., then supervising the choice of subjects for the frescoes at the New Palace of Westminster. The pamphlet concludes with a long letter from Eastlake and a series of lithographs of Châteauneuf's design for the proposed mansion in a Picturesquely Italianate style. Situated on the water's edge and dominated by an asymmetrically placed tower, it recalls designs by Barry such as Trentham Hall, Staffordshire (1834–9), and his unexecuted scheme for the lakeside palace of Clumber, Nottinghamshire, of 1857. Its irregular grouping was consciously Picturesque in accordance with the recommendations of Prince Hermann von Pückler-Muskau whose *Andeutungen über Landschaftgärtnerei*, Stuttgart 1834 (Hints on Landscape Gardening) Châteauneuf quotes in his seventh letter.

Alexis de Châteauneuf's designs of 1840–2 for the earliest railway station in Hamburg, for the Hamburg-Bergerdorf line, express perhaps for the first time in railway architecture the departure and arrival sheds as a pair of colossal arches. This powerful motif, which anticipates Lewis Cubitt's celebrated front of King's Cross Station, London (1850–2), was repeated in Châteauneuf's station for the Hamburg-Berlin line, executed in 1844–9.

111 Axel Bundsen:
Friedhofskapelle,
Flensburg, 1810–13.

112 Axel Bundsen (?):
Landhaus Brandt,
Hamburg-Othmarschen,
1817.

CHAPTER VI

Leo von Klenze

IT seems a remarkable coincidence that Germany in the 1780s should have produced two architects of such international stature, with such closely parallel achievements and careers, as Schinkel and Klenze. Both were not merely architects whose numerous public and private buildings, palaces and museums, gave a totally new identity to their respective capital cities, Berlin and Munich, but both became nationally respected public figures, partly as a result of their close association with the ruling houses of Prussia and Bavaria. Indeed Klenze, somewhat in the manner of Rubens, was occasionally employed by his sovereign on ambassadorial missions. Both architects were talented painters of landscape, topography and architecture; both were indefatigable writers on architecture, a subject which they approached with solemn dedication and high intellectual ideals; and both were prolific self-advertisers, publishing descriptions and engravings of their own buildings. Klenze, in addition, was a Greek archaeologist of some distinction. While Schinkel's visionary schemes for hilltop palaces at Orianda and Athens remained on paper, Klenze's Walhalla was actually built on its breathtaking site above the Danube. The climax of the whole Greek Revival, the Walhalla can also be seen as the realization of Gilly's design for a monument to Frederick the Great, the sight of which had moved both Schinkel and Klenze to adopt the profession of architecture.

Yet Klenze has received very little attention from architectural historians: only one published monograph, no *Lebenswerk* series, no comprehensive exhibitions, very few articles. Why? The answer may partly be that whereas the apparent modernity of Schinkel's work and career, with its interest in industrial techniques, is thought, rightly or wrongly, to have a relevance to present-day problems, Klenze's career entirely lacks these overtones. But this is no reason for ignoring an architect of commanding genius whose Walhalla is surely a landmark in the history of Germany and of Western architecture.

Klenze was more fortunate in his principal patron, the extraordinary Crown Prince Ludwig of Bavaria (1786–1868), than Schinkel was in his. From the start Ludwig not only had more power and more money than Schinkel's patron, Crown Prince Friedrich Wilhelm of Prussia, but he ascended the throne in 1825, whereas Friedrich Wilhelm did not succeed until 1840, the year before Schinkel's death. If the fantastic palaces of Linderhof, Herrenchiemsee and Neuschwanstein, built by Ludwig's grandson, Ludwig II of Bavaria, are the best-known examples of the Wittelsbach building mania, the transformation of an entire modern city by Ludwig I is in some ways the more remarkable achievement. A complex and contradictory character who made his children live on black bread in the Residenz while he poured out millions on building palaces, temples and museums, he was obsessed by a nostalgia for the south which he shared with men as varied as Winckelmann, Burckhardt, Ruskin and Pater. Their search for a paradise warmed by a southern sun was akin to a religious pilgrimage. Their vision of Greece and Italy changed the face of the modern world, as we shall see in our study of one small part of it, Bavaria.

113 Leo von Klenze: Roman Room of Glyptothek, Munich, 1816–30.

Despite the fact that Klenze spent virtually his entire professional career in the service of the Wittelsbachs of Bavaria, he was not himself a south German. Born in 1784 at Schladen near Brunswick into a prosperous Catholic family, he attended the Collegium Carolinum at Brunswick from 1798 to 1800. He moved to Berlin University in 1800 where his father, a lawyer, wanted him to pursue legal studies. Finding these boring he switched to architecture under the dynamic influence of the young Friedrich Gilly whose heroic and poetical designs captivated him as they had Schinkel a year or so earlier. Soon he was living in the Gilly household where he met Schinkel and, after Gilly's death, copied his designs for the National Theatre and Exchange in Berlin, as well as his drawings of the Gothic Marienburg. Mere stylistic imitations were not enough, and Klenze soon began to search for the norm between the two poles of the antique and the newly developed technical possibilities in the field of construction. In the teaching at Gilly's school of Alois Hirt Klenze found a firm direction. His ambition became clear: to develop Greek form further in his work, not merely to imitate it. As he wrote to Crown Prince Ludwig in 1817, 'Just as Palladio became great and immortal through an inspired adaption of Roman architecture to the exigencies of his own time and country, I shall attempt to do likewise with the works of the Greeks; that is the only way to be anything more than a pale plagiarist.'

In 1803 he travelled to Paris where he came under the influence of Durand at the Ecole Polytechnique and worked for a time in the office of Percier and Fontaine. He visited southern France and Italy in 1803–4 where a nobleman whose palace he was sketching in Genoa was so struck by his combination of architectural talent and courtly demeanour, that he recommended him as court architect at Kassel. Here Napoleon's brother Jérôme presided from 1808 over a hedonistic court in the palace at Wilhelmshöhe, formerly the seat of the Landgraves of Hesse. Klenze's first executed work, which still survives, is the court theatre of 1812–13 at Wilhelmshöhe, temporarily graced by the name of 114 Napoleonshöhe. Intended for French comedies and comic opera, this is a freestanding rectangular building in a simple Palladian style with an interior, holding 400 to 500 persons, which was modelled, according to Klenze, on the semicircular amphitheatres of the ancients at Segesta, Catania and Pompeii.

Jérôme, who had become king of the newly created kingdom of Westphalia in 1807, fell with Napoleon in 1813, the year of Klenze's marriage. Jérôme begged

114 Klenze: design for the theatre at Wilhelmshöhe, 1812–3.

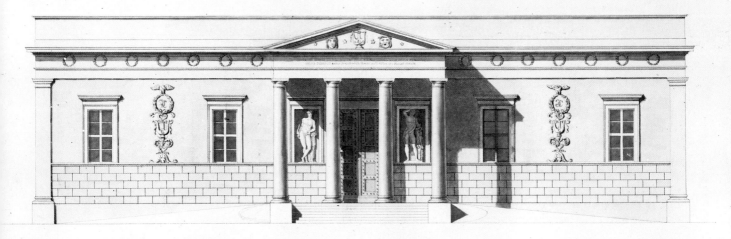

him to continue in his service in Italy, but Klenze returned with his young Italian bride to Paris where he designed a 'Monument à la Pacification de l'Europe', a vast temple raised on a podium inspired by that of Gilly's monument to Frederick the Great. Hoping, mistakenly, to find a new patron amongst the princes gathered at the Congress of Vienna, he set off for Vienna, but stopping at Munich on the way in February 1814 was introduced to Prince Ludwig. He describes their meeting, which was to change the course of his life, as follows: '"Ah-ha, a German!" – thus the Crown Prince of Bavaria hailed me, seizing a handful of my blond hair, "A warm welcome to you".' Despite this encouraging start, no architectural commission was forthcoming, though earlier in the same month the Munich Academy had announced a competition for a military hospital, a German national monument (Walhalla), and a museum for antique sculpture (Glyptothek). These schemes were part of Ludwig's ambition to turn a cosy little Residenz town of scarcely 50,000 inhabitants into a large European royal capital which would vie as a cultural centre with Rome, Paris or Vienna. In 1809 Karl von Fischer (1782–1820), a pupil of Maximilian von Verschaffelt in Munich, was appointed Königlicher Oberbaurat in Munich, where he was the leading town planner until the arrival of Klenze who quickly supplanted him. Fischer made proposals as early as 1809–10 for a Königsplatz with the sculpture gallery on its north side. The Königsplatz owed its origin to the competition of 1808 for the enlargement of the city, which followed the creation of the monarchy in 1806. The centre of the new Maxvorstadt (Max suburb) was Fischer's circular Carolinenplatz of 1808–12 with the as yet unbuilt-up area of the future Königsplatz to the west.

In 1811 Ludwig commissioned designs for the sculpture gallery from the Italian architect Giacomo Quarenghi and in 1813 from Karl Haller von Hallerstein (1774–1817), a former pupil of Friedrich Gilly and a leading Greek archaeologist. The gallery was to be 'ein Ur-Werk', 'a work of primordial originality,' which was to be known in Greek fashion as a Glyptothek. Arguably the first public museum of its kind in the world, this sumptuous building was paid for entirely by Ludwig out of his annual savings from his privy purse. It was Ludwig, moreover, who, from the time of his Grand Tour of Italy in 1804–5, had been responsible for accumulating its treasures, notably the Late Archaic pedimental sculpture from the temple at Aegina which had been discovered in 1811 by C.R. Cockerell, Haller von Hallerstein, Foster and Linckh.

In July 1815 Ludwig went to Paris with the allied leaders where he met Klenze again. Sharing Klenze's passion for antiquity, he favoured him as architect for the Glyptothek and persuaded him to submit designs. Klenze drew up his first plans in Paris and, later in the year, elaborated them into a competition entry which comprised three sets of designs – one Greek, one Roman, and one Renaissance. Haller, a meticulous but imaginative draughtsman, submitted ravishing Graeco-Egyptian designs, while the cross-section of Fischer's project, with its Corinthian portico, Pantheon hall and colonnaded gallery, recalled Paine's Kedleston of 1759–60, though the outer walls were totally blank in the manner of French Grand Prix designs. The competition was now extended until the beginning of 1816 and the entries were submitted for his comments to Ludwig's art agent in Rome, the painter Johann Martin von Wagner (1777–1858). Klenze and Fischer reworked their designs in 1816 but it was the designs of the former of which Ludwig laid the foundation stone on 23 April that year.

115
116

Ludwig enjoyed playing off his architects against each other, and Klenze's account of their relationship at this time does not shed an attractive light on the prince's character:

On the next day the prince said to me cheerfully, 'But Klenze, what a source of continual annoyance it will be to Fischer to have to watch your building, the Glyptothek, rising daily before his very eyes!' I replied that I hoped this would not be the case and that if it were, it would grieve me greatly – but the whole idea seemed to amuse the crown prince enormously. Fischer lived right on the square where the Glyptothek was to be built – he had been the architectural first love of his Royal Highness, had served him loyally and with the best intentions for six to eight years, was now ill and at death's door and deserved sympathy and consolation rather than this *Schadenfreude*. O Princes! Princes!

In 1816 Ludwig appointed Klenze Hofbaumeister and sent him on a mission to Paris to purchase further antique sculpture for the Glyptothek. The aloof marble façades of Klenze's gallery, built from 1816 to 1830 on the north side of what was to become the Königsplatz, incorporated Greek, Hellenistic and Renaissance elements, handled with Greek austerity: Greek the Erechtheum-inspired Ionic capitals of the portico; Hellenistic the pilaster capitals; Renaissance the round-headed aedicules. The whole building, and especially its sumptuous interior decoration, offers itself as a commentary on its contents with which it enters into a kind of suggestive dialogue. This synthetic allusive approach is rather different from the uncompromising severity of Schinkel's first building in Berlin, the Neue Wache, which is exactly contemporary with the Glyptothek. The façade of the Glyptothek gives no impression that it fronts one 117

115 Karl von Fischer: design for the Glyptothek, Munich, *c*.1816.

116 (Opposite above). Klenze: preliminary design for the Glyptothek, Munich, elevation and section, *c*.1816.

117 (Opposite below) Klenze: the Glyptothek, Munich, 1816–30.

range of a four-sided courtyard which is thus one of the unexpected charms of the building. Another surprise is, or was, the two handsome rooms for Ludwig's entertainments and dinners in the centre of the north range. Elaborately frescoed by Peter Cornelius and his pupils with scenes from Greek mythology and history, these emphasized that the collections, though open to the public, were still seen as a background to a princely way of life. Inspired by a design published in Durand's *Précis*, the ranges of the museum are one-storeyed with virtually no windows apart from high side-lighting looking into the central courtyard, and top-lighting.

Klenze placed the sculpture in a series of polychromatic interiors which 113 increased in decorative richness as the visitor moved round the museum in clockwise direction, beginning with the earliest sculpture in the Egyptian Room and ending in the Roman Room which occupied the whole east range. The walls of the Roman Room were faced with violet marble scagliola up to the prominent white and gold cornice, while the white and gold domes were enriched with crimson and pink coffering and bas-reliefs by Schwanthaler. This decoration was lost during bomb damage in the Second World War. Sadly it was not reinstated during the disastrous 'restoration' of the 1960s which has resulted in marble statuary being displayed incongruously against walls of exposed brick. This completely contradicts Klenze's belief that 'a well-ordered splendour in the surroundings charms the eye and immediately establishes a suitable atmosphere; a lively coloured background makes even the most undistinguished antique sculpture appear fresh and pure.'

In 1816 Klenze was also engaged on the first of his many domestic buildings in Munich, the Leuchtenberg Palais, built for Napoleon's step-son, Eugène de 118 Beauharnais, viceroy of Italy. He had married Crown Prince Ludwig's sister, Princess Augusta, in 1806 as part of the alliance with Napoleon which the Elector of Bavaria had been persuaded to make by his minister, Montgelas. After the fall of Napoleon, Beauharnais found refuge in Munich where he was created Duke of Leuchtenberg and reactivated his scheme for a town palace for which Fischer had provided designs in 1810 and 1814. With the appearance on the scene of the dynamic, suave and ambitious Klenze, Fischer's chances of executing this, or indeed any other, commission, dramatically receded. The duke had entertained ambitions of building his palace near the Glyptothek in the Königsplatz, but Ludwig, reluctant to admit domestic architecture into this area, wrote hysterically to Klenze, 'Never, never, never will I permit it, if you go through with this, you have damned yourself for ever in my eyes'. Klenze, who was vigorously engaged with plans for replanning the area near the Schwabinger Tor in front of the Residenz, persuaded the duke to build his palace there. Adapting Fischer's plans, he accordingly erected for the duke what was the first building in the new Ludwigstrasse running north from the Residenz in territory outside the old city wall.

Fischer's drawings, prepared when Eugène de Beauharnais was viceroy of Italy, were labelled in Italian, Klenze's in French. Fischer had adopted a Palladian pattern for his façades which Klenze remodelled along the lines of the Palazzo Farnese. The style of Raphael, Peruzzi and Antonio da San Gallo, as opposed to the later and more widely imitated Palladio, was familiar from the plates in Percier and Fontaine's *Palais, maisons, et autres édifices modernes, dessinés à Rome* (Paris 1798). Klenze had originally shown the eleven-bay south entrance front with an entrance door framed by a simple arch, as at the Palazzo Farnese, but, on the crown prince's orders, this was fronted with a four-columned portico supporting a first-floor balcony. The interiors, colourfully decorated in the

118 Klenze:
Leuchtenberg Palais,
Munich, 1816.

Empire Style of Klenze's old masters Percier and Fontaine, contained Eugène's rich collection of paintings by Italian sixteenth- and seventeenth-century artists, as well as by contemporary German artists.

The first monument of the Neo-Renaissance in nineteenth-century Germany, this 253-roomed palace set the tone for the development of central Munich. Its assembly of Renaissance prototypes according to the lessons of Durand was echoed in adjacent buildings by Klenze such as the Arco Palais (1824) and the Alfons (or Ludwig Ferdinand) Palais (1825), both in the Wittelsbacher Platz, and the Max Palais in the Ludwigstrasse (1828; demolished 1936). The crown prince's development of the Ludwigstrasse and its neighbourhood far outstripped the actual demand for buildings, so that much of Klenze's new residential accommodation was still unoccupied in the mid-1830s. Unlike other recently developed areas of the city such as the Carolinenplatz, laid out by Fischer with freestanding villas almost in the manner of a garden-suburb, Klenze's Ludwigstrasse, with façades designed by him and approved by the crown prince, was wholly urban, a straight closed street which excluded views outwards of the adjacent Hofgarten and Englischer Garten. One of the first buildings was the Haus Kobell, built in 1817–18 as no. 1 Ludwigstrasse, on the corner of the Gallerie Strasse, for Franz von Kobell, a minister of state. This was followed by houses in similar Florentine Renaissance styles for Count Mejean, head of the French colony left in Munich after the fall of Napoleon, and no. 3 Ludwigstrasse, for Jean-Baptiste Métivier, a court architect and decorator who was a colleague of Klenze. At no. 30, further down the street, the building contractor Rudolf Röschenauer built an apartment block from Klenze's Florentine designs. Amongst the books which Klenze used in the design of these buildings was *Architecture toscane* (Paris 1815) by A.-H.-V. Grandjean de Montigny (1776–1850) and A. Famin, of whom the former, a pupil of Percier and Fontaine, had worked at Kassel for King Jérôme in *c.* 1808–10. The crown prince's own passion for Italy, to which he paid over fifty visits in the course of his life, was inexhaustible. In 1827 he bought the Villa Malta on the Pincio in Rome, a house which had long been the centre of the German artists' colony. He had stayed here in 1818 when on a visit to Italy with Klenze, the carefree mood of his visits being captured in an enchanting painting of 1824 by Franz Ludwig Catel of 'Crown Prince Ludwig in the Spanish Inn in Rome'. Far from the ritual of court life, the prince is shown in a modest *taverna*, calling for more wine in the company of a group of roistering companions including Thorvaldsen, Wagner, Schnorr von Carolsfeld, Veit, Catel, and, sitting on his left, Klenze.

However, Klenze and the crown prince were engaged in fundamental debate at this time about the style appropriate for the development of the Ludwigstrasse area of Munich. This came to a head in 1817 with the commission for a substantial house at no. 31, Ludwigstrasse from the wealthy locksmith Korbinian Meyer. The crown prince entertained visions of a grandiose street lined with neo-antique buildings in the style of the Glyptothek or with showy Italianate palaces. Klenze rejected both these proposals by arguing that 'the antique heroes were not forced to live in storeys one on top of the other', and, in a letter of 17 June 1820, that 'Unfortunately Munich is not Rome and Mr Meyer is no Farnese or Pitti.'

Klenze's aim was to adapt the more modest façade types of fifteenth-century Florence with their frequent windows, such as the Strozzi, Medici Riccardi and Pitti palaces. In 1818 he pointed out the beauty of these to the crown prince who insisted that the ideal model was the Palazzo Torlonia Giraud in Rome, a monumental early-sixteenth-century pile, inspired by the Cancelleria, with massive wall spaces and widely separated window openings. 'Make the windows far apart, dear Klenze,' observed the crown prince, 'for without that the large cannot appear impressive and the small merely looks small.'

One obvious solution, adopted at the Schmid-Bertsch Haus, for example, was to unite several smaller dwellings behind a single palace façade. This principle, which was adopted successfully at Weimar by Coudray in 1817–27, did not appeal to Schinkel when he saw Nash's terraces in London in 1826, but it was one which Klenze was obliged to follow in 1826 in the design of the Odeon, the Greek-named city concert hall and ballroom. Its site off the Ludwigstrasse had been intended by the crown prince as early as 1818 to be occupied by a symmetrical pendant to the adjacent Leuchtenberg Palais. Shortly after ascending the

V Klenze: fantasy reconstruction of Athens in ancient times, 1862.

throne, Ludwig commissioned designs from Klenze for a building which, despite its totally different function, would duplicate the external appearance of the Leuchtenberg Palais. Thus Klenze cleverly buried the concert hall in the heart of the building so that it makes no appearance from the outside at all. Surrounded by a two-storeyed colonnade, the sumptuous concert hall, richly adorned with stucco-work and terminating in a great apse containing busts of German composers, was destroyed in the Second World War. The subsequent restoration of the stuccoed façades of the Odeon, together with those of its similarly damaged twin, the Leuchtenberg Palais, cannot fully compensate for this loss.

With its domestic-looking façades, the Odeon flatly contradicted Klenze's dictum that 'A building is an organic whole and architectonic effect comes from the interior and is expressed on the exterior, but never and at no point the other way round'. However, his Pinakothek, designed in 1822 and executed 1826–36, clearly expresses its function as an art gallery which is more than can be said for either Schinkel's Altes Museum or Smirke's British Museum. It was built to house the celebrated Wittelsbach collection of paintings which Ludwig generously gave to his people. The novel exterior is conceived entirely within a Neo-Renaissance vocabulary – the ground floor inspired by the Palazzo Cancelleria, and the upper floor by the Vatican Belvedere Courtyard – which may be considered appropriate for a building largely designed to house Renaissance paintings. Unlike the Altes Museum and the Glyptothek, which both contained Pantheon-like rooms, the Pinakothek did not contain a collection of antique sculpture. Its original and influential plan disposes the seven principal galleries along the centre of the body of the building on the first floor. They are entirely top-lit so that the windows which feature so prominently along the south front do not light galleries but a twenty-five-bay-long loggia. This was decorated by Peter Cornelius and others in the High Renaissance grotesque style of Raphael and Giovanni da Udine so as to represent the development of painting, beginning with Italy at one end and northern Europe at the other, and meeting in the middle with a climax provided by Raphael on whose birthday the foundation stone of the building was laid. Balancing the loggia on the north side of the building was a series of small cabinets, opening into each other and into the main galleries, for the display of smaller pictures. This unusual disposition was subsequently adopted for the galleries at Dresden, Frankfurt and Brunswick.

Ludwig's ascent to the throne on the death of his father in 1825 enabled him to turn his attention to the modernization of the vast and rambling Residenz. Schemes for the reconstruction of this rich ensemble of medieval, Renaissance and Baroque buildings had been prepared between 1799 and 1809 by Maximilian von Verschaffelt, Charles Pierre Puille, Andreas Gärtner and Karl von Fischer. There was no question of replacing this historic if disorderly complex with some Neo-classical dream palace, but of tidying up its outer façades and providing private and state apartments in the latest classical styles. Klenze's chief additions between 1826 and 1842 were the new southern wing, the Königsbau (1826–35); the court church of All Saints (1826–37) to the east; and the refacing of the whole north front, the Festsaalbau (1832–42), providing a magnificent colonnaded throne room, ballroom and new grand staircase.

The Königsbau, facing on to the Max Josephs Platz, recalls well-known Florentine sources: the Palazzo Pitti combined with the pilaster system of a building like the Palazzo Rucellai. Interestingly, Karl von Fischer on his second visit to Italy in 1812 had made detailed drawings of the Palazzo Pitti, which Klenze used in designing the Königsbau. It is not known whether the crown prince ordered the drawings from Fischer in the first place or whether he saw

VI Klenze: Propyläen, Munich, 1846–60.

151

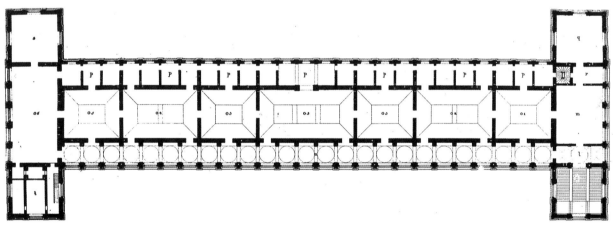

119, 120 Klenze: Alte
Pinakothek, Munich,
façade and plan at main
gallery level, 1826–36.

them for the first time in Klenze's studio after Fischer's death. The internal
planning of the Königsbau was intimate and asymmetrical, despite the
emphatically regular exterior. The interiors were decorated in an Empire Style 122
enriched with fresco cycles from Greek poetry in the king's apartments and from
German poetry, particularly Schiller, in the queen's. The large team of artists
included the painters Heinrich Hess, Georg Hiltensperger, Rockl, Schnorr von
Carolsfeld and Kaulbach, and the sculptors Thorvaldsen and Schwanthaler.
Klenze himself designed appropriate furniture and light fittings. The king
wanted his subjects to be able to admire these ambitious interiors and therefore
opened the palace to the public one day a week while work was in progress. They
were shown round at intervals of about a quarter of an hour in groups of twenty
or thirty, exactly like modern tourists.

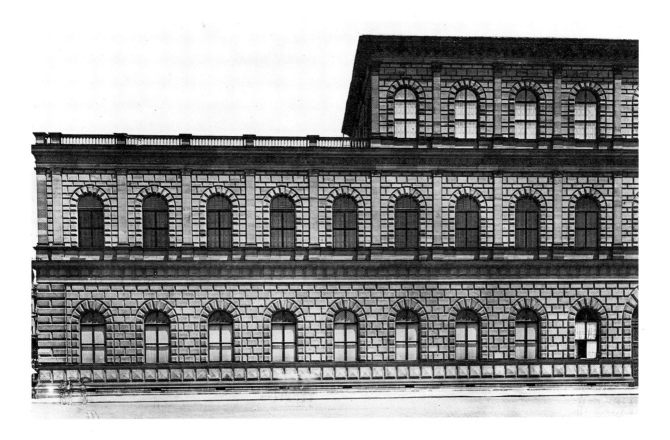

121, 122 Klenze: exterior and interior of the Königsbau, Munich, 1826–35.

153

In a picturesquely theatrical stroke Klenze provided the south side of the Max Josephs Platz opposite the Königsbau in 1836 with a head post office directly inspired by Brunelleschi's Foundling Hospital in Florence. The square thus became a museum of styles like the plates in Durand's *Recueil* or, less augustly, a souvenir of holidays abroad. The square nonetheless has undoubted charm and, on the eastern side, a touch of real monumentality provided by the octastyle Corinthian portico of Fischer's National Theatre of 1812. This was restored by Klenze after a serious fire in 1823.

Klenze's lengthy Festsaalbau of the Residenz, facing the Hofgarten to the 123 north, is a rather unadventurous Palladian composition echoing a design which VII Fischer had made in 1809 for the Königsbau, inspired by Palladio's Basilica at Vicenza. Far more interesting was the court church of All Saints, with an interior designed, at the king's request, on the basis of the twelfth-century Palatine Chapel at Palermo. Ludwig had twice spent Christmas at Palermo, once in 1817 and again in 1823 in the company of Klenze on the occasion of a tour of southern Italy and Sicily. Early in 1826 Klenze travelled to Venice which he had visited with the crown prince on their Italian journey of 1817–18. He now paid particular attention to St Mark's from which he borrowed features such as its shallow-domed nave for his court chapel at Munich. The interior of the chapel, 124 built from 1826 to 1837, dispenses with the curious Moslem pointed arches and honeycomb roof of his model at Palermo, while the exterior is a competent if unexpected essay in the later Romanesque style of Northern Italy and Germany. The building was a stylistic amalgam forced by the king on a reluctant Klenze. It contained a glowingly memorable interior, destroyed in the war, in which frescoes and mosaics with liberal use of gold ground were provided at enormous expense by Heinrich Hess. With a front of Kelheim sandstone, as opposed to the rendered brick of other parts of the Residenz, the church was a costly statement of some of the ideals Klenze had expressed in his *Anweisung zur Architektur des christlichen Kultus*, Munich 1822 (Directions on the Architecture of Christian Worship). Like many of his generation who adopted the *Rundbogenstil*, Klenze saw Early Christian architecture as having preserved something of the spirit of antique architecture. The *Rundbogenstil* thus appealed as a compromise between antiquity and the Middle Ages. The Early Christian basilica also appealed to liberal Christians like Klenze who felt that the church had lost spiritual as well as architectural sincerity in the Baroque period.

125 Klenze: Catholic cathedral of St Dionysius, Athens, 1844–53.

Klenze, unlike Schinkel, designed very few churches. Indeed the court chapel is his only church in Munich. In Athens, of all places, he designed the Catholic cathedral of St Dionysus (1844–53) as a Neo-Renaissance basilica with a 125 Romanesque campanile, though this was partly to satisfy the wishes of King Otto. The last building he ever designed was the richly adorned Stourdza Chapel at Baden Baden of 1864–6. The fine Hellenistic exterior of this little-known building with its Ionic portico and octagonal lantern is close to the plates in his *Anweisung* of forty years before. In complete contrast, the interior of this Roumanian Orthodox church, designed as a mausoleum for the Stourdza family, is in a richly marbled Renaissance style and is dominated by a gilded iconostasis.

It may be thought that we have strayed far from anything that could be considered Neo-classical, but we have to remember that Klenze had convinced himself that the principles of Greek architecture lived on in the round-arched style. He gave his views on this subject in the introduction to his *Sammlung architecktonischer Entwürfe* which he began publishing in 1830:

> Never has there been, and never will there be, more than one art of building, namely, that which was brought to perfection at the epoch of the prosperity and civilization of Greece. ... Grecian architecture alone is marked by universal propriety, character and beauty, although any mode of architecture is capable of affecting us, and has a certain value of its own, when it is a really national style, and has grown up out of the religious and civil habits of a people. This Grecian architecture, taking it in the most exclusive sense of the term, comprehends two leading epochs of its formation; namely, that in which all the apertures and intervals are covered by horizontal lines, and that when the arch was discovered and applied to similar purposes. If we examine and attend to this two-fold development of Grecian architecture in its elementary principles, and in forming a style for ourselves, keep in view those precious remains of art which are as yet preserved to us both in Greece and in Italy, Grecian architecture can and must be the architecture of the world, and that of all periods; nor can any climate, any material, any difference of manners prove an obstacle to its universal adoption.

This uncompromising view was backed by the detailed knowledge he had acquired of Greek architecture during his study tour of southern Italy and Sicily in 1823. During the 1820s he published the results of his researches, which were largely concerned with reconstructing the Greek temples at Selinus, Agrigentum and Paestum. The remaining buildings by him which we have to consider are public monuments in which he was able to give free rein to his passion for antiquity. The first and finest of them is the Walhalla, built near Regensburg from 1830 to 1842. As the greatest temple of its kind erected since the ancient world, it has some claim to be regarded as the climax of the whole Neo-classical movement. The vision of a temple in a timeless landscape, begun with the Grecian Temple (later Temple of Concord and Victory) at Stowe of *c*.1748, continued with Stuart's epoch-making Greek Doric temple at Hagley a decade later, and carried to the new world by Jefferson in his Virginia State Capitol of 1785–99, is central to the cultural history of the later eighteenth and early nineteenth centuries. The Walhalla of Ludwig and Klenze, inspired in its form by what they regarded as the noblest monument in the world, the Parthenon, dedicated to the greatest Germans of all time, and set in one of the finest natural landscapes in Germany, was a compelling, high-minded yet poetical attempt to define what it might mean to be a German in the nineteenth century. The photographs now openly displayed inside of a visit from Hitler need not persuade us that the idea of the building was not in its day a noble one. Bavaria is a country rich in much-visited Baroque and Rococo pilgrimage churches, to which the Walhalla, not incongruously, is a secular and Neo-classical counterpart.

The idea of a great German national monument came to Ludwig when, aged only twenty-one, he visited Berlin in 1807. The sight of an occupied German city smarting under Napoleon's yoke, with its royal family exiled to Königsberg, filled him with the passion to erect a monument to pan-German unity. Such an ambition might be considered ironic in a German whose own country of Bavaria had recently allied itself with Napoleon. Nonetheless, Ludwig's detestation of Napoleon was real, if partly inspired by what he saw as Napoleon's spoliation of his beloved Italy, and partly by the customary opposition of crown princes to their fathers' politics. With as yet no firm idea of the architectural form the monument might take, Ludwig began commissioning busts, of which there were to be a hundred in all, from Schadow, Rauch and other Berlin sculptors. Ludwig may have been inspired at this time by the kind of moral garden of busts of heroes which had been described by Hirschfeld in his seminal book, *Theorie der Gartenkunst* (5 vols, Leipzig 1779–85). A professor of philosophy and fine arts in the university of Kiel, Hirschfeld was important for combining English theories of garden buildings and landscape design with French theories of appropriate architectural character. He described how 'All the towns, all the public places, even the main streets of Greece, were crowded with superb monuments erected to do honour to merit. . . . Tombs were not hidden like ours but exposed along the main roads to the view of passers by. Numerous places of public promenade were embellished with statues of the wisest and most valiant citizens. A number of buildings were even erected with the sole purpose of housing such honourable monuments.' Elsewhere he writes stirringly of a 'new and fertile field of patriotic garden art', complaining that 'Very little thought has been given in our time to decorating places consecrated to public enjoyment with works of art recalling useful merit. . . . In the neighbourhood of our great Residenz cities one could make public national gardens.'

It was the Swiss historian Johannes von Müller, with whom Ludwig was in correspondence over the selection of those to be commemorated with busts, who suggested the title 'Walhalla' on the basis of his study of Nordic and Ossianic legend. Ludwig's first title of a 'Pantheon of Germans' implied a building modelled on the Roman Pantheon, which he had seen on his first visit to Italy in 1805, or even on Soufflot's Panthéon in Paris, which he had seen in the following year. Seeking an appropriate architect he visited Weinbrenner in Karlsruhe but, dissatisfied with his works, approached Karl von Fischer for designs following his return from Berlin to Munich in 1807. In 1809–10 Fischer submitted two impressive schemes for a site on a hill near Munich, one a cruciform building with a Pantheon-like centre approached through a Greek Doric portico, the other a combination of the Parthenon and the Basilica at Paestum. Impressed by the second of these, Ludwig invited Haller von Hallerstein to send in designs from Athens in 1813 and, following the defeat of Napoleon at Leipzig, announced a prize competition for the Walhalla and other public buildings in Munich in February 1814. The terms of the competition stipulated that it should be a Greek temple on a three-tiered platform because Ludwig, who desired a building in what he called the 'renovated Antique style', believed that it was better to have a 'worthy imitation of all that was great in antiquity, than a less beautiful original creation'.

Of the fifty-one architects who entered the competition of 1814–16 we know the names of only a few, though these include Klenze, Schinkel, Andreas Gärtner, Ohlmüller, Speeth and Hübsch. Only a small number of designs has survived. The terms of the competition provoked criticism from those who, still moved by Goethe's rapturous identification of Strasbourg Cathedral with the German soul, argued for the adoption of a 'German style'. Influenced by C.L. Stieglitz's *Von altdeutscher Baukunst*, 2 vols, Leipzig 1820 (On Ancient German Architecture), the painter Peter von Cornelius, to whom Ludwig gave much employment, wrote to the crown prince in November 1820:

126 Karl von Fischer: second design for the Walhalla, 1810.

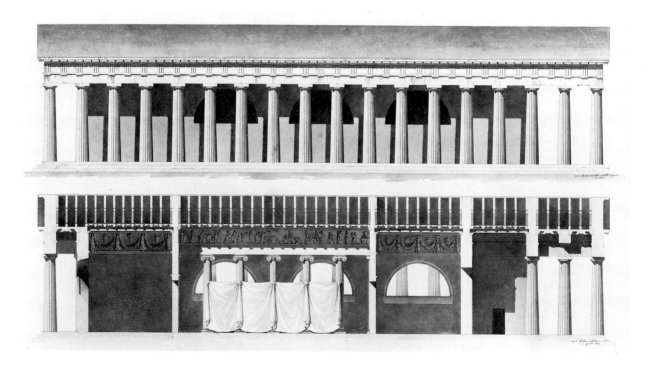

127 Klenze: the Walhalla,
near Regensburg,
1830–42.

Although the realization that a great and worthy monument is to be erected, at long last, to the greatness of Germany makes our hearts beat faster and, above all, reminds us, and makes us profoundly aware, of our German nationality, the proposed design nonetheless prompts the question as to why this great and exclusively German monument should be so completely Grecian. Are we not being inconsistent when we try to glorify our nation by the erection of a great building whilst ignoring the great and splendidly original German style of architecture?

That Greek could be invested with the same symbolism as Gothic was shown by Schinkel, who in 1815 painted two parallel pictures of high romance entitled 'Greek Town by the Sea' and 'Medieval Town on a River'. However, it must be confessed that the conventional Greek temple which Klenze submitted as his competition entry in 1816 is much less gripping than Ohlmüller's three-tiered centrally planned Gothic fantasia containing a vaulted hall of Fonthill-like drama. This, of course, had no more chance of success with Ludwig than did Schinkel's Neo-Gothic Camposanto project. The most attractive classical design we have is Haller's, sent in from Athens in 1815. It shows how far both he, and doubtless Ludwig also, had moved from the garden envisaged by Hirschfeld on the basis of English sources such as the Temple of British Worthies at Stowe. A version of the Parthenon rises above great stepped platforms on the top of a wooded acropolis at the foot of which a monumental gateway flanked by Egyptian pylons guards the approach to a sacred way for national processions.

Ludwig was preoccupied for the next few years with the Glyptothek. No winner was announced in the prize competition for the Walhalla and in 1819 he commissioned new designs from Klenze, by now his favourite architect. Klenze's own preference at this stage was for a centrally planned building which he felt would better symbolize the pan-Germanic elysium. In 1819–20 he drew up several plans for a circular Walhalla, some inspired by Fischer's project of 1809 and others by the Pantheon, by the mausolea of Hadrian and of Cecilia Metella, and by Bramante's project for St Peter's. In the meantime, his visit to Paestum and Sicily with Ludwig in 1817–18 had more than ever convinced the latter that the Walhalla must be a modern equivalent to these temples and must enjoy a similar natural setting. In 1819 Ludwig, who had earlier considered various sites in gardens in and near Munich, wrote emphatically to Klenze that the Walhalla could not stand in a town. In the same year various sites on the Danube were considered though the final choice was not made till after Ludwig had ascended the throne. Klenze began preparing the final designs in 1821 and the building was erected in 1830–42.

What exactly is Klenze's Walhalla? In Norse mythology Walhalla is the 127 palace in which the souls of slain heroes feasted, having been brought there by the Valkyries. But the Walhalla built above the Danube was more than a glorified war memorial. Despite believing in different styles, Ludwig and Cornelius, whose letter about the style of the Walhalla we have quoted, were in agreement that the purpose of the building was to 'make us profoundly aware of our German nationality'. Ludwig, indeed, went so far as to declare that 'The Walhalla was erected that the German might depart from it more German and better than when he had arrived'.

The richly marbled interior is a novel development from the cella of a Greek 128 temple, and is one of the most striking examples of the interest in polychromy which dominated much architectural and archaeological debate in the 1830s and 40s. Its walls are lined with portrait busts, mainly by Rauch, Schadow and Tieck, of field marshals like Blücher and Schwarzenberg, saints like Thomas à Kempis, composers like Gluck and Mozart, philosophers like Leibniz and Haller, poets like Schiller, and painters like Mengs. Some of them were accompanied by curious inscriptions composed by the king, of whom a statue by Schwanthaler, dressed in a Roman toga, dominates the room. The entablature supporting the richly ornamented gilt-bronze ceiling is carried by fourteen painted and gilded figures of the Valkyries, carved in marble by Schwanthaler in the form of Greek caryatids, though wearing northern bearskins! The temple is top-lit through a lantern as reconstructed by Cockerell in the temple of Apollo at Bassae. A further similarity with that temple is the incorporation of a marble figured frieze *inside* the cella. The work of Johann Martin von Wagner in 1837, this depicts the early and legendary past of Germany from the initial immigrations up to the proclamation of Christianity by St Boniface. The first scene shows the departure from the Caucasus. The Caucasian theory, inspired by the writings of Johannes von Müller, was an essential part of the racial and cultural explanations proposed by Klenze in his publication of 1821, *Versuch einer Wiederstellung des toskanischen Tempels nach seinen historischen und technischen Analogie* (Attempt at a Restoration of Tuscan Temples according to their Historical and Technical Analogies). Klenze argued that the two primary places of population on the earth were the Himalayas and Kashmir, and the Caucasus mountains. From the Caucasus the whole of Europe was populated and civilized by two streams of people, one moving towards the north along the Volga, the other moving through Asia Minor across the Bosphorus and along the Danube into the

128 Klenze: interior of
the Walhalla, near
Regensburg, 1830–42.

heart of Western Europe. One of the first resting places in this move from the
Caucasus was Thrace, so that the Hellenic and German peoples have the same
root. Klenze found further support for his view in both linguistics and
architecture, in particular in the polygonal stonework of the Greeks which was
echoed in various primitive monuments in northern Europe, and in the
vernacular buildings of Tuscany, Switzerland, the Tirol and the Bavarian
uplands, which supposedly echoed the construction and decoration of Greek
roofs.

The establishment of these links between the ancient Greeks and the Germans
was, of course, an important justification for the Doric temple as a hall of fame for
immortal Germans. Like the Parthenon, the pediments of the Walhalla are filled
with historical and allegorical sculpture. Carved in marble by Schwanthaler,
these depict the defeat in 9 AD in the Teutoburger Wald of Augustus's legions,
under Varus, by the united tribes of central and north-western Germany, under
Arminius who thereby 'saved' the country from Roman domination; and, at the
other end of the building overlooking the Danube valley, a female figure
representing Germany surrounded by war heroes representing the lost provinces
returned between 1813 and 1815. The iconographical programme suggests a
parallel between these victories and the Greek victory over the Persians from
which Greek unity was supposed to have been derived.

The crypt inside the substructure served as a waiting hall for the busts of
celebrated living figures awaiting only death to be transported by the Valkyries
to the Walhalla above. Klenze referred to this hall as a 'hypogaion', a term used
by archaeologists at that time in connection with Etruscan tomb chambers. Not

the least imposing aspect of the whole Walhalla is the gigantic substructure of stepped terraces and staircases on which it hangs three hundred feet above the Danube. The superhuman scale of this recalls not merely recent projects such as Gilly's Monument to Frederick the Great and Klenze's own 'Monument à la Pacification de l'Europe', but an archaic world of ziggurats and reconstructions of the Tower of Babel. The lowest of the terraces is constructed of polygonal masonry, an archaic form which Klenze described as 'Pelasgic' in his account of the Walhalla.

The building captured the imagination of the painter Turner, who visited it when it was nearing completion in 1840. The characteristically diaphanous quality of his celebrated painting, 'Opening of the Wallhalla [*sic*] in 1842', hints obscurely that the antique may be tantalizingly unattainable in the modern world. Unfamiliar with Turner's steamy romance, the Germans derided it for its topographical inexactitude when it was exhibited at Munich in 1845. The building was opened with much pomp by the king on 18 October 1842, the same day on which he had laid the foundation stone twelve years before, the anniversary of the Battle of Leipzig in 1813. This brooding temple of unpolished grey marble, this costly shrine to Teutonic self-regard, is approached as in some act of pilgrimage either on foot through the forests behind it, or by water along the Danube and thus up a daunting flight of 240 steps. Untouched by bomb damage, it survives more perfectly than any major building by Schinkel as perhaps the most memorable building of the classical revival in Germany.

In describing Schinkel's career we touched on the significance of the creation of the kingdom of Greece under the protection of France, Russia and England, and the offering of its throne by the Congress of London in 1832 to Prince Otto, not yet twenty-one, second son of Ludwig I of Bavaria. Ludwig was overjoyed at this Romantic realization of his ambitions for a link between Greece and Germany. Otto called on his father's architects to lay out his capital city, surrounded himself with Bavarian advisers and assistants and kept large sections of the Bavarian army permanently on call. As Ludwig had made Munich the Athens of the nineteenth century, so Otto may be said to have started the process of turning Athens into a second Munich, though the difficulties and intrigues with which he was surrounded eventually led to his deposition. Ludwig, difficult, impatient, autocratic yet often irresolute, and made suspicious by his deafness, found the suave and distinguished architect, Klenze, a useful ambassador. Klenze's diplomatic mission to Athens in 1834 in connection with an accusation of treason levelled against Count Armannsperg led to his producing a city plan and designs for the Royal Palace, the Catholic cathedral, a museum and government buildings. Of these only the cathedral was executed. However, he also made proposals of fundamental importance for protecting ancient sites from decay and looting, and drew up a conservation scheme for Athens including the rebuilding of the ruins on the Acropolis, then threatened by proposals to incorporate a new palace and military buildings with them. Especially remarkable was his unexecuted design of 1836 for the museum or 'Pantechnion', a completely asymmetrical tripartite building which forms an astringently Hellenistic parallel to the Italianate Picturesque manner of Schinkel.

Klenze echoed the façade treatment of his Athenian Pantechnion in the far greater museum which he was invited to build in St Petersburg on the strength of his international reputation. On his visit to Munich in 1838 the Emperor of Russia, Nicholas I, was shown round the Glyptothek and the Pinakothek by Klenze, whom he invited to St Petersburg in the following year. The old Winter Palace had been burnt in December 1837, thus encouraging Nicholas to think of

building a new Hermitage Museum for the imperial collections on a truly vast scale. Klenze's new building linked with Rastrelli's Winter Palace and Quarenghi's Hermitage Theatre to form an extravagant setting for court entertainment.

The huge grey marble museum containing three courtyards within an overall rectangular plan rose on the banks of the Neva from 1832 to 1852. A triumph of co-operation between German and Russian architects, artists and craftsmen, it is one of the greatest cultural monuments of the classical revival. All four of the trabeated Schinkelesque outer façades are subtly different. The south entrance
129 front is marked by a portico supported by pairs of massive telamones carved in grey granite by A.I. Terebenev from models made in Munich by Halbig following Klenze's drawings. The telamones echoed the mysterious figures of giants on the temple of Olympian Zeus at Agrigentum, of which both Klenze and Cockerell had made restorations. The north front on to the Neva is adorned with porches supported by Greek caryatids, while the longer east front has a first-floor gallery supposedly inspired by the Vatican *logge*. The building materials were novel, including iron for the roofs, zinc-coated galvanoplastic copper for the statues, reliefs and adornments, and green bronze for the balcony railings and window surrounds.

129 Klenze: portico of the Hermitage Museum, St Petersburg (Leningrad), 1842–51.

The internal planning and distribution of the museum is wholly asymmetrical, each wing being separately planned for its specific function. The ground floor was reserved for antique and modern sculpture, prints and drawings, and the library. A monumental staircase leads to the first floor where the paintings were arranged according to the various European schools, separate rooms being devoted to Rembrandt, Rubens, Van Dyck and Wouwerman. This arrangement recalled that established at Schinkel's Altes Museum, as did the hanging of the paintings on low screens projecting at right angles from the walls. Also on the first floor were the collections of Renaissance armour, vases and luxury objects, as well as an immense two-storeyed coin room with a bizarre disproportion between its scale and that of the objects it housed. The staircase, too, has a megalomaniac grandeur calculated to deter ascent on the part of all but the hardiest museum visitors. It should be remembered, however, that we are in St Petersburg where further along the Neva the Admiralty, erected in 1806–23 by Zakharov, boasts a façade a quarter of a mile long. Klenze's staircase is the climax of a type flanked by colonnades inspired by Chalgrin's at the Palais du Luxembourg of 1803–7 and given noble expression by Friedrich von Gärtner at the Bavarian Court and State Library (1832–43) in the Ludwigstrasse in Munich. The floor, the twenty-two-foot-wide steps and the capitals of the columns are of white Carrara marble; the columns are of white-grey granite; and the walls are lined with yellow Siena marble. The ceilings and ornaments are of metal plates or galvanoplastic copper. Here, as throughout the museum, Klenze made drawings at the Tsar's request for every architectural and ornamental detail, including the furnishings.

Klenze was fortunate in having such a major commission during the 1840s, for his architectural relations with Ludwig cooled somewhat as the king became more attracted by the Romantic and medievalizing ideals of architects like Gärtner, who will be discussed in the next chapter. Also, in 1846 Lola Montez, born in County Limerick and known as the most wanton woman in Europe, arrived in Munich to seduce the amorous sixty-two-year-old monarch and to cause such political chaos that he abdicated two years later. His son, who succeeded him as King Maximilian II in 1848, had very different architectural tastes, so that Klenze's three major buildings of the 1840s were privately financed by Ludwig who had commissioned them all between 1817 and 1836. The three

131 Klenze: Hall of Fame, Munich, with colossal bronze figure of Bavaria by Schwanthaler, 1843–54.

132 Klenze: interior of the Befreiungshalle, Kelheim, with sculpture by Johann Halbig, 1836–44.

buildings, with their significantly lofty titles, are the Befreiungshalle (Hall of Liberation), 1842–63; the Ruhmeshalle (Hall of Fame), 1843–54; and the Propyläen, 1846–60. Originally designed in 1817, the Propyläen, of 130 Untersberger marble, is the gateway to the Königsplatz which, in its present form, is one of the major contributions to Munich of Ludwig and Klenze. We have already traced the early history of this square. Once he had secured the commission for the Glyptothek on its north side, Klenze drew up proposals for the square in 1817 including a church on the south side, balancing the Glyptothek, and an impressive gateway on the west side, marking the entrance to Munich from the royal summer palace of Nymphenburg a couple of miles west of the city. The idea of the church, built in a neo-Romanesque style by Ziebland in 1834–50, came from Fischer's designs of *c.*1813 for a memorial on this site to the fallen of the Bavarian army, incorporating a domed chapel. Finalized in 1823, Klenze's lofty statement of the civic ideals of Neo-classicism, with its Ionic museum, Doric gateway and Corinthian church of the Apostles, forms an eloquent counterpart to the image of a city projected in Schinkel's contemporary painting of a 'Medieval Cathedral by the Water'.

A delay of many years ensued during which Ludwig contemplated other sites for the Propyläen, such as the end of the Ludwigstrasse where Gärtner erected the Siegestor (Gate of Victory) from 1843 to 1852, modelled on the Arch of Constantine in Rome. It was thus not until 1846 that work began on the construction of the Propyläen, by which time Ludwig had decided to make it commemorate the Greek War of Independence. The pediments and friezes were carved by Schwanthaler with scenes from the war and from the reign of Otto I, though ironically he was deposed in 1862, only two years after the building's completion. A further change concerned the actual architectural design which in 1817 had been close to the Athenian Propylaea and to Langhans's paler echo of that in Berlin. By 1846 the design had become heavier and more powerful, the principal change being the replacement of the flanking gatehouses with huge VI pylons, towering over the central portico, while the number of Ionic columns flanking the internal carriageway was increased from six to sixteen.

On the third day of his reign Ludwig had surprised Klenze by seeking designs from him for a Bavarian Hall of Fame to be erected on the Sendlinger Höhe in Munich, a site which Klenze had once proposed for the Walhalla. Klenze made a sketch which he forgot about for seven years until in 1833 the king commanded him, Gärtner, Ohlmüller and Ziebland to enter a competition for the Ruhmes- 131 halle, the site of which was now determined as the slope overlooking the Theresienwiese on the south-western edge of Munich. The choice of style – Greek, round-arched or pointed-arched – was left to the architects, except that copies of the Walhalla or the Parthenon were not required. Klenze's design, erected in 1843–54, was for a U-shaped Doric stoa or colonnade raised on a high platform. It is a remarkable indication of his deep feeling for ancient architecture that it should be so close in form to the great Hellenistic altar at Pergamum, which had not at that date been discovered. The colonnade behind its forty-eight Greek Doric columns sheltered busts of eighty prominent Bavarians, including artists, architects and composers such as Holbein, Dürer, Altdorfer, Ohlmüller, Gärtner, Schwanthaler, Hess, Cornelius, Gluck, and even Count Romford, the American-born Minister of War and Police to the Elector of Bavaria, and inventor of the chimney-cowl. The two pediments and ninety-four metopes of the frieze, containing allegorical figures representing Bavaria, war, peace, art and trade, were carved by the ubiquitous Schwanthaler, who also found time to execute in 1850 the colossal bronze female figure of Bavaria in the forecourt.

VII Klenze: design for the wall decoration of the Festsaalbau, Munich, 1832–42.

VIII Klenze: sculpture gallery of the Hermitage Museum, St Petersburg (Leningrad), 1842–51.

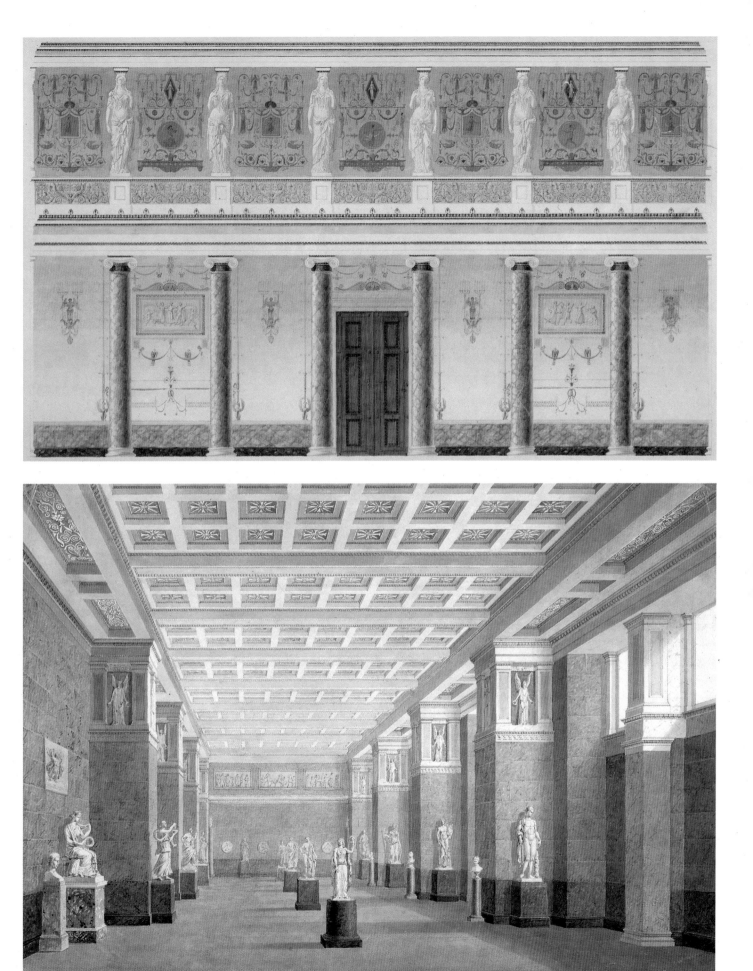

With its tall pedestal this reaches a total height of a hundred feet.

Ludwig's monument mania knew no bounds. While in Greece in 1836 he visited the ruins of Tiryns with Gärtner. Here, musing on the parallels between Greek and German history in a country still shaken by its war of liberation against the Turks, he determined on a definitive German monument, a Befreiungshalle, to the Wars of Liberation against Napoleon. He envisaged a centrally planned building like that proposed by Klenze in 1819 for the Walhalla, containing shields bearing the names of battles with the names of field marshals and military leaders above them. Gärtner produced numerous sketches modelled on Hadrian's Mausoleum and the Pantheon, but the selected design was for an eighteen-sided domed building resembling Early Renaissance projects such as Bramante's St Peter's, and Gärtner's own entry in the competition for the Ruhmeshalle. Its eighteen sides reflected Ludwig's wish for a commemoration of the fact that the battles of Leipzig and of Waterloo were both fought on the eighteenth day of the month.

The site chosen in 1838, under thirty miles from the Walhalla, was the Michelsberg near Kelheim, a wooded hill 1500 feet above the point where the Danube and the Altmühl merge. The transport of materials was made easy by the presence nearby of the Ludwig-Danube-Main canal, built by Ludwig from 1836 to 1844. The foundation stone was laid by Ludwig on 19 October 1842; he could not make it on the 18th because he was busy opening the Walhalla. Work proceeded very slowly. In 1844 Gärtner ordered from Schwanthaler the marble winged Victories which line the interior, but three years later all that was completed of the building was the foundations and two of the three great socles on which it rests. At this point Gärtner died aged fifty-five. Klenze, who was used to the conveniently premature deaths of his rivals – Fischer had succumbed at the age of thirty-eight, Haller von Hallerstein at forty-three – stepped magnanimously in and was given a free hand to alter the design by the king. He revolutionized Gärtner's timid but faintly sentimental *Rundbogenstil* design at a stroke by completely eliminating the encircling arcade and round-arched windows. The building became a sculptural object, proud and bare like a petrified ancient tumulus monument, uncluttered with windows. Its naked cylindrical volume is dominated by a ring of eighteen great buttresses upon which stand female figures, twenty feet high, representing the German provinces, carved by Johann Halbig. Above them is a continuous Doric colonnade of fifty-four marble columns.

The top-lit interior, like that of the Walhalla, is a masterpiece of polychromatic marble. The vast domed space is encircled by a ring of thirty-four angels or winged Victories in Carrara marble. Each adopting a different pose, they stand in strangely life-like fashion with linked hands resting on circular shields of gilt bronze. Behind them is a tall arcade of segment-headed arches above which a Tuscan colonnade supports the dome with its aggressive diagonal coffering. Work was temporarily arrested in 1848 by the abdication of Ludwig and the death of Schwanthaler, but thereafter continued relentlessly for fifteen years, until the laying of the magnificent patterned floor of Tegernsee marble in the summer of 1863 came as the conclusion of years of painting, carving, gilding, marbling, and cutting of inscriptions recording the names of generals, battles, and captured fortresses. On his favourite day, 18 October, the aged ex-king Ludwig and Klenze, who was to die three months later, mounted the hill for the grand opening in 1863. When the two entered the building alone, Ludwig embraced his architect, exclaiming through his tears, 'Klenze, never have I dreamed of so beautiful, so beautiful a building'.

IX Klenze: Befreiungshalle, Kelheim, 1836–44.

CHAPTER VII

Neo-classicism in South Germany: 1815–45

KLENZE did not build in south Germany anything like as extensively as Schinkel did in north Germany. Nonetheless, his influence was powerful, above all on his principal rival, Gärtner, whose career we will investigate at the end of this chapter. We begin with the work of Weinbrenner who was an important forerunner of Klenze. Weinbrenner is a parallel to architects in the north such as Krahe and Laves who might have rivalled him in significance had they been given the same opportunities in Brunswick and Hanover which he was given in Karlsruhe.

Karlsruhe under Friedrich Weinbrenner (1766–1826) affords one of the most striking examples in Germany of the application of Neo-classical principles to the development of a nineteenth-century town. Weinbrenner's career falls into two different parts divided between the eighteenth and nineteenth centuries, so that it has been difficult to decide how to treat him in the present book. His visionary designs of the 1790s, which we have seen in Chapter III, are in the Franco-Prussian style of Friedrich Gilly, while his more sober executed buildings in Karlsruhe provided a realistic model for the expansion of German towns in the immediate post-Napoleonic period.

Born in Karlsruhe of a long line of carpenters and joiners, Weinbrenner was trained in carpentry by his father and, following a two-year stay in Switzerland, briefly studied mathematics and architecture at the Academy in Vienna. As we saw earlier, he was in Berlin in the 1790s where he made friends with the pioneers of the new style such as Langhans and Genelli. His designs produced at this time for a church at Karlsruhe show a Pantheon-inspired building approached through a Greek Doric portico, a type which was subsequently taken up by Fischer, Klenze and Gärtner. The instruction in drawing and the art of perspective which he received from Vincenz Fischer at Vienna influenced his architectural drawing technique with its characteristic sharp lines and strong rendering in light and shade. In about 1792 he travelled to Italy with the painter Asmus Jacob Carstens whose chill and precise outline drawings similarly influenced the way in which Weinbrenner represented his buildings and theories in his own publications.

On his return to Karlsruhe in 1797, following the Napoleonic invasion of Italy, Weinbrenner found support from the Margrave of Baden who had been attracted by the visionary Piranesian drawings he had sent from Rome. Appointed Bauinspektor in 1797, his earliest building in Karlsruhe was the 200 Synagogue (1797–8; burnt 1871). This powerful if bizarre Graeco-Oriental building was the only executed work in the imaginative style of his youth. It is paralleled in interest by the synagogue which Krahe designed for Düsseldorf at about the same time.

Following its alliance with Napoleon, Baden was created a duchy in 1806 and gained additional territory in the southern part of the country. The expanding capital of Baden, which grew from 3,000 inhabitants in 1780 to 10,600 in 1810,

133 Georg Moller: staircase hall of the Ducal Palace, Wiesbaden, 1835–7.

134 Friedrich
Weinbrenner: the
Marktplatz, Karlsruhe,
planned 1797, executed
1806–26.

had been founded in 1715 by Margrave Karl Wilhelm of Baden-Durlach. At its core was the three-winged palace built by Kesslau from 1749 to 1771 on the basis of designs by Balthasar Neumann. The astonishing plan of Karlsruhe, with thirty-two avenues radiating out from the palace, gives striking Baroque expression to the Margrave's absolutist rule as a mini-Sun King. Consideration had been given from the 1760s to the development of a civic focus south of the palace, but Weinbrenner's unsolicited plan for the Marktplatz, sent from Berlin in 1791, proposed a novel asymmetrical disposition for the Town Hall and 201 Protestant church. This plan, elaborated in 1797, formed the basis of what he was 135 to erect slowly between 1806 and his death twenty years later. The porticoed 134 church (1806–20) and adjacent grammar school face the Town Hall (1807–14) 136 across the Marktplatz which contains the centrally placed monument of 1825 to 202 Margrave Karl Wilhelm. Behind the church and Town Hall rise single towers which echo but do not repeat each other. The monument takes the form of a solid pyramid of red sandstone which is the heir of the abstract monuments to genius of the visionary classicism of late-eighteenth-century France. It commemorates a Baroque princeling whom it nonetheless confronts with the characteristic civic monuments of a bourgeois town of the nineteenth century. Weinbrenner has left us a clear explanation of his aims in the design of the Marktplatz:

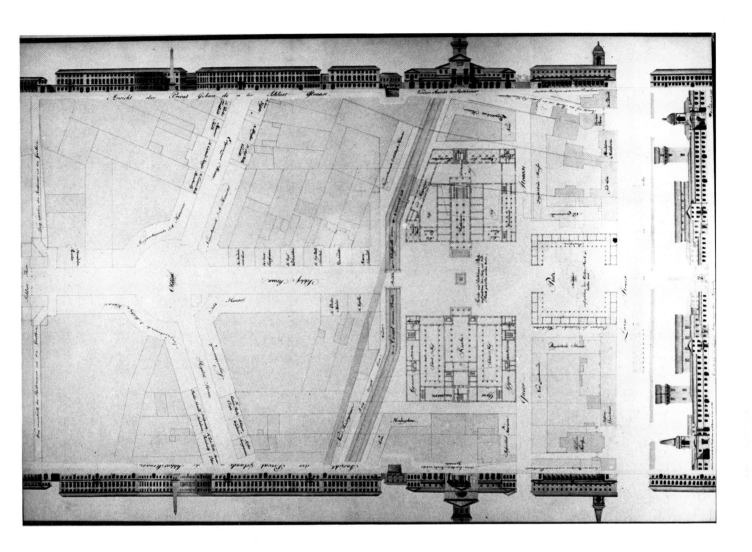

135 Friedrich Weinbrenner: project for the Marktplatz, Karlsruhe, 1797.

136 Friedrich Weinbrenner: Town Hall, Karlsruhe, 1811–25.

137 Friedrich
Weinbrenner: Ettlinger
Tor, Karlsruhe, 1803.

A fine and most appropriate model for our market place is provided by the
markets of antiquity. Pausanias described the market and other public places
of Athens in his first book, and has thereby left us a most favourable picture of
the ancient Greeks' agora. None of our public squares is at all comparable.
While some of them have been produced by accident, others have been built
clumsily and purposelessly owing to the depraved taste of our architecture. It
seems to me, therefore, that it would be very wrong when building our market
place, which is to be designed from scratch, if we were not to consider its
function and the aesthetic principles of our time. . . . it is not my intention to
change Karlsruhe into an Athens, but, with the money available, to build this
square in a practical and functional manner.

Weinbrenner's relaxed but spacious Marktplatz was one of a series of incidents
in the leisurely progress of his Schloss Strasse (today Karl-Friedrichstrasse)
which, begun in 1799, led from the palace southwards to the Ettlinger Tor 187
(1803). Like Nash's Regent Street in London, the street is remarkable for the fact
that its major accents are carefully and deliberately asymmetrical in relation to
each other. This asymmetry reflects similar tendencies in other German town-
extension schemes, for example at Düsseldorf, Brunswick and, a little later,
Moller's projects for Darmstadt. The Ettlinger Tor was an archaeologically
purer version of Langhans's Greek Doric Gate in Berlin. At right angles to it was
Weinbrenner's own house (1803; demolished 1873), an impressive mansion with
a portico of engaged columns in an unfluted Greek Doric order echoing those of

the gate itself. Again, there is a parallel with Nash who chose to emphasize his status by building a handsome house and office for himself in his new street.

North of the Ettlinger Tor the Schloss Strasse opens out into the octagonal Rondellplatz, dominated by the large Corinthian portico of Weinbrenner's Margrave's Palace (1803–14), behind which Weinbrenner contrived an elaborate Picturesque garden containing a Palladian garden pavilion. With its plan in the form of a broad truncated 'V', the palace was a grandiose example of a solution Weinbrenner was forced to adopt in numerous more modest buildings as a result of the frequent intersection of the radiating streets of the Baroque town with streets running east and west, in particular the Lange Strasse (today Kaiserstrasse). This kind of corner treatment was to become familiar in later nineteenth-century urban architecture, for example by Moller in Darmstadt and by Haussmann in Paris.

In the Friedrichsplatz, further west, is Weinbrenner's Catholic church of St Stephen (1808–14) which was a product of the religious toleration of Napoleonic Baden. This impressive domed building combines references to the Pantheon and the Roman baths with a large bell tower which is medieval in general form though not in detail. It takes its place in a line of Pantheon-inspired Catholic churches, which leads from St Hedwig's in Berlin to Moller's St Georg's in Darmstadt.

The buildings we have so far seen were the highlights of Weinbrenner's Karlsruhe but what was remarkable about his achievement was his ability to stamp his image on all aspects of the town. Thus as early as 1804 he was designing model dwellings for all classes which he was able to persuade private builders to adopt. The provision of model dwellings was a common feature in town development schemes in the late-eighteenth and early-nineteenth centuries.

138 Friedrich Weinbrenner: Margrave's Palace on the Rondellplatz, Karlsruhe, 1803–14.

139 Friedrich Weinbrenner: Catholic church of St Stephen, Karlsruhe, 1808–14.

Some of Weinbrenner's took the form of terraced housing while others were free-standing houses in streets, for example the houses for General von Beck and for the chemist Sommerschuh. He also built the Court Theatre (1807–8; burnt 1870); Museum (1813–14; burnt 1918); Chancellery (1814–16); Assembly 140 Rooms and shops.

Like so many of his contemporaries he promoted his vision of a new German architecture in publications of his own designs and theories. These included his *Architektonisches Lehrbuch*, Tübingen 1810–17 (Architectural Textbook), and *Ausgeführte und projektierte Gebäude*, Karlsruhe 1822–35 (Executed and Projected Buildings). His ambitions were clearly not confined to Karlsruhe. He later recalled:

> My devoted study of the buildings of Italy necessarily altered my artistic conception greatly, and as I accept the principles of antique architecture, I wished also to take these as a standard for buildings in Germany. With the sole exception of Gothic architecture, which is entirely original and complete in itself, the modern buildings, which I had previously found so beautiful and knowledgeably composed in all parts, seemed now less complete. Thus I returned from Italy with the intention of exerting an influence over the education of young architects in my fatherland, where I had decided to practise my art.

Thus in 1800 he founded a school of architecture in his own house in Karlsruhe. Described by Goethe as the only place where the 'True' was to be found in Germany, it was given ducal support and in 1825 was incorporated into the newly founded Polytechnic, today Karlsruhe University. Upholding the classical ideals of Winckelmann, Hirt and Goethe, tempered by an emphasis on constructional practicality and modesty, Weinbrenner trained over a hundred architects including some, like Hübsch, Moller and Châteauneuf, who were to be the leaders of the next generation.

In 1827 Weinbrenner was succeeded as Baurat (building inspector) in Karlsruhe by Heinrich Hübsch (1795–1863). He need not detain us long in the present book because his attacks on the teachings of Hirt and Weinbrenner effectively brought to an end the classical ideals which had been upheld since the time of Winckelmann. The title of his celebrated treatise of 1828, *In welchem Stil sollen wir bauen?* (In what style shall we build?), asked the question which was to plague the whole of the nineteenth century. It suggested the pluralism of the new century, even though Hübsch himself had a very specific answer to his question.

From 1813 to 1815 Hübsch studied at Heidelberg University where he came under the influence of Friedrich Creuzer (1771–1858), whose *Die Historische Kunst der Griechen in ihrer Entstehung und Fortbildung*, 1803 (The Historical Art of the Greeks from its Origins and Development), was a pioneering work of historiography and an important statement of empirical ideals in the study of history. Hübsch was subsequently a pupil of Weinbrenner at the Karlsruhe Bauakademie from 1815 to 1817 and then, following the advice Weinbrenner gave to all his pupils, travelled extensively in Italy from 1817 to 1820. Reacting against the Doric idealism of Weinbrenner's teaching in Karlsruhe and Hirt's in Berlin, Hübsch published a pamphlet entitled *Über griechische Architektur* (On Greek Architecture) in 1822 which rejected Hirt's belief that the forms of the Doric temple originated in earlier wooden constructions. The significance of this rejection was that it was based on a belief which he developed in *In welchem Stil sollen wir bauen?* that architecture is so rooted in function, materials, climate and social and economic conditions, that it would be as impossible for the forms of the Greek temple to be imitations of earlier wooden forms as it would be for contemporary architects to imitate the temples of the Greeks.

140 Friedrich Weinbrenner: drawing for the north façade of the museum, Karlsruhe, 1813.

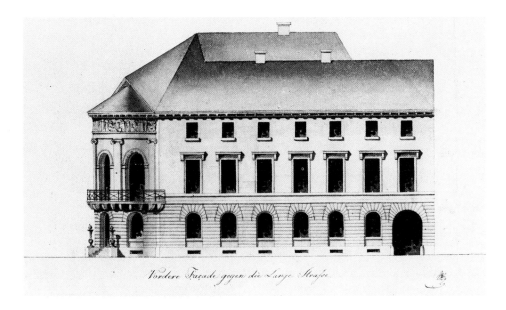

In welchem Stil sollen wir bauen? was published on the anniversary of Dürer's birth in 1828 as a manifesto for a meeting of Nazarene artists gathered in Nuremberg for the Dürer Festival. Like the Nazarenes, who sought a total renewal of art by rejecting classical idealism, Hübsch proposed a new non-Greek architecture based on the vaulted buildings of the Romanesque period. This, he felt, was a rational and flexible style of which the forms, like those of Greek architecture, had been determined functionally. He disapproved of Roman architecture, arguing that it 'actually ceased to be true and real, and began much more to become an optical art'. Hübsch's functionalist and mechanistic position was opposed to Hirt and Weinbrenner, who emphasized beauty and form in architecture. It was, of course, close in some ways to the defence of Gothic in terms of construction and truth proposed by Pugin and Viollet-le-Duc. This in itself was rooted in one aspect of French Neo-classicism: the rationalist theories of Rondelet's *L'Art de Bâtir* (1802–3) and of Durand's *Précis* which was available in a German translation as *Abriss der Vorlesungen über Baukunst* (1831) (Outline of Lectures on the Art of Building).

Refusing to uphold absolute ideals or privileged historical moments, Hübsch studied history as a process. In so doing he implied that it could be manipulated and developed to provide a basis for a new architecture which for him could only be the *Rundbogenstil*. He gave physical expression to his ideal in his best-known building, the Trinkhalle (pump-room) of 1837–40 at Baden Baden. This 141 impressive building was nearer to Weinbrenner's Assembly Rooms (1821–4), with their broad Corinthian colonnade, than the Old Pump Room which Weinbrenner had built in the old town. Hübsch was important for giving the *Rundbogenstil* a theoretical foundation. However, after Schinkel's death, it tended to become a straightforward historical revival, especially in Hübsch's native Rhineland, with strongly nationalist overtones.

The development of spa towns in the early nineteenth century – such as Baden Baden, Wiesbaden, Bad Ems and Bad Brückenau – provided new opportunities for the expression of Neo-classical ideals in town planning. Weinbrenner worked extensively in Baden Baden, providing numerous bath buildings as well as the Antiquitätenhalle (1804) and the Palais Hamilton (1808), while the leading architect in Wiesbaden was his pupil Johann Christian Zais (1770–1820). As part of his scheme for the Wilhelmstrasse in Wiesbaden, Zais built the Prinzenpalais (soon converted into a museum, and now offices) in 1812–18 in a 250 simplified Palladian style with a seventeen-bay façade. His Kurhaus (1808–10) 249 has a Vitruvian colonnaded interior in a tradition which goes back to Burlington's assembly rooms at York. Zais also built the Vier Jahreszeiten (1817–18), a palatial hotel for spa visitors, and the museum (1812–18), originally planned as a town palace. The modest theatre of 1826–7 in the Wilhelmstrasse at Wiesbaden was designed by the architect Zengerle. At Bad Brückenau, the favourite spa of Ludwig I of Bavaria, Joseph Thürmer (1789–1833) and Johann Gottfried Gutensohn (1792–*c*.1844) provided modest Neo-Renaissance designs for the Kursaal in a style derived from Weinbrenner. Gutensohn's designs were executed in 1827–35 with open loggias provided at the king's request. Gutensohn, a court architect at Munich, also designed extensive bath buildings at Bad Ems, including the Kursaal of 1836–9.

Georg Moller (1784–1852), director of architecture in Hesse-Darmstadt, was the architect largely responsible for the Neo-classical modernization of Darmstadt, a quiet little Residenz town which had grown from 6,700 inhabitants in 1794 to 21,000 in 1828. Unfortunately it was particularly badly damaged during the War so that its centre today has little historical flavour.

141 Heinrich Hübsch:
Trinkhalle, Baden Baden,
1837–40.

Born in Diepholz, which subsequently became part of the Napoleonic
kingdom of Westphalia, Moller was trained by Christian Ludwig Witting,
Hofbaumeister at Hanover from 1801, and Weinbrenner at Karlsruhe from 1802
to 1807. On a study tour of Italy in 1807–10 he met leading German artists and
intellectuals in Rome such as Karl von Fischer, Rauch, Kestner and the
Humboldts. In 1810 he returned via Paris and Karlsruhe to Darmstadt where he
began to put into practice the lessons in architecture and urban planning which
he had learned from Weinbrenner. He specialized in unassertive and modest
buildings, empirically grouped, such as his houses of 1811–25 in the Rheinstrasse,
Neckarstrasse, Wilhelminenstrasse and Wilhelminenplatz; his Freemasons' Hall
(1817–20); Court Theatre and Opera House (1818–20); and New Chancellery
(1826–31), which somewhat recalls Klenze's contemporary Leuchtenberg Palais
in Munich. As a town planner Moller was important for his street compositions
like the Neckarstrasse and lower Rheinstrasse where, in a residential setting, he
favoured detached houses with low Italianate hipped roofs, linked by arched
gateways. The repetitive use of arched window and door openings was modified
by subtle variations in the width and decorative treatment of the elevations.
Indeed Moller was responsible for introducing to Darmstadt a new sophisticated
elegance in the design of urban façades and a greater emphasis on decorative
features, with the result that the system of ducal support which had previously
taken the form of 'elevation grants' was altered to one of 'embellishment grants'.

Moller's most arresting single building in Darmstadt was his Catholic 142
Ludwigskirche (1820–7), a monumental rotunda with a bare exterior containing 143
a noble domed space ringed by twenty-eight free-standing Corinthian columns.
With roots in the French Revolutionary architecture of Boullée and Ledoux, it is
close to the Pantheon-inspired schemes of Fischer, Klenze and Gärtner for the
Walhalla and Befreiungshalle. It was not completed in full accordance with
Moller's intentions and, after gutting in the Second World War, has been
restored in drastically simplified form. Placed in the middle of the
Wilhelminenplatz, the church commands picturesque views over the town as
well as serving to close the vistas from north and south along Moller's
Wilhelminenstrasse. Immediately north-west of the church was the palace which
Moller built in 1837–41 for Prince Carl, brother of the future Grand Duke
Ludwig III. This was a chaste cubic block in the manner of Schinkel with a
carefully designed plan: on the ground floor the prince's apartments were on the
right-hand side with rooms for visitors on the left-hand side; the princess's
apartments and the principal reception rooms were on the first floor; and rooms
for servants and children on the second floor. The centre of the garden front
projected in a demi-rotunda like Bélanger's Bagatelle, so as to allow for a circular
room on each floor. The undemonstrative character of this building reflects the
'bourgeois' tendency of the day in the design of palaces for royalty and nobility:
for example, the Rotes Palais at Kassel, the Schloss at Wiesbaden, the
Margrave's Palace at Karlsruhe and Schloss Charlottenhof at Potsdam.

Similarly Schinkelesque was the grand-ducal mausoleum that Moller built in
the Greek Revival style in 1826–31 on the Rosenhöhe in the eastern outskirts of
the town. It contains the tombs by Rauch of the infant Princess Elizabeth and the
grand duchess.

Moller built several Catholic and Evangelical churches in the Rhineland such
as St Georg at Bensheim (1825–30), a Neo-classical version of an Early Christian
basilica, and the more modest churches of c.1816 at Birkenau and Gräfenhausen.
His Villa Flotow at Darmstadt (1840) was a Neo-grec essay recalling the plates in
Krafft and Ransonnette's *Plans, coupes, élévations des plus belles maisons . . . à Paris*
(Paris, c.1802). His theatre of 1829–33 at Mainz also followed a French model:
the design for a theatre after the manner of the ancients in Durand's *Précis* of
1802–5. With its semicircular auditorium treated externally with arcades like the
Colosseum, this influenced Semper's celebrated theatre at Dresden.

Moller's ambitious but dull plans of 1833 for rebuilding the Schloss at
Darmstadt were not executed, though he remodelled both it and the Altes Palais
in the Luisenplatz in 1841–2, providing the latter with a splendid staircase hall
and other fine interiors. In the Luisenplatz he built the monument to
commemorate Grand Duke Ludwig I who had died in 1830. Completed in 1844,
this is a fluted Doric column of red sandstone, 144 feet high, surmounted by a
bronze statue of Ludwig by Schwanthaler.

Outside of Darmstadt Moller worked for Landgrave Friedrich VI Joseph of
Hesse-Homburg (1769–1829) and his wife, Princess Elizabeth (1770–1840), a
daughter of King George III of England and an enthusiastic architectural
patron. At Homburg Moller built for them the Gothic House (1823–4) in the
English castle style, and also remodelled the seventeenth-century Schloss (1825–
41), heightening it and providing elegant new interiors including a grand
entrance vestibule and Ionic staircase. At Wiesbaden he was employed by Duke
Wilhelm of Nassau in 1837–41 to rebuild the Schloss completely. He provided a 144
highly successful piece of street architecture on a corner site which reflects in its
angle treatment some of his designs for buildings in Darmstadt such as the Kasino 183

142, 143 Georg Moller: Catholic church of St. Ludwig, Darmstadt, 1820–7, exterior and interior.

144 Georg Moller: Ducal
Palace, Wiesbaden,
1835–7.

and shops in the Theaterstrasse. The subtle plan is dominated by a diagonal cross axis through the centre of the building which forms a processional way on different levels leading, via two staircases, to a handsome rotunda with a vaulted ground floor supported by a central Doric column. The staircase was flanked with six statues in sandstone of antique gods and goddesses carved by Schwanthaler, who also provided the Festsaal with female statues of dancers in Carrara marble.

Moller was a man of wide-ranging sympathies and a medieval architectural historian of some importance. He was also interested in new materials and utilitarian buildings, designing the 125-foot-high viaduct at Goehltal near Aachen in 1841. It was, by contrast, he and Sulpiz Boisserée who discovered the lost medieval plans for Cologne Cathedral in 1814 which were used in its spectacular completion. His fine drawings of the cathedral were published by Boisserée in the 1820s. Moller also published *Denkmäler der deutschen Baukunst* (3 vols, Darmstadt 1815–21), which was published in English translations by Priestley and Weale in 1824 and, as *Moller's Memorials of German Gothic Architecture*, by W.H. Leeds in 1836. Moller was in close touch with the remarkable group of architects and architectural historians who made England one of the major European centres of architectural scholarship in the first half of the nineteenth century. He visited England in 1830 where his contacts included William Whewell, John Britton, C.R. Cockerell, Owen Jones, Edmund Sharpe, Henry Gally Knight and T.L. Donaldson. Moller's book was important as one of the earliest accounts of Romanesque architecture, which previous writers had not always separated from Gothic. One of the buildings illustrated is Mainz Cathedral, where in 1827 he provided a remarkable metal dome (replaced after 1870) over the east choir.

Despite his study of medieval architecture he was not prepared to see it widely imitated in the nineteenth century, although he prepared an elaborate design in *c*.1820 for a Gothic Schloss for the Grand Duke of Hesse and another in 1843 for Prince Ludwig Wittgenstein at Friedrichsberg near Sayn. He did not adopt the full *Rundbogenstil* but remained faithful to Weinbrenner and to the principles of Greek architecture which alone, he believed, had permanent validity.

Schloss Fasanerie near the cathedral town of Fulda in the modern *Land* of Hesse at the heart of Germany is a Baroque palace begun in 1710 but largely dating from a building campaign of 1739–50 by the Italian Andrea Callasini for Prince Bishop Amandus von Buseck. In 1804 it was given by Napoleon to Marshal Duroc but after the Congress of Vienna it was restored not to the bishopric but to the Electors of Hesse. Having been badly damaged during its use as a hospital in 1812–13, the building was restored in 1825–7 by Elector Wilhelm II of Hesse-Kassel who employed his court architect, Johann Konrad Bromeis (1788–1854), to remodel the main rooms in the *corps de logis*. The delicacy and quality of his interiors make us regret all the more the destruction of his work for the Elector in the Rotes Palais at Kassel which we noted in Chapter V. Bromeis's best interiors at Schloss Fasanerie are the Galeriesaal (or Antikensaal) with its segmental vault painted with trompe l'oeil coffering, and the Audienzsaal where crisp bas reliefs in grisaille impart a Pompeian flavour. A notable feature of this apartment is the cylindrical stove surmounted by a tall statue of an antique warrior made of clay to retain the heat. This recalls Soane's Greek Doric entrance vestibule of 1798 at Bentley Priory, where a figure of a man in armour performed a similar function on top of a stove.

Further north, in Frankfurt, capital of the Napoleonic Grand Duchy of Frankfurt under Karl Theodor von Dalberg but once more a free city of the German Confederation from 1815, the leading architects were Johann Georg Christian Hess (1756–1816) and his son Johann Friedrich Christian Hess (1785–1845). The younger Hess's State Library (1820–5) is a routine Neo-Palladian essay with a large Corinthian portico, while his other works include the Museum of Natural History, Law Courts, Custom House, and the spire and interior of St Paul's church, a building begun by his father in 1789 from designs by F.A. Liebhardt. The now demolished Exchange (1840–4) at Frankfurt is the earliest independent work of Friedrich August Stüler (1800–65) who had been one of Schinkel's principal assistants from 1827. It was a powerfully inventive building in a Schinkelesque manner with a polychromatic exterior and an astonishing main hall in which fan vaults rose poetically from classical columns.

145, 146

145, 146 Friedrich August Stüler: exterior and main hall of the Exchange, Frankfurt, 1840–4.

During the reign of King Wilhelm I of Württemberg (1816–64) Stuttgart became an important centre of late Neo-classical ideals. As we saw in Chapter III, Nicolaus Friedrich von Thouret (1767–1845) had arrived here in 1803 to work for Wilhelm's predecessor, Duke Friedrich of Württemberg. The court architect from 1817 to 1839 was the Florentine-born émigré, Giovanni Salucci (1769–1845), who built the summer residence of King Wilhelm and Queen Katharine, Schloss Rosenstein (1824–29), on the outskirts of Stuttgart. The principal interior of this long, low Schinkelesque building is the Festsaal, a domed and barrel-vaulted gallery surrounded by an Ionic colonnade carrying a continuous figured frieze. Salucci's winter palace for King Wilhelm, the Wilhelmspalais in Stuttgart (1835–40), recalls the style of Laves in Hanover, while his hilltop mausoleum for Queen Katharine of 1820–4 on the Rotenberg near Stuttgart is an echo of Palladio's Villa Rotonda. A centrally planned building with four Ionic porticoes, it is capped by a Pantheon dome. In Stuttgart Gottlob Georg Barth (1777–1848), a pupil of Durand, built the Museum and Academy of Arts (1838–43) in an elegant Greek Revival style. Numerous schemes for this building had been submitted between 1833 and 1838 by Thouret and Zanth, the former adopting a range of arcuated Durandesque styles.

149 Giovanni Salucci:
Festsaal, Schloss
Rosenstein, 1822–30.

185

150 Johann Michael Knapp: Königsbau, Stuttgart, designed c.1837, executed 1857–60.

Dr Karl Ludwig Wilhelm Zanth (né Zanik, 1796–1857), son of Jérôme Bonaparte's Jewish doctor, was trained as an architect in the atelier of Percier and settled in Stuttgart as a court architect around 1830. He was also an archaeologist who had worked with Hittorff in 1822–30 on the books on ancient and modern architecture in Sicily in which Hittorff published his important discoveries of Greek polychromy. Zanth subsequently acquired a doctorate from the University of Tübingen with a dissertation on Pompeian domestic architecture. His only major executed work was the Villa Wilhelma, built in 1837–51 for Wilhelm I below the hill on which Schloss Rosenstein stands. This unusual asymmetrically planned villa, rich in constructional and decorative polychromy, was designed, at the king's request, in the 'mauresque' style. It seems to be inspired by the literary imagery of the *Arabian Nights*, published in French in 1704–17; by Nicolas de Pigage's Mosque at Schwetzingen (1778–95), from which it borrows the theme of kiosks, trellises and a larger pavilion grouped round a pool; and by the preoccupation with polychromy in Hittorff's circle in the 1830s.

Another archaeologist-architect who worked for King Wilhelm was Johann Michael Knapp (1793–1861) who had lived mainly in Rome from 1819 to 1840 in which year he became court architect at Stuttgart. He designed the Jubilee Column (1842–8) in the centre of the Schlossplatz to commemorate King Wilhelm's silver jubilee, and remodelled various interiors in the Schloss in 1853. He also built several villas in Stuttgart such as the Villa Notter, near Berkheimer Hof, in the Pompeian style. One of his most impressive works, designed in c.1837 but not executed till 1856–60 when it was stylistically somewhat anachronistic, was the Königsbau on the north-west side of the Schlossplatz opposite the 150 Schloss. This is a combination of assembly room and shops with an Ionic colonnade along the ground floor, incorporating two Corinthian porticos, surmounted by a high attic storey articulated with a grid of Schinkelesque piers.

Christian Friedrich Leins (1814–92), the executant architect of the Königsbau, was trained by Zanth and then by Labrouste in Paris. He became the favourite architect of Crown Prince Karl of Württemberg whom he accompanied on an Italian study tour in 1845–6. For the prince he built the Villa Berg near Stuttgart, 1845–53, an Italianate composition inspired by Schinkel.

151 Christian Friedrich Leins: Villa Berg, near Stuttgart, 1844–53.

A stray building of markedly Schinkelesque character can be found as far south as Lindau on Lake Constance in Bavaria. This is the Villa Lindenhof, built, 1842–5, as the first work by the prolific Munich architect and engineer, Franz Jakob Kreuter (1813–89), for the merchant Friedrich Gruber. At the centre of this ambitious villa with its colonnaded conservatories is a circular domed vestibule, galleried and richly decorated. The building is set in a Romantic park landscaped by the Düsseldorf gardener, Maximilian Friedrich Weyhe (c.1775–1846).

The astonishing transformation of Munich by Klenze under Ludwig I had comparatively few repercussions in Bavaria generally. In the charming medieval and Baroque court town of Regensburg, the French-born Jean-Baptiste Métivier (1781–1853), court architect and decorator at Munich, designed an impressive riding school and mews in 1828–31 for Prince Maximilian Karl von Thurn und Taxis. In a Neo-Florentine style influenced by Klenze's court riding school of 1818–22 at Munich, this contained an impressive hall adorned with plaster casts by Schwanthaler of equine subjects. At Augsburg the Stock Exchange of 1820–30 is the work of Johann Nepomuk Pertsch (1780–1835). He was indebted for this commission to Ludwig I of Bavaria who, though the building was privately financed, took the keenest interest in it. The original design, for a large triangular building in the Ludwigsplatz in the form of an arcuated rusticated palazzo inspired by Durand and Klenze, was much modified in execution.

For twenty vital years from 1827 Friedrich von Gärtner was the leading architect in Munich after Klenze. In some ways he was more influential than his rival, because whereas Klenze maintained the ideals of the Greek Revival into the 1840s, when others had abandoned them, Gärtner trained numerous pupils such as F. Bürklein, Riedel and Semper, to continue his own more varied and, in some ways, more realistic approach to contemporary architectural tasks. Like Klenze, he was an architect whose professional career was entirely determined from start to finish by the patronage of Ludwig I, with his consuming passion for building.

Gärtner was born in Koblenz in 1792, the son of Andreas Gärtner (1744–1826), a talented architect who was Hofbauintendant at Munich from 1804 to 1826. Friedrich studied architecture at the Munich Academy under Karl von Fischer from 1808 to 1811, under Weinbrenner at Karlsruhe in 1812, and under Durand and Percier in Paris from 1812 to 1814. On a study tour of Italy in 1814–17 he met the German artistic colony in Rome, including Wilhelm von Humboldt and Johann Martin von Wagner, who revolved round Crown Prince Ludwig of Bavaria. He studied the Greek temples at Paestum and Sicily and in 1819 published a book of lithographs entitled *Ansichten der am meisten erhalten griechischen Monumente Siciliens – nach der Natur und auf Stein gezeichnet von Friedrich Gärtner* (Views of the best preserved Greek monuments in Sicily – drawn from nature and on stone by Friedrich Gärtner). In 1819 he visited England at C.R. Cockerell's invitation and worked with Cockerell's friend, the lithographer Charles Hullmandel. Like Schinkel six years later, he also became interested in the problems of industrialization and in the new building techniques.

On his return to Munich in 1820, he was appointed professor of architecture at the Academy in succession to his old master, Karl von Fischer, and, in 1822, artistic director at the Nymphenburg porcelain manufactory. During these architecturally unproductive years in his career he was forced to watch the spectacular rise of Klenze as the darling of the crown prince. However, once he had ascended the throne in November 1825, Ludwig found it impolitic to rely so completely on the services of a single favourite architect. Gärtner now saw his chance and, urged on by Wagner, Ludwig's art agent in Rome, put his case to the king in person in June 1827 at Colombella, a country house near Perugia at which the king was staying. Impressed by the young architect, Ludwig entrusted him with the commission for building the State Library.

Gärtner's first design for the library in 1827 was for a site on the south side of the Königsplatz balancing Klenze's Glyptothek of which he reproduced the portico, though with a Corinthian order. His main library was round the corner in a simple, Italianate, round-arched style. There was now a delay of several years during which the site was shifted to the Ludwigstrasse and Klenze submitted a *Rundbogenstil* design of his own in 1832. The brick-built library which 155 rose in the Ludwigstrasse from Gärtner's designs in 1832–43 is in a simplified Palazzo Pitti style. Gärtner complained in a letter to Wagner in 1830 that in his desire for economy the king wanted a building 'without projection, columns or portico, nothing but round-arched windows à la Fiorentina, a boring barracks for books', which would be just another version of the Palazzo Ruspoli (built by Ammanati in Rome in 1558). Nonetheless, Gärtner responded well to these constraints. Like Schinkel, he had studied the brick buildings of Bologna and Ferrara, and he produced a building which makes an overwhelming impact by the sheer scale of its twenty-five-bay-long façade, by the unbroken horizontality of its skyline and, inside, by its marble staircase, a monument to megalomania 152 inspired by Chalgrin's at the Luxembourg Palace and anticipating Klenze's at the Hermitage Museum.

Gärtner's first executed building in the Ludwigstrasse was not the State

152 Friedrich von Gärtner: staircase of the state library, Munich, 1832–43.

Library but the Ludwigskirche, for which he made the first drawings in 1828, the year after the commission for the library. Built in 1829–44, it stands next to the library to which its tall twin-towered façade forms a lively contrast in the street scene. Klenze made a design in 1828 in the form of a simple Early Christian basilica, while Gärtner's executed designs are in an Italian Romanesque style with conically capped towers oddly reminiscent of that of Weinbrenner's church at Karlsruhe of 1806–20. The building seems cold and mechanical, though this may partly be due to restoration after war damage. The interior is dominated by Peter Cornelius's epic fresco at the east end of the Last Judgment, sixty feet high and thirty-six feet wide. Designed in Rome in 1834–5, this ambitious monument of the Nazarene school was painted entirely by Cornelius's hand in 1836–9. Alas, the rather flat cold style with elements borrowed from Fra Angelico and Signorelli, did not appeal to Ludwig who, prompted by Klenze and Gärtner, offered Cornelius no further employment. No more popular were the five chill figures in niches on the west front carved by Schwanthaler in 1834.

Opposite his church and library Gärtner built a row of three enormous buildings in a similar style to the library: these are the Blinden Institut (Institute for the Blind), of 1833–5; the Damenstift (women's charitable foundation), of 1835–9; and the Salinendirektion (Saltworks Administration Building), of 1838–43. The last of these was built of an immensely durable exposed brick inspired by the later works of Schinkel. Nearby, at the north end of the Ludwigstrasse, Gärtner laid out the Universitätsplatz, a large new square to contain the university which Ludwig had transferred from Landshut to Munich in 1826. Gärtner's university, built 1835–40, occupied the west side, with the Georgianum (seminary), of 1835–40, and Max-Joseph-Stift (girls' school), of 1837, facing it on the east side. An important part of this square is the Siegestor (Gate of Victory) which closes it a little way to the north. This idea originated with Klenze who in 1826 had proposed terminating the Ludwigstrasse with a circular *place* containing a triumphal arch in the centre, rather like the Place de l'Etoile in Paris. Gärtner's buildings were all in his plain Florentine style, though each is slightly different from the other. The square contains two impressive fountains of 1840, for which Gärtner had to fight the king who wanted a circular *place* with obelisks inspired by the Piazza del Popolo in Rome.

153   Gärtner's great Gate of Victory was built in 1843–54 to vie with the Roman triumphal arches recently erected in Paris, London and Milan. He designed it in 1840, though triumphal arches had already been proposed in Munich by Karl von Fischer at the Karlstor in 1810, by Gärtner's father Andreas at the Schwabingertor in 1814, and by Klenze, as we have seen, at the Universitätsplatz in 1826. Modelled on the Arch of Constantine in Rome, Gärtner's arch was dedicated to the Bavarian army and richly adorned with sculpture from the designs of Johann Martin von Wagner. This included six circular reliefs in the attic, symbolizing the Bavarian provinces; eight goddesses of victory surmounting the Corinthian columns; four reliefs of battles from that of Duke Arnulf over the Waren to the war against the French of 1814; and a grandiose quadriga surmounting the whole building.

154   With the commission in 1840 for the Feldherrnhalle (Hall of the Field Marshals), which closes the Ludwigstrasse at its southern end, Gärtner was entering an area where all recent buildings had been designed by Klenze: the Festsaalbau of the Residenz, the Hofgartentor and the Odeonsplatz. However,

153 (Opposite above). Friedrich von Gärtner: Gate of Victory, Munich, 1843–54, with a view of the Ludwigsstrasse and the Ludwigskirche on the left.

154 (Opposite below). Friedrich von Gärtner: Feldherrnhalle, Munich, 1841–3.

155 Friedrich von Gärtner: the Ludwigstrasse, Munich, showing the Ludwigskirche, 1829–44, and State Library, 1832–43.

Klenze disqualified himself by submitting designs for the Feldherrnhalle exclusively in the Doric style, and refusing to produce a copy of the fourteenth-century Loggia dei Lanzi in Florence which was what Ludwig really wanted. It is hard for us to enter Ludwig's mind sufficiently to understand exactly what prompted him to begin and end the street named after him with versions of the Arch of Constantine and the Loggia dei Lanzi, but he doubtless appreciated the incipient classicism of the Florentine building which, though supposedly Gothic, featured giant round arches. Apart from its higher podium, Gärtner's loggia is surprisingly close in all its dimensions to its model. The ornamental carving was executed by Sanguinetti from designs by Sickinger, while the bronze statues of the military leaders, Tilly and Wrede, were designed by Schwanthaler. Built of Kelheim stone, the Feldherrnhalle was paid for by Ludwig with his own funds. The foundation stone was laid on 18 June 1841, the anniversary of the battle of Waterloo, and, no less inevitably, it was opened three years later on 18 October, the over-commemorated anniversary of the battle of Leipzig.

One of the few really unhappy consequences of the forcing of styles on reluctant architects by the Bavarian royal family was the Wittelsbacher Palais, built a little way west of the Odeonsplatz by Gärtner for Ludwig's son, Crown Prince Maximilian. Begun in 1843, it was completed five years later by Klenze, after Gärtner's death. This enormous symmetrical pile of red brick and terracotta, remotely modelled on English and Venetian Gothic models, was heartily disliked both by Gärtner and by Ludwig, who complained that it might do for Nuremberg but not for Munich. Nonetheless, he had to live in it following his abdication in 1848. Its subsequent history was no brighter. Having become the seat of the Communist government in 1918–19, it was the Ministry of Social Welfare under the Weimar Republic and the headquarters of the Gestapo from 1935 to 1945. Bombed in the war, its unloved ruins were subsequently demolished without regret. Far happier is the Kursaal at Bad Kissingen, the chief spa in Bavaria, which Gärtner designed with Ludwig's approval in 1834. With its long, round-arched colonnades looking on to a fountain court, this compares favourably with the better-known Trinkhalle at Baden Baden by Heinrich Hübsch of 1840.

In December 1835 Gärtner travelled to Athens with Ludwig where in the following year he designed the Royal Palace for the young King Otto. Completed in 1841, it is a rather featureless classical pile but its interiors are richly decorated by a large team of artists with Pompeian wall paintings and scenes from Greek mythology and history, including the Greek War of Independence.

Ludwig's concern with what he saw as stylistic appropriateness and with the national image of Bavaria found a fitting outlet in his restoration programme for a number of medieval cathedrals and churches which had been altered in the Baroque period. He became responsible for ecclesiastical architecture following the secularization of religious property which had been carried out as part of his father's liberal reforms. The completion of Cologne Cathedral, begun in 1823, inspired the whole of Germany as an act of faith and patriotism, and also encouraged Ludwig to announce in 1826 the restoration of the Romanesque cathedral of Bamberg to its original style. Indeed, it seems that Ludwig had been the first to suggest, in 1814, that 'the Germans ought to complete Cologne Cathedral entirely in its own style as a monument to their liberation'. An extensive programme of restoration was carried out at Bamberg Cathedral between 1829 and 1837, which was supervised for the last two years by Gärtner. In 1837 he began restoring the Gothic cathedral of Regensburg and, in the

following year, the important Romanesque abbey at Heilbronn. He also restored
at this time the fourteenth-century Isartor in Munich, though his plans for
restoring the medieval cathedral at Speyer were interrupted by his death in 1847.

A more important work stopped by his death was the Befreiungshalle at
Kelheim, the construction of which was begun in 1842. This great circular
monument to the Wars of Liberation was close in form to his Early Renaissance
designs of 1833 for the Ruhmeshalle in Munich. As we saw in the last chapter, it
was transformed in a strikingly original way by Klenze who took over the
commission in 1847. However, it was to Gärtner not Klenze that Ludwig
entrusted the design of two elaborate villas which he built for himself in the 1840s
156 – the Pompeian House at Aschaffenburg, and the Villa Ludwigshöhe near
Edenkoben in the Rhine Palatinate. Both brought the king nothing but
unalloyed pleasure. Though the former is only marginally an urban building,
and the latter not at all, it seems appropriate to discuss them at this point.

156 Friedrich von
Gärtner: Pompeian
House, Aschaffenburg,
1842–6.

In compliance with Ludwig's expressed wish for 'an image of a Roman building with all its arrangements on German soil', Gärtner travelled to Naples and Pompeii in 1839 to gather information. The German passion for Pompeian art, which Gärtner fully shared, went back at least as far as Goethe's visit to Pompeii in 1787. The Pompeian House should be seen as the climax of the numerous Pompeian rooms which had been created in palaces up and down Germany during the previous half century. The celebrated Pompeian House which Alfred Norman built in Paris for Prince Jérôme Napoleon, 1854–9, was a very different affair. Its façade was in the modern Neo-grec style of Hittorff, only its atrium being an archaeological exercise in the Pompeian style.

The model selected for an, on the whole remarkably faithful, reproduction at Aschaffenburg from 1840 to 1848 was the Late Roman House of Castor and Pollux in Pompeii. It is charmingly placed in a garden on the side of the hill near the enormous Schloss Johannisburg, a late Renaissance building with corner towers which group picturesquely with the belvedere tower of the Pompeian House. With its Doric triclinium, open to the sky, its enchanting colonnaded *viridarium* or courtyard garden, and its rich neo-antique interior decoration comprising mosaics, wall paintings, stucco-work and sculpture provided by a large team of artists and craftsmen, the Pompeian House was a source of constant joy to Ludwig.

No sooner was the Pompeian House ready for occupation than the indefatigable king was laying the foundation stone in May 1846 of yet another private dream house, the Villa Ludwigshöhe. Embedded in vineyards at the foot of a wooded hill, this was the realization of a romantic ambition which Ludwig had nursed since 1826 of 'building an Italian villa in the mildest part of the kingdom'. The choice of site was made on the occasion of the marriage in 1842 of his son, Crown Prince Maximilian, to Princess Marie of Prussia.

Gärtner provided a substantial two-storeyed villa forming a rectangle, eleven bays by seven, with a central courtyard surrounded by a corridor on all four sides. The state apartments were on the ground floor, the private apartments for Ludwig, his family and guests, on the first floor. Its somewhat stark exterior design echoed that of his Royal Palace in Athens, and was more appropriate for this smaller building in its more luxuriant setting. The only external adornment is the open two-storeyed colonnade on the east entrance front with a row of six free-standing columns on each floor, Doric below and Ionic above. This was a Neo-classical version of Palladio's Palazzo Chiericati in Vicenza, which had already been attractively reflected at West Wycombe Park, Buckinghamshire, in the 1750s. The Pompeian interiors were completed after Gärtner's death by Klenze, who had provided similar decorative schemes in 1818 at Schloss Ismaning, for Eugène de Beauharnais, and Schloss Pappenheim, and from 1832 at the Munich Residenz.

The Pompeian House and the Villa Ludwigshöhe are appropriate buildings with which to end this book since they are ambitious late expressions of the fundamental Neo-classical desire, stimulated by a passion for Italy, to create a new classical synthesis in which images culled from antique and Renaissance sources would combine suggestively in a landscape setting.

THE story of classicism in Germany after the closing date of the present book would continue with the impact of Schinkel in Berlin. For over twenty years after his death in 1841 his architectural language was widely imitated by a number of very able followers such as Friedrich August Stüler (1800–65), Johann Heinrich Strack (1805–80), Friedrich Hitzig (1811–81) and Martin Gropius (1824–80). Echoing Schinkel's stylistic versatility though not always his intellectual control, they provided Berlin with countless villas, mansions, apartment blocks, churches and public buildings in a variety of neo-antique, Neo-Romanesque, Neo-Renaissance and Neo-Gothic styles. Perhaps the ablest was Stüler, whose Frankfurt Exchange, designed in 1839, we have already noticed in Chapter VII. In 1843–50 he built the Neues Museum in a style harmonizing with Schinkel's adjacent Altes Museum and, in collaboration with Strack, he added the Nationalgalerie nearby in 1865–9. This was based on a sketch by King Friedrich Wilhelm IV which was distantly inspired by Gilly's proposed monument to Frederick the Great. Gropius, who designed several handsome Schinkelesque villas, combined with Heino Schmieden to design the Kunstgewerbemuseum (1876–81) in Berlin, a late and sumptuous echo of Schinkel's Bauakademie and Klenze's Hermitage Museum.

The most important German architect and theorist of the nineteenth century after Schinkel and Klenze was Gärtner's pupil, Gottfried Semper (1803–79). His principal buildings in Dresden and Vienna are in a Neo-Cinquecento and Neo-Baroque manner which, following the establishment of the German Empire in 1870, became the norm in German architecture right into the twentieth century. Three characteristic monuments in Berlin of this somewhat turgid style are the Reichstag Building of 1884–94 by Paul Wallot (1841–1912), the Cathedral of 1888–1905 by Julius Raschdorf (1823–1914), and the Kaiser Friedrich (now Bode) Museum of 1896–1904 by Ernst von Ihne (1848–1917). In Bavaria the building mania and the stylistic eclecticism of the Wittelsbachs were carried to extreme lengths by Ludwig I's celebrated grandson, Ludwig II (1845–86). His Neo-Rococo Schloss Linderhof (1870–86) and Versailles-inspired Schloss Herrenchiemsee (begun 1878), both designed by Georg von Dollmann (1830–95), and his fantastic Wagnerian Schloss Neuschwanstein, begun in 1869 by Eduard Riedel, are probably visited by more tourists today than any other buildings in Germany. Linderhof, indeed, has considerably more *élan* than many subsequent Neo-Baroque buildings by leading architects such as Raschdorf.

In reaction to this full-blown style a more fastidious revival of indigenous sixteenth- and eighteenth-century modes, often inspired by the vernacular tradition of southern Germany, occurred around 1900 in the work of Ludwig Hoffmann (1851–1932), Theodor Fischer (1862–1938), and Alfred Messel (1853–1909) who had made measured drawings of Gentz's Berlin Mint on its demolition in 1886. Messel's offices for the Allgemeine Elektrizitäts-Gesellschaft (1905–6), on the Friedrich-Karl-Ufer in Berlin, and his Nationalbank (1906–7) in the Behrenstrasse, both contained superb Greek Doric vestibules and staircases inspired by Gentz's at Weimar. In Munich similar work with strong Neo-classical overtones was being carried out by German Bestelmeyer (1874–1942), for example his university extension in 1906–10, insurance company headquarters (1916) and technical high school (1922). A revival of interest in the austere and supposedly 'Prussian' style of Gilly and Schinkel is evident in the work of Peter Behrens (1868–1940). Sometimes regarded as a 'Pioneer of the Modern Movement', he is of relevance to us as the inventor of a kind of Neo-Schinkelesque stripped classicism which, despite the Expressionist and Bauhaus episodes, was to colour much German architecture up to 1945. Behrens's principal buildings in this style, all begun in 1911, are his Wiegand House at Berlin-Dahlem, German Embassy at St Petersburg, and Continental Rubber Company offices at Hanover. Paul Bonatz (1877–1951) produced work in a similar style, including his masterpiece, Stuttgart railway station of 1913–27. At Oldenburg, in a more conventional Neo-classical style, he built the Ministry buildings (1912–14) and colonnaded Legislative Assembly buildings (1912–16) of the Grand Duchy of Oldenburg, the last grand ducal monuments of their kind ever to be built in Germany.

The arresting and austere architecture of Behrens and Bonatz was accompanied by a scholarly reassessment of the great age of German classicism in such books as Paul Mebes' *Um 1800, Architektur und Handwerk im letzten Jahrhundert ihrer traditionellen Entwicklung* (Around 1800. Architecture and Handicraft in the Last Century of Traditional Development), 1908, Paul Klopfer's *Von Palladio bis Schinkel. Eine Charakteristik der Baukunst des Klassizismus* (From Palladio to Schinkel. The Characteristics of the Architecture of Classicism), 1911, and monographs on Erdmannsdorff by E.P. Riesenfeld in 1913, on Gentz by Adolph Doebber in 1916, and on Weinbrenner by Arthur Valdenaire in 1926. This remarkable investigation of Neo-classicism, not paralleled at that moment elsewhere in Europe, was accompanied by a flow of monographs on Schinkel, for example by Fritz Stahl in 1912, Hans Macknowsky in 1922, and August Grisebach in 1924. This culminated in the magisterial sequence of *Karl Friedrich Schinkel Lebenswerk* (The Works of Schinkel) volumes edited by P.O. Rave of which the first appeared in 1939. A related interest in the startling work of Schinkel's mentor, Gilly, resulted in a luxurious study of him by Alste Oncken published in 1935 and another by Alfred Rietdorf in 1943. Produced in wartime Berlin, Rietdorf's book reminds us that the language of Gilly and Schinkel, revived by Behrens, also inspired architects in the Third Reich like Paul Ludwig Troost (1878–1934), as in his Haus der Deutschen Kunst (1933) in Munich, and Albert Speer (1905–81) in his Chancellery in Berlin (1938). Leading architects in their sixties such as Bestelmeyer, Behrens, Bonatz and Kreis all worked for the National Socialist government. Wilhelm Kreis (1873–1956), who before 1914 had produced over forty national monuments, many of them to Bismarck, in a militantly monumental style, was a natural choice in 1941 as general architectural adviser for the building of military cemeteries. His proposals for monuments like the vast memorial pyramid to be erected on the River Dnieper echo the obsession with tombs and mausolea of the Neo-classical period. Indeed, the quest for a monument to Frederick the Great, which was a leitmotiv of German architecture for over thirty years after his death in 1786, was revived under Hitler. Thus in May 1943 Goebbels recorded in his diary that, 'thanks to English air raids . . . we have had to remove the coffin of Frederick the Great from the Garrison Church and place it where it is safe from bombs. The Führer will never restore it to the Garrison Church. Either an imposing mausoleum in the Greek style is to be built for Frederick the Great in the park of Sanssouci or he is to be laid to rest in the great Soldiers' Hall of a new War Ministry yet to be constructed.'

The language of classicism naturally took a long time to recover from its use by the National Socialist Party as a vehicle for the expression of political ideals. But classicism is older and better than National Socialism and though German architects have been slower to return to it than, say, those in the United States or Great Britain, there is no doubt that the interest now being taken in Schinkel will lead to the rehabilitation in Germany of the classical language of architecture.

PART TWO

Gazetteer of
Neo-classical Buildings

NORTH
SEA

DENMARK

SWEDEN

BALTIC
SEA

SCHLESWIG-
HOLSTEIN

Altona
Hamburg

Bad Doberan
Heiligendamm

MECKLENBURG

POLAND

NETHERLANDS

Oldenburg
Bremen

HANOVER

BRANDENBURG

Osnabrück

Hanover

Potsdam
Berlin

WESTPHALIA

Brunswick

Münster

Krefeld

Kassel

Dieskau

Elberfeld

SAXONY

Düsseldorf

Bad Lauchstädt

Aachen
Cologne

Weimar

Dresden

BELGIUM

Bonn

THURINGIA

RHINELAND

Koblenz

Bad Homburg

Coburg

Bad Ems

Wiesbaden

Frankfurt

Darmstadt

Aschaffenburg

CZECHOSLOVAKIA

Bensheim

Würzburg

Mannheim

PALATINATE

Ansbach

Karlsruhe

Stuttgart

BAVARIA

N

FRANCE

Baden Baden

WÜRTTEMBERG

Bad Buchau

Munich

Lindau

AUSTRIA

0   80 Miles

SWITZERLAND

0   120 Km

198

THE FOLLOWING GAZETTEER is intended to supplement the text by listing, town by town, the main Neoclassical buildings of Germany, both extant and destroyed. To avoid unnecessary repetition, certain cities, notably Hamburg, Berlin and Munich, are not included, since these have been given sufficient coverage in the text; country palaces described in the text are also omitted. For a list of publications arranged by locality, see the final section of the bibliography.

Aachen

Famous as Charlemagne's residence and the coronation place of thirty German kings up to 1531, Aachen became increasingly prosperous in the 18c. through industry and growing popularity as a spa. Because of this and the fact that the town was not the seat of a court, domestic architecture assumed an importance that it did not have in nearby Düsseldorf or Cologne. Some of the grander houses are modelled on the French *hôtel* type. During the French occupation (1795–1814) Aachen was the capital of the department of Roer; afterwards it became part of the Prussian Rhine Province, with its own jurisdiction and parliament. As a result there was a demand for civic architecture, and, in the 1830s, some town planning.

The main architects working in Aachen were *Johann Joseph Couven* (1701–63) and his son *Jakob Couven* (1735–1812). The official Prussian architects were *Joseph Peter Cremer* (1785–1863) and *A.F.F. Leydel* (1785–1838).

Major buildings

Altes Kurhaus/Old Pump Room (1782–6, *J. Couven*) Contains a splendid first-floor ballroom, later concert hall. Extended 1900–1903.

Monopteros on the Losberg (1815–16, *A.F.F. Leydel*) A tholos on the sandy Losberg.

Stadttheater (1822–5, *Cremer*, with major design modifications by *Schinkel*) After the Elisenbrunnen, the most important Neo-classical building in Aachen. Splendid temple front with sculptured pediment representing Melpomene and Thalia receiving laurels from a genius, designed by Schinkel after Cremer and executed by *W.J. Imhof.* Auditorium based on the Odéon, Paris. Enlarged 1836, restored 1878, enlarged 1900–1901; rebuilt with original façade after part destruction in the war.

Elisenbrunnen (1825–7, *Schinkel*, based on a design by *Cremer*) Schinkel's best building in the Rhineland, built over a spring in the centre of town near the cathedral and intended to revitalize the old spa. A Doric colonnade emphasized by a central rotunda with a magnificent tented roof, originally planned with murals. Rebuilt after the war.

157 Cremer and Schinkel: Elisenbrunnen, Aachen, 1825–7.

Regierungsgebäude/Regional Government Offices (1828–31, *Cremer*) A simple, dignified building in the austere Prussian style. Partially rebuilt after war damage, when the Prussian royal arms in the pediment were replaced by the arms of Rhineland-Westphalia. The interior had a richly decorated council chamber and murals by pupils of Schadow, and vaulted corridors.

Königstor (1836), **Neubad** (1836) and **Belvedere on the Losberg** (1838), all by *A.F.F. Leydel.*

Zollgebäude/Customs House (1846–9, *Cremer*)

Domestic architecture

Early classical houses by *J. Couven*: **Eckenberg, Eckenbergstrasse 6–8** (1788); **Haus zum Kardinal, Alexanderstrasse 12** (1790). Others, by unknown architects, at **Alexanderstrasse 10, Paulstrasse 88, Dahmengraben 2**, and **Franz-Strasse 6.** Classical houses by *A.F.F. Leydel* at **Hackgraben 12** and **Hindenburgstrasse 57–8.**

Ansbach

Known for its Schloss and surviving Baroque layout, the town has been the seat of the margraves of Ansbach-Bayreuth since 1456, and since 1806 part of Bavaria. There are some very early signs of French classicism in parts of the **Schloss** (façade to the Reitbahn, 1731) and in some houses; a later example is the **Karlshalle** (1777, *J.C. Wohlgemut*), a Catholic chapel designed externally like a town house to disguise its function (as with the two Protestant churches in Frankfurt by F. Mack). Yet the most important Neo-classical building is the Catholic **Ludwigskirche** (1834–40, *Leonhard Schmidtner*): with its magnificent Doric temple front it forms a somewhat curious accent on one corner of the Baroque Karlsplatz.

Aschaffenburg

Seat of the archbishops of Mainz since *c*.975. After secularization in 1803 Aschaffenburg became a principality under the archbishop-Elector of Mainz Karl Theodor von Dalberg. In 1814, after the collapse of the Napoleonic Empire, it became part of Bavaria.

In the last quarter of the 18c. Aschaffenburg gained a renewed importance due to Friedrich Carl Joseph Freiherr von Erthal (1774–1803), the energetic and ambitious last archbishop of Mainz. Extensive building projects were an integral part of his political schemes, devised with the aid of his minister Count Wilhelm von Sickingen. Progressively minded, he appointed the Paris-trained Portuguese architect *Emanuel Joseph von Herigoyen* (1746–1817), formerly Sickingen's own architect, who erected buildings in the most up-to-date Louis XVI style. Herigoyen also worked later for Karl Theodor von Dalberg. The last impressive Neo-classical contribution to Aschaffenburg was the Pompeian House, built for Ludwig I of Bavaria by *Friedrich von Gärtner* (1792–1847).

158 Emmanuel Joseph von Herigoyen: east wing vestibule of Schloss Johannisburg, Aschaffenburg, 1774–84.

Schloss Johannisburg (1774–84, *Herigoyen*) The old castle was remodelled around a magnificent new staircase based on French models such as those of the Petit Trianon and the Hôtel Salé in Paris. Destroyed in the war, and partially restored as a museum.

Schloss Schönbusch (1778–82, *Herigoyen*) Some details are still in a transitional Rococo/classical mood, but the composition is markedly forward-looking, with an emphasis on plain surfaces. The decoration of the ceiling of the Festsaal or banqueting hall is taken from George Richardson's *Book of Ceilings* (1776).

English influence also permeated the layout of the **park**, partly designed by *L.F. Sckell*, the gardener of Schwetzingen, which ranks among the finest *jardins anglais* in Germany. A variety of garden pavilions and ornamental structures were also designed by *Herigoyen*, e.g. the Dining Hall (1788–92), a version of Robert Morris's idea for a Summer Room in his *Architectural Remembrancer* (London 1751). The Temple of Friendship (1792 or 1799–1802) is based on Chambers's Temple of Bellona at Kew. The Temple of Philosophers may also have been inspired by Herigoyen's visit to England in 1789.

Later works by *Herigoyen* were the **Town Hall**, Dalbergstrasse 15 (1790) and the **Theatre** (1809–11, restored 1959).

Pompeijanum/Pompeian House (1840–48, *F. Gärtner*) A lavish villa built for Ludwig I in a commanding situation overlooking the Main. It is a copy of the House of Castor and Pollux at Pompeii, but with two storeys. Restored after the war.

Other Neo-classical buildings: **Kasino**, Karlsplatz (1823); **Hospital** (1824); and good houses at **Stiftsstrasse 1** (1770); **Dalbergstrasse 49a** (1803); **Webergasse 4** (1804); **Metzgergasse 11–13**.

Bad Buchau am Federsee

Bad Buchau is chiefly famous for its convent, an early medieval foundation for ladies of the nobility, and for the **convent church of SS. Cornelius and Cyprian**, remodelled in 1773 by *Pierre Michel d'Ixnard* (1723–95), on the pattern of his masterpiece, the monastic church of St Blasien, South Germany's most perfect evocation of early classicism.

D'Ixnard had been called in in 1769 to restore the convent buildings and make some slight modifications to the church. He succeeded, however, in persuading his patrons to accept a more ambitious scheme whereby the early 15c. basilica was transformed into a remarkable hall-church with aisles almost as tall as the nave. He ingeniously created a feeling of spaciousness with widely spaced shallow pillars and galleries set in like balconies (similar to the circular gallery at St Blasien). The classical decorative programme is expressed within a firm architectural frame of Ionic pilasters supporting a rich entablature. The ceiling frescoes (in the nave by *Adrian Brugger*, in the aisles by *Johann Georg Messner*) are also framed and treated like easel paintings within the otherwise white and gold decorations. Regrettably the spectacular setting planned for the high altar was never realized: an apse was to contain a cross on a high rocky base, mysteriously lit from above – a dramatic effect recalling that in the Baroque church of Weltenburg but probably inspired by the Lady Chapel of St Sulpice in Paris, and destined to become a favourite motif of Revolutionary architecture.

Bad Doberan

Created in the 1790s by Grand Duke Friedrich Franz I of Mecklenburg-Schwerin as Germany's first seaside resort and his own summer residence, Bad Doberan became celebrated for its remarkable uniform Neoclassical town ensemble. *Carl Theodor Severin* (1763–1836), a pupil in Berlin of Langhans and Friedrich Gilly, was entrusted with the master plan centred around a triangular public space, called 'Kamp'. Between 1800 and 1825 Severin developed Doberan in a style bearing the imprint of the austere Berlin classicism of the pre-Schinkel era. The scheme included Heiligendamm, 6 km away, founded in 1793 to enjoy immediate access to the sea (see p. 232).

Kurhaus/Assembly Rooms (1801–2) A white stuccoed two-storeyed building of severe geometric forms, with an emphasis on plain wall surfaces contrasted with bold cornices. The projecting centre is impressively accentuated by an unusually tall attic, while shopping arcades are a feature of the side wings. All the banqueting rooms were placed at the back facing the garden. A banqueting hall of considerable grandeur was added here in 1819–21 with sumptuous Empire decorations, particularly in the ceiling and the elaborate balustrade of the surrounding gallery. In 1879, with the building's transformation into a town hall, the exterior was remodelled in Renaissance style to suit the richer taste of the time. Fortunately in 1956 it was restored to its former glory.

159 Carl Theodor Severin: Palais am Kamp, Bad Doberan, 1806–9.

Palais am Kamp/Summer Palace (1806–9) The focal point of the entrance front is a giant recessed Ionic portico rising to an impressive cornice which dominates the two-storeyed building. Slightly projecting corners terminate the otherwise restrained stuccoed façade. Of the rich Empire interiors only the Gartensaal survives, still with its original pictorial wallpaper of *c.*1820 by *Johann Christoph Xaver Mader le Pere*, representing in grisaille frivolous stories of Cupid and Psyche. Most of the palace is used today for offices.

Haus Medini (1825) *Severin's* last authenticated work in Doberan still displays the reductive style of some twenty years earlier, but with a curiously ponderous use of a Palladian window as a central feature. The projecting corner pavilions recall those of the Summer Palace.

Bad Ems

Renowned since Roman times for its waters, Bad Ems achieved international celebrity and royal patronage as a spa during the 19c. The principal attraction for the fashionable world, however, was gambling. That was the source of the town's wealth, which in turn created its fine civic architecture. The spa's most spectacular classical building is the Kursaal. During the second half of the century the town grew rapidly: whole streets like the Römerstrasse and Lahnstrasse were created, and many hotels and private villas built, most of them variations on the classical theme which is still very much felt today.

Kursaal/Assembly Room (1836–9, *Johann Gottfried Gutensohn*) By designing an H-shaped building with tower-like wings framing a lower two-storeyed central block, the Bavarian court architect successfully complemented the romantic setting along the river Lahn, with picturesque wooded hills rising behind. A Palladianesque Doric loggia stretches between the wings, with a massive row of arcaded windows above in a clear reference to the Munich *Rundbogenstil*. In the gambling hall inside, the arrangement is reversed, and an order rises above an arcade. Decoration of the greatest opulence was achieved here by combining Raphaelesque references with Grecian and Pompeian motifs, such as a saucer-domed arcade contrasted with the principal space covered by a deeply coffered ceiling with sumptuous gilded rosettes.

After a first extension in 1862, a major addition followed in 1913–14, adding on to the west front new banqueting rooms and a theatre ending in an elegant rotunda facing the gardens. The classical style of the 1830s was successfully recaptured; the former symmetry of the design was replaced by a picturesque grouping, though without diminishing its monumental impact.

Baden Baden

Picturesquely situated in the valley of the river Oos, Baden Baden was already known as a spa in Roman times. In the Middle Ages it became the seat of the margraves of Baden, and although they established a larger residence in nearby Rastatt in 1700, Baden Baden remained their summer seat and spa. It was considerably revitalized by the last of the margraves, August Georg, in the 1760s: he had assembly rooms built on virgin ground west of the Oos, thereby laying the foundations for a new town centre. With the takeover in 1771 of the Baden-Durlach line, then residing in Karlsruhe, the spa's further development had to wait until the beginning of the 19c. Then, profiting from Karlsruhe's increasing power, Baden Baden grew rapidly and received many new spa buildings. From 1830 to 1880 it was Europe's most fashionable summer resort, famous for gambling but also for the spectacular beauty of the surrounding wooded hills and luxuriant vineyards. By then the Assembly Rooms had grown to a palatial size. 'In the height of summer,' a 19c. writer vividly observed, 'the noise of the crowd of visitors blended with music . . . and the fragrance of the most beautiful flowers brings before us, as it were by magic, a picture from the *Arabian Nights*.'

All the official buildings, and some of the major private houses, were designed by the directors of public buildings of the Grand Duchy of Baden – *Friedrich Weinbrenner* (1766–1826) and then *Heinrich Hübsch* (1795–1863). Weinbrenner himself was responsible for no less than six public buildings and one private house: the Antiquitätenhalle or Sculpture Gallery (1804), the Palais Hamilton (1808), the Neue Armenbad (new baths for the poor, 1809), Pferdebad ('horse baths', 1810–11), and Alte Dampfbad (old steam baths, 1819), the grand Kurhaus or Assembly Rooms (1821–4), and finally the Old Pump Room (1822–4). By Hübsch are the Trinkhalle or New Pump Room (1837–40) and the Neue Dampfbad (new steam baths, 1846–8).

Klenze is represented in Baden Baden by his last commission, the Stourdza Chapel (1864–6).

Badischer Hof (converted 1807–9, *Weinbrenner*) A strange, intriguing transformation of a former Capuchin monastery into a grand hotel. The church was successfully turned into a majestic banqueting hall, music and conversation rooms, but the most startling change was that of the cloister into a dining hall. With a monumentality reminiscent of his visionary Roman schemes, Weinbrenner spanned the cloister with a gigantic barrel vault supported by eighteen giant Doric columns with galleries on three floors. A skylight as the main source of illumination must have produced that mysterious atmosphere aimed at in Weinbrenner's imaginative reconstruction of Hippias's Bath (1794). Not surprisingly, in the later 19c. such a monumental space was thought more appropriate for a staircase hall' and was adapted accordingly.

Palais Hamilton (1808, *Weinbrenner*) Built for the physician Dr Maier; sold in 1824 to Grand Duke Leopold, whose descendant Princess Maria marrying the Duke of Hamilton gave the house its present name. Austere and geometric in style, the Palais impresses by the powerful disposition of its masses with the main block vigorously accentuated in front and at the rear by bold central projections. In the front a raised giant Doric order supporting a heavy pediment marks the entrance. The uncompromising Revolutionary style is expressed as much in major motifs, such as the low wide entrance arch, as in the general reductive vocabulary of architectural forms. Its character had been ruthlessly destroyed by several 19c. alterations, but recent skilful restoration has successfully recreated the original effect. Having served at one stage as a library, the building is now a bank.

Kurpark The layout of the English garden around the Assembly Rooms is said to have been partially the work of the great Munich court gardener *Sckell* in 1817. The original plan, however, as executed in 1810–11, was by the Baden Baden court gardener *Hertwig*. The extensive flooding of the river Oos in 1825 occasioned a totally new layout.

Boutiquen/Shops The approach to the old Assembly Rooms had been enhanced by an avenue of four rows of chestnut trees, and soon small shops began to appear. In order to maintain the original intention, in 1816 Weinbrenner was asked to submit an overall design. His plan of two rows of wooden shops was executed during his absence in Leipzig – so ineptly that most of them had to be rebuilt on his return. In 1839 there were 25 little shops. In 1867–8 they were replaced by the more permanent stuccoed structures that exist today.

Kurhaus/Assembly Rooms (1821–4, *Weinbrenner*) The scheme of 1821 required Weinbrenner to incorporate the existing assembly rooms into his design. He had to provide a variety of entertainment and gambling rooms together with a majestic banqueting hall and a large theatre (to replace a wooden structure of 1810). His first project consisted of pavilions linked by lower wings to a main block, the south pavilion being the former hall heightened by one storey. This was balanced to the north by a similar pavilion for the theatre, while a giant Corinthian portico marked the banqueting hall in the centre. A Baroque massing of separate rooflines crowned the impressive Palladian composition. A yet more palace-like grouping resulted when, in the interests of fire precaution, loggias with shops were introduced between the wings and pavilions. The stuccoed elevations are themselves rather conventional, the central portico forming a traditional climax. However, at the rear Weinbrenner's design is bolder, particularly on the theatre side, where it recalls the geometric language of his earlier Roman days.

As early as 1853–4 the northern half of the building was rebuilt, luckily retaining the original façade (at Hübsch's insistence). In 1912–16 the same was done with the south pavilion, leaving the centre as the only survival of Weinbrenner's work. One-storeyed build-

160 Friedrich Weinbrenner: Kurhaus, Baden Baden, 1821–4.

ings now encase most of the wings, destroying the unity and elegant flow which Weinbrenner had considered so important in his building.

The interior too has mostly vanished, after several modernizations. The banqueting hall was originally adorned at both ends by striking screens of giant columns with galleries between them (as in Weinbrenner's Evangelical church in Karlsruhe). The walls were articulated by pairs of pilasters framing niches; they and the flat ceiling were decorated with feigned architectural elements in paint by the Berlin artists *Fritz* and *Orth the elder*. Most of the remaining interior decoration was in a rich Pompeian style, now lost.

141 **Trinkhalle/New Pump Room** (1837–40, *Hübsch*) Only thirteen years after Weinbrenner's Pump Room had been completed in the centre of town, the authorities commissioned a new building nearer to the Assembly Rooms. Conscious of the panoramic views, Hübsch designed a monumental arcade opening towards the town with elegant segmental arches inspired by Schinkel's Bauakademie. As a synthesis of Renaissance architecture (Foundling Hospital, Florence) and Hellenistic design (in the architrave-portico arrangement), the Trinkhalle, with its subtle polychromy of strawberry-coloured sandstone, red brick and brownish-yellow terracotta, is recognized today as a turning point in Hübsch's oeuvre towards a more mature and relaxed attitude, freed from rigid classical dependence. The emphasis on decorative features is also remarkable. The entrance is marked by a three-bay projection

crowned by a rich figurative pediment by *Xaver Reich* representing 'Healing by the Nymphs of the Spring'. The arcaded rear wall of the loggia is dominated by a vivid mural scheme of the 'Schwarzwald' saga by *Jakob Götzenberg* (chosen in preference to Moritz von Schwind's design simply because it cost one-fourth as much).

The pump room itself was originally just a single 'elegant drinking saloon' behind the arcade on the central axis, whose vault was supported 'by a column of coloured marble with pipes from which the hot mineral water spouts into the basin of the fountain'. Additional rooms were built in 1952. The Trinkhalle remains as described in 1880, 'one of the most beautiful ornaments of the watering place'.

Stourdza Chapel (1864–6, *Klenze*) An exotic and provocative synthesis both in plan and imagery of Greek temple architecture and Byzantine church design, rising out of the wooded hills above Baden Baden on the Friesenberg. It is Klenze's last work, executed after his death by *G. Dollmann*, a local architect. The picturesque site had originally been intended by the Romanian refugee Prince Stourdza for a hilltop villa, but after his son's tragic early death in 1863 it was devoted to a memorial chapel cum mausoleum. Square in plan with extensions at either side for chancel and vestibule, the chapel is vividly marked by its red and white polychromatic exterior crowned by an originally gilded lantern dome. The vestibule takes the form of a small Ionic prostyle temple with four marble columns – a classical allusion to the building's solemn function.

Within, one is captivated by the opulence of the rich Greek Orthodox church interior, the style of which is in strange contrast to the two white marble groups facing each other in the central axis. As if in permanent dialogue, the son on the right (modelled by *Rinaldo Rinaldi*) touchingly confronts his mourning parents on the left (by the French sculptor *Gabriel Thomas*). The four sarcophagi of the Stourdza family are in a frescoed vault below. In 1867 the chapel was handed over to the town of Baden Baden.

161, 162 Leo von Klenze: Stourdza Chapel, interior and exterior, Baden Baden, 1864–6.

Bad Lauchstädt

Bad Lauchstädt gained more fame as the favourite spa of Grand Duke Karl August of Weimar and his kinsman, friend and chancellor Goethe than it did for its waters or indeed for being the summer residence of the dukes of Saxe-Merseburg. In fact it was the Weimar court who revived the town each summer and it was here that the grand duke, devoted to the muses, built himself a **theatre** for his entertainment. The Berlin architect *Heinrich Gentz* (1766–1811), then designing the Schloss at Weimar, was entrusted with the project, which was supervised by Goethe and his *concilium*. Built in 1802, the theatre is rather a modest structure yet with an elegant interior including Pompeian decorations, which culminate in the barrel-vaulted ceiling with its delicate painted ribbing suggesting rippling canvas.

Bensheim

Close to the once-powerful Benedictine abbey of Lorsch, Bensheim was ruled after the abbey's decline by the Palatinate and, from 1803, by the house of Hesse-Darmstadt. The **Catholic church of St George**, an 8c. foundation, was impressively remodelled in classical style by the Darmstadt architect *Georg Moller* (1784–1852); his design of 1824–5 was executed by the local architect *Ignaz Opfermann* in 1826–30. Moller's most important church after the Ludwigskirche in Darmstadt, which is similarly sited on a height, St George's surprises by the dramatic contrast between its restrained, austere exterior and its monumental interior. The nave and aisles are separated by an arcade of tall, florid Corinthian columns which support a coffered barrel vault over the nave and lead to a coffered apse containing the high altar. After severe war damage, the church was rebuilt in 1950 with two flanking towers instead of the original single west tower; the interior was restored in 1962, when the Corinthian columns were happily reinstated (unlike the unfortunate restoration of the Ludwigskirche in Darmstadt).

Bonn

When at the end of the 13c. the archbishops of Cologne were forced to flee from their rebellious citizens they chose Bonn as their residence. The town reached its zenith during the Baroque and Rococo period under the patronage of the two Wittelsbach Electors Joseph Clemens (1688–1723) and Clemens August (1723–61). They were the creators of the extensive Residenz Schloss, the Palais at Poppelsdorf, the majestic Schloss Brühl and the enchanting Falkenlust hunting pavilion. Following the French occupation (1794–1814) Bonn became part of Prussia. In 1818 the University was reinstituted by Wilhelm III. The Schloss was adapted to house it, and several new buildings were duly erected under Prussian surveillance. The architects in charge were *Friedrich Waesemann*, from 1818 to 1830, and *Peter*

Joseph Leydel (1798–1845), from 1830 to 1845. Between 1820 and 1840 Bonn grew rapidly. There was no formal town planning, but during this period (and later) streets such as the Friedrichstrasse were laid out. *Leydel* was one of the chief architects involved.

Anatomiegebäude/Anatomy Theatre (1824–5, *Waesemann*, with major design modifications by *Schinkel*) Waesemann had originally projected a domed structure on a square plan with a Pantheon-like dissection theatre. To improve the poor lighting Schinkel replaced the dome with a round lantern, with the same elegant tent-like roof he had designed for the Elisenbrunnen in nearby Aachen. Schinkel also simplified and unified Waesemann's design. The building was, however, badly constructed and a new anatomy theatre had to be built in 1874. In 1883–4 the old building was adapted to house the University's collection of casts from the antique, and regrettably the circular windows of the main floor were cut into rectangular shapes. Later additions were made to the south front.

Sternwarte/Observatory (1840–45, *P.J. Leydel*, with major design modifications by *Schinkel*) Leydel's original design (1837) showed an unrelated grouping of elements with restless elevations in both Gothic and Romanesque modes. Schinkel stripped and simplified the façades and combined them into a uniform austere design. The brick structure (similar to Schloss Kamenz) with its dramatic pylon-like corner towers still survives unaltered.

Bremen

Bremen is Germany's second largest seaport after Hamburg. Once known as 'the Rome of the North' because of its missionary and cultural activity, the town had been an archiepiscopal seat since 850. In spite of this it was quickly seduced by Protestantism during the Reformation and indeed became a stronghold of Calvinism. Important as a trading centre, Bremen already had a powerful burgher class which was dominant from the 16c. onwards and which influenced the town's architectural history throughout the centuries, notably in the splendid array of medieval and Renaissance public buildings surrounding the cathedral. Neo-classicism is best seen in domestic architecture, responding to the needs of the wealthy citizenry. An ideal setting was created with the dismantling of the Baroque ramparts in 1802–9, and their transformation into a landscaped park with the Strasse Am Wall as the inner and the Contrescarpe as the outer ring. A first wave of building followed the Wars of Liberation, while the main activity gathered momentum during the 1840s. Single-family houses became the pattern through which classicism remained supreme right up to the end of the century.

Five main architects worked in Bremen. *Johann Georg Poppe* was a master builder with a wide range of private commissions. *Jacob Ephraim Polzin* (1776–1851), from East Prussia, spent time in Berlin in the circle of Gilly and Gentz and then worked for Hansen in Copenhagen

163 P.J. Leydel and K.F. Schinkel: Observatory, Bonn, 1838–45.

before arriving in Bremen in 1814. Here he married Poppe's daughter and built up a successful practice, introducing Berlin refinement. *Friedrich Moritz Stamm* (1794–1843) was a Prussian clerk of works who after an interlude in Munich settled in Bremen. In 1822 he became head of the Hochbauwesen or board of building works. *Dietrich C. Rutenberg* and *Lüder Rutenberg* were the leading architects after 1840 working in the classical idiom.

Public buildings

With historic civic buildings in existence, there was no immediate demand for new public architecture in the late 18c. and 19c., and even when new needs prompted new buildings, such as the Theatre and Museum, they were conceived in modest terms as if intended not to clash with existing architecture.

St Petri Waisenhaus/Orphanage (1783–5, architect unknown) The first building in Bremen to announce a change of style. Although still firmly grounded in the tradition of French Baroque classicism, the elongated building with its central tower above a pedimented entrance is more severe, and shows a controlled handling of architectural features emphasizing horizontality.

Theatre (1792) In Calvinist Bremen theatrical performances were unpopular, and the building of a theatre was organized by a few enthusiasts, who barely managed to raise 5,000 Thaler for a simple wooden structure which was erected within six months. To give the building some architectural importance a tetrastyle portico of wood was attached to the entrance in 1802, replaced by a stone one in 1826. A new theatre was built in 1843 (see below).

Museum (1806–8, *Hinrich Averdieck*; 1834 and 1836, *Polzin*) Bremen was one of the first towns to have a Museums Society, formed as early as 1783 out of a Natural Science Society established in 1776. After over 20 years in rented accommodation the society acquired the old Hanoverian garrison headquarters and in 1806 commissioned *Averdieck* to convert the building. He created a new two-storeyed façade emphasized by an Ionic tetrastyle portico clumsily attached to the centre. In 1834 *Polzin* added at the rear a charming banqueting hall for the increasing social activities of the society, which was effectively turning into a gentlemen's club. Polzin was also responsible for the ambitious remodelling and enlargement of the clubhouse in 1836. By adding another storey and redesigning the ground floor he gave the impression of the whole structure being lifted on a huge pedestal. The portico now appeared as a towering decorative feature, enhanced by acroteria in a Schinkelesque manner. Polzin had emphatically improved the building's appearance by applying his Berlin-influenced style. In 1873 it was replaced by a new building, now serving solely as a club.

Am Brill Waisenhaus/Orphanage (1817, *Averdieck*) A simple structure framed by small protruding wings and emphasized by a steeply pitched roof. Demolished.

Arbeitshaus Auf der Herrlichkeit/Workhouse (1830–31, *Stamm*) One of the architectural casualties of the last war was Bremen's extraordinary workhouse. Monumental in scale, it consisted of three parallel three-storeyed blocks, each *c.* 50 m long, arranged behind one another and linked by pairs of small corridor wings. Not only the sheer size but the palatial appearance were astonishing. The façade was punctuated by rows of framed windows, those on the ground floor round-headed and set in an imposing arcade, and its centre was marked by a pedimented feature with giant pilasters taking in the two upper storeys. The centre was further enriched by sculptural decorations: a remarkable female figure personifying Bremen stood on the apex of the pediment, flanked by lions, and there were fire-bowls at the ends of the pediment. Above the central arches of the ground-floor arcade were roundels with busts of classical gods – Artemis, Zeus, Aphrodite and Poseidon. Inside, there were vast workrooms on the first floor, with dormitories above, and on the ground floor kitchens, service rooms and dining halls. Stamm seems to have ignored the building's lowly function, giving his largest and most important commission an incongruous grandeur.

Haus der Gesellschaft Union/Clubhouse of the Union Society, Am Wall 206 (1835, *Polzin*) With his progressive design for this building Polzin introduced to Bremen the latest wave of German mature Neo-classicism – the *Rundbogenstil* of the then emerging Neo-Renaissance. This is the more astonishing as there exists an earlier project by Polzin showing a fairly traditional porticoed structure. The final design, however, bore the Berlin hallmark: round-arched windows in rectangular frames, decorated with acroteria, were set sparingly in the two-storeyed façade, thus emphasizing the flat wall surfaces and stressing horizontality. The composition was carefully balanced. The central entrance, with a wider flight of steps leading up, was flanked by lamp-posts and surmounted by a tripartite window, equal in width to the stairs below, while pairs of windows on each storey framed the whole. As in all of Polzin's work, the details were exquisite, showing Schinkel's influence. One of the main features of the interior was a concert hall, for long the largest in Bremen. The building was pulled down as uneconomical in 1903.

Rembertistift/Almshouses (1842–6, *D. Rutenberg*) A venerable institution, founded in 1305, rebuilt in a modest style. The only notable feature of the two-storeyed blocks along the Rembertiring and Rembertistrasse is a monumental entrance arch in the latter façade forming a carriageway with a dense tripartite arrangement of round-headed windows above. Later additions in 1856 and 1869 extended the complex almost into a quadrilateral structure, followed by further expansions in 1877–8 and 1900.

Stadttheater am Wall (1840–43, *Heinrich Seemann*) Bremen's theatre was built as a private enterprise, after nearly fifteen years of fund-raising, to the design of a local builder. Prominently situated on the landscaped ramparts above the former town moat, it looked more like a palatial town house than a theatre. The designer had doubtless studied Schinkel's Berlin Schauspielhaus, though more for details than for the compositional formula. The idea of an overpowering centre block flanked by side wings is transformed here into an H-shaped arrangement of lesser impact with two short side wings protruding at each end from the massive centre. Windows dominate the three-storeyed elevations. One of Schinkel's most characteristic devices, used in the Schauspielhaus – the pilastered window-band – is only partly understood and copied to emphasize the centre of the fronts. Elegant cast-iron railings, accentuating the centre of the first floor of the principal façades, and acroteria were the only decorations in a design which relied on simplicity for its charm.

In 1849, after the dissolution of the Theatre Society, the architect Seemann himself bought the building, which his heirs eventually sold for 47,600 Thaler to the city of Bremen in 1855. Additions were made in 1862 and subsequently. The building did not survive the war.

Kunsthalle/Art Gallery (1847–9, *L. Rutenberg*) Built ten years later than the adjacent Union Clubhouse, the gallery also subscribed to the *Rundbogenstil*. 'A more cheerful rather than a ponderous structure' had been desired by the commissioning Society of Arts (founded in 1823) when they announced a competition for a design in 1844. Rutenberg won the commission but had to revise his design when the Society decided on a new site, in a parkland setting at the Ostertor, and issued a new set of requirements for the projected building. They seem also to have invited designs from other architects. There exists a rough design by the Hanover architect Laves, owing much to Stüler's Stockholm Museum and the Neues Museum in Berlin yet externally still in a smooth academic classical style typical of Laves's earlier years. Rutenberg, on the other hand, drew his inspiration from Hübsch's Kunsthalle, just being finished in Karlsruhe. As in the latter, the façade focuses on a pedimented central projection of Italianate extraction with three monumental arches leading into a vestibule and emphasized by sculpture above. The main gallery floor is similar, indicated by pilaster strips separating huge round-headed windows. The arrangement of this main floor, used for regular shows of contemporary art for sale, comprised a vast exhibition room with a row of small cabinets behind. To give more hanging space, the great room was divided by partitioning walls, as Schinkel had devised for the Altes Museum in Berlin. Galleries for the permanent collection of sculpture and plaster casts were on the ground floor. More than the architecture – similar to the clubhouse nearby – it is the sculptural decoration which points at the building's function: reliefs in the pediment represent architecture, painting and sculpture, while statues of artists, two Italian (Raphael and Michelangelo) and two northern (Dürer and Rubens) are placed above the entrance arches. Substantial extensions by *Eduard Gildemeister* and *Albert Dunkel* in 1900–1902 greatly changed the original structure.

Ramparts development

The original scheme for transforming Bremen's ramparts into a sequence of avenues was given up in 1802 when the ducal gardener of Oldenburg, *Christian Ludwig Bosse* (1771–1832), was called in, and he suggested instead a picturesque park *à l'anglaise*, with the moat retained as a romantic rivulet. Bosse stayed only a year, however, and it was under Bremen's town gardener, *Altmann*, that the grand project materialized. The old town, stretching along the river Weser, was surrounded by an attractive half circle of green parkland with the Strasse Am Wall as the inner and the Contrescarpe as the outer border and between them the picturesque zigzag line of the Baroque moat. In place of the Baroque town gates, new Neo-classical toll- and guard houses were built. The first of these was the now lost Doventor.

Doventor (1805–9, *Carl Matthaey*) A pair of single-storeyed but striking square blocks with tented roofs and small loggias opening towards the street.

Ansgaritor (1806, *Poppe*) The gatehouses, larger than those of the Doventor and rectangular in plan, were emphasized by a Doric portico in antis stretching along two-thirds of the façade. The first of the gatehouses was pulled down in 1815, followed by the second in 1842.

Buntentor (1819–21, *N. Blohm*) Similar in concept to the others but two-storeyed and of monumental appearance, the Buntentor gatehouses had powerful Doric porticoes and an extraordinary reductive arrangement of a rectangular window surmounted by a semi-circular lunette. Destroyed in the war.

Werdertorwache (1820, *N. Blohm*) Much more basic than the Buntentor. Also destroyed in the war.

Ostertorwache (1825–8, *Stamm*) The most monumental of the gates, and an important civic structure since it included the town prison. Porticoes of baseless Doric columns on each of the street façades protrude from blocklike fronts pierced simply by rows of bare rectangular windows with striking keystones. The latter indicate with bold carvings the respective functions of the gate buildings – to the north the prison with emblems of war, to the south the guard house with symbols of peace. That the buildings have two storeys is only revealed in the side elevations. The prison is also disguised: three ranges surround an internal courtyard behind the north building, with cells towards the courtyard and corridors on the outside so as not to upset the exterior with a display of barred windows. The Ostertorwache survived the war.

Hohentorwache (1826, *Stamm*) Another pair of guard houses, a smaller and less ambitious replica of the Ostertorwache. Destroyed in the war.

Domestic architecture

In Bremen, as in most of the north German towns, the dual influence of French academicism and English Palladianism inspired in the latter part of the 18c. the earliest phase of Neo-classicism. At first the change of style manifested itself by the simple absorption of classical motifs into the native traditions, such as decorating the traditional gabled houses with Louis XVI urns, festoons and Greek key. In fact the gabled house type survived up to the beginning of the 19c. and the final break only occurred with the Wars of Liberation. The three-bay house was at first the more common type, proving ideal for the Palladian formula of temple fronts. An early example was the house at **Markt 15** (1790). With the Lohmann house, at **Langestrasse 34**, built in 1805 for the collector Lohmann, this use of the Palladian temple façade reaches perfection – a belated tribute to Stuart's Lichfield House in London (15 St James's Square). As a centrepiece the temple motif reappears in the contemporary seven-bay house erected for Senator Dr Jur. B. Castendyk at **Sandstrasse 5**, with amazingly original capitals in its giant pilaster order.

With the arrival of the Berlin-trained architect *Polzin* in 1814, new life was breathed into Bremen's domestic architecture. The house he built in 1819 for the merchant C.T. Brunn, **Schlachte 1**, must have created a sensation with its radical statement of stripped classicism, inspired by Gentz's Mint in Berlin. It was an exciting reinterpretation of the conventional Bremen gabled façade, renouncing the use of any order in favour of a decorative handling of architectural forms emphasizing wall surfaces. Above a low rusticated ground floor pierced by three round-headed windows, the main storey was stressed by three large windows linked by a balcony with its balustrade decorated by giant palm leaves which appeared to spring from the supporting brackets. A huge lunette window like the one Gentz had used in the Mint surmounted the whole on an otherwise plain surface. The composition was steeply roofed, creating the effect of a pyramid and highlighting the geometric quality of the façade. The outstanding character of this design, facing the river Weser, was never matched again, even by Polzin. In a later house, **Schlüsselkorb 1**, erected in 1830 for the wine merchant Engelbert Wilhelmi, *Polzin* reverted to traditional fenestration, though his unusual style was still expressed, albeit in a muted form, in the extraordinary ground floor rustication and refined decorations in relief. Polzin's achievement is the more appreciated in comparison with the stodgy classicism of a similar house at **Brautstrasse 26**, designed *c.*1825 by *Johann Christian Lührig* for the West Indian merchant Hagedorn. **Brautstrasse 15**, constructed in 1825 for J.G.N. Eylers, was a more elegant version of this type of house, distinguished by integral sculptural decoration. Unfortunately all these houses have now gone.

The larger type of house was accentuated either in the centre or at its extremities, the latter recalling Krahe's houses in Koblenz and Brunswick. As a regional feature the customary high hipped roof remained – as distinct from the flat roofs customary in Berlin and south Germany. In 1816 the architect *Poppe* built for himself a house, **An der Herrlichkeit 14–16**. A symbol of his professional success, this was in fact a combination of three houses under one general design, not unlike the houses of Soane and Nash with their similar commercial aspect. The focal point of Poppe's façade was a three-bay pedimented centre projection with a strip-like full-length arched recess marking the entrance, surmounted by the only framed window and a remarkable lunette on the second-floor level. Rows of plain windows marked the side wings; the only interruption was a boldly carved frieze placed high up. Poppe's own house is an echo of the Revolutionary style of the Vieweg House in Brunswick by David Gilly, and it may be that Poppe's Berlin-trained son-in-law Polzin introduced him to the Gilly-Gentz style. Stylistically similar but smaller was the house *Poppe* designed for his nephew S.A. Poppe in 1820, **Buchtstrasse 67–8**. Here he followed Krahe's Brunswick device, with slightly projecting ends and a wide recess in the centre. An acanthus frieze with griffins formed a bold horizontal line above the ground-floor windows, while pediments emphasized the end projections. **Domshof 20** (1823) is a larger but less powerful version of the same formula. The house *Polzin* designed for Christian Hasselhoff in 1825 at **Wachtstrasse 27–8** reflects the elegant life-style enjoyed by Bremen's wealthy merchant class. It is a subtle composition: a wide but otherwise unemphatic centre projection, marked only by more opulent decoration, an attic storey and richer first-floor windows, cleverly counterbalances the horizontal window line and the unusual and brilliantly executed rustication of ground and first floor. Polzin's style has changed here from a radical to a compromising nature, above all in the refined and rather old-fashioned decoration. The interior was noted for the high quality of its design and execution. **Wachtstrasse 40** (1842) and **Stintbrücke 4–5** (1843, *H.H. Meier*) are impressive examples of the more dogmatic and academic classicism derived from Berlin, while **Domsheide 3** (1848, *Johann Heinrich Schröder*) is a worthy tribute to Schinkel's Bauakademie.

Strasse Am Wall and **Alten Wall** As in many northern German cities, the transformation of the Baroque ramparts into landscaped parkland provided a scenic setting for domestic architecture. The avenue created along the line of the ramparts soon became a fashionable spot for the rich and successful to build their houses. An especially attractive feature was the panoramic view of open country, which was guaranteed by allowing only one side of the street to be built up. Otherwise there were no restrictions. As a consequence, individuality was the order of the day and between 1815 and 1845 a picturesque array of noble houses resulted. Although they differed in height and width, and were sometimes grouped together and sometimes widely spaced, unity was achieved by the demand for elegance. Some of the more important houses were:

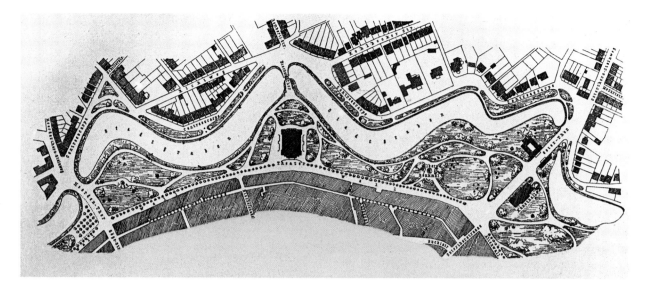

164 Map showing the transformation of the former ramparts of Bremen into promenades, early 19th century.

Am Wall 200 (1816, *Polzin?*) One of the earliest houses, built for Senator J.G. Iken. The two-storeyed façade, with its emphasis on tower-like end bays framing a wide central recess, followed a type much favoured by Poppe and probably copied from Krahe. Giant pilaster strips topped by a segmental arch stressed the end bays, with button-like roundels high up and impressive sphinx reliefs between ground-floor and first-floor windows. In the centre the latter were replaced by voluptuous festoons under Egyptian-style heads protruding from the wall, while a delicate acanthus frieze ran below the roof line. Demolished in 1905.

No. 206 (1817, *Poppe*) Built for the Senator Dr Jur. Johann Pavenstedt. A portico in antis formed the focal point. Similar houses by *Poppe* were **nos. 111, 151** and **165**.

No. 119 (1817, *Poppe*) One of its architect's more conventional three-bay houses, focused on the first floor with boldly carved window heads.

No. 146 (1818) Another example of the more modest type of house, three bays wide and surmounted by a pediment, built for the merchant Kulenkampf.

No. 145 A larger five-bay house focused on a central Palladian window.

Nos. 196, 197 Two adjacent houses which illustrated to perfection the extreme individuality which flourished in the Strasse Am Wall and the picturesque effect achieved. Different in height and width and expressing the classic formula in different ways, they harmoniously complemented each other. No. 197, built in 1829 for the merchant D.J. Visser, may be attributed to *Polzin*. A giant round-arched centre recess dominated the façade with an elegant portico in antis surmounted by the most startling arrangement of a central window flanked by four descending plaques with a relief like a filigree brooch above. No. 196 (demolished) had a more conventional central emphasis, with a giant Doric pilaster

order supporting a low pediment, but with a similar monumental effect. Mutilated by later changes, No. 197 still survives.

No. 113, Lürman'sche Haus (1833, *Polzin*) This epitomized the high standard of patrician life in Bremen. The architect paid respect to Schinkelesque classicism with a noble façade of relaxed composition characterized by plain surfaces and widely spaced windows emphasized on the first floor by elegant cast-iron balconies. The central entrance door in particular formed an elegant feature, with its carefully designed aedicule framing and acroteria, and it was flanked by lamp-posts of exquisite quality. Destroyed by bombing, a serious loss.

Alten Wall 16–22 (1830) This unusual terrace of four Neo-classical houses was constructed in a Nash-like manner as a single composition emphasized by pedimented end sections. A similar arrangement was created in 1850 out of **nos. 21–3**, originally built *c*.1839.

No. 9 (1831, *Polzin*) Designed for the widow Albers. A fairly large house, composed in noble simple terms. The broad façade was accentuated by a low-pedimented shallow centre projection with an overpowering first-floor balcony on brackets to which three French doors gave access, in an arrangement remotely suggestive of a Palladian window. The entrance door was asymmetrically placed to the right.

Contrescarpe Bremen's other picturesque setting for domestic architecture was created a generation later on the other side of the town moat, as the outer ring to the Strasse Am Wall, following the zig-zag line of the walls. It took its name from the vocabulary of fortification, having been the outer slope of the ditch. Until 1849 this area was excluded from the privileges of the free town, and so it was used only for summer villas. Of these a distinguished example was the charming one-storeyed villa built by *Polzin* in 1822 for Konsul Lürmann (**Contrescarpe 22**) which owes much to the influence of Schinkel. This influence was increased almost accidentally after a remodelling by *Heinrich Müller* in 1866 when the hipped roof was replaced by a second floor, in which a tripartite window echoed the Doric portico below, topped by a bold unbroken frieze below the roofline. Ten years previously the house had received the spectacular addition of a large Erechtheum-like verandah with caryatids recalling classical Athens, designed by *H. Rauschenberg*. Next door, at **no. 21**, *Müller* designed at the same time a similarly grand villa for Lürmann's brother. The grandeur of these late classical villas for Bremen's upper class in the Contrescarpe also appears in **no. 142** (1862, *D. Engelken*) and **nos. 143–4** (1865, *H. Deetjen*). On a less prestigious scale are **nos. 29, 30** and **36** (all of 1852), and **nos. 33** and **34** (1853).

Other late classical street ensembles are the **Adlerstrasse** of 1853–6, chiefly designed by *Hermann Rauschenberg*, and the **Mendestrasse** of 1860–61.

Country houses

Since the late 18c. wealthy citizens of Bremen had built themselves country villas nearby for the hot summer months. Especially favoured were Oberneuland, northeast of Bremen, and Vegesack to the north-west. The majority of these charming retreats were one-storeyed structures with large hipped or saddleback roofs and temple-like portico arrangements (often tetrastyle), a classical reference in a faint Palladian tradition.

BREMEN-HORN-LEHE
Haus Landruhe, Am Rüten 2 (*c*.1795, *Joachim A. Deetjen*) Built for Consul Cassel, the villa featured a two-storeyed pedimented centrepiece stressed by giant Ionic pilasters of some grandeur. The subsequent construction of a cast-iron Tudor orangery in 1850 created a picturesque contrast.

Teahouse, Marcus Allee 1 (*c*.1820, *Polzin*) Alderman Everhard Delius erected this handsome teahouse as a Greek Doric 'temple of friendship', which still exists.

BREMEN-OBERNEULAND
Landgut Heinekens, Oberneuländer Landstrasse 151–3 (*c*.1800) Originally built in the second half of the 18c. and then rebuilt in a more severe academic classical style. Still extant.

Landgut Holdheim, Apfelallee 30 (*c*.1809) Another villa emphasized by a Doric portico with Palladian overtones in the design of the entrance door.

Haus Rockwinkeler, Oberneuländer Landstrasse 65 (*c*.1800) The Neo-classical interiors, which still survive, testify to the high standard of these summer retreats.

Haus Hoogenkamp, Oberneuländer Landstrasse 33 (*c*.1825) Distinguished by a central domed rotunda and a Doric portico.

Landgut Böving-Muhle, Oberneuländer Landstrasse 65–7. A converted farmhouse with a new main

façade facing south marked by the conventional feature of a pedimented portico.

Villa Caesar-Ichon, Oberneuländer Landstrasse 70 (1843, *A. T. Eggers*) A late classical villa also formed out of a farmhouse. The main front, to the garden, is a balanced Neo-classical composition, proudly highlighted by the family crest in the central pediment.

BREMEN-BURGLESUM
Lesumbroker Landstrasse 110 (1770) Recent additions have unfortunately diminished the purity and elegance of this early Neo-classical country house constructed for the physician Dr C. von Ransfeld.

Haus Lesmona, Am hohen Ufer 60–62 (after 1814) A design of restrained elegance, with a variation on the portico theme in the form of a column-supported balcony emphasizing the entrance.

BREMEN-VEGESACK
Vegesack became famous as Germany's first man-made harbour, created in the early 17c. to replace that of Bremen. The natural beauty of its countryside, however, especially the hilly banks of the river Weser, attracted wealthy Bremen merchants and bankers to build their villas. The most impressive was the **house of Senator Fritze** (1827). Although small in size, it achieved monumental grandeur by a raised Ionic portico with a majestic flight of steps leading up to it. This picturesque scene of classical villas has regrettably vanished.

Brunswick

In the late 18c. Brunswick was just emerging from a severe period of retrenchment, and architectural activity was at a very low ebb. However, thanks to the cautious and prudent rule of Duke Carl Wilhelm Friedrich (1780–1806), 'a tall military-looking man' trained in Prussia, conditions improved and in the last decade of the 18c. the duke was able to put into effect two major improvement schemes – the architectural embellishment of the town and the transformation of the ramparts into parks and residential areas.

The town scheme was successfully inaugurated in 1797 when the Berlin publisher Friedrich Vieweg was persuaded to settle in Brunswick with the promise of a prominent site in the Burgplatz for his publishing house, the Vieweg House. Immediately next to it Baron von Veltheim-Derstedt commissioned a grand town palace, also actively supported by the duke. Except for a town residence for his fourth son, the duke's own projects were for public buildings: a museum-cum-academy and an observatory, both for economic reasons utilizing existing structures.

The most ambitious scheme of all was that for the ramparts. The duke soon realized that the task was far beyond the capacity of *Christian G. Langwagen* (1753–1805), who had been appointed architect in 1782 and since 1785 had been court architect and head of the building department. A combination of fortunate circumstances led to the appointment in 1803 of *Peter Joseph Krahe* (1758–1840), recommended by Vieweg

165 Ernst Wilhelm Horn: Council Chamber, Brunswick, 1764.

and his Berlin architect David Gilly. Krahe, who had been working in Koblenz, designed an impressive Neo-classical layout with a succession of grand avenues punctuated and linked by spaces of varying shape forming a picturesque ensemble encircling the old town. Work was abruptly stopped in 1806 by the French invasion. The monumental rampart scheme was resumed under Krahe's direction in 1815 and successfully completed but none of Krahe's imposing projects for embellishing the centre of the town – the Von Hontheim Palais, the Prinzenpalais, the museum-cum-academy or the observatory – was realized. Thus Brunswick was deprived of what would have been some of its most striking Neo-classical buildings, of which the Vieweg House is a powerful reminder. Their importance warrants their inclusion as projects in this gazetteer.

Other architects working in Brunswick between 1750 and 1850 were *Karl Christian Wilhelm Fleischer* (1727–97), court architect from 1766; *Ernst Wilhelm Horn* (1732/3–1812), inspector of public buildings; *Karl Wilhelm von Gebhardi* (1738–1809), court administrator and head of the building department 1771–82; *Heinrich Ludwig Rothermund* (1753?–1833), a building official with a varied private practice; and the gifted *Carl Theodor Ottmer* (1800–1843), who succeeded his teacher Krahe as court architect 1829–43, and is best remembered for the Residenz Schloss, which he rebuilt after a fire in 1830!

Major buildings

Herzogliche Kammer/Council Chamber (1764, *Horn*) A foretaste of Neo-classicism in Brunswick. A giant order on a rusticated ground floor firmly controls the façade; a pediment adorned with the ducal arms (by *J.H. Peters* and *J.H. Oden*) proclaims the building's official purpose.

38
39 **Schloss Richmond** (1769, *Fleischer?*) A surprising and unique example of early French classicism in Brunswick, commissioned by Crown Princess Augusta, the daughter of Frederick, Prince of Wales. The plan consists of a square placed diagonally, with circular rooms at the ends of the diagonal axis – to the south the entrance hall and to the north a circular Gartensaal. Between them is an elegant top-lit oval banqueting room, to which paired pilasters alternating with large grisaille roundels of scenes from Greek mythology give a certain Adam flavour. The entrance hall still shows the gaiety and frivolity of Rococo decoration, although restrained by a classical framework. These three rooms rise the full height of the building. Flanking the banqueting hall, two-storeyed ranges face outward, providing a surprising number of private apartments on an intimate scale.

The exterior is marked by a crisp pilaster order, above which a balustrade concealed the roof and its lantern. The present lantern, designed by *Langwagen* to improve the lighting of the oval hall, is more prominent than the original.

166 Attributed to Karl Christian Wilhelm Fleischer: entrance hall of Schloss Richmond, Brunswick, 1769.

Outbuildings, with mansard roofs, look earlier but are actually a later addition, also by *Langwagen*.

Foundling Hospital (1785, *Fleischer*) A plain building distinguished only by a central pediment.

Residenz Schloss, **Graue Hof** (1784–8, *Langwagen*) Langwagen sympathetically added a new *corps de logis* to the Baroque Schloss. His work was remodelled internally in 1809–12, and destroyed by fire in 1830. Langwagen also rebuilt the palace mews, or **Ackerhof**, which survived and was in use up to the war.

Landschaftsgebäude/Chamber of Deputies (1794–9, *Langwagen*) A powerful early application of Neo-classicism to a public building, making full use of the impact of a monumental Ionic portico. After heavy bombing, the portico survives as an impressive ruin.

168 David Gilly: Vieweg House, Brunswick, 1800–7.

167 Christian Langwagen: Chamber of Deputies, Brunswick, 1794–9.

45 **Vieweg House** (1800–1807, *David Gilly*) As if following a timetable, at the dawn of the new century Brunswick moved into the limelight of German Neo-classicism with one of the most remarkable houses of the period. The building, for the publisher Vieweg, combined offices and private dwellings, and occupied a prestigious but awkward site in the centre of the medieval town, with a narrower façade to the Burgplatz and a longer facade to Vor der Burg, slightly at an angle, with a courtyard behind. Each façade is subtly individual, yet they combine to create a monumental effect. The nine-bay Burgplatz front is given a powerful horizontal accent by a Paestum-like Doric portico, while the thirteen-bay side elevation has a vertical emphasis provided by a delicately modelled frontispiece, which, with its crisp, unorthodox Soanian character, is the most compelling feature of the entire design. The two façades are unified by a band of Greek key running below the first floor windows. Although this is David Gilly's best known building, it is also unlike anything else in his *oeuvre*. The design may well have been influenced by his son *Friedrich Gilly* or by *Gentz*; its similarities to *Krahe's* design for the adjacent Palais von Veltheim-Derstedt (unbuilt: see below) and to his Villa Salve Hospes make one suspect the Brunswick architect's involvement.

Prinzenpalais (designed 1804, *Krahe*) Commissioned by the duke for his favourite son, Friedrich Wilhelm, on part of the newly dismantled ramparts. The building had risen to a height of three storeys when the French invaded Brunswick and work stopped. It was to have had a remarkable projecting centre crowned by a pediment, in a reductivist cubic style similar to that of the centre of the Vieweg House, but even more rigorous with an exotic Egyptian-style entrance gate. Acanthus decorations carefully placed on the wings stressed the palace's more festive character. Krahe no doubt considered this his most important work to date, for he personally paid for the building's protection when the French besieged Brunswick. In 1814 he sadly had to witness the demolition of its unfinished shell.

Observatory, project (*c.*1804–5, *Krahe*) By building an observatory the duke hoped to attract the famous astronomer Carl Friedrich Gauss to Brunswick in furtherance of his plan to make his court a centre of learning. Supported by expert advice, Krahe converted a former powder magazine and produced what appeared to be a completely new building. The remarkable geometric design comprised a prismatic ground-floor block supporting an oval and two smaller circular cylindrical structures, the first with a Corinthian pilaster order, the latter with domes like pepperpots. Again the French invasion terminated the project.

Gallery, museum and academy of arts, projects (*c.*1804–5, *Krahe*) An enlightened early scheme to establish a public museum and art academy, by concentrating all the ducal collections in the Paulinenkloster where part had been housed since 1764. The convent was to be rebuilt and enlarged, and the importance of the proposal is reflected by the fact that no fewer than three different projects were prepared. The most striking is the first, owing much to Gentz's Berlin Mint, with a contrast between a strongly rusticated ground floor and plain surfaces above, accented by a monumental figurative frieze running across and a vast thermal window filling the pediment. The two other projects, though on a larger scale, were less remarkable. None was realized.

Von Veltheim-Derstedt Palais, project (1805, *Krahe*) This ambitiously large palace, which remained unbuilt, would have been a remarkable neighbour for the Vieweg House in the Burgplatz. It was to be the same height, and to be linked visually by a similar Greek key frieze at first-floor level. The compelling simplicity of the forms contrasted with linear and carved decoration of Roman and Renaissance origin applied sparingly like jewellery to the façade. The focus was again on a bold central feature, this time with a Palladian window and a curious segmental pediment.

Residenz Schloss, Graue Hof, interior remodelling (1809–12, *Krahe*) After years of inactivity during the French occupation Krahe was asked to modernize the Schloss as a second residence for King Jérôme. It was a challenging task, involving the remodelling of forty rooms in Langwagen's range and in the north wing. Together with *Louis Catel*, Krahe created some outstanding Empire interiors. Destroyed by fire in 1830, they may still be appreciated from surviving drawings.

Reithaus/Riding School (1816) and **Kanzleigebäude/Chancellery** (1826) Two later buildings by *Krahe*, in a less original style than his early work. Both were destroyed by fire – the Chancellery in 1830, the Riding School in 1865.

95 **Residenz Schloss** (1831–8, *Ottmer*) After the fire of
96 1830 Krahe had hoped for the commission to rebuild the palace, but he was passed over in favour of the younger architect and his more fashionable academic classicism. The twenty-nine-year-old Ottmer produced a reversed Baroque plan, with a central range and two wings extending to the rear, rather than forming a courtyard in front. That the palace now faced onto a public square reflected the changed role of German rulers. Curved Doric colonnades were planned to extend from the palace and embrace the square, but never realized. Above a rusticated ground floor a giant Corinthian order encircled the building in the form of pilasters and, at the corners and in the centre of the façade, as detached colonnades. The projecting centre, crowned by a quadriga, was balanced on the garden side by a domed rotunda.

Ottmer's love of circular, apsed and oval rooms left its mark on the plan, as did Krahe's teaching, immediately felt in the majestic entrance and staircase hall in the rotunda with its massive arches, impressive Greek Doric columns and crisp Greek decoration. From here the two arms of a semicircular staircase formed a dignified ascent to the reception rooms above.

After another disastrous fire in 1869 the Schloss was again rebuilt, but this time significantly Ottmer's design was retained. It is the shame of Brunswick that the war-damaged palace was pulled down in 1960 to make way for a department store. At least the portico has been preserved.

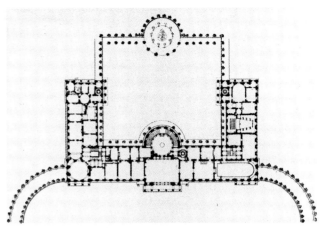

169 Karl Theodor Ottmer: plan of the Residenz Schloss, Brunswick, 1831–8.

Theaterverwaltung und Kulissenhaus (*c*.1840, *Ottmer*) Offices designed as an annex to the theatre. The three-storeyed building formed a visual accent in the Wilhelmstrasse, with a picturesque domed rotunda at the corner articulated by giant Corinthian pilasters and crowned by a balustraded cornice.

170 Karl Theodor Ottmer: Theaterverwaltung, Brunswick, *c*.1840.

Railway Station (1843–5, *Ottmer*) The architect's last 171 building, replacing an earlier Neo-Gothic station. The entrance is marked by an imposing triumphal arch. The side entrance, behind, is composed as a monumental tholos with a splendid coffered dome supported on tall Corinthian columns. Converted in 1963–6 into a bank's head office.

171 Karl Theodor Ottmer: Railway station, Brunswick, 1843–5.

Other domestic architecture in the town centre

In the last quarter of the 18c. rich courtiers and wealthy merchants commissioned larger town houses, some with palatial interiors. Most were in a transitional style based on French classicism with Baroque reminiscences, exemplified by **Eiermarkt 7** (1779, *Fleischer*), *Langwagen's* **Palais von Veltheim** at Damm 16 (1786) and above all his **Palais Riedsel**, Augusttorplatz 1 (1786–9). A purer and more advanced classicism was displayed by the **Gravenhorstsche Palais**, Kalttreppeln 22 (1784, *Gebhardi*). There were remarkable interiors in **Sack 1** (*c*.1780) and **Hagenmarkt 13** (remodelled in 1787 for the courtier von Sierstopff). The house opposite the Vieweg House, **Vor der Burg 2–4** (*c*.1802, *Rothermund*), is built on a similar scale; its less original Neo-classicism provides a foil for its remarkable neighbour.

Ramparts development

Brunswick's greatest urban achievement was undoubtedly the transformation of its ramparts into a green belt of Elysian scenes embracing the town. By 1803, when *Krahe* was appointed, three great parks had already been envisaged, guaranteeing a certain grandeur for the project. The most eminent was planned by the duchess herself as an English garden to be formed out of a vast plot of land in the east; another in the south was intended for the Villa Krause (known as the Villa Salve Hospes), and a third in the north-west for the Villa Bierbaum. Between these established points Krahe laid

out avenues, wherever possible straight, linking an amazing ensemble of crescents, ovals, circuses, triangles and squares. His scheme was started in 1804, shortly before the French occupation, and completed afterwards (1815–23).

As a grand entrance to the town from the south, the area of the Baroque **Augusttor** was laid out in 1804–6. On the model of the Piazza del Popolo in Rome, a semicircular open space was created from which three streets radiated – two leading left and right to the circumferential roads, and one straight ahead to the Augustplatz. The approach, by a bridge across the surviving water moat, was flanked by a pair of massive cubic buildings comprising guard house and tollhouse; the new gate itself was connected by elegant curved railings echoing the crescent shape beyond. These two buildings were designed in a vigorous Revolutionary geometric style that proclaimed their custodial function, much like Soane's lodges at Langley Park, Norfolk (1784–6). The most remarkable structure at the Augusttor, however, was the **Neue Hauptwache**, a clever conversion of the old Baroque gate into a guard house and prison which had in fact dictated the entire layout. Once the earthen ramparts that abutted it were removed, it became freestanding, and it now formed one corner of the Augusttorplatz, to the west of the main axis leading to the Augustplatz. Its eastern face, towards the street, was given a façade with a monumental Paestum Doric portico set in front of archaically plain walls, decorated with trophies of arms to indicate this side's function as a guard house. On the west side, blank walls relieved only by three deeply recessed arches were identified as those of the prison by carved stone chains.

This grand Neo-classical square was sadly remodelled by modern planners to become the Kennedy Platz, and the portico alone of the Hauptwache survives, now set as a romantic ruin in the Bürger Park.

174 Peter Joseph Krahe: the Steintor, Brunswick, 1804–6.

172 Peter Joseph Krahe: Neue Hauptwache, Brunswick, 1804–6.

173 Peter Joseph Krahe: drawing of the rear elevation of the Neue Hauptwache, Brunswick, 1804–6.

Some of the lesser of the seven gates, such as the **Steintor**, **Fallersleben Tor** and **Wendentor**, survive to give an idea of the scheme's former splendour, as does the layout of the green belt; but the **Löwenwall**, *Krahe's* final feat of grandiose planning, an elegant oval with an austere obelisk in the centre designed as a war memorial, has now been ruthlessly isolated north-east of the former Augusttor by modern rebuilding.

Domestic architecture obviously flourished most in the newly landscaped ramparts. Although initially private builders had to be encouraged, once the planting had become established the area was fashionable, and an official map of 1822 could list 76 properties. The scheme was carefully supervised by *Krahe* and each design had to be approved by the duke, who as a rule provided the building material. The first houses were built in the north-west, near the Petritor and Wilhelmtor. Of these the largest and most impressive was the **Villa Bierbaum**, Inselwall (1805, *Rothermund*). Less prestigious were the **house of H.W. Cole**, an English merchant (1803–5, *Rothermund?*), later occupied by the architect Ottmer and sadly demolished in 1960, and the **house of A.F. von Löhneysen**, a courtier (1804–6). Some of the villas were merely summer retreats, single-storeyed *Gartenhäuser* dotted about in a picturesque fashion like little temples, but often of an imposing nature, such as those built by *Krahe* for Wilmerding and Haeckel. Krahe had designed five villas specifically as part of the layout of the ramparts before the French occupation; only three were built, including the Hans Opitz and Hans Schuster-Jorn, but of those only one – the Villa Salve Hospes – survives.

Wilmerding's Gartenhaus (1804, *Krahe*) The façade's 175 on the Wolfenbüttler Allee, though only three bays wide, displayed a monumental recessed arch containing the entrance door and a lunette window above. At the rear, the house opened to the garden through a central arcade. The most remarkable feature of the interior was the domed entrance rotunda, of crisp geometric perfection. Demolished in 1886.

Haeckel'sche Gartenhaus, Theaterwall 19 (1805, *Krahe*) A pavilion-like house with a façade marked by two full-height Tuscan columns screening a vestibule. The two-storeyed nature of the building was revealed only at the back. The villa was built on the north side of the ducal park, and was taken over by the duke in 1832.

175 Peter Joseph Krahe: Gartenhaus Wilmerding, Brunswick, 1804.

176 Peter Joseph Krahe: entrance hall of the Villa Salve Hospes, Brunswick, 1805–8.

Villa Salve Hospes (1805–8, *Krahe*) Designed for the wealthy merchant D.W. Krause, this villa sums up to perfection the originality of style achieved by Krahe and his free handling of the classical formula. Its inspiration is both Palladian and Parisian, with a central block and service wings framing a forecourt. It is in fact both a country house and a town house, situated at the edge of town and opening at the front to a formal urban vista and at the back to an informal prospect of the country. Standing to the west of the Augusttor, it was carefully conceived as the first urban incident on the western axis, with a square in front linked via an avenue to the Augusttorplatz. It is set back from the street, and its design suggests a monumental gateway. On each façade the centre projects vigorously from a severely unadorned windowed block, in a free reworking of the triumphal arch motif (wider on the garden front), and bears the building's only decoration, a powerful blend of Greek, Roman and Cinquecento elements. Also on both fronts a ramp-like arrangement of steps leads up in ceremonial fashion recalling Revolutionary ideas. The villa takes its name from the inscription over the entrance door, 'SALVE HOSPES' ('Welcome, guest'), in the position at first designated for a sculptured frieze inspired by Gentz's Berlin Mint. The most dramatic use of Revolutionary features is in the Durand-like arcades of baseless Doric columns which front the stables.

The main feature of the interior is, as suggested on the exterior, a domed circular entrance hall rising the full height of the building, with a gallery at first floor level giving access to the flanking rooms. Its exquisite decoration, richer than originally planned, is as crisply carved and powerful as on the exterior.

The villa has since 1927 belonged to the town, and is now used as an exhibition gallery.

Haus Opitz, Petritorwall 31 (1804–6, *Krahe*) The first of the larger houses with flanking outbuildings. The façade was marked only by a large thermal window over the entrance, and depended for its grandeur on the simplicity and massing of its forms. Demolished.

Haus Schuster-Jorn (1804–5, *Krahe*) Two houses combined into a single design with the same compelling simplicity as in the Haus Opitz. A variation on the Palladian motif was used here to mark the entrance.

Less spectacular, but expressed in the same impressive geometrical language, are *Krahe's* two later villas, the **Villa Amsberg**, Friedrich Wilhelm Platz 3 (1827), now the Marcard Bank, and the exactly contemporary house at **Wendentorwall 7**.

From the 1830s onwards the ramparts area was rapidly built up under the supervision of Krahe's successor, *Ottmer*. Several of the villas he designed survive, showing him as a gifted late classicist. In his houses he realized a fluency and freedom in the classical language, blending Krahe's massiveness and his fondness for heavy ornament sparingly deployed with Schinkel's subtle manipulation of plain surfaces enhanced by finely carved decorations. In the **Villa Bülow**, Cellerstrasse 1 (1839), tower-like projections at the corners contrast with crowded elevations on the long north and south fronts where closely-set windows are arcaded on the ground floor and tightly framed within a pilastrade above. The villa now houses the Georg Eckert Institute. The villa at **Wilhelmtorwall 29** (1841) has massive tower-like end bays framing a recessed centre with an applied giant triple arcade. Other examples of Ottmer's villa architecture are **Wendentorwall 17** (1840), and almost certainly **Hohetorwall 16** where the rich, heavy acanthus scroll decoration in the pediment is reminiscent of Krahe's ornament.

In the work of *Ebeling*, the classical tradition was carried on into the 1860s and 1870s. Fine examples are **Löwentorwall 8** (1864) and **Theaterwall 18** (1867).

177 Karl Theodor Ottmer: Wilhelmtorwall 29, Brunswick, 1841.

Wolfenbüttel-Halchter

Gutshof Wätjen (*c.*1820, *Krahe*) An unpretentious stuccoed farmhouse with a pedimented frontispiece as its main feature. Inside is an oval entrance hall, a simplified but elegant variant of the one in the Villa Salve Hospes.

Coburg

Formerly the residence of the dukes of Saxe-Coburg-Gotha, Coburg gained importance during the 17c. and 18c. and was from 1826 to 1918 joint capital with Gotha. It is now part of Bavaria.

Schloss Ehrenburg, alterations (1811–15, *Schinkel*, executed 1812–40 by *André Maria Renié*) Shortly after his accession Duke Ernst of Saxe-Coburg decided to enlarge and modernize the 16c. Schloss. The whole of the exterior was encased in a Neo-Gothic style, carried out by Renié, a pupil of Vaudoyer and Percier. The Silberbau Wing is a range of 1623 by Giovanni Bonalino substantially enlarged by Schinkel, with a façade in a free Italian style. Neo-classical interiors were provided for the private apartments of the ducal family, together with a splendid Marble Hall and Throne Room with Corinthian columns set off by red velvet hangings.

Landestheater (1837–40, *Karl Balthasar Harres*) Built in a simple classical style. Foyer and auditorium retain their original decoration.

Bürglass Schlösschen (*c.*1800) Good Neo-classical domestic architecture.

Cologne

The town's Roman origin and medieval growth shaped its structure in a way that is still evident today. Though an archiepiscopal seat, Cologne was never the residence of an Elector, and consequently it had no single unifying influence or imposing buildings. A stronghold of the Gothic style, it can show only a few Neo-classical buildings.

After the French occupation (1794–1814) the Prussians took over. Architecturally, this change of rule found an expression in the erection of administrative buildings. Though supervised by Berlin, the independent-minded citizens of Cologne tried to retain their architectural freedom. The architects in charge were *Johann Peter Weyer* (1794–1864) and *Matthäus Biercher* (1797–1869).

Appelationsgericht/Appeal Court (1824–6, *Weyer*) The design, carried out despite opposition from Berlin, was influenced by the remodelled Palais Bourbon in Paris: D-shaped in plan, it consisted of a crescent linked to an arcaded front range by five two-storeyed structures.

Regierungsgebäude/Regional Government Offices (1830–32, *Biercher*) A long tripartite building with a taller central section featuring a modest Tuscan portico. Built rapidly with a minimum of interference from Berlin, this was nevertheless one of the more important examples of the Schinkel style in the Rhineland. In 1912 the two-storeyed wings were raised to the height of the central block.

Theatre (1827–9, *Biercher*) Built seemingly without consulting Berlin. An unpretentious building with a pedimented façade and giant Corinthian pilasters above the ground floor, its purpose proclaimed by the inscription 'Ludimus Effigiem Vitae' ('we act the image of life') high up. Destroyed in 1859 by a spectacular fire.

178 Johann Heinrich Strack: Zivil kasino, Cologne, 1831–2.

179 C.F. Busse: guard house in the Heumarkt, Cologne, 1841–2.

180 C.F. Busse: the three guard houses, Cologne, 1841–2. Top: Waidmarkt; centre, Zeughaus; bottom, Heumarkt.

Zivilkasino/Assembly Rooms, Augustinerplatz 7 (1831–2, *Johann Heinrich Strack*, executed by *Biercher*) The Berlin architect's design was carried out with several damaging modifications. The three-storeyed building is rusticated on the exterior, with the centre emphasized by a simple Tuscan portico, similar to that of the Government Offices. Inside, it was particularly noted for a double-height banqueting hall with a surrounding gallery supported by columns, faintly resembling Schinkel's Blaue Saal in the Berlin Schauspielhaus. Demolished in 1938.

Guard houses (1841–2, *C.F. Busse*) The last buildings approved by Schinkel in the Rhineland. New plans were prepared by Busse after Berlin's rejection of the original designs by the Cologne architect *Major Schuberth*. The Hauptwache in the **Heumarkt** is an impressive single-storeyed building in the manner of Schinkel with a deep arcaded wall filled by windows and doors surmounted by a heavy cornice with Prussian eagles on the four corners. The **Zeughaus** (Arsenal) Wache was similar but two-storeyed. It was re-erected after bombing. That in the **Waidmarkt** is the smallest of the three. Its more conventional character, with a pedimented centrepiece, suggests an adaption of *Schuberth's* original design.

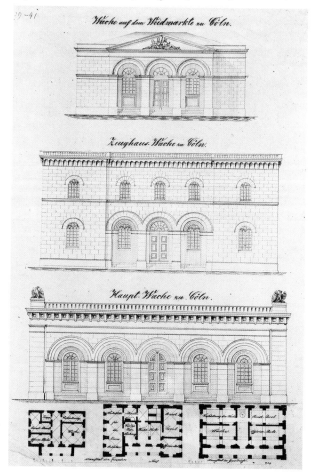

Darmstadt

Like so many other capitals of small German states in the 18c. and 19c., Darmstadt was entirely dependent on a court. The town grew up around the moated 14c. castle of the counts of Hesse-Darmstadt, who in 1567 had designated this their principal seat. The first major extension was Duke Ernst Ludwig's (1678–1739) Baroque venture of a new town fronting the castle, planned to attract Huguenot settlers. They failed to come, and only parts of the plan were executed, yet it determined all future town expansion. Under Ludwig IX (1768–90), a dedicated soldier, Darmstadt could boast the largest barracks in Europe – one of the few extravagances of the economical duke, who successfully restored the finances of the state. His wife, Caroline of the Palatinate, made Darmstadt a cultural centre attracting such people as Herder, Klopstock and Goethe. While her daughters were married off to leading courts of Europe (Berlin, St Petersburg, Weimar, Karlsruhe) her son Ludwig X – later Grand Duke Ludwig I (1790–1830) – a much loved and enlightened ruler, and as musical as his mother, considerably increased the state's size and power. After Napoleon had made him grand duke in 1806, he and his architect *Georg Moller* (1784–1852), appointed in 1810, ambitiously set out to transform Darmstadt into a modern capital with a variety of new public buildings, streets and squares similar to nearby Karlsruhe, where Moller had been trained under Weinbrenner. Most of Ludwig I's Darmstadt sadly disappeared in the severe bombing of the last war.

Under Ludwig I the administration of the board of works saw several changes. A major reorganization in 1804 left it still under the control of the Treasury. In 1811 it passed under the direct control of the grand duke. Finally in 1819 a new constitution gave some controlling power to the town.

In addition to Moller, four other main architects were active in Neo-classical Darmstadt. *J.M. Schuhknecht* (1729–90) was first appointed in 1764 as court carpenter; in 1770 he became consulting architect, and from 1777 to 1790 he was the official court architect. His major work was the great army Exerzierhaus. His talent was not equal to his position, and his designs for the Kollegienhaus (Government Offices) were rejected. *Johann Helfrich Müller* (1746–1830) began as assistant to Schuhknecht 1774–6; after a spell as Landbaumeister in Giessen he returned to Darmstadt in 1790 and in 1796 was appointed director of building. He was chiefly responsible for the town expansion plan. His most charming and important architectural work was the Prinz Christian Palais. His real interest was physics, and he gained fame as the inventor of one of the first calculators. *Michael Mittermeyer* (1758–1816) appeared on the scene in 1803 and was appointed court architect in 1808, though he was mostly occupied teaching drawing to the grand-ducal family. The conversion of the former barracks into a palace for the crown prince, the Altes Palais, was his major work; he also designed the grand-ducal mews. The last is *Franz Heger* (1792–1836),

a pupil of Moller, who trained abroad on his master's recommendation and then became his assistant. He was mainly concerned with the construction of barracks.

Town extension

Throughout the 18c. several town expansion schemes had been suggested in Darmstadt. Most of them were based on the earlier project for a Huguenot town laid out to the west of the Schloss on a regular grid plan, of which the first range of houses (1696–1701) reached as far as an intended square, the future Luisenplatz. On the north side of this square in 1777–81 new government offices were built (the Kollegienhaus), promoted by the forward-looking chancellor Karl von Moser, who intended them as the first phase of a more ambitious scheme. Moser combined his progressive and ambitious ideas with rational planning: he not only pushed through building laws to secure a generous scale of development, but also called in experts such as the Stuttgart town planner *Christoph von Fischer*. Although nothing further materialized, Moser's vision influenced later plans for the town.

Immediately after his accession in 1790 Ludwig ordered a new urban scheme from the court architect, *Müller*. In preparation, he legalized the expropriation of land (on the Prussian model). Müller suggested a grid of parallel streets on either side of a central axis (the Rheinstrasse), as in the Huguenot plan, but nearly double the size, and punctuated by two squares instead of one. Following Stuttgart practice introduced by Fischer, he divided his layout into lots, which would allow either one large five-bay family house or two smaller houses. Strict regulations governing the height and width of buildings were imposed to achieve architectural unity and also to distinguish between major and minor thoroughfares (three storeys in main streets), while financial incentives, which later included a free site, were introduced to encourage private builders. Within an area extending over 20 blocks, 208 building units were planned. Lack of private funding, however, forced the duke to consider an alternative scheme of using public lotteries to finance the construction of individual houses, which were later known as 'lottery houses'. Only seven houses had been built when Napoleon's first threat to Europe called a halt to the work. Building resumed after the Peace of Campo Formio, but progressed slowly in spite of Darmstadt's rapid growth from 6,700 inhabitants in 1794 to 15,183 in 1815. Economic reasons apart, this slowness was mainly due to a lack of firm architectural leadership. Ludwig, newly created grand duke, dreamed of achieving Parisian grandeur, represented by an inept scheme centred on the Rheinstrasse as a *Via triumphalis*. By now Müller's formal plan was in trouble. Although the Rheinstrasse had been established as the central axis and two-thirds of the street had been built with the Luisenplatz as its grand eastern termination, symmetry no longer prevailed. Instead of developing on either side of the Rheinstrasse, the new town had grown to the south-east.

Moller's first task when he took over in 1810 was thus to tidy up the unplanned expansion. To recreate a

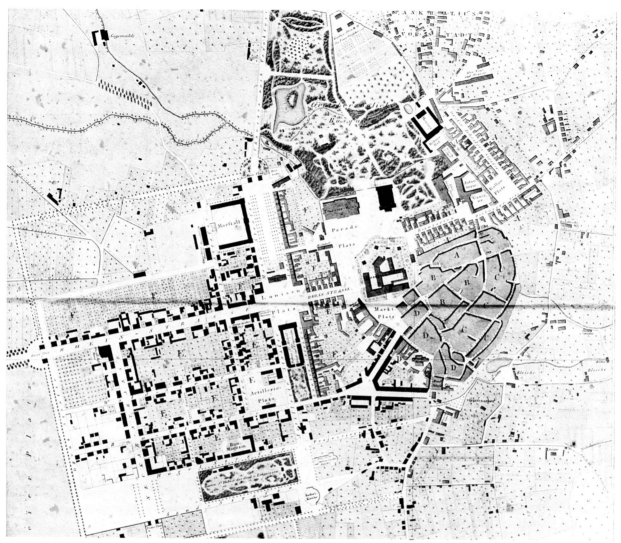

181 Plan of Darmstadt showing the extensions of the 18th and 19th centuries. The Luisenplatz is in the centre; to its north stands the Kollegienhaus and to the west the Rheinstrasse with the new grid of streets to its south. Moller's Neckarstrasse meets the Rheinstrasse at right angles.

balance he introduced on the north-south axis a second avenue, the Neckarstrasse, with a grand southern termination, the Neckartor, for the main approach from the south. Still in line with Müller's original grid plan, Moller created new quarters to the west, but also extended them to the south-west and later to the south-east, divided by new streets, the Hügelstrasse and Sandstrasse, with a square in the south-east corner, the Wilhelminenplatz, which reflected and balanced the Neckartor ensemble. This perfect geometric arrangement was later enclosed by a by-pass to keep out north-south traffic and to facilitate military movements.

To link old and new towns Moller ingeniously modified the formal pattern by creating a picturesque layout of a triangular open space and radiating streets stretching from the new town to its medieval parent, flanked by imposing three-storeyed commercial and office blocks skilfully combined in one uniform design.

Although conditioned by previous schemes, Moller was able to create his own townscape dominated by long impressive vistas. Street compositions such as the Neckarstrasse and Lower Rheinstrasse were his main concern. There he placed Italianate detached houses, varying in width and in the play of arched window and door openings, linked by arched gateways. Moller introduced to Darmstadt façades a more sophisticated, decorative character, and the duke's 'elevation grants' were replaced by 'embellishment grants'. In interior decoration Moller was even more influential in changing the town's standards by providing a pattern for more civilised and elegant living.

From 1819 onwards, with the new constitution leaving less under ducal control, Moller's official involvement changed. However, by then the framework had been created which determined Darmstadt's future development.

Luisenplatz Conceived as part of the ill-fated late-17c. Huguenot town project, the square was only realized over a hundred years later. Its east side, with a generous recess towards the Upper Rheinstrasse, remained for long the only built section (1709–27). The erection of the vast Kollegienhaus on the north side in 1777–81 eventually revived the project and decided the square's dimensions. Its symmetrical layout, however, was a Neo-classical idea, formulated in 1791 by *Müller* who, contrary to the original project, designed the west side to match the east, a scheme gradually executed in 1793–1804. With the creation of the Altes Palais, begun in 1803 on the south side as a counterpart to the Kollegienhaus, the square was successfully completed.

Although built at different times and varying in height and style, the houses of the square presented a consistent appearance, disciplined by the two monumental blocks of the Kollegienhaus and Altes Palais. By far the finest building was the Berlin-influenced Prinz Christian Palais (1793–6) at the south-west corner with the Rheinstrasse. The contemporary building opposite, the **house of Judge Schenk**, was more typical of the chaste Darmstadt tradition with its restrained elevations and its entrance simply marked by giant pilasters. Similar to this was the **house of the Treasury Secretary Zimmermann** (1798, *Johann Heinrich Hill*), in the south side of the square, at the corner of the Wilhelmstrasse, which represented the type of house built by lottery funding. The last house to be built in the square, filling in the north-west corner, opposite the Zimmermann house, was the **house of the courtier Moldenhauer** (1804, by the Mainz architect *G. Schmittermeyer*): it presented a rounded angle to the square, which required official sanction as it compromised the geometric layout, and it was also the first of the houses to offer the refinement of a bold decorative frieze on the exterior. In 1862–4 it was rebuilt on a larger scale for Prince Alexander of Hesse with the addition of an elegant portico to the rounded corner, similar to Moller's Schloss at Wiesbaden. The square gained an emphatic Neo-classical embellishment in the monumental **Victory Column** (28 m high) designed by *Moller* in 1837 and erected in 1841–4 to commemorate Darmstadt's remarkable ruler Ludwig I, portrayed in a bronze statue by *Schwanthaler*.

182 Georg Moller: Victory Column, Darmstadt, erected 1841–4.

the width of the Luisenstrasse. The interior is unpretentious except for the splendid first-floor assembly room with its fine stucco-work. In 1826–31 *Moller* added a north wing (the New Chancellery) towards the Mathildenplatz with an impressive monumental façade in Florentine palazzo style. After severe bombing the building was extensively restored in 1952–4, but without the sculpture which emphasized the entrance.

Major buildings

Kollegienhaus/Government Offices (1777–81, *Cancerin/Scheidel*; 1825–6, *Moller*) The erection of government offices, which would symbolize the new policy of enlightenment, was the idea of the chancellor Karl von Moser. He was actively supported by the crown prince (later Ludwig I), who even contributed his marriage settlement to finance the project. A first design, by Schuhknecht, was rejected, as was the second, by the Hanau architect *F. von Cancerin*. Finally the latter's project was adapted by *Thomas Scheidel*, a builder from Frankfurt, and executed by *Schuhknecht*. Conventional in design, the building surprises by its sheer size. Situated on the north side of the Luisenplatz, it determined the future layout of the square and dictated

Prinz Christian Palais, Rheinstrasse 10 (1793–6), converted into **Ständehaus/Chamber of Deputies** (1832–4, *Moller*) The palace was built for Ludwig IX's brother Prince Carl as a replica of the Darmstadt Embassy in Berlin (1787). The plans were sent from Berlin, and *Müller* was commissioned to supervise their execution. Since the embassy was on a corner, a site was chosen for the palace at the south-west corner of the Luisenplatz and Rheinstrasse, one of the most prominent locations in the newly developed area. The elegant French classical building, emphasized on both fronts by a central giant portico rising from a first-floor balcony, must have been a startling addition to provincial Darmstadt. Due to a quarrel between the duke and the prince, and the latter's move to Neustrelitz, the palace remained unfinished for some time. From 1803 to 1830 it was lived in by Prince Christian. It was then acquired by the newly formed government and altered to serve as a chamber of deputies. In addition to extensive remodelling of the interior, introducing new staircases and entrances, Moller enclosed the inner courtyard of the U-shaped building to provide for a monumental chamber. Elegantly decorated and surrounded on three sides by a gallery of Corinthian columns above amphitheatre seating, the hall was one of Darmstadt's finest Neoclassical interiors. It was destroyed in the war.

Altes Palais (1803, *Mittermeyer*; remodelled 1841–2, *Moller*) Mittermeyer converted the Dragoon Barracks, prominently situated on the Luisenplatz opposite the Kollegienhaus, into a palace for the crown prince, the future Ludwig II. His work involved major internal changes and substantial extensions to the rear wings stretching as far as the Wilhelminenplatz. The resulting building was on a palatial scale but with little architectural merit externally. Moller too concentrated on the interior when Ludwig II, having decided to remain in the palace after his accession, commissioned a remodelling in 1839. By extending Mittermeyer's covered central carriageway with its paired columns à la Vignola into the courtyard, he created an impressive approach to a magnificent new staircase hall. The ascent from a dark vestibule to a bright upper hall, in concept not unlike the famous staircase at Würzburg, produced an effect of surprise and grandeur, the upper hall being adorned with sculptured niches set in a framework of paired Doric pilasters supporting a vaulted ceiling pierced by a skylight. From there one entered the grand banqueting hall placed by Moller over the carriageway, with exquisite Corinthian pilasters round the walls and refined white and gold decoration. Like most of Moller's work in Darmstadt, this was lost in the war.

Marstall/Mews (1810–12, *Mittermeyer* and *M. Spiess*) A vast complex on the west side of the new Mathildenplatz. Rather traditional and severe in style, the building consisted of a range stretching the length of two blocks, with two wings extending out at the rear, and impressed above all by its enormous scale. Towards the square tall domed pavilions, accentuating the centre and extremities of the façade, created a palace-like impression.

Kasino, Rheinstrasse 36 (1812, *Moller*) Moller initially adapted a design he had made earlier for the Kasinogesellschaft in Karlsruhe, a similar learned social club. The Darmstadt society, however, had grander ideas and asked him to add a banqueting and concert hall, which complicated the internal arrangement but produced the building's most charming feature. This consisted of a hall placed diagonally behind two ranges at right angles maximizing the impact of the important corner site in the Rheinstrasse. Inspired by imperial Roman baths, Moller created a sense of hidden spaces with apsidal bays on three sides screened by paired columns, while a monumental window in the wall facing the entrance provided superb views into the country. Externally the

183 Georg Moller: Kasino, Darmstadt, 1812.

hall was indicated by a striking pepperpot rotunda at the junction of the two façades, adorned with Ionic pilasters and delicate friezes – an idea clearly taken from Weinbrenner. Destroyed in the war.

Freimauerloge/Freemasons' Hall, Sandstrasse (1817–20, *Moller*) The design convincingly succeeded in expressing the secrecy generally connected with such societies. The only inviting feature of the windowless façade was a temple-like Ionic portico of monumental proportions. Sphinxes framing the entrance, by *Johann Baptist Scholl*, added to the mysterious character. Inside was a gigantic hall. Although the grand duke had donated the site he seems not to have been involved with the society. In 1870 a dining room was added on the south side to the design of *Ludwig Harres*. After serious war damage the building was extensively restored.

Hoftheater und Opernhaus/Court Theatre and Opera House (1818–20, *Moller*) Opera was the grand duke's ruling passion. Darmstadt had had one of the first opera houses, converted as early as 1710 by Rémy de la Fosse from a riding school, remodelled in 1783 by Schuhknecht, and (following Weimar's example) soon opened to the public. Now the first major public building commissioned by the grand duke from Moller was a theatre and opera house (contemporary with Schinkel's in Berlin and Fischer's in Munich). Moller based his rational design on Gilly's famous project for a National Theatre in Berlin, the functional organization being reflected externally in simply related geometrical shapes. The distribution of the staircases on either side of the entrance hall was (as in Fischer's Munich building) modelled on the classic example of the Odéon in Paris. The impressive Corinthian *porte cochère* was likewise inspired by Parisian examples. The stage exceeded in extent all others of the time in Germany. A disastrous fire in 1871 led to rebuilding in 1873–9 by *Christian Horst*, generally following Moller's design. In 1904 *Fellner* and *Helmer* added a new stage-tower, cleverly expressed by a second pediment in the manner of Schinkel's Schauspielhaus. After severe bombing the Opera House survives as a remarkable ruin awaiting restoration.

Ludwigskirche/Catholic church of St Ludwig (1820–7, *Moller*) In choosing the popular Pantheon formula for his design Moller was inspired perhaps more by the prominent site than by iconographical considerations. Rising majestically from the Riedelsberg – a hill south of the Schloss – the rotunda dominates all views and closes the vista along the Wilhelminenstrasse, one of the principal avenues of the new town. Lack of funds from the Catholic community (emancipated only in 1790) forced Moller to abandon some of his more grandiose ideas. He gave up the flanking school and clergy buildings and stripped the rotunda itself of its splendid Ionic portico and concealing attic storey. The latter unfortunately destroyed the elegance of the design as well as the composition's architectural clarity. Portico and attic had expressed the structural reality of the dome being actually supported on an inner circle of columns rather than on the encircling walls. So limited were the financial resources that the twenty-eight Corinthian columns – copied from the rotunda of S. Stefano – were constructed of brick (plastered only in 1909) while the dome was of wood, painted with *trompe l'oeil* coffering. In 1958–9 after severe war damage the rotunda was substantially rebuilt, using concrete for the dome and omitting the capitals of the columns, to the detriment of Moller's design; at the same time the formerly open oculus was glazed.

Mausoleum on the Rosenhöhe (1826–31, *Moller*) Built on a hill outside Darmstadt for the grand duke's daughter, the Princess Elizabeth, who had died tragically at the age of five. The sober block-like exterior, unadorned except for the columned entrance and the gilded inscription below the pediment, gives no preparation for the spatial surprises within, where a sense of mystery is produced by the placing of a square barrel-vaulted chancel behind a coffered rotunda. The latter contains the tomb, which displays a touching sculpture of a sleeping child by *Rauch* (1827–31). In 1837 the grand duchess's remains were placed with those of her daughter, and she is commemorated by another sculpture by *Rauch*. In 1870, colonnaded wings continuing the Ionic order of the mausoleum were added by *H. Wagner* to contain the tombs of Ludwig I and Prince Emil.

Münze/Mint, Mathildenplatz 12 (1831, *Moller*) A squat two-storeyed structure of uncompromising solidity, in a free Renaissance palazzo style. Its rusticated ground floor with deeply recessed round-arched windows created an appearance of security entirely appropriate to the nature of the building, while the architecture of the first floor was less ponderous, reflecting its use as residential apartments. Demolished.

Prison (1832–4) Several projects were proposed by *Heger*, including a remarkable design which prevented visual contact between prisoners' cells. Finally, however, the authorities decided on a totally new design based on the prison at Giessen, then considered to be exemplary. This was executed after revisions by *Moller* and the result was an uninspired structure of frigid classicism.

Prinz Carl Palais, Wilhelminenstrasse (*c.*1834, *Moller*) Built as a town residence for the younger son of Ludwig II, this is one of Moller's most enchanting designs, with a garden façade centred on a half-rotunda. The layout ingeniously combined official and domestic purposes within a subtle manipulation of space. Arranged around the central top-lit staircase were private apartments on the right and state rooms on the left, linked behind the grand garden bow by a circular library on the ground floor and a great dining room on the first floor. The decorations were more patrician than palatial, reflecting the owner's domestic inclinations. In 1900 the villa was sadly converted into offices for an insurance company and raised in 1927 by an additional storey.

Schloss: remodelling (1842, *Moller*) One of Moller's first tasks in Darmstadt was to produce designs for the ducal seat, a 14c. moated castle encased and vastly extended during Renaissance and Baroque times and famous for its wings by Rémy de la Fosse. His main project (1812) proposed enlarging the building into a unified structure of four ranges round a courtyard, the courtyard to be covered by a magnificent Pantheon dome. Neither this nor an even more ambitious project commissioned by Ludwig III was ever realized, and Moller's work was finally limited to an interior remodelling which provided rooms for the exhibition of the ducal art treasures.

Army buildings

In the late 18c. Darmstadt was famous for its **Exerzierhaus** (1772, *Schuhknecht*), Europe's largest drill hall, designed for the soldier-duke Ludwig IX. This was technically remarkable but stylistically plain, the only notable feature of the façade being a curiously monumental wooden pediment above the entrance (by *Johann Paul Eckhard*) containing the duke's coat of arms and name framed by trophies. The structure survived until 1892 when it made way for a museums complex.

At the beginning of the 19c. military architecture flourished owing to the considerable growth of the armed forces, prompted by the grand duchy's increase in size and power. Most of the buildings were designed by *Heger*. They included **Dragoon Barracks** (1825–7) in the Marienplatz, in a dignified *Rundbogenstil*, with stabling for 425 horses; **Horse Artillery Barracks** (1826) in the Grafenstrasse, on a less prominent site and a more modest scale; the **Army Hospital** (1827) at Alexanderstrasse 27, marked also by functional simplicity grounded in classicism; and finally a totally new block fronting Alexanderstrasse as an enlargement of the old **Ernst Ludwig Barracks** for the infantry (1829–30). None of these buildings survives.

Dieskau (near Halle)

Hoffmann'sche Mausoleum, St Anna (after 1750, *Adam Friedrich Oeser?*) A notable example of early classicism in East Germany. Opening off the south side of the 15c. church, redecorated in the Baroque period, it comprises a monumental coffered apse mysteriously seen through a massive arch supported by paired Ionic columns in the manner of a giant Palladian window. The focal point within is a funerary group, sculpted in a style transitional between Rococo and classicism.

Dresden

The history of Dresden seems characterized by destruction. Seat of the Wettiner dynasty from 1485, it rose to fame as a Renaissance cultural centre when it became an electorate under the Elector Moritz in 1547. Following its destruction during the Thirty Years War, it made a splendid recovery as a Baroque capital of European significance during the reign of Augustus the Strong (1694–1733). During the Seven Years War it suffered heavy bombardment at the hands of Frederick the Great in 1758–60, when 790 houses and 5 churches were destroyed. Again the city recovered, only to undergo the most devastating destruction of all in the Second World War.

Dresden grew round two settlements on both sides of the Elbe. The right bank, though the older part, became known as the Neustadt (new town) due to its extensive rebuilding after a fire in 1685. The left bank is known as the Altstädter Seite (old town side). It is architecturally the more important, containing the principal public buildings.

It was above all Augustus the Strong who made Dresden famous. Under him French architects introduced academic classicism, though of course the Baroque was also strongly represented. The architects who led the trend towards increasing severity were *Zacharias Longuelune* (1699–1748) and *Jean de Bodt* (1670–1745), who was in Dresden from 1728. It was during the last few years of Augustus's reign that French classicism emerged, for example in the Blockhaus by *Longuelune*, a building which served as the Neustädter Wache or guard house from 1755. One of the preliminary designs shows two buildings with stepped pyramids on top, one surmounted by an equestrian statue of Augustus the Strong and the other by a statue of Minerva. The guard house, begun in 1732 to a modified design by Longuelune, contained the seeds of the later so-called 'Lisenen' (pilaster-strip) façades. It was not completed till 1749, by Longuelune's pupil, *Johann Christoph Knöffel* (1686–1752).

Further evidence of the impact of French academic classicism can be seen at the Japanisches Palais (1726–37) by *Pöppelmann, Longuelune, Knöffel* and *De Bodt*. This is a quadrilateral structure extended and rebuilt out of the former Holländisches Palais. Longuelune designed the wing facing the Palaisplatz; the entrance hall is by De Bodt, and the roofs by Pöppelmann. The centrepiece of the façade recalls that of Perrault's east front of the Louvre. The building was adapted in 1782–6 as a museum housing coins, antique sculpture and a library.

Although the Rococo style was dominant under Augustus's son, Augustus II (1733–63), this period also saw the birth and early development of Neo-classicism. Appreciation of classical ideals emerged above all in the circle of Crown Prince Friedrich Christian and his cultured wife Maria Antonia. The leading architects were *Friedrich August Krubsacius* (1718–89) and *Johann Georg Schmid* (1704–74). As early as 1745, in his first book, *Betrachtungen über den Geschmack der Alten in der Baukunst* (Observations on the Taste of the Ancients in Architecture), Krubsacius was investigating the relevance of antique architecture for modern purposes. In his second book, *Ursprung, Wachstum und Verfall der Verzierungen in den schönen Künsten*, 1759 (Origin, Development and Decay of Decoration in the Fine Arts), he openly attacked Baroque architecture. In 1763 he became professor at the newly founded Academy of Arts whose Director, Christian Ludwig von Hagedorn (1713–80), also played an important role in the development of the new style. Other significant figures were the painters Adam Friedrich Oeser (1717–99) and Anton Raphael Mengs (1728–79). Oeser, in Dresden 1739–56, there taught Goethe and also Winckelmann, who arrived in 1754. Mengs's celebrated collection of casts passed into the grand-ducal collection after his death.

Dresden became more important as a centre of Neo-classical theory than of building, the most significant executed work of this period being the Landhaus, designed by Krubsacius. With *Christian Traugott Weinlig* (1739–99), *Christian Friedrich Schuricht* (1753–1832) and *Gottlob Friedrich Thormeyer* (1757–1842) Neo-classicism became established. Weinlig, a pupil of the Rococo architect Julius Heinrich Schwarze, studied in Paris with Blondel and Le Roy, and then in Rome, before returning to Dresden in 1770. Here his best works are his famous Pompeian interiors, e.g. in the Basemann'sche Concert Hall or (still surviving) in the Marcolini Palais. Mainly an interior designer, his only important buildings are the Riding School and the circular Ionic garden temple at Schloss Pillnitz.

While Weinlig worked mainly in the Louis XVI style, Schuricht and Thormeyer belonged more to the school of Gilly and were influenced by French Revolutionary architecture. Thormeyer was involved with the layout of the area of the ramparts, demolished on the orders of Napoleon in 1806. Work only started in 1817, but by 1824 the encircling avenue, punctuated by squares, was completed. Because some of the former bastions of the Altstadt had already been built on (e.g. the Brühlsche Terrasse), it was the Neustadt which benefited most. The most famous element of the new layout, the Bautznerplatz (now Platz der Einheit), is a rond-point with ten radiating avenues similar to the Leipziger Platz in Berlin.

The age of Schinkel is represented architecturally by *Joseph Thürmer* (1789–1833) and by Schuricht and Thormeyer from the older generation. By the 1820s Dresden was again as popular as it had been during the reign of Augustus the Strong.

Other architects active in Dresden were *Christian Friedrich Exner* (1718–98); *Johann Friedrich Knöbel* (1724–92), a pupil of Knöffel; *Johann Daniel Schade* (1730–98); *Gottlob August Hölzer* (1744–1814); and *Johann August Giesel* (1751–1822).

Early classicism

Kreuzkirche (1764–92, *Schmid, Exner* and *Hölzer*) Built in a transitional style, and at the centre of a debate between protagonists of Baroque and of classicism. The plan and interior are due to Schmid. Krubsacius criticized Schmid's design and was called in as adviser in 1765. Exner's exterior is in the style of French academic classicism. The spire, originally won in competition by Exner, was completed in 1788 by Krubsacius's pupil Hölzer.

Prinz Georg Palais (1764–70, *Krubsacius*) Built for the Chevalier de Saxe, illegitimate son of Augustus the Strong. Still reminiscent of French architecture of *c.*1700, but with Louis XVI details. Destroyed in 1945. An English garden, laid out in 1782, included a sunken Doric temple.

Gewandhaus/Drapers' Hall (1768–70, *Knöffel*) The most important public building in Dresden in the period immediately after the Seven Years War, built in the Kreuzstrasse to replace the old Drapers' Hall in the Neumarkt. The entrance façade was conventional, with a pediment over the central projection containing the arms of the city. The ground floor contained a meat market. Converted into a bank in 1925; demolished after the war.

36 **Landhaus/Chamber of Deputies** (1770–76, *Krubsacius*) The first important administrative building in Dresden designed by Krubsacius and the largest of its time in the city. The main front, 77 m long, is inspired by the style of Soufflot and has a severe Tuscan portico. The composition of this elevation with its colossal Ionic pilasters on the third and fourth floors is dense, as is required by its situation in the narrow Landhausstrasse. There is a certain tension in the building between Baroque and classical elements but the fine staircase is still largely Baroque. In 1945 it suffered severe bomb damage but in 1963–7 it was restored as an historical museum.

Palais Max (1742; remodelled 1783 by *Giesel*) Originally built by G. Chiaveri for himself; 'modernized' for Prince Max, brother of the crown prince, with the addition of Ionic demi-columns to the centre projection, swags, and royal arms. The belvedere was used as an observatory. The outstanding Louis XVI interior was a joint effort by Giesel, his brother *Ludwig Giesel, Schuricht* and *Weinlig*. Demolished in 1890. The park was one of Dresden's most famous English gardens.

Villa Sorgenfrei (1786–9) U-shaped building whose architect is unknown. The last Louis XVI villa, similar to the rebuilt Palais Max, with an exceptional belvedere.

184 Friedrich August Krubsacius: Chamber of Deputies, Dresden, 1770–6.

Reithalle/Riding School (1794–6, *Weinlig*) Weinlig's only large building, behind the Zwinger. The severe reliefs over the entrance are clearly derived from interior decoration. The pediment was carved by *Franz Pettrich* (1770–1844).

Neo-classical architecture from Schuricht to Thürmer

Belvedere on the Brühlsche Terrasse (1814, *Schuricht*) Built for Prince Repnin in an arresting French Doric style influenced by Ledoux, replacing a former Rococo structure. In the first design a Pantheon-like rotunda surmounts a Doric colonnade, but in the final version the surmounting feature is a cubic pavilion and the Doric colonnade has become more primitivist or Revolutionary in character. Replaced in 1845 by one designed by *Wolframsdorf*.

Gatehouses in the Grosse Garten (1814, *Thormeyer*) In a similar but less arresting reductive Revolutionary style. Now in ruins and awaiting a proposed restoration.

Country house in Helfenburg (*c.*1814, *Thormeyer* or *Schuricht*) Remodelled in the Revolutionary style as then practised by Gentz, Krahe and Speeth. The inset reliefs are by *Franz Pettrich* with the gods of Greece as the main feature in the middle and allegories of paintings on the left, and of architecture on the right.

Trinitatis Cemetery mortuary and chapel (1815–16, *Thormeyer*)

Calberlasche Zuckersiederei/Calberla Sugar Refinery (1819–20, *Thormeyer*?) One of Dresden's earliest industrial buildings, built for the sugar refiner Wilhelm Calberla on the former 'Sol' bastion, in the form of a group of three blocks set in a quadrant and linked by single-storeyed ranges. The whole composition and the Palladian style are reminiscent of Bath. Facing the Elbe, the refinery bordered the Theaterplatz and later determined its layout. In 1853 it became the Hotel Bellevue. Damaged during the war, it was finally demolished in 1950.

Antonsplatz (1826, *Thormeyer*) An urban development designed in connection with the demolition of the ramparts, consisting of a square flanked on two sides by shops with open arcades on the ground floor. At the top of the square a U-shaped Post Office was added by *A. Geutebrück* and *Thürmer* in 1830–32, successfully connecting the two ranges. In 1846 the fourth side was closed by a Technical School by *G. Heine*, whose Renaissance style destroyed the whole composition. Bombed, and demolished in 1950.

Antonstrasse Also part of the ramparts scheme but now in the Neustadt, running on the northern axis behind the Bautzner Platz. Of the stuccoed detached houses with a Greek key frieze below the eaves in a Schinkelesque manner no. 8 still survives.

Leipziger or **Weissen Tor** (1827–9, *Thormeyer*) A pair of square gatehouses, each with Tuscan porticoes on three sides, forming an ambitious composition inspired by Ledoux's *barrières*. The north-east gate was restored in 1950.

Altstädter Hauptwache/main guard house (1830–32, *Schinkel*, executed by *Thürmer*) The finest Neo-classical building in Dresden. Hexastyle portico in antis in the Erechtheum Ionic order flanked by two lower wings with typically Schinkelesque trabeated treatment. In the pediment on the main front facing the Schloss is a figure of Saxonia by *Joseph Hermann* (1800–1869), a pupil of Thorvaldsen. In the pediment on the other side, facing the theatre, a figure of Mars by *Franz Pettrich*. Restored in 1955–6.

185 Schinkel and Thürmer: Altstädter Hauptwache, Dresden, 1830–2.

Palais Lüttichau (*c.*1830, *Thürmer*) Similar to Weinbrenner's Haus Beck in Karlsruhe (1805). Flanked by two single-storeyed glazed wings, one of which contains the main entrance, projecting at right angles towards the street.

Some of the more outstanding examples of Neo-classical domestic architecture were **Landhausstrasse 18** and **27**, **Pillnitzer Strasse 26**, **Johannesstrasse 23**, **Pirnaische Strasse 50**, **Polierstrasse 19**, and **Gewandhausstrasse 7**.

186 Joseph Thürmer: Palais Luttichau, Dresden, *c.*1830.

Düsseldorf

Since the days of the Great Elector, the avid collector and connoisseur Johann Wilhelm (1690–1716), Düsseldorf has always had the reputation of being a centre for the arts. First selected as a residence by the dukes of Berg (from 1289), it was linked through Johann Wilhelm to the Palatinate and later through the Elector Karl Theodor (1742–99) to Bavaria (1778), which established Düsseldorf's dazzling connection to such cultural centres as Munich, Nymphenburg, Mannheim and Schwetzingen. Though Düsseldorf ceased after Johann Wilhelm's death to be a permanent residence, the Electors continued to have an influence, as may be seen in Karl Theodor's creation of Schloss Jägerhof

(1748–63), the formally planned Karlstadt (1787), and the charming jewel-like Schloss Benrath (1755–69) by *Nicolas de Pigage* (1723–96). When the area of the former ramparts was laid out Düsseldorf received its most charming feature, the Hofgarten, designed by *Maximilian Friedrich Weyhe* (1775–1842). The scheme was conceived and begun under Bavarian rule, in 1801–4, but it was mostly carried out, with further embellishments, when Düsseldorf had become the Grand Duchy of Berg (1806–13). Surprisingly, however, the majestic Champs-Elysées-like Königsallee, 82 m wide and 812 m long, on the eastern edge of the new development was a pre-Napoleonic creation, designed in 1801 and executed in 1802–4 by the Bavarian court architect *Kaspar Anton Huschberger*. The French simply rounded off the design with a corresponding but less spectacular western avenue, the Alleestrasse of 1808 (now Heinrich Heine Allee). Further town planning followed to a design by Vagedes of 1822, modified and ultimately sanctioned by a Prussian decree of 1831.

Düsseldorf's foremost architect in the Neo-classical period was *Adolf von Vagedes* (1777–1842). Others included *Anton Schnitzler* (1796–1873), *Rudolf Wiegmann*, and *Carl Adolf Krüger* (1803–75), working in the Schinkel style. Yet the impressive urban layout with its emphasis on domestic architecture remains the town's only significant architectural contribution to Neo-classicism. No public building of real importance was erected, and projects like the theatre, for which designs were made by *Schinkel* and *Weinbrenner*, the leading architects of the day, were never realized.

93 **Ratinger Tor** (*c.*1810, *Vagedes*) Designed as part of the layout of the Hofgarten. Austere temple structures with an impressive three-sided Doric colonnade inspired by the Propylaea.

Regierungsgebäude/Government Offices (1825, *Schinkel* and *Vagedes*) A former Jesuit monastery with an unpretentious façade, remodelled by Schinkel to express its new function as a government building (his only known work in Düsseldorf). The interiors were by Vagedes.

Gymnasium/School (1828–31) Original design by *Vagedes*, modified by the Berlin board of works. A simple well-proportioned cube, known locally as 'The Box'. Demolished 1904.

Hontheim'sches Palais (early 18c., remodelled between 1806 and 1813 by *Vagedes*) Re-cast as a residence for the Grand Duke of Berg with splendid interiors.

In domestic architecture, examples of *Vagedes's* classicism can still be seen in the Karlstadt: **Bilker Strasse 24–8**, **Bastionstrasse 13–23**, **Hohe Strasse 27–9**, and **Kurze Strasse 3** (all *c.*1820). A more patrician type of house, with rusticated ground floor and giant order, and elongated round-headed windows giving a vertical emphasis, is **Schwanenmarkt 8** (1836), designed by *Schnitzler* in a style still indebted to Vagedes. Later *Schnitzler* followed the more academic Schinkelesque classicism of Berlin, best seen in his houses at **Poststrasse 24–6** and **Südstrasse 1–3** (all after 1843).

187 Adolf von Vagedes: Gymnasium, Düsseldorf, 1828–31.

188 Adolf von Vagedes: stucco decoration in the Hontheim'shes Palais, Düsseldorf, 1806–13.

189 Anton Schnitzler: house at Schwanenmarkt 8, Düsseldorf, 1836.

Elberfeld (Wuppertal)

Wuppertal was created in 1929 by the amalgamation of six communities, among them Barmen and Elberfeld. As part of the Prussian Rhine province in the Neoclassical period, both were subject to sanction from Berlin, and major buildings were designed by the Prussian building inspectors *Adolf von Vagedes* (1777–1842) and *Joseph Peter Cremer* (1785–1863).

Elberfeld, a stronghold of Protestantism and famous for the sheer variety of its reformed sects, possesses a few notable buildings of the period under consideration. Thanks to its growing textile industry, helped by Napoleon's sea blockade in 1806 which stopped foreign imports, the town prospered and expanded rapidly, and in the 1820s could contemplate commissioning a town hall of some grandeur.

Catholic church of St Laurence (1825–35, *Vagedes*) Often mistaken for a work by *Schinkel*. The first design was by Cremer; it was passed over in favour of a more economical design by Vagedes, but the latter's final scheme proved just as expensive, even though the school, planned to balance the vicarage in a grand composition flanking the church, was never built. Vagedes's original design for the façade had a simple geometric character, with a block-like attic above the entrance arch, from which rose short stout spires. The final version presents a more successful and fantastic synthesis of late Roman and late medieval architecture, stressing simplicity of form: a monumental pedimented arch marks the entrance on the south front (begun in 1828), above which tall pointed spires rise on either side. By choosing a hall-church model Vagedes created a vast, impressive interior.

Rathaus/Town Hall (1829–42, *Cremer*) The dominant nature of this building reflects the increasing civic power exercised by some Prussian provincial towns. Italian Quattrocento architecture served as a model to create a majestic three-storeyed building of massive forms with deeply recessed window arcades as the major feature. Bold horizontal lines in mouldings and cornice and crowning balustrade underline the composition's strength. A flight of steps framed by lions with a balcony above marks the entrance. The building's official function is clearly indicated by the Prussian eagle at the top of each corner. Schinkel very much approved of Cremer's achievement, which still survives as one of the foremost buildings of its time in the Rhineland. Most of it is now used by a museum, while the ground floor has unforgivably been turned into shops.

Railway Station (1846–50, *Hauptner* and *Ebeling*) A charming Neo-classical structure overlooking the town from an elevated site. As a focal point in the long façade an elegant Corinthian portico surmounted by a pediment with acroteria rises in the centre on an arcaded

190 Joseph Peter Cremer: Town Hall, Elberfeld, 1829–42.

ground-floor block forming the entrance. The building was altered in 1882 and 1908, and in the 1960s the ground floor was crudely encased by a glass structure from which the classical upper stories sadly rise.

Landgerichtsgebäude/County Court (1848–53, *C.F. Busse*) A splendid combination of Greek and Quattrocento styles, designed by Busse after he had freed himself from the influence of Schinkel. The façade's main feature is a light and airy first-floor loggia, on a firm ground floor base, connecting two temple-like blocks which rise like towers on either side.

Neo-classical domestic architecture was well represented in Elberfeld, and there are still some good examples in Neuenteich, Luisenstrasse, and above all in the fine square surrounding the church of St Laurence.

191 F. Busse: County Court, Elberfeld, 1848–53.

Wuppertal-Barmen

Catholic church of St Anthony (1824–9, *Vagedes*)
Vagedes's first designs, made in 1819, were strongly
criticized by Schinkel, but he eventually triumphed. In
plan the church is a strange combination of basilica and
Greek cross, expressed externally in a picturesque
grouping with an Ionic tetrastyle portico at the west
end and a tower at the east. Extensively restored after
the war.

Hanover

To the British Hanover is best known for the dynastic
alliance by which the Electors of Hanover were also
kings of England from the accession of George I in 1714
until 1837. Yet Hanover, the summer residence of the
dukes of Calenburg (the Guelphs) from 1636, had
already risen to fame as a cultural centre under
George I's parents, Duke Ernst August (1629–98, ascending in 1679) and his celebrated wife Sophie, the
niece of Charles I. The splendour of their reign is
recalled in the vast Baroque gardens of Herrenhausen.
Their descendants as kings of England naturally
focused less on their homeland. This was especially
true of the English-born George III, who left Hanover
to the care of governors, the most famous being Count
Münster. It was due to Münster's influence that the
electorate became a monarchy after the Congress of
Vienna, and he became its *de facto* ruler, although
George IV had appointed his brother, the Duke of
Cambridge, as governor.

Ambitious aspirations to transform Hanover into a
modern capital became apparent with the appointment
in 1816 of the promising young architect *Georg Ludwig
Friedrich Laves* (1788–1864), a nephew of the Kassel
architect Jussow, as royal building inspector. For half a
century he controlled architecture here, during which
time Hanover changed from a small court town into a
large modern city. However, Laves's grand vision was
never realized and his ambitious town-planning
schemes remained incomplete, as did the project for
rebuilding the palace (the Leineschloss). Political insta-
bility partly accounts for this, as does the Duke of
Cambridge's easy-going nature. In 1837, on the accession of Queen Victoria, Hanover became a totally
independent kingdom under Ernst August, the former
Duke of Cumberland, and remained so until 1866. It
was then taken over by Prussia, with the result that
pupils of Schinkel, such as *Hitzig* and *Stier*, came to work
here.

Of *Laves's* extensive town-planning schemes, the best
surviving example is the large oval Waterlooplatz
(1826–32). This contains the Waterloo Column, a
Tuscan column surmounted by a gilt copper figure of
Victory on a globe by *August Hengst. Laves* was also
responsible for the layout of the Railway Station as part
of the north-south axis he attempted to create.

Although many of Laves's projects remained dreams
he designed some of the city's finest public buildings
and created the framework which shaped its townscape.

The tradition was not lost when Hanover was virtually
rebuilt after the last war by *R. Hillebrecht*, who followed
many of Laves's original ideas.

Other architects working in Hanover at the same time
as Laves were *Hermann Humäus*, who introduced the
Rundbogenstil and took over many commissions for
domestic buildings from Laves in the 1830s; and *August
Heinrich Andreae*, who competed with Laves, above all in
the layout of the new Ernst August Stadt to the north.

Leineschloss (1817–35 etc., *Laves*) In 1816 Laves first 97
suggested a vast structure at the top of the Herrenhäuser
Allee, with four ranges round a courtyard in the manner
of the monumental French-orientated schemes of his
student years, with grand porticoes and terminal pavilions accenting long elevations. The project proved far
too ambitious and it was decided to adapt and extend
the old palace along the river Leine, a historic structure
originating in a Minorite monastery secularized in 1533.
For this Laves quickly drew up three different projects in
February–March 1816. *Jussow* was also called in, and
submitted two designs. A final design by Laves of
August–September was approved in December that
year. Although work started immediately in 1817 the
building was never completely finished and was several
times modified during its construction. Most of the work
was completed in 1835.

Illustrative of the complicated building history is the
story of the throne room. After a first design in 1826
Laves submitted four further projects in 1840 (one after
Schinkel); in the meantime, however, *Klenze* had also
been called in. He submitted yet another design, as did
an architect named *J. Molthan*. Finally the throne room
idea was abandoned and a concert hall executed instead
to a new design by Laves (1841–3).

Laves also triumphed over an alternative design by
Klenze for a conservatory added to the river front in
1841–5. This now looks like a Neo-classical addition to
an older building, but the façade had only been
completed some ten years before by Laves to match the
adjoining Kammerflügel, a mid-18c. addition to the
north-west by *Johann Paul Heumann*.

In his design of the main front facing the Leinestrasse
Laves was free to follow his own ideas and apply his
rather dogmatic and academic style marked by crisp
detailing. With a Corinthian portico designed as a porte
cochère cleverly set back in a receding centre, Laves
managed to achieve a remarkably monumental effect in
the narrow street. The portico, completed in 1834, was
enhanced by rich and refined decoration and its
pediment was adorned with the Hanoverian arms. The
south-west wing was never executed, but its absence did
not seriously harm the power of the design.

When the Leineschloss was restored after the war by
Dieter Oesterlen in 1958–61, the missing wing was added
in a modern style, creating a hideous effect. On the other
hand a new square in front was sensitively laid out and
linked to the building by a majestic flight of steps to the
portico.

The interior, which took over forty years to complete,
was mainly designed for official court functions in a rich
late classical/Empire Style, of which the barrel-vaulted

banqueting hall (1835) was an impressive example. (The interior was adapted during the postwar rebuilding to serve the Leineschloss's present function, as the seat of local government.)

The royal family actually lived in a more domestic setting in a palace across the street at no. 29, the **Altes Palais** (1752), which was remodelled and enlarged by incorporating two adjoining houses by *Laves* in 1817–20. At one stage Laves suggested connecting the two residences by a bridge over the Leinestrasse.

192 Georg Ludwig Friedrich Laves: vestibule in the Leineschloss, Hanover, 1817–35.

Gärtnermeister Wohnung/Chief Gardener's House (1817–20, *Laves*) Built as a gardener's house but dominated by an impressive rotunda intended to provide shelter on wet days for visitors to the Grosse Garten and Berggarten. It is situated at the end of the Herrenhäuser Allee, where Laves intended it to serve as a *point de vue* for the vast palace he projected at the beginning of the Allee. The two-storeyed rotunda has a rich interior with a raised circular colonnade of free-standing Corinthian columns below a coffered dome. In 1852 the building was converted into a botanical library.

Laves's own houses (1819–20, 1822–3, *Laves*) The architect's social and professional ambitions are clearly indicated in the two imposing houses he built for himself, the first on a site along the river Ihme, though with a street frontage as well, and the second at Friedrichstrasse 15 next to the Wangenheim Palais. The first (demolished in 1910) was a five-bay three-storeyed house with a handsome D-shaped staircase. In the even more ambitious second house, with a seven-bay frontage, the main staircase led only to the first floor and Laves may have let some of the accommodation.

193 Georg Ludwig Friedrich Laves: house in the Friedrichstrasse, Hanover, built for himself, 1822–3.

Wangenheim Palais (1829–33, 1844, *Laves*) At first the intention was to convert the old palace in the Archivstrasse, and Laves prepared nine different schemes in 1827–8. Then in 1828 it was decided to erect a wholly new building in the Friedrichstrasse, and Laves prepared seven designs of which three incorporated a *cour d'honneur*. An alternative design presented by Georg Moller of Darmstadt forced Laves to make his own design more cubic and to eliminate the *cour d'honneur*. The result is a grave composition in a chaste Schinkelesque style. This was offset within by a splendid staircase of outstanding elegance. In 1844 Laves added to the western side a semicircular winter garden of unusual grandeur, surpassing the one he had just added to the river front of the Schloss. From 1913 until 1956 the building served as the Town Hall. It is now the Ministry of Industry.

194 Georg Ludwig Friedrich Laves: Wangenheim Palais, Hanover, 1829–33.

Mausoleum in the Berggarten, Herrenhausen (1842–7, *Laves*) Placed as the focal point of an avenue of lime trees planted in 1727, this block-like building with its Greek Doric portico in a garden setting recalls Schinkel's of 1810 at Schloss Charlottenburg. Laves made several alternative designs, including one in the Egyptian style. The centrally-planned interior with its shallow dome contains the tomb of George I of England and those of Ernst August (d. 1851) and his wife Friederike of Mecklenburg-Strelitz, both carved by *Rauch*.

Hoftheater/Court Theatre, later **Royal Opera** 99 **House** (1845–52, *Laves*) The last great classical building of Hanover, this occupies the triangular site of a former bastion in the city ramparts. It is also placed in axis with the Leineschloss, in accordance with Laves's town-planning proposals. Laves's first designs of 1843 were for a more classical and Schinkelesque building but in 1844–5 he modified them in a Neo-Renaissance manner which is transitional between Schinkel and Semper. The sumptuously decorated building contained a concert hall as well as a theatre, like Schinkel's Schauspielhaus in Berlin (early schemes for incorporating a ballroom were abandoned). Bombed during the war, it was rebuilt with slight alterations by *W. Kallmorgen* in 1947–51.

195, 196 Georg Ludwig Friedrich Laves: Mausoleum, Hanover, 1842–7. Above: unexecuted design in the Egyptian style. Below: interior of executed building.

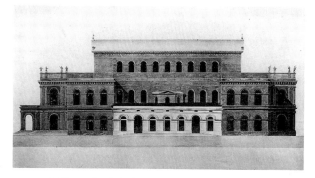

197, 198 Georg Ludwig Friedrich Laves: Royal Opera House, Hanover, 1845–52. Above: drawing of side elevation. Below: foyer.

Heiligendamm

Heiligendamm became known as the 'white town by the sea' on account of the large number of stuccoed classical villas erected here around the 1840s. The most striking building is the *Kasino* (1814–16) by *Carl Theodor Severin* (1763–1836), devised to enhance the young seaside resort. With his design of a large Ionic colonnade in front of a massive block emphasized by an austere giant pediment, Severin created a monumental effect remarkable for the pre-Schinkel era. Reliefs of nereids, tritons and Hygeia decorate the back wall of the colonnade. As indicated by the exterior massing, the main feature within is a central banqueting hall with reception, reading and entertainment rooms in the side wings. The rear of the building was partly rebuilt and extended in 1856.

Homburg vor der Höhe

Up to the First World War Homburg was one of Germany's many small principalities. The legendary Friedrich II of Hesse-Homburg (1633–1708), immortalized in Kleist's play *The Prince of Homburg*, commissioned the impressive Baroque **Schloss** (1680–85), a vast structure round two courtyards which remained uncompleted. Fortune returned with the marriage of Friedrich VI Joseph to Elizabeth of England, a daughter of George III, as her immense dowry allowed extensive alterations. *Georg Moller*, the architect to the prince's ducal relations at Darmstadt, was called in and between 1825 and 1841 he remodelled several of the interiors, and added another storey to the main (east) wing and two storeys to the south corner block. In the east wing Moller designed a majestic staircase with a splendid screen of mauve marble Ionic columns at the top. In the west wing, dining room, library and the enchanting Pompeian Room give an impression of the elegance created by Moller.

Karlsruhe

Karlsruhe is the conception of the ambitious Baroque ruler Margrave Karl Wilhelm of Baden-Durlach (1709–38), who in 1715 laid the foundation stone of his new residence in the midst of his favourite hunting forest. It took the form of an octagonal tower from which thirty-two avenues radiated, of which twenty-three fanned out to the adjoining woods while nine led into the town, built as a small segment of crescents of houses. In 1717, when Karlsruhe became the official capital, the tower was extended into a palace with three wings and people of all denominations were invited to settle in the town, thus necessitating a major expansion from 1765. Baden itself increased in size and power when the margraves of Baden-Durlach rose to ascendancy in the house of Baden in 1771 and above all when Napoleon bribed them with the creation of the Duchy of Baden in 1806 and with vast territorial additions in the south.

Although the first proposals for an urban centre were made in the 1760s and although the need for administrative buildings and a new church had become pressing in the late 1770s, wars and shortages delayed Karlsruhe's architectural evolution.

Friedrich Weinbrenner (1766–1826) returned to his home town in 1797, after formative years in Berlin and above all Italy. From Berlin he had sent in 1791 his first project for the Marktplatz, but from Rome came fantasies of Piranesian grandeur and unrealistic dreams of an ideal Karlsruhe. On his return to Karlsruhe he was appointed Bauinspektor – though as yet without significant commissions. The frustration of these years is reflected in a multitude of designs centred around the new market square and projected public buildings. However, his first commission was a private one, by the Jewish congregation for a synagogue (1797–8). Only after the death of Karlsruhe's Bauinspektor *Jeremias Müller* in 1801 could Weinbrenner set about realizing his urban vision. By the time his projects were completed, in the 1820s, his style seemed somewhat dated, and was criticized by his pupil and successor, *Heinrich Hübsch* (1795–1863), who introduced a new architectural language to Karlsruhe. Yet happily by then Weinbrenner's impressive Neo-classical urban ensemble, forming a triumphal route from the palace to the Ettlinger Tor, punctuated by two varied spaces, the Marktplatz and the Rondellplatz, was secure.

Architecture and planning by Weinbrenner

As early as his plan of 1791 Weinbrenner suggested the placing of a town hall and Protestant church on the west and east sides of a square on the major axis, the Schloss Strasse (now Kaiser Wilhelmstrasse). The layout was finalized in the 1797 plan, which remained the pattern for development over the next twenty-five years. The major cross-axis to the all-important Schloss Strasse was the Lange Strasse (now Kaiser Strasse), forming a screen between the town and palace. From there the Schloss Strasse first opens into the Upper Marktplatz, surrounded by a series of shops and focusing on an allegorical figure of the city of Karlsruhe in the centre. This was later modified and the famous pyramid built instead. The Upper Marktplatz led immediately into the main square with the Protestant church and Town Hall, leaving the central vista to and from the palace open. For both those buildings Weinbrenner suggested very similar designs, and campaniles to form a triangle with the palace tower. At first more sculptural and dense, the designs were later substantially modified so as to achieve greater individual expression, especially in the different towers. The **Rondellplatz**, lined with palatial houses, formed the second highlight of the Schloss Strasse on its way to the Ettlinger Tor, where Weinbrenner placed his own house. This progression of spaces of varying shape was dramatized by a careful massing of the buildings as if part of a single sculptural composition.

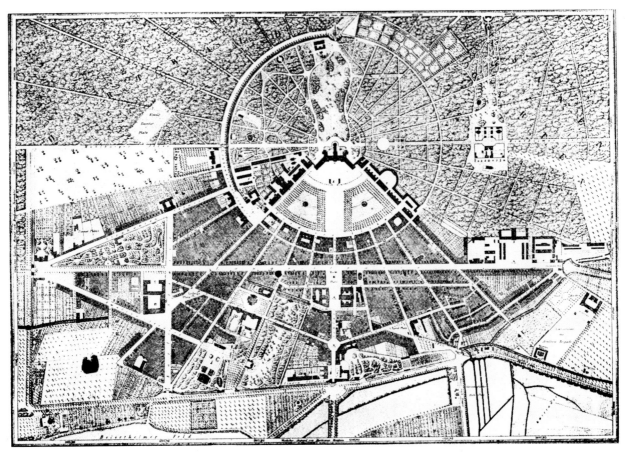

199 Plan of Karlsruhe. The radiating streets and avenues go back to the 1715 plan, but the central axis with its

vistas and squares belongs to Weinbrenner's scheme of 1797.

Synagogue (1797–8) Weinbrenner's earliest building in Karlsruhe, a large complex combining synagogue with schools and apartments for the rabbi, on a prominent but difficult triangular site at the corner of Lange Strasse and Kronenstrasse. The exotic design recalled his fantastic projects sent from Rome: an exterior with Egyptian battered walls, and an interior derived from Roman domestic and early medieval church architecture, decorated in an oriental manner, all grouped around an internal courtyard with a Doric peristyle. Destroyed in 1871.

200 Friedrich Weinbrenner: Synagogue, Karlsruhe, 1797–8.

Ettlinger Tor (1803) A Greek Doric gate inspired 137 ultimately by the Athenian Propylaea and by the Brandenburg Gate in Berlin, which it resembled in its scheme of a main portico flanked by lower colonnaded pavilions set at right angles. The pediment facing the country was filled with a complex composition in which Cybele was surrounded by Mercury and Ceres and children representing science, agriculture and the arts.

Weinbrenner's own house (1803) At right angles to the Ettlinger Tor Weinbrenner built for himself a substantial Palladian villa with a three-bay engaged Greek Doric portico in the centre. Here he ran his celebrated school of architecture. Demolished in 1873.

Markgräfliches Palais/Margrave's Palace (1803– 138 14) An exceptionally sensitive and original urban composition: the wings flanking the Corinthian entrance portico are brought forward at canted angles so as to define the near-octagonal shape of the Rondellplatz, while three-storeyed secondary wings are concealed behind. The two-storeyed centre block contains a magnificent staircase hall with apsed ends screened by pairs of Ionic columns and an elliptical barrel vault decorated in Pompeian style. On the first floor the staircase is flanked by two ballrooms, one facing the square and the other the garden.

233

Weinbrenner also made unexecuted designs for another ambitious palace in the Rondellplatz, an imaginative building with two prominent corner towers, laid out on a pentagonal plan, following in part the lines of the square.

Evangelische Stadtkirche/Protestant church (1806–16) The façade has an impressive hexastyle Corinthian portico, while behind rises a campanile capped by a tall pyramidal spirelet. The Corinthian order is carried over into the interior, where the nave is bordered by giant free-standing columns behind which rise galleries over the aisles.

202 Friedrich Weinbrenner: staircase of the Town Hall, Karlsruhe, 1811–25.

201 Friedrich Weinbrenner: Protestant Church, Karlsruhe, 1806–16.

139 **Katholische Stadtkirche St Stephan/Catholic church of St Stephen** (1808–14) One of the family of Neo-classical churches based on the Pantheon idea. In an early design the rotunda rose from a cube, with a projecting portico and flanking towers, creating a mosque-like effect. The final version shows a successful combination of rotunda and Greek cross plan, with the portico continuing in side colonnades. Inside, the dome is flanked by short side bays with dramatic barrel vaults screened by paired Corinthian columns. The effect of spatial mystery thus produced was destroyed in the post-war rebuilding, when the wooden dome was replaced by reinforced concrete.

Rathaus/Town Hall (1811–25) A Palladian tripartite 136 composition with a five-bay pedimented centrepiece flanked by two five-bay wings with pedimented three-bay terminations. The centre has an Ionic order *in antis*; the pediment above lost its crowded figure sculpture in a recent restoration. A handsome entrance hall lined by free-standing fluted Greek Doric columns in the manner of Gentz leads to the grand staircase, where the columns are unfluted.

Museum (1813–14) Weinbrenner accentuated the 140 corner of Lange Strasse and Ritterstrasse with a startling motif: a three-quarter rotunda, marked by giant Ionic pilasters rising from a first-floor balcony between large round-headed windows, the whole surmounted by an impressive classical frieze. Privately financed by a learned society, this was an ambitious project more like a clubhouse than a museum building. The treatment of the corner later inspired Moller's design for the Schloss in Wiesbaden, and became a popular device in later 19c. urban design. Extended by Hübsch 1835. Demolished in 1918.

Palais der Markgräfin Friedrich (1816–17) An enchanting summer villa with direct access to the garden from the *piano nobile* via external stairs on two fronts. The central pavilion was carried on an open archway treated as a grotto, a romantic idea recalling Bélanger and Ledoux. It contained a Pantheon-like hall with a coffered ceiling. Demolished.

Ständehaus/Chamber of Deputies (1820) Two long façades, three storeys high and articulated by flat pilasters, meet at a right angle which Weinbrenner treats as a projecting rotunda and further marks by round-headed windows. The interiors are in Empire Style, the finest of them being the semi-circular council chamber surrounded by free-standing columns with palm-leaf capitals.

203 Friedrich Weinbrenner: Palais der Markgräfin Friedrich, Karlsruhe, 1816–7.

204, 205 Friedrich Weinbrenner: exterior and council chamber (below) of the Chamber of Deputies, Karlsruhe, 1820.

Münze/Mint (1826) In this his last work, Weinbrenner returned to the Franco-Prussian style of Gentz and Krahe. It is an ambitious building, with a three-bay centre flanked by two four-bay wings. The colonnade of engaged Greek Doric columns on the upper floor suggests the solidity required of a mint. The structure also provided lodgings for the mint director and engraver, and in addition housed the Baudirektion.

206, 207 Friedrich Weinbrenner: exterior and interior of the Mint, Karlsruhe, 1826.

208 Karlsruhe in 1845. In the centre is the Town Hall. The other buildings (beginning top left and going clockwise) are: the Ettlinger Tor, the Ministry of Finance, the Residenz, the Mint, the Durlacher Tor, the Museum, the Protestant Church, the Mühlburger Tor, the Academy, a palace in the Rondellplatz, the Polytechnic, the Ludwigs Tor and Military School, the Catholic Church, and the Chamber of Deputies.

Kassel

'Cassel stands partly at the bottom, partly on the steep ascent, and partly on the summit of an eminence washed by the Fulda. No two parts of a city can be more distinct in external character than the lower and the upper towns. The former is huddled together on the river, at the bottom of the hill; its streets are narrow, dark and confused, the houses consist mostly of a frame of woodwork. . . . The upper town, . . . originally begun by French refugees who brought their arts and industry to Cassel on the revocation of the Edict of Nantes, is light, airy, and elegant, from its style of building as well as from its site.' This is how Kassel appeared in 1825, after the town's decisive architectural evolution.

Seat of the house of Hesse-Kassel since 1277, the town's fame was established under the dynamic Baroque ruler Landgrave Karl (1670–1730), the creator of Kassel's two landmarks, the famous garden of the Karlsaue and the unique cascade of Wilhelmshöhe. But Karl was also a realistic ruler and, in furtherance of the country's industry, he invited the Huguenots to Kassel. To build them a town on the former vineyards above the medieval town outside the ramparts he employed one of their countrymen, *Paul du Ry* (1640–1714). It was not until the reign of his grandson, the Landgrave Friedrich II (1760–85), that the Huguenot town or Oberneustadt was finally linked up with Kassel proper. Like his grandfather, Friedrich II pursued ambitious architectural schemes – with the assistance of *Simon Louis du Ry* (see below), the gifted grandson of Paul du Ry. In the latter half of the 18c. they transformed Kassel into an exemplary modern town, much admired by visitors such as Goethe and Anna Amalia of Weimar. Upper and lower town were ingeniously linked by a scheme which included the Friedrichsplatz, the largest square in Europe at the time, the Königsplatz, a circus with radiating streets, and the Königsstrasse.

An enlightened ruler, inspired by the example of his great-uncle Frederick the Great, Friedrich was a benefactor of charitable institutions as well as a champion of the arts and sciences, ventures which he supported by hiring out a mercenary army of 12,000 men to the British during the North American war. As a patron of public institutions he sponsored many buildings: a museum and library, theatre, opera house, almshouses, hospital and exhibition halls. He was also concerned with major town improvements and introduced a special meat tax to finance the building of roads; sewers and pavements were laid, and finally the custom of driving cattle through the town was terminated.

His son Wilhelm IX (1785–1821), who became the Elector Wilhelm I in 1803, known as the banker of Germany, was parsimonious and disliked opera and ballet, but inherited Friedrich's enthusiasm for architecture. More of a traditional absolutist than his enlightened father, he spent most of his fortune on his own residences. Schloss Wilhelmshöhe and its park (begun by Friedrich) and the extraordinary castellated folly, the Löwenburg, were his principal creations. During the French occupation of 1806–13 Wilhelm went into exile and Kassel became the capital of Jérôme Bonaparte's Kingdom of Westphalia. The most regrettable effect of the French rule was the destruction of the Rennbahn-Paradeplatz ensemble for a parade ground. This was the first of many acts of vandalism towards Du Ry's carefully planned urban layout. Under the Elector Wilhelm II (1821–31) the damage continued with the building-up of the east side of the Friedrichsplatz. Although some individual buildings of importance were created, the great days of Kassel's architecture were over. Development in the later 19c. encroached on the 18c. town, which was finally destroyed by heavy bombing and unfeeling postwar reconstruction.

Several major architects were involved in the creation and transformation of Kassel. Chief among them, as we have seen, was *Simon Louis du Ry* (1726–99), who began in 1756 as building inspector at Wilhelmsthal, the Rococo castle commissioned by Landgrave Wilhelm VIII. After his father's death a year later he became the leading architect of Kassel and was until his own death responsible for all major works. *Heinrich Christoph Jussow* (1754–1825) first trained as a lawyer, then started his architectural career in 1778 as building assistant to Du Ry in the department of public works. Following travels abroad he was back by 1788, when he prepared designs for Wilhelmshöhe. His most important works were all connected with Wilhelmshöhe, but he also designed public buildings in Kassel, some under Jérôme. In 1799 he succeeded Du Ry as court architect. Jérôme also employed *Leo von Klenze*, who designed a theatre north of the palace at Wilhelmshöhe (built in 1808–9) and submitted designs for several other ambitious schemes, and *A.-H.-V. Grandjean de Montigny*, who made alterations and extensions to the Museum Fridericianum. Finally, *Johann Konrad Bromeis* (1788–1854) succeeded Jussow in 1825 as court architect. He was responsible for works at Wilhelmshöhe and public buildings in Kassel, but is best known for the Rotes Palais, Wilhelm II's town palace in the Friedrichsplatz.

Improvements by Simon Louis du Ry, 1763–99

Friedrich II took up his ambitious building schemes in 1763, immediately after the Seven Years War, even though country and people were impoverished. With the decision to demolish the ramparts, which had proved useless during the war, vast opportunities opened up for town improvements and above all for the connection of the Huguenot Oberneustadt with the old town, which had long been desired. Du Ry as court architect was entrusted with the master plan. To link the two he conceived a combination of two squares and a circus in a triangular arrangement which connected the formal plan of the Huguenot town with the irregular medieval one. While the squares were partly inspired by the plans of earlier architects, the circus was novel. By far the most impressive link was provided by the Friedrichsplatz in the west, a vast square forming a monumental bridge to the upper town. As a southern connection the 16c. race course, the Rennbahn, facing the castle was redesigned in conjunction with a new parade ground, laid out on the former castle moat.

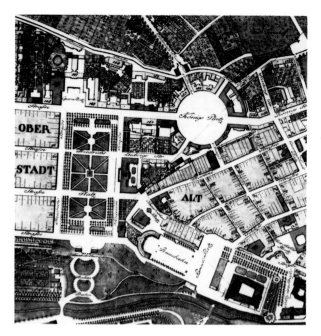

209, 210 The centre of Kassel in about 1803 (left) and the town in 1830 (below). In the earlier plan the basic elements of the classical layout are clearly shown: the circular Königsplatz, the rectangular Friedrichsplatz (laid out as a formal garden) and to the south the old Schloss facing the apsidal-ended Rennbahn and Paradeplatz. Under Jérôme (1806–13) the trees lining the two latter were swept away and the Friedrichsplatz cleared of its garden. At the southern end of the Friedrichsplatz is the Auetor (pl. 213). The Schloss shown on the later plan is in fact the projected Chattenburg (pl. 216) begun in 1818 and never finished.

The most notable of the new buildings are depicted round the border. The upper row is the east side of the Friedrichsplatz (compare pl. 31), consisting of the Palais Jungken, the Rotes Palais (not yet built in the earlier plan), the Museum Fridericianum, the Hofverwaltungsgebäude (also a new building) and the church of St Elisabeth (pl. 212). The rest, going clockwise, are: the Fürstenhaus, Privy Council, military academy, theatre, Auetor, Guards' Barracks (forming three sides of the Kasernenplatz fronting the Königsstrasse), Wilhelmshöhertor, Messhaus, War Department, Ministry of State and Schloss Bellevue.

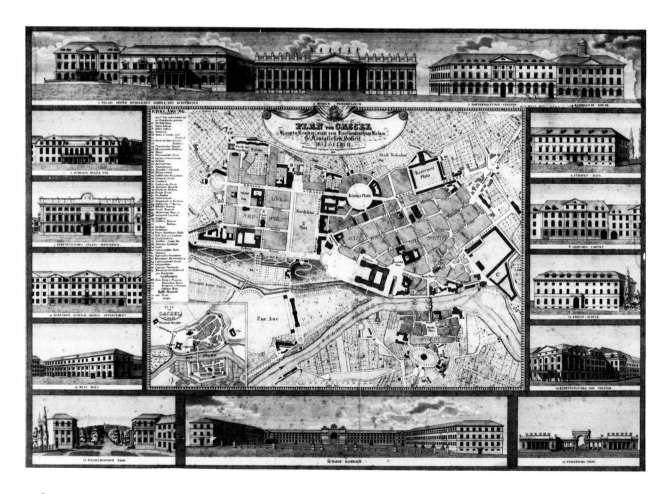

Rennbahn and **Paradeplatz** (1763–mid-1770s) This was the first of Friedrich's urban projects. To provide a magnificent *point de vue* from the castle, and accentuate the apsidal end of the former race course which had been laid out on the pattern of a Roman circus, Du Ry designed an impressive colonnade with a triumphal arch as a central feature. The whole was topped by sculpture by *Johann August Nahl* symbolizing princely and military virtues alternating with trophies. The colonnade itself contained statues of Greek and Roman gods in niches recalling garden statuary but on a monumental scale. The Dioscuri at the castle end and a pair of Roman gladiators and figures with slings flanking the exedra accentuated the classical feel of this arrangement. Avenues of lime trees following the colonnade enclosed this space and served to screen the newly extended Bellevuestrasse to the south, which now connected the castle with the Friedrichsplatz and the Huguenot town. Along the north side arcades – built by Landgrave Karl as part of a project to convert the race course into a fairground – partly hid the medieval houses behind, which Landgrave Friedrich intended to conceal behind false façades. Jérôme Bonaparte destroyed the Rennbahn ensemble by transforming it into a vast drill ground.

Komödienhaus/Theatre, Rennbahn (1773) A rebuilding of a small theatre created in the early 18c. out of a banqueting hall immediately in front of the race course. The simple façade, with many windows and a pedimented centre bay, hardly suggested a theatre except for the unusual number of doors, which were in fact exits. The main entrance was on the side, through the neighbouring arcades built by Landgrave Karl. The size of the interior did not allow large productions. In 1787 the lighting required for an artificial moon set fire to the building, destroying the whole fabric. Du Ry was later asked to design a dummy façade to conceal the resulting vista of medieval houses.

Königsplatz Simultaneously with the Paradeplatz and Rennbahn Du Ry laid out this all-important north-east connection, in the form of an imposing circus from which the Upper Königsstrasse ran westwards as a triumphal route along the edge of the new extension. There it focused on the Königstor, conceived by Du Ry as a triumphal arch for the Wilhelmshöher Allee, the landgrave's new avenue to his palace on the hill. The triumphal character of the Upper Königsstrasse was heightened by the fact that it was both long and straight, whereas the four other streets radiating from the circus, including the Lower Königsstrasse continuing eastwards, were either short or crooked. This combination of one long and four short vistas was highly admired at the time, not only for its appearance but for the echo it produced, 'sounds uttered by a person standing in the centre being repeated six times'.

Except for two houses Du Ry designed the whole circus. Maintaining a uniform impression by equal heights and similar architectural features, he avoided monotony by an individual treatment of the façades, which could differ as much as the **house of Major**

Consens (1770) with its restrained elevation and the **house of the plasterer Brühl** with its extraordinary decorative embellishment verging on the Rococo. The first of the houses to be built was the **Palais Hessen-Rotenburg** at the south corner of Königsstrasse and Königsplatz (1769, *Diede*). As the town house of the Landgrave of Hesse-Rotenburg it was by far the most palatial, with a magnificent staircase hall and Rococo decorations on its façades, of which its shorter one, to the circus, was next to the outstandingly ornate Haus Brühl. Its demolition in 1911 was a serious loss. Two other grand town houses were the **residence of Generallieutnant von Schlieffen** (1772) later famous as the Hôtel Zum König von Preussen, and the house of Major Consens. One whole segment was taken up by the **Post Office** (1771–2), which was as grand as the town houses. So too were the commercial buildings occupying the two remaining segments on the south, whose true function as factories and warehouses was disguised. Their position, on what used to be the town moat, allowed only two-storeyed elevations with a mezzanine instead of the customary three storeys. In spite of all the varying functions and the different heights, Du Ry achieved an appearance of unity, balancing space and architectural volume. He considered this his finest work, and Tischbein's portrait shows him displaying its plans. Later rebuilding without due attention to height wrecked Du Ry's subtle harmony.

Friedrichsplatz (1767–8) An architectural composition of remarkable unity conceived on a grand urban scale, bordered by the Königsstrasse to the north, the Huguenot town to the west, and the natural slopes to the medieval town to the east and the Karlsaue to the south. There had been earlier proposals for a square on this site, such as those by *De Paije* and *Dumont* in their *Plan des villes de Cassel avec ses environs et ses projets* (1760), but not on such a scale – which was made possible by the demolition of the ramparts in 1767. Also unprecedented was the idea of creating a civic forum dominated by a public building rather than a ruler's palace. Sparked off by the Enlightenment ideals of the landgrave, it was Du Ry's masterly handling and compositional strategy which gave the square its grandeur. Building began with the Haus Kopp on the north side and the Palais Jungken on the north-east corner.

Palais Jungken (1767–9) Built for the courtier Generalmajor Friedrich Christian Arnold von Jungken, the palace was generously subsidized by the landgrave to ensure a suitably grandiose structure, with a richer façade towards the square. The dominant feature is a classical frontispiece enriched with rather Rococo decoration. In 1772 the palace was bought, on the orders of the landgrave, for the diets of Hesse, and it was later used by Jérôme as law courts. After the fall of the French, Crown Prince Wilhelm, later Wilhelm II, took up residence and commissioned *Bromeis* to remodel and extend the building. Two ranges were added at the rear, completing a square. Further changes took place when the Rotes Palais was added in 1821.

31 **Museum Fridericianum** (1769–79; altered 1808–10 by *Grandjean de Montigny*, *Klenze* and *Johann Heinrich Wolff*) The controlling feature of the Friedrichsplatz. The building originated with the landgrave's wish to concentrate his collections and library, and even more with his enlightened decision to make them more accessible to the public. According to Du Ry he also chose the site, between the eastern extensions of the Karlstrasse and Frankfurterstrasse, making it the centre of the new square (Du Ry almost certainly influenced his choice). Du Ry's layout still distantly pays homage to formal palace design. The buildings flanking the Museum – the Palais Jungken to the north and the Catholic church of St Elizabeth to the south – are treated like terminal pavilions, while the square itself seems to serve as a *cour d'honneur* for the Museum (which is in fact labelled 'corps de logis' in one of the drawings). Friedrich's statue in the centre of the square, by *Johann August Nahl*, faces the Museum as if to call attention to it. The Museum was also emphasized by the planting of lime trees, which surrounded the square, leaving a gap in front of it and clustering more thickly in the spaces between Museum and flanking buildings. Quite as important as the positioning of the building was the height, which needed to be carefully considered, as the ground sloped in both directions. Du Ry was criticized for the low proportions of his building, but he argued that the Museum's height had to be in proportion both to the higher-placed houses of the Huguenot town (forming the west side of the square) and to the lower ones in the medieval town. The foundations had to be 8.6 m deep, as the building was erected over the former ditch of the ramparts.

211 Grandjean de Montigny: Ständesaal added to the Museum Fridericianum, Kassel, 1806–13.

The long low structure of the Museum, some 80 m long with wings extending 41 m to the rear, is articulated by giant Ionic pilasters which balance the strong horizontality of the rows of windows and the heavy architrave topped by a balustrade with urns. The main accent is the majestic hexastyle Ionic portico with its cubic attic crowned by six statues representing architecture, philosophy, painting, sculpture, history and astronomy sculpted by *Heyd* and *Samuel Nahl the younger*. The temple motif refers to the function of the building as Temple of the Muses.

The Museum was very much the landgrave's personal toy and to speed up its construction, which took ten years, he doubled the building budget each year. He did not interfere with the design, but he did take an active part in the presentation of the collections. Still in the tradition of the Renaissance cabinets of curiosities, these even included a waxwork collection. The sculpture collection, displayed in two galleries flanking the entrance hall, was outshone only by those of Munich and Berlin. The library formed an important part of the holdings – not unlike the British Museum – and took up the first floor of the main block.

During the reign of Jérôme Bonaparte the Museum was altered to provide a **Ständesaal** or 'Palais des Etats' by *Grandjean de Montigny*, assisted by *Klenze* and *Wolff*. The staircase at the back was replaced by a spectacular semi-circular chamber for the diet with a splendid coffered ceiling. In 1882 the room was divided horizontally into two storeys by *Bromeis*.

The Museum also included an observatory, cleverly installed in a medieval watchtower at the south-east corner.

The interior was gutted in the war and awaits restoration.

Catholic church of St Elizabeth (1770–76) Balancing the Palais Jungken south of the Museum Fridericianum was the court chapel of the convert Friedrich II. To secure Protestantism in Hesse Crown Prince Friedrich had to sign the Assekurationsakte, which forbade the official practice of Catholicism and the building of Catholic churches, but permitted the prince to worship privately as he pleased. The church was therefore given a palace façade which perfectly suited Du Ry's idea of harmony and symmetry for the square. The interior, skilfully planned with unostentatious opulence, was a surprising achievement behind the secular façade. All the features required to make the building look like a palace were brilliantly turned to advantage for the design of the church, such as the multitude of windows and the frontispiece projection, cleverly used for a short transept. Inside, the dramatic domed crossing is surmounted by an upper gallery with Ionic columns which continues the galleries over the narrow aisles. In effect the interior was a sophisticated reinterpretation of the splendour of south German Baroque (a remarkable achievement for a Huguenot), while the exterior was severely classical. The church was entered not from the square but from a lesser street to the north; this was necessitated by the plan, which also incorporated at the south end a flat for

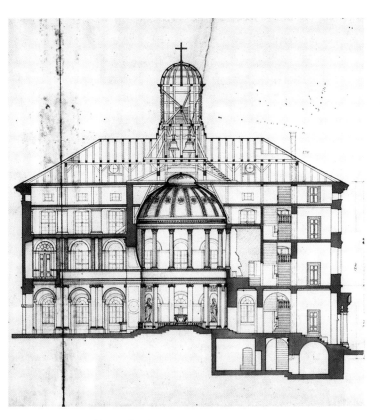

212 Simon Louis du Ry: section of the church of St Elisabeth, Kassel, 1770–6.

the chaplain and above the church a Betsaal. In 1810, under Jérôme's Catholic emancipation, it was thought necessary to signal the building's function by a small clock tower designed by *Jussow*. The church no longer exists.

Auetor or **Friedrichstor** (1779–82) More of an ornament than an actual town gate, consisting of a curved platform protruding from the Friedrichsplatz like a belvedere, framed by a pair of lodges whose recessed Tuscan porticoes, crowned by Roman trophies

by *Johann August Nahl*, faced the square rather than each other, as function would have demanded. The design marked the triumph of Du Ry and his distinctive flair for spatial handling over the monumentality of Ledoux. To the south the Friedrichsplatz commanded magnificent views over the countryside, reminiscent of Tuscan hill towns. With his early taste for the Picturesque, Du Ry wished to integrate this natural scene into the architectural setting of his square. He was obliged to fight for his vision when an ambitious scheme by *Ledoux* in 1775–6, consisting of a large and elaborate triumphal arch flanked by screens of columns, threatened to destroy this privileged view. In order to persuade the infatuated landgrave of the unsuitability and extravagance of the Ledoux project Du Ry had a life-size model erected *in situ*, proving his point, which is said to have prompted Ledoux to leave Kassel. Du Ry's own design was then built.

However, a generation later, in 1824, *Bromeis* compromised Du Ry's idea of an open vista by filling in the gap between the lodges with a triumphal arch, as if to avenge Ledoux. The arch, intended to be crowned by a quadriga, was adorned with a group of warriors in 1870–71 and in 1876 by the Prussian eagle, when Kassel became part of Prussia. The whole ensemble was pulled down in 1906 to make way for a theatre, but Bromeis's arch was re-erected on the east side of the square.

213 Simon Louis du Ry and Johann Konrad Bromeis: Auetor, Kassel, 1779–82 and 1824. The Prussian eagle was added in 1876.

214 Claude-Nicholas Ledoux: design for the Auetor, Kassel, 1775–6.

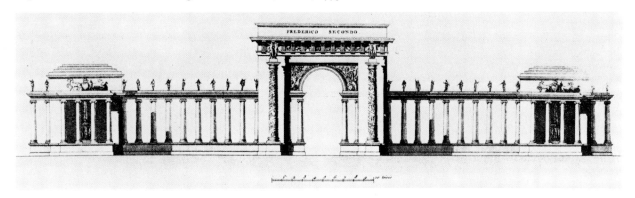

Opernplatz (1763–70) An intimate little square of charming stage-like design, opening off the west end of the north side of the Friedrichsplatz. The whole composition evolved from the landgrave's desire for a grand **Opera House** to be created out of the existing Palais Maximilian, which fronted the Friedrichsplatz. This proved far too small, and substantial extensions were built on at the rear (north) to house the auditorium, while the palace was converted to serve as foyer and public rooms. These extensions, composed as a picturesque sequence with impressive mansard roofs, were built in 1766–9 and formed the first part of the Opernplatz, its west side. In 1770 the east of the square was formed by the rear extension of **Haus Roux**, which like the Opera House fronted the Friedrichsplatz. At the same time the north side of the square was closed by the **Palais Waitz von Eschen**, which stood on the highest point of the sloping ground and provided the dominant feature of the ensemble. A classical remodelling of the rear elevation of the Rococo Schloss Wilhelmsthal, the four-storeyed palace was made to seem even grander by Du Ry's clever design of the square: the lower Opera House and Haus Roux appeared like its side wings, and the square itself suggested its *cour d'honneur*.

Du Ry's composition was sophisticated and balanced, stemming from Baroque tradition but with a decided striving towards classicism in the restraint and cubic forms of the elevations. The Opera House – the fourth in Europe, after Berlin, Bayreuth, and Milan – was demolished in 1910, while bombing and redevelopment after the war destroyed the rest.

Königsstrasse (1767–*c*.1775) In this scheme Du Ry extended the northern axis of the Huguenot town, which had been established by his father, eastwards to form a triumphal link between his new squares, leading along the north side of the Friedrichsplatz in a straight line to the Königsplatz. The street became a fashionable setting for the houses of the aristocracy and wealthy patricians, most of them courtiers. The first to be built, in 1767, was the **house of Philipp Kopp**, who was Du Ry's brother-in-law – a relationship which may explain the fact that although it is the smallest of all the houses it has a prominent site overlooking the Friedrichsplatz. By the mid-1770s the street was completely lined with three-storeyed houses with majestic broad façades, most of them accentuated by a central pediment, creating a uniform impression although they were designed separately. Even such individual expressions as the exuberant Rococo decorations on **no. 41**, the house of the sculptor *Nahl*, with its lower side wings, did not destroy this unity. The palatial size of the houses allowed some of them to be converted later into public buildings: **no. 47**, the house of the courtier Zanthier, was acquired in 1778 by the landgrave and transformed into a school, the famous Lyceum Fridericianum. The **house of the privy councillor Robert** was used 1781–5 for lotteries to raise money and later as an additional residence for the landgrave's family. With its neat row of houses, its pavements, and its street lamps, the Königsstrasse was in the forefront of contemporary town planning, and was readily admired even by widely-travelled visitors such as Goethe.

CONSTRUCTIONS IN THE EXISTING TOWN

In addition to the complex of the new street, squares, and circus, to realize their grand vision of a modern Kassel the landgrave and Du Ry projected the final completion of the Huguenot town (the Oberneustadt) and improvements to the medieval town extension (the Unterneustadt). They also built a new wall around the town.

For his modification to the Huguenot **Oberneustadt**, Du Ry again focused on a square, the **Wilhelmsplatz**, which he created by dividing the quarter by a new street, the Philippstrasse. On the east side stood the **Berlepp'sche Haus**, which Du Ry had already converted in 1762 into an exhibition building for the twice-yearly Kassel trade fair. Now (1767–9) extensive wings were added to the rear as far as the Königsstrasse, one along the Amalienstrasse, the other along the north-east side of the new square. The Wilhelmsplatz was conceived as a new civic centre, with on the south the **Town Hall** (1771–5) and on the west the **French Hospital** (1770–72). The Town Hall was given an imposing Palladian façade with an up-to-date applied Ionic portico in the centre, but the other buildings were designed to blend with the rational style of the Huguenot quarter. The north side of the square, facing the Königsstrasse, was to have been filled by a building of unusual size and character, a **Museum of Architecture** to hold the models collected by Landgrave Karl. Its four-storeyed exterior would have been plain, but monumental in scale; its interior, on the other hand, would have been astonishing, with a vast hall containing the extraordinary 63-metre-long model of the Wilhelmshöhe cascade, rising the full height of the building, and around this hall galleries supported on Ionic columns providing further exhibition space. The project was never realized, and the old Modellhaus south of the Rennbahn was simply re-erected in 1789 in the Kornmarkt.

In the **Unterneustadt**, Kassel's medieval extension south of the Fulda, the demolition of the ramparts allowed the layout of another open space, the **Leipziger Platz**. Here Du Ry opted for an oval, with a curve towards the new Leipziger Tor, Kassel's main entrance from the south-east. The **Charité** hospital (1772) was the largest and most ambitious of all Friedrich's charitable foundations. While the French Hospital only catered for the Huguenots, the Charité served the whole of Kassel. The building, in an even more reduced functional style than the French Hospital, impressed by its sheer scale and monumental simplicity. The **Anatomy Theatre** (1777) of the Carolinum, an academic institution founded by Landgrave Karl and revived by Friedrich II, was built in axis to the Leipziger Tor. The large theatre with its tiered seating was famous as the first of its kind in Germany, and when the Carolinum moved to the University of Marburg it was dismantled and re-erected there.

In 1767 a new **town wall**, 3.5 m high, was built to enclose all the area which the landgrave and Du Ry planned to improve. Of its many gates a few were designed on a grand scale, either as part of a larger

Kassel

scheme or because they marked an important approach to the town. Thus the **Weissensteiner Tor** (1768–70), on the north-west, lay on the principal road to Wilhelmshöhe. It had lodges with Tuscan porticoes supporting richly decorated pediments, which on the town side were linked to an octagonal open space. The gate lost its importance with the construction of the Wilhelmshöher Allee, begun in 1777. Next to the Weissensteiner Tor Du Ry built vast **Artillery Barracks** for the Garde du Corps (begun c.1768). Their varying mansard rooflines, picturesquely arranged, formed an attractive feature of the conventional arrangement of centre and corner pavilions linked by extensive lower wings. The **Königstor** or **Wilhelmshöher Tor** occupied an important site at the end of the Königsstrasse, and many designs were made for it, of which Du Ry favoured a copy of the Arch of Septimius Severus opening into a three-quarter-circle piazza with three radiating streets echoing the Königsplatz. The latter was built, but neither Du Ry's arch nor one later designed by *Jussow* (see below) ever materialized. Similarly part of an urban scheme was the **Auetor** (1779), which has been discussed in connection with the Friedrichsplatz (above).

Works by Jussow

Jussow's buildings in Kassel are few. For a considerable time his career was overshadowed by the powerful Du Ry, whom he succeeded only in his mid-forties, and then his commissions suffered first from the French occupation and then from Wilhelm I's reluctance to spend money on public projects.

Unterneustädterkirche (1802–8) Designed as a replacement for the Magdalenenkirche, demolished for a new approach to the re-sited Fulda bridge. Its prominent position, in the middle of Du Ry's oval Leipziger Platz, called for special care to be given to the design, and between 1800 and 1802 Jussow prepared several projects, one of them a spectacular version of the Pantheon and another an early exercise in Greek Revival, with a severe hexastyle portico of baseless Doric columns. Financial restrictions in the end dictated a far more modest design, but that suited the austerity of the reductive Revolutionary style that Jussow favoured. The church is impressive for its severe cubic massiveness, its unadorned windows and its sparse architectural features.

Messhaus/trade hall (1809) Occupying an important site in the Upper Königsstrasse near the Königstor, the main entrance to the town, Jussow's building formed a fourth side of the enormous complex that Du Ry had created out of the Berlepp'sche Haus (see Oberneustadt, above). Although it was a utilitarian structure, Jussow prepared several preliminary designs. The long façade was given distinction by giant pilasters supporting an impressive architrave at second-floor level, which served to integrate the three-storeyed structure into the ensemble of the street. The Messhaus was demolished at the beginning of the 20c. to make way for a new town hall.

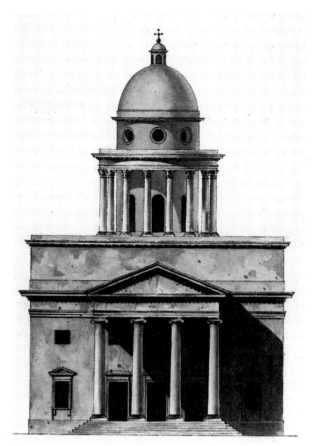

215 Heinrich Christoph Jussow: design for the Unterneustädterkirche, c.1802.

Wilhelmshöher Tor (1803–6?) The commission is said to have been connected with Wilhelm IX becoming Elector in 1803, and that might explain why Jussow took up the theme of the triumphal arch suggested a generation earlier by Du Ry, although victory columns and a stepped pyramid were also considered. The scheme had changed considerably, however, for the gate was now to be sited not in axis with the Königsstrasse but at the beginning of the Wilhelmshöher Allee, which Wilhelm conceived as a *via triumphalis* leading to his favourite palace, Wilhelmshöhe. Jussow proposed a design based on the Brandenburg Gate in Berlin, with alternative suggestions for the central feature, one based on Du Ry's arch, another modelled on Ledoux's project for the Auetor with a columned screen, and a third virtually a copy of Langhans's original. The French invasion in 1806 prevented the construction of anything but the flanking lodges. Majestic cubes three storeys high with tetrastyle porticoes facing the street, these still guard the road and leave no doubt about the intended monumentality of the scheme. Their solemn austerity, heightened by the bare masonry, suggests the Revolutionary style at its purest, though the effect is due to their unfinished state. The northern gatehouse became famous as the home of the Brothers Grimm.

Fürstenhaus Palace for the electoral family (1806) A somewhat undistinguished building the size of a patrician town house, erected south of the Wilhelmshöher Tor and lived in by the Elector intermittently from 1813.

Arnold's Wallpaper Factory Opposite the Electoral Palace and far more impressive, in a grand domestic style, with a centre marked by giant Ionic pilasters and arcaded side wings. The design has been attributed to Jussow.

Mausoleum for Wilhelmine Karoline of Hesse (1826) A perfect example of the Greek Revival, this small mausoleum for the widow of Wilhelm I has a Doric portico *in antis* and a coffered vault within. It survives, but sadly as a ruin.

Other schemes by Jussow remained unrealized dreams. These included an impressive urban improvement plan around the Fulda bridge and a monumental drill hall facing the Königsstrasse. The saddest of these unfulfilled projects is one which was actually begun, and then abandoned: the **Chattenburg**, an ambitious town palace commissioned by Wilhelm I in 1815 to replace the Renaissance castle which had been destroyed by fire. The building, which is known from many detailed drawings and a remarkable model, would have been Jussow's masterpiece. It was to be an enormous pile arranged around two spacious courtyards, with a multitude of giant Ionic columns – eighty-four in all – accentuating central porticoes and corner pavilions all the way round the building. The centre of the entrance front was to be crowned by a colossal quadriga flanked by tholos-like lanterns. One storey had been built by 1821 when Wilhelm died, and with him the project. The shell of red sandstone lingered as a bizarre ruin until 1870, when the material was re-used in the construction of the Art Gallery, and the site covered by the Law Courts.

Works by Bromeis

Wilhelm II came to power in 1821, having inherited from his father not only enormous wealth but also an obsession with grandiose palace schemes. He abandoned the Chattenburg project because Jussow's majestic style did not appeal to him. A lover of the Empire Style, he appointed as his court architect *Bromeis*, whom he had already employed while crown prince. He had extensively enlarged his beloved Palais Jungken (see above), and he now commissioned a further extension, the Rotes Palais. This building and the **Hofverwaltungsgebäude** (1826/7–9), administrative offices in an unsuccessful version of the style of the neighbouring church of St Elizabeth, demonstrated Bromeis's insensitivity to the subtle layout of the Friedrichsplatz, whose harmony and balance they destroyed.

Rotes Palais (1821–6/31) No money was spared, and the best materials were used to create Germany's finest Empire interior, a near-perfect fulfilment of the Parisian ideal. The sophisticated decorative schemes mixing Grecian, Roman and Pompeian motifs, inspired by and partly copied from Percier and Fontaine, were of great elegance and jewel-like finish. Such were the Festsaal or ballroom, famous for its precious inlaid floors, the Throne Room, a modification of Napoleon's bedroom in the Tuileries, and the Egyptian Boudoir. The interior of the Palais Jungken was integrated into this great scheme and redecorated in the same Empire Style.

The exterior of the Rotes Palais was in a marked contrast. Lower than the Palais Jungken, it formed a somewhat unhappy neighbour to the earlier building's balanced and well-proportioned composition, and was soon nicknamed 'the locomotive'. A heavy portico with pilasters above, and a variety of different window forms in the wings, created a restless impression. The palace was bombed, and its site built over by a department store, tastelessly re-using the surviving portico as a side entrance.

216 Heinrich Christoph Jussow: model for the Chattenburg, Kassel, 1818.

217 Johann Konrad Bromeis: Festsaal of the Rotes Palais, Kassel, 1821–6/31.

218, 219 Johann Konrad Bromeis: staircase and (below) south-east front of internal court of the Rotes Palais, Kassel, 1816.

Koblenz

A dazzling but brief chapter opened for Koblenz when Clemens Wenzeslaus, Elector and Archbishop of Trier (1768–94), decided in the 1770s to move his court there from nearby Ehrenbreitstein. Son of the Saxon Elector and King of Poland August III, Clemens Wenzeslaus had been brought up in Dresden, one of the most splendid and cultivated courts of Germany. Looking across the Rhine to Koblenz from his old castle he must have visualized a new palace and town to rival his father's in the picturesque setting along the river immediately south of the medieval town. For Koblenz this meant an enhanced status. The centre was shifted south away from the Moselle to the Rhine, where a new town rose in the 1780s. The francophile Elector also injected a new artistic impulse, Blondel's modern French classicism, with which he had been acquainted at his father's court. Limited means (Clemens did not match his father in wealth or power) and the French occupation from 1794 to 1815 allowed him to realize the gigantic scheme only partially, but still on a monumental scale. It was finally finished under Prussian rule, from 1815. The new town was rapidly built up and the Residenz Schloss was restored for the use of the Prussian King Friedrich Wilhelm IV and later his brother the German Emperor Wilhelm I. As a military stronghold, called 'the Gibraltar of the Rhine' by the English traveller John Aiton, Koblenz became in 1824 the capital of Rhenish Prussia. Though extensive fortification work was carried out and barracks were erected, no public building of importance was built. Clemens's palace remained Koblenz's foremost Neo-classical construction.

Clemens's first court architect was *Johannes G. Seiz* (died 1779), who drew up initial plans for the new Residenz Schloss with his son *Karl*. The Elector changed his mind several times, obtaining plans from a number of architects and commissioning *Pierre-Michel d'Ixnard* (1723–95) before changing to *Antoine-François Peyre*, the younger brother of the famous Marie-Joseph Peyre. Other architects working at Koblenz include *Peter Joseph Krahe* (1758–1840), who was there from 1787 to 1803 (from 1790 as official court architect), the town architects *N. Lauxem*, *J. G. von Lassaulx* (1781–1848) and *Ferdinand Jakob Nebel* (1782–1860).

Residenz Schloss (1777–86, *D'Ixnard/Peyre*) Although one of the last buildings of its class, the Residenz Schloss at Koblenz was designed in a markedly forward-looking style, a startlingly early intimation of French Revolutionary architecture in Germany. Change of architects, and above all financial problems, threatened the project, which was never completed. In the winter of 1776–7 *Salins de Montfort*, *Poggi* and *D'Ixnard* submitted designs. In 1777 D'Ixnard was appointed architect. The Elector may have regretted his choice, for after several visits to Koblenz and the actual start of the work in 1778 D'Ixnard confessed in the spring of 1779 that 'the design was not yet finished, but still under preparation'. In the meantime the clerk of works had twice been replaced – the first time by *Christian Trosson*, and the second time by the Dresden-born, Paris-trained *Andreas Gärtner*. Seiz intrigued against D'Ixnard. Finally the Elector referred the whole matter to the Académie d'Architecture in Paris. The outcome was the appointment of *Peyre* as D'Ixnard's successor late in 1779. Many problems had to be overcome before the Elector finally moved into his new palace in the winter of 1786. Banqueting hall, chapel and several of the important guest-rooms were not yet finished. Although hall and chapel were finally completed in 1792, many of the guest-rooms were still untouched when the Elector fled before the French army in 1794.

D'Ixnard's first scheme was not as grandiose as the one he presented in 1779 and later published in his 26 *Recueil d'Architecture*. Indeed, only after his visit to Koblenz early in 1777 did he learn the actual site of the palace, south of the city walls along the Rhine. He accordingly modified his design, and from a simple U-shaped Baroque composition the palace design finally grew into an impressive, vast ensemble of visionary quality with a second set of flanking wings in front connected by huge pavilion-punctuated crescents to the main block and directly linked across the courtyard by one-storeyed colonnades. A Propylaea-inspired gate closed off the quadrangle and one-storeyed structures surrounded the whole. It was a remarkable composition of controlled spaces and simply related geometrical shapes, a fusion of square and circle. Ludwigsburg's double *cours d'honneur* and Schloss Benrath's theme of flanking crescents, both known to D'Ixnard, seem here to be transformed into one monumental design.

When *Peyre* took over, D'Ixnard's *corps de logis* had already risen to one third of its height and the foundations of the wings were laid. Thus Peyre had little scope for originality; furthermore, financial restrictions forced him to reduce the scheme. The composition was impaired when he was forced to fill in the foundations of the wings and erect the two crescents over them, linked by small pavilions for stables and servants' quarters. However, in the elevations Peyre was still able to express his own more advanced ideas, the reductive vocabulary of the young Revolutionary style with its sharp contrasts of light and dark, its emphasis on geometric shapes and plain surfaces. On the town front this was achieved with a Durand-like arcade on the ground floor, austere rows of windows above and an emphasis on bold horizontals in cornices and above all in the roofline, D'Ixnard's traditional central dome being suppressed. The octastyle Ionic portico reflects those of the most up-to-date Parisian buildings – Gondoin's Ecole de Médecine and Rousseau's Hôtel de Salm. (Peyre had even suggested an eighteen-column portico as a definite commitment to Revolutionary classicism.) On the Rhine front the portico motif was repeated in the form of six giant Ionic columns supporting an attic with the building's only decoration, a sculptured relief by *Sebastian Pfaff* representing the Rhine and Moselle as female figures flanking the Elector's coat of arms.

D'Ixnard's interior arrangement was basically maintained. The southern part of the *corps de logis* received the Elector's private suite of rooms, the northern the guest-rooms, while entrance hall and Gartensaal with the banqueting hall above remained the dominant central features. One notable change was the rearrangement of the staircase into a single monumental flight of steps leading, not unlike Würzburg, from a dim lower vestibule, its vault supported by four columns, to a lofty upper hall with side galleries (anticipating Chalgrin's staircase in the Palais du Luxembourg). Another change was the relocation of the chapel in the north-east corner of the *corps de logis*.

Peyre's decorative scheme combined Greek motifs with the monumental language of Roman architecture and its Renaissance derivatives, as his brother had taught him. This style reached its apogee in the interiors of the banqueting hall and the chapel. The former was designed with a majestic barrel vault rising over a rich acanthus leaf entablature of an elegant Corinthian pilaster order, the latter with a dome over a Greek cross lavishly decorated using the full classical vocabulary. Some of Peyre's richly carved yet controlled architectural ornament and crisp overdoor reliefs still survives, in the first and second ante-chambers, the Salle d'Audience (with a fresco by *Januarius Zick*), the Elector's drawing room, and his bedroom (also with a ceiling by *Zick*). *C.W. Coudray* worked with his father on the execution of the interior decoration.

A considerable part of Peyre's interior was later overlaid by *Stüler* and *Lassaulx's* insensitive redecoration scheme for the king of Prussia in 1842–5. They disfigured the banqueting hall by placing strange temple fronts high up on the side walls and by cutting the graceful round-headed doors into rectangles.

Severe war damage unfortunately resulted in the loss of the splendid chapel and other interiors, though the *corps de logis* was restored to its former glory. The corner pavilions and curved wings were rebuilt in a free style for modern needs.

Clemensstadt, later Neustadt

A new town in association with the palace was part of the Elector's ambitious original scheme, and was also necessary to accommodate the court. The first proposal by *D'Ixnard* in 1777 suggested a Nancy-inspired sequence of crescents and circuses within a grid plan, which also determined *Peyre's* planning of the Clemensstadt in 1782–3. Although Peyre himself, according to his *Traité*, had visualized in front of the palace a monumental square similar to the one by Gabriel in Rennes, the Elector favoured D'Ixnard's crescent idea. Peyre therefore established a central axis running westward from the Schloss, the Clemensstrasse, now Schloss Strasse, which includes at the palace end a crescent that echoes the palace's own more monumental curved wings. As a cross-axis, between the Schloss and the Crescent he created the Residenzstrasse, leading north to the Clemensplatz (now Deinhardtplatz). *Faber*, another architect involved with Peyre, had intended to complete the scheme with a corresponding square to the south, which regrettably was never realized. The northern area of the grid plan between Schloss Strasse and Residenzstrasse was the first part to be built. Peyre's idea of a progression of spaces responding to and framing the palace was one of remarkable grandeur. With the long row of houses stretching from the Crescent along the Residenzstrasse to the Clemensplatz he had conceived an impressive scenic setting at a respectful distance from the Schloss but also with an integrity of its own. This stretch became known as Clemensstadt and later as Neustadt.

To encourage private builders the Elector granted tax concessions, helped with timber for building, and promised to plant one oak tree per bay of each house. To achieve a unified design he empowered a building commission to establish strict rules for the height of the houses, the number of storeys and the general design. However, there was still considerable freedom for individual expression. The scheme was announced in all the major papers in April 1786.

With the move of the court to Koblenz, building activity started. The architects involved were *Krahe*, not yet court architect, who made designs for at least fifteen houses only two of which can be identified; *Christian Trosson*, the second clerk of works for the palace; the town architect *Lauxen*; court carpenter *Josef Wirth*; court architect *M. Wirth*; and the builder *Johann Mäckler*.

The years of French occupation and the Wars of Liberation interrupted the realization of this impressive Neo-classical town ensemble. However, by the end of the century most parts north of the Schloss Strasse had been developed – the houses between the Crescent and Clemensplatz (Neustadt 1–14), then the north side of the square leading west into the Schanzenstrasse (confusingly, now called Clemensstrasse) with the south side of that street. Neustadt 18 was for a long time the only house in the southern quadrant of the Crescent, with no. 21 isolated further south, while the Schloss Strasse could only boast three houses. The slow development in the south was partly due to the city ramparts. The Prussians, however, after taking over in 1815, demolished these and completed the scheme according to the 1782–3 masterplan, again supervised by a building commission. First the Schloss Strasse and Löhrrondell and then up to 1853 the transverse streets – Löhr-, Casino-, Gymnasial-, Friedrich-, Victoria-, and Magazinstrasse – were developed with many houses designed by *Lassaulx*.

Neustadt A considerable part of the 18c. development survives and determines the character of the area facing the Schloss. **No. 1** (1786, *Josef Wirth*, probably after *Trosson*), built for the courtier Hürten, later became the famous Trierischer Hof inn, which housed such illustrious guests as Madame Mère and Metternich. Its dignified façade towards the Clemensplatz is accentuated by a pedimented three-bay centre framed by giant Ionic pilasters on piers corresponding to the corners of the house. **No. 2** is the Theatre (see below). **No. 3** (1786, *Lauxem*), built for Madame Grant, is larger than

220 Three houses in Neustadt, Koblenz. No. 1 (on the right) by Wirth, 1786; No. 2, the Theatre by Krahe, 1787; No. 3 (on the left) by Lauxem, 1736.

no. 1. The main feature of its façade is the entrance door, framed by fluted pilasters supporting a ponderous architrave; the interior has a splendid Empire staircase. When the house was restored in 1950 it was still in the hands of the Deinhard family, owners since 1810. **No. 6** (1789, *Krahe*), built for Revisionsrat von Hontheim, was after the Theatre the most impressive façade in the row, with an Egyptian flavour in its Revolutionary style. Austere pylon-like corner towers containing gateways flanked a composition punctuated by simple rows of windows and a heavily framed entrance door set in the centre of the rusticated ground floor. A frieze between ground and first floor and a massive crowning cornice complied with the requirements of the master plan for the district. The main rooms were on the first floor, of different shapes and grouped around a staircase at the rear. A small banqueting room reflected the high social position of the owner. In 1935 this house and the adjacent **no. 7** were pulled down for a bank. **No. 8** (*c.*1790, *Trosson*) is a smaller house, only five bays wide, designed for Freiherr von Thümefeld. The entrance is off-centre and emphasized by Doric columns supporting an architrave. **Nos. 9 and 10** (after 1788, architect unknown) were commissioned by the Abbey of St Maxim of Trier in 1788. A first plan was prepared by *Krahe*, but rejected by the building commission. Situated at the corner of Neustadt and the Crescent, the design echoes on a larger and more monumental scale the corresponding corner house, no. 1: a giant Ionic order marks the centre bay and the cornice is bolder. The balconies are a later addition. In 1788 *Krahe* submitted a design for the **Crescent** similar to the curved wing composition of the Schloss with three-storeyed corner blocks framing a two-storeyed arcade probably intended for shops. His scheme was not built. What was constructed was later spoiled by rebuilding and bombing. **No. 21** (*Trosson*), designed for the alderman Franz Josef Eltz and the most individual of all the houses of the earlier period, was the first to be erected south of the Crescent. The picturesque design with an apse-like centre bay was hesitantly sanctioned by the commission on condition that a wall would be built to preserve the street line. Finally, however, two projecting gatehouses were built in line with the street (and the bay) framing the recessed house. Balustraded windows give importance to the first floor, which is surmounted by a heavy cornice continuing the roofline of the gatehouses, with another floor above. The interior was particularly noted for the dramatic barrel vaulting in some of the first-floor rooms. In 1823 the Prussian government acquired the house as official residence for the town commandant.

Theatre, Neustadt 2 (1787, *Krahe*) Krahe's first building in Koblenz, erected in only seven months. Commissioned by the courtier Franz Josef Schmitz (financial secretary of the Elector's sister) on a prominent but restricted site, it was a private enterprise encouraged by the Elector. While in Rome in 1784–5 Krahe had drawn up schemes for an imaginary theatre which he used for his Koblenz design, fused with remarkable new ideas. As a drawing in the Koblenz Archives suggests, he adopted the three-quarter-circle form for the audi-

torium from Victor Louis's theatre at Bordeaux (1782). As Ledoux had done only a few years earlier at the theatre of Besançon (1778–84), Krahe also eliminated the Baroque tiers of boxes in favour of amphitheatre balconies. Financial restrictions undoubtedly suited his preference for simplicity, and only the proscenium was prominently set off by Composite columns and pilasters. Externally, due to the restrictions of the site, there was only room for a street façade. Various alternative schemes were contemplated. In the final design, with a Tuscan giant order rising above a heavy rusticated and arcaded ground floor, Krahe was inspired by Italian Renaissance models. This scheme, more conventional than another proposed by Krahe with pylon-like end bays, was probably suggested by D'Ixnard's design for the front pavilion of the Residenz Schloss, which was also combined with a similar extraordinarily steep pitched roof.

On 23 November 1787 the theatre was opened with a spectacular performance of Mozart's *Seraglio*. Its modernity was not immediately appreciated by provincial Koblenz, although the building found admirers. The Empress Josephine in 1804 enthusiastically proclaimed it 'une des plus jolies salles que j'ai vues'. As late as 1835 the leading Koblenz architect *Lassaulx* recommended it as 'the true model for theatres of this size', finding the proscenium the most attractive he could recall. One of the earliest public theatres, no longer exclusively designed for the entertainment of a court, it survived as a private undertaking till 1864 when it was taken over by the town. An impressive restoration has just been completed, recreating even the original colour scheme.

Festungsschirrhof (1787–8, *A. Gärtner*) A utilitarian building of some grandeur, designed for various court purposes, consisting of a low range of buildings around a quadrangle with a western façade towards the Neustadt and an eastern one towards the Rhine. The latter, inspired by Krahe, included a Ledoux-like monumental triumphal arch.

Rheintor (1779, *A. Gärtner*) An early Neo-classical town gate towards the Rhine.

221 Ferdinand Jakob Nebel: great hall of the Civilkasino, Koblenz, 1826–8.

Civilkasino (extension 1826–8, *Nebel*) A grand banqueting hall added to the clubhouse of the Kasinogesellschaft, a proud and aspiring civic society founded in 1808. *Lassaulx* had initially received the commission, but after a quarrel it was given to his local rival, designer of the Civilkasino in nearby Neuwied. Above a low ground storey is a distinguished hall dominated by an elegant apse with a screen of Corinthian columns continued as pilasters round the walls, and covered with a segmental barrel vault. An effect of great splendour is achieved by the refined decoration in scagliola. No separate entrance was required, so externally the main emphasis was on the smaller garden front which faced towards an important new street then under construction. As a focal point Nebel introduced a pedimented four-columned portico raised on a solid ground-floor block. The building had an enormous influence on all future extensions and determined the impressive remodelling of 1869–71 which created a vast complex in a late classical style.

Mortuary (1825–30, *Nebel*) A notable polygonal building.

Krefeld

In the 17c. and early 18c. Krefeld became a haven for religious refugees, and from humble origins it grew rapidly into a prosperous town famed for its silk and velvet industry, and experienced four major expansions within only fifty-five years. Its wholly secular background found expression in a selfconsciously democratic grid layout without any axial focus on a palace. Ultimately this also conditioned the Neo-classical planning which was necessary when, after the Napoleonic interlude, Krefeld was restored to Prussian rule.

In 1817 *Adolf von Vagedes* (1777–1842) projected an ambitious scheme based on a Greek cross, but he was forced by Berlin to retain the grid pattern. This he dramatically extended and surrounded with a grand rectangle of four avenues as a principal feature. From 1824 onwards the works were carried out, and within one generation an impressive Neo-classical townscape was created, albeit of a predominantly bourgeois residential character. The lack of major public buildings was only remedied towards the end of the 19c.

The most notable house was the town residence of the Von der Leyen family, which became known as the **Schloss**. It was built in 1791–4 by *Martin Leydel* in a Palladian style probably dictated by the owner. The white stuccoed façade is dominated by a hexastyle Ionic portico, raised as a giant order above a rusticated ground floor with entrance arcades. The house was acquired by the corporation in 1859–60 to serve as the town hall, and a pair of Prussian eagles was installed on top of the portico in a Schinkelesque manner. In 1891 a north wing was added in Renaissance style.

Another expansion scheme was drawn up in the 1830s and built from 1843 onwards. Though much of Krefeld's Neo-classical heritage has been destroyed, either by rebuilding during the *Gründerjahre* around 1900

222 Martin Leydel: house for the Von der Leyen family known as the Schloss, Krefeld, 1791–4.

or by bombing during the war, much still survives. Good examples of Neo-classical houses are to be seen at **Ostwall 119** (1840), **Ostwall 121** (1835–40), and **Westwall 81** (1830–35).

In the district

The country round Krefeld is punctuated by several Neo-classical villas and country retreats, some of which are remarkable.

Bockum: Haus Sollbrüggen (*c*.1785) An elegant white stuccoed manor house with a first-floor arcade of windows as the main central feature. Within is a banqueting hall on the first floor with refined Neo-classical stucco decoration.

Linn: Greiffenhorst (1838–43, *O. von Gloeden*?) A hunting lodge built for Cornelius de Greiff, probably by a Prussian building inspector rather than by *Vagedes*, to whom it is usually attributed. The remarkable design

223 Attrib. to O. von Gloeden: Schloss Greiffenhorst, Linn, near Krefeld, 1838–43.

consists of a three-storeyed octagonal tower with four square arms rising to second-floor level. The composition was unified by a balustrade which produced a pagoda-like effect. The geometrical clarity of the design and the austerity of its flat surfaces gave the building a Prussian flavour. Now in ruins, it awaits restoration.

Ürdingen, a little neighbouring town, suddenly gained importance thanks to the free trade policy of the Napoleonic period. This is well reflected in several good Neo-classical town houses, such as **Oberstrasse 20** (*c.*1800). The **Herbezhäuser** (1832) are the outstanding examples. They are a group of three houses, commissioned by the wealthy sugar merchant Balthasar Herbez for himself and his two brothers, as a terrace forming a dominant feature in the market square. They are identical, all three-storeyed, their entrances marked by first-floor balconies, and their rooflines united by a cast-iron balustrade. Most remarkable are their splendid interiors. In each, a charming semicircular staircase leads up to the *piano nobile*, on which is a splendid banqueting room with Composite pilasters round the walls, elegantly stuccoed and enhanced by refined painted decoration. Towards the end of the 19c. the houses were turned into a town hall, a pharmacy, and county offices. In 1967 they were restored and painted yellow.

Lindau

Lindau is best known for the beauty of its setting on Lake Constance, guarded by snowcapped mountains, and for its two principal buildings – the late medieval Town Hall and the splendid Baroque Haus zum Cavazzen. The picturesque lakeside scenery tempted the rich to build villas here set in landscaped parkland.

Villa Lindenhof (1842–5, *Franz Jakob Kreuter*) Commissioned from the young Munich architect by the widely travelled merchant Friedrich Gruber, a native of Lindau, the villa combines an elegant interior with an impressive exterior. Decidedly Schinkelesque in style, the plan seems to have been inspired by the Palladian layout of C. F. Hansen's villas in the Hamburg suburb of Altona. The exquisitely decorated rooms, some of them in a delicate Pompeian style, are arranged around a domed top-lit rotunda rising the full height of the building. The main front looks out from a gently sloping hillside across a terrace towards the lake. The centre, flanked by one-storeyed wings, is accentuated by a portico-like semicircular bay echoing the rotunda within. The villa still survives, surrounded by a magnificent park laid out by the Düsseldorf gardener *M. F. Weyhe*.

Villa Lotzbeck (*c.*1830, *Jean-Baptiste Métivier*) Another early example also designed by a Munich architect, but less grand. Recently pulled down for redevelopment.

Schloss Alwin (1853, *St Galler Sutter*) An imposing late classical pile built for Georg von Gruber, surrounded by vast Italianate terraced gardens.

Mannheim

Nowhere else does the Baroque chequerboard layout survive better than in Mannheim, with its parallel streets and squares still maintaining their curious mathematical labelling (such as M1, O2, P3) and still to some degree providing confusion by their monotonous uniformity. The town rapidly gained importance after 1720, when the Palatine rulers moved their residence from Heidelberg to Mannheim and created a court second in splendour only to Dresden. The vast palace, rivalling the monumentality of Nymphenburg, was to become a centre of learning and the arts known all over Europe, especially for its music. Yet in terms of classicism what gave Mannheim its distinction was its outstanding gallery of casts from the Antique, open to the public from 1769 onwards. It was here (and later in the Dresden Gallery) that young Germans had their first visions of Antiquity and were inspired by the classical world. Goethe exclaimed after his visit in 1769: 'J'en ai été extasié.' However, all that came to an end with the Elector Karl Theodor's succession to the Bavarian throne in 1778 and the removal of the court to Munich. The town's population dwindled by a third, to recover only around the mid-19c. Thus Neo-classical architecture never really developed in Mannheim and is confined to a few examples, mainly of the very early period.

Two architects, both serving under Karl Theodor, but of totally different personalities, left their mark: *Nicolas de Pigage* (1723–96), court architect from 1748/9, and then *Peter Anton von Verschaffelt* (1710–93), who originally came as court sculptor in 1752.

Major buildings

Schloss: interiors (1752–96, *Pigage*) As the fourth architect to the Schloss, Pigage was chiefly concerned with the embellishment of its interiors. Two of his most enchanting designs were the main library in the east wing (burnt during the war) and the cabinet library for the Elector's wife (1755–7, restored after 1945). Their exquisite and subtle decorations combine the elegance of Rococo forms with a controlled classical framework in a way similar to Pigage's work at Schloss Benrath.

Sternwarte/Observatory (1772–4, *Johann Lacher*) A curious, impressive structure built for the brilliant Jesuit court astronomer Christian Mayer. It consists of a five-storeyed octagon, the successive storeys progressively smaller and marked by different patterns of fenestration.

The style contains references to Greek, Renaissance and Baroque architecture. With its 160 steps the building was popular as an observation tower, and its visitors' book can show many famous names including Mozart and Goethe. It continued to serve as an observatory until 1880. In 1958 it was restored and converted into artists' flats.

National Theatre (conversion, 1776–7, 1780–81) The awakening of nationalist pride and consciousness found early expression in Mannheim in the foundation of a National Theatre by the Elector Karl Theodor, fostered by the Kurpfälzische Deutsche Gesellschaft founded in 1775. Instead of erecting a new building, the old Arsenal was converted to provide a theatre, concert hall and ballroom. The exterior was given considerable grandeur by side wings and a wide frontispiece, added to the design of *J. Quaglio* to provide new entrances and staircase halls. Coupled Tuscan columns supported a balcony with giant pilasters above, crowned by a sculptural pediment. The main entrance was adorned in Baroque fashion by statues on balcony and pediment, by *J. M. von den Branden*. Inside there were splendid decorations in a dignified Louis XVI style, with rich coffered ceilings, graceful overdoor reliefs, fauns and herms in niches, and paintings on the ceilings of theatre and concert hall. The paintings were by *Leydensdorff*, while most of the stucco-work was carried out by *M. Pozzi*. It was here that Schiller's *Die Räuber* had its premiere in January 1782. The theatre was modernized at various times, chiefly in the extensive rebuilding of 1855–6 by *Joseph Mühlendorff*, and destroyed by bombing in the war.

Zeughaus/Arsenal (1777–9, *Verschaffelt*) Verschaffelt's more vigorous style, Roman Baroque in origin but subdued by French classicism, finds its most decidedly Roman expression in this majestic building. Resembling a 17c. palazzo, the heavy block-like structure is punctuated by a monumental entrance arch whose architectural framework dominates the whole of the façade. Now Museum of Local History and Archaeology.

Palais Bretzenheim (1782–8, *Verschaffelt*) Verschaffelt's other important work in Mannheim, built for the illegitimate children of the Elector, presents an extraordinary contrast to his monumental Arsenal. Set among the residential buildings facing the Schloss it had to conform to the urban ensemble, but although subordinate, it gains grandeur by the sheer length of its twenty-one-bay façade. Reticent elevations, punctuated by rows of windows with the only notable emphasis on the entrance and some sparse Louis XVI swags, give the exterior a chilly solemnity. The interior, however, is a sudden surprise: what had appeared chaste and subdued externally is splendid and elegant within. Behind a vestibule the staircase ingeniously winds up on either side of a central courtyard, its two arms swiftly leading to the top landing, which in fact forms a bridge over the entrance passage similar to the spectacular arrangement in the Schloss itself. The upper hall is an exquisite example of French classicism, with a firm architectural framework of pilasters and architraves

filled chiefly with delicate trophy decorations beneath putti reliefs and niches with statues of Mars and Venus. The other interiors are of the same sophisticated elegance, some with curious vestigial Baroque features.

Neckartor An astonishing Neo-classical restatement of a Baroque town gate (similar to the Augusttor in Brunswick), in the form of a bold triumphal arch in correct Greek Doric forms, originally crowned by a famous Atlas figure by *Paul Egell*. Designer and date are both uncertain. Demolished in 1841.

Domestic architecture

Haus Düringer, L4, 4, is typical of the grander town houses built in the last quarter of the 18c., similar in style to the early classicism of the Palais Bretzenheim, with an unostentatious exterior but often elegant and delicate interiors. Far more powerful externally were the houses built in the 1820s and 1830s by *Johann Friedrich Dyckerhoff*, who was also responsible for some of the 19c. interiors in the Schloss. His **Haus Lamney, R7, 46** (1828) still bears the imprint of the reductive Weinbrenner and Krahe style with an emphasis on mass and unadorned wall surfaces. His corner house, **D6, 9** (1830), however, was more Schinkelesque, marked by an impressive giant pilaster order in the upper storeys surmounted by a bold cornice and crowned by a tower-like attic storey for the central hall. None of these buildings by Dyckerhoff survives.

Neuwied near Koblenz

Civilkasino (1825–7, *Ferdinand Jakob Nebel*) A simple two-storeyed structure for a club, with a curious façade dominated by an impressive Greek Doric portico in a crowded pedimented centre. The commission was an unfortunate one for Nebel, ending in a ten-year lawsuit; but he nevertheless was commissioned to design at almost the same time an extension to the Civilkasino in Koblenz, within whose territory Neuwied fell.

Niederselters near Koblenz

Brunnenwache (1791–2, *Peter Joseph Krahe*) A charming little guard house with a Doric portico *in antis* designed to protect the spa spring. The pediment is adorned with the coat of arms of the Elector of Trier to whose territory the spa belonged, which also explains the commissioning of his architect Krahe. Originally two flanking detached wings were projected forming a minute *cour d'honneur* as in some of Krahe's later work in Brunswick. The building is now the town hall.

Oldenburg

The town rose to fame in the mid-17c. under the last count of Oldenburg, creator of the remarkable Renaissance castle. After his death, however, the region fell for a hundred bleak years under Danish rule; finally it was presented by Tsar Paul I of Russia in 1773 to his cousin, the prince-bishop Friedrich August von Lübeck (1773–85). Now a duchy and the seat of the house of Holstein-Gottorp, Oldenburg regained importance, especially under the prince-bishop's successor Duke Peter Friedrich Ludwig and his son, Grand Duke Paul Friedrich August. A man of progressive thoughts and inspired by the ideals of classicism, Peter Friedrich Ludwig (1785–1829) was one of the enlightened paternalistic German rulers typical of his age. His seat at Eutin, where he gathered around him men like the painter Tischbein, Voss, the translator of Homer, and Goethe's friend Count Stollberg, was hailed as the Weimar of the north. Oldenburg, as the regional capital, was the focus of his architectural attention. Aspiring to create a modern city, he promoted several schemes, in particular the vast project of transforming the ramparts into a series of promenades, with the crescent of the Haarentorplatz as a grand entrance in the north-west and the Damm as an impressive avenue in the south-east leading from the Schloss to the open country, lined by important civic and private buildings. What the father had begun the son, Paul Friedrich August (1829–53), continued with even more gusto. He embellished Oldenburg (since 1815 a grand duchy) with a number of public and court buildings, while the extension of his army was reflected in his emphasis on military architecture. Basking in the democratic rule of this grand duke, domestic architecture flourished and Oldenburg grew rapidly. A firm predilection for classicism created a uniform townscape, which continued into the 20c. with buildings such as *Paul Bonatz's* government offices (1917). Most of the Neo-classical ensemble survived the fires of the last war, only to be disfigured by rapid and unfeeling postwar redevelopment.

The first court architect to work in a Neo-classical mode was *Peter Richter*. He is best known for the Ducal Mausoleum, designed in association with *Johann Heinrich Gottlob Becker*, who came from Hanover and served in Oldenburg as Bauinspektor until 1798. *Johann Bernard Winck* (1751–1812), who arrived in 1791 from Münster, succeeded Richter as court architect and was responsible for several public projects such as the rebuilding of St Lambert's and the Haarentorplatz. *Georg Sigismund Otto Lasius* was a Berlin-oriented architect influenced by Friedrich Gilly. *Carl Heinrich Slevogt* (c.1784–1832), who succeeded Winck as court architect, was born in Eutin and spent his formative years in Berlin. Most of his work is official court architecture. *Heinrich Strack the elder* (1801–80) studied with Hansen 1818–22 and was influenced by his master's Palladianesque style. He returned to his native Oldenburg in 1824 to start his career in the building department, soon became second in command to Slevogt, and finally succeeded him as

court architect. He was responsible for a variety of public structures, above all the impressive range of civic and court buildings facing the Schloss. *Hero Dietrich Hillners* (1807–85) was one of the leading late classicists in Oldenburg.

Schloss (1775–8, *Georg Greggenhofer*; 1787–1832, *Slevogt* and others) The first classical addition to the Renaissance castle was a substantial new east wing, commissioned by Friedrich August shortly after his accession. Known after the cabinet minister Holmer as the Holmer Wing, it was built to provide apartments for the highest civil servants, with a banqueting room on the first floor. The latter's enchanting and still extant interior shows to perfection the high standards of early classicism in Oldenburg.

The Library Wing which followed, built at right angles to the Holmer Wing, was the contribution of Peter Friedrich Ludwig. To maintain external unity the mansard roof of the main building was continued. Within is a stunning 'Antiquarium' decorated c.1800 in Pompeian style. A fourth wing was added in the 1890s in Renaissance style. In 1923 the castle was turned into a museum for the ducal collections.

Fürstengruft/Ducal Mausoleum (1786–90, *Richter* and *Becker*) The mausoleum, a stripped-down version of the Maison Carrée at Nîmes, formed a striking *point de vue* from the northern town gate, the Heiligengeisttor, whence it appeared across the newly laid out Pferdemarkt with the Gertrude Cemetery in the distance. Its stark cubic form is in the boldly experimental reductive style of the Revolutionary architecture beginning to grip Europe. French influence is even more apparent inside, where a simple row of three niches (the centre one emphasized by a temple-like frame) for the urns faces the entrance, and illumination is provided by a Pantheon-like oculus in a coffered vault. The interior was enriched later by two impressive marble monuments by the Stuttgart sculptor *J. H. Dannecker*, one commemorating Prince Georg (1824) and the other Princess Adelheid (1831).

Church of St Lambert (1791–5, *Winck*) When Oldenburg's renowned late Gothic Protestant Stadtkirche collapsed in 1791 and had to be rebuilt the use of the Pantheon formula for church design was still novel in Germany. The Hamburg architect *E. G. Sonnin* seems to have been the first to suggest it for St Lambert's, but the commission went to Winck. The foundations of the old hall church had to be used, so the new design was encased in a rectangular block. The dome, with a central lantern, is supported on a circle of twelve Ionic columns resting on a gallery upheld by piers. An additional gallery, probably inspired by D'Ixnard's St Blasien with its solemn Corinthian rotunda, runs high up behind the ring of columns like theatre boxes. A similar theatrical effect is created by the duke's box in the main gallery opposite the altar, which is emphasized by a screen of columns set within an arch containing a sculptural arrangement of the ducal coat of arms.

The original free-standing bell-tower was replaced by an attached west tower in 1873–4, and in 1882–7 four round towers for new staircases were added and the whole exterior was Gothicized, creating a picturesque ensemble in total stylistic contrast to the interior.

224 Johann Bernard Winck: church of St Lambert, Oldenburg, 1791–5.

Haarentorplatz and church of St Peter (1797–1814, *Winck*) The laying out of the area around the Haarentor, initiated by the dismantling of the ramparts, became a vital part of Duke Friedrich Ludwig's town improvement scheme. It was conceived as the grand entrance from the north-west, in the form of a crescent with radiating streets leading directly into the centre and communicating laterally with the newly created avenues on the ramparts. Its Palladian composition, with an alternation of one- and two-storeyed blocks, centred on the Catholic church of St Peter. Any emphasis on Catholic churches was forbidden in the Protestant north (they could not have steeples), and Winck's design was a subtle way of overcoming this rule. This unecclesiastical-looking St Peter's survived until the 1890s when the congregation moved to a Neo-Gothic building in Peterstrasse. Completion of the scheme was delayed until 1814 by the French occupation. Rebuilding from 1900 onwards destroyed the original elegance of the crescent, known today as Julius Mosen Platz.

Schlossgarten (1806–17, *C. F.* and *Julius Bosse*) Having created English gardens at Eutin and Rastede, Duke Peter Friedrich Ludwig desired one near his Oldenburg residence. Since this was in the middle of the town, land was acquired from 1803 onwards immediately outside the ramparts but near the castle, along the river Hunte in the direction of Everston, and here the court gardener and his son created a park of scenic beauty with charming garden buildings and meandering streams, entered through pilastered entrance lodges.

Tea pavilion in the Schlossgarten (1817, *Slevogt*) The pavilion, to which a Schinkelesque conservatory is attached, is remarkable for its severe cubic form. The strong, smooth wall surfaces are articulated by bold classical elements; a contrast is provided by delicate carvings, sparsely applied.

Gartenstrasse, originally a simple country road facing the Schlossgarten, became after the completion of the park in 1817 a fashionable setting for the villas of the rich.

Damm, a formal avenue leading in a straight line from south of the Schloss into the country, was the most ambitious of Peter Friedrich Ludwig's improvement schemes. Although the first houses built in the 1790s (on the east side) were modest in scale, the duke's vision was one of important public buildings and great private houses. He himself set the example, with the Prinzenpalais for his Russian grandchildren Alexander and Peter.

Prinzenpalais (1821–6, *Slevogt*; extended 1860–63, *Boos* and *Strack*) The palace that Slevogt built, on a corner at the top of the Damm, was a three-storeyed stucco building in a rather strict Neo-classical style, the façade towards the Damm emphasized by a pilastered central projection. The interior was more remarkable, with an exceptionally fine staircase hall and a striking Pompeian Room (1825) with precious inlays and murals by *Presuhn*. In 1860 the building was doubled in size by an extension to the south, and the exterior was unified by continuing the pilastrade over all the façades. The palace now sadly serves as offices.

The Damm's most important buildings are of late Neo-classical design. They consist of a range of civic structures on the west side and generously spaced private houses on the east, which were built first. The three houses at **nos. 39, 41 and 43**, two storeys tall, owe their air of grandeur not to any architectural emphasis but to their scale and balanced composition. The same cannot be said of the **Kastellanei** (1840) at no. 46, offices for palace administration, the first of the official structures built on the west side, which is totally without architectural distinction. The adjacent **Library and Archive Building** (1840–42, *Hillners*, to the design of *Otto Lasius*) is an altogether more remarkable building, in an elegant *Rundbogenstil*. The last in the row is the **Natural History Museum** (1876–9, *Gerhard Schwitger*), which was meant to balance the Kastellanei in scale and style, but emerged in an overcharged Renaissance-Baroque composite mode.

Schlossplatz Of all the urban improvements in Oldenburg the most spectacular was opposite the Schloss. Here, as an imposing architectural shield towards the medieval town, Grand Duke Paul Friedrich August sponsored an array of grandiose classical buildings, most of them designed by *Strack*. Closest to the Schloss is the **Hauptwache** (1839), a stuccoed guard house with a Doric portico, which is clearly a re-working of Schinkel's Neue Wache. The flanking **Kavaliershaus** (1839) and **Reithalle** (Riding School) and **Mews** (1835) all expressed the same smooth dignified language of mature classicism. That the latter three were pulled down in 1958–60 is an unforgivable and irreparable loss to Germany's architectural heritage.

Peter Friedrich Ludwig Hospital (1838–41, *Strack*) A monumental two-storeyed building accented by a hexastyle Tuscan portico.

Osnabrück

Seat of a bishop since 785 and a member of the powerful Hanseatic League in the Middle Ages, Osnabrück was from early times a centre of intellectual and personal freedom. The Treaty of Westphalia, signed here in conclusion of the Thirty Years War, gave the town its curious *successio alternativa*, whereby it was ruled alternatively by a Catholic bishop and a Protestant prince-bishop, the latter appointed by the house of Brunswick-Lüneburg. It was in the late 18c., under the last of the Protestant prince-bishops, George III's second son Frederick, Duke of York and Albany, that Osnabrück enjoyed its golden age. This was largely due to the enlightened chancellor Justus Möser (1720–94), a writer and historian, who was partly trained in London and who ruled Osnabrück for the Hanoverians. Möser's liberalism, combined with his keen patronage of the theatre and literature, exerted a profound influence on the town's development. International refinement was introduced at the end of the century by French refugees from the Revolution, who affected the life of the town for over a decade.

Between secularization in 1802 and the departure of Jérôme Bonaparte in 1813 Osnabrück changed hands a number of times between Hanover, Prussia and the French, ending up part of the Duchy of Hanover and finally, in 1866, part of Prussia.

The strong medieval character of the town and its liberal traditions, resistant to the authoritarianism necessary for ambitious urban schemes, ensured that Neo-classicism in Osnabrück, though important, was chiefly expressed in domestic terms. There are almost no monumental public buildings, and the one proposed grand avenue, the 'Boulevard du Roi de Rome', was begun in 1811 under Napoleonic rule and never completed. The heyday of domestic architecture was *c*.1785–1800, when it was marked first by early French classicism and then by the English Palladianism of the

town's leading architect, *Georg Heinrich Hollenberg* (1752–1831). After 1815 the influence of Schinkel was felt from Berlin.

In addition to Hollenberg – who was also an architectural writer, publishing *Praktische Baukunst* in 1804 – two other main architects were active. Classicism was introduced by *Schaedler*, the court architect, who is best known for his Kanzleigebäude and remodelling of the interior of the palace. *Clemens Lipper* was the brother of the famous Münster architect Ferdinand Wilhelm Lipper. He received no formal training, and although he is said to have visited Italy the Parisian character of his work suggests the influence of his brother.

Kanzleigebäude/Episcopal Chancellery (1782–5, *Schaedler*) A first design to replace the 16c. building was made by *Lipper* in 1779; a new design by Schaedler was presented in 1782 and built in 1783–5. It is still in a style transitional between late Baroque and early classical, but it marked a turning point in the town's architectural history. The cubic, restrained exterior, marked by an impressive pediment decorated with the arms of Hanover, reflects the new ideas of classicism, and the decorations are Louis XVI. The high roof follows local northern tradition. Additions in 1851 destroyed the purity of the design.

225 Schaedler: Kanzleigebäude, Osnabrück, 1782–5.

Schloss: interiors (1785–90, *Schaedler*) Remodelled in association with the Berlin court painter *Verona*. The entrance hall was redesigned, an impressive free-standing colonnade of paired columns forming an oval within the rectangular hall.

Clubsaal/Assembly Rooms (1793, *Hollenberg*) The centre of Osnabrück's cultural and social life: a set of public rooms attached to the Von der Busche Haus, in an up-to-date Neo-classical style which revolutionized interior design in the town.

Heger Tor (1817, *Hollenberg*) The medieval gate was transformed into an impressive triumphal arch to commemorate the battle of Waterloo, and porticoed lodges were added to serve as toll- and guard house.

In domestic architecture Osnabrück's Neo-classicism presented a rich and varied picture. The type of house most favoured was either three or five bays wide, and often still had the traditional high roof. They were mainly merchants' houses, the ground floor being used for business purposes while reception rooms and living rooms took up the first floor. Often in the case of the five-bay houses the centre was occupied by a ballroom flanked by smaller rooms or cabinets, a disposition clearly indicated by a central decoration on the façade. Thomas Mann gives a good account of this type of Hanseatic patrician house in *Buddenbrooks*, describing his childhood home. The development can be divided into three different phases: a French-influenced period, 1785–95; the Hollenberg era of Palladianism, 1795–1815; and Schinkelesque Neo-classicism, 1815–40.

The first period is best exemplified by three houses. The **Schwartzesche Haus**, begun in 1765 but practically rebuilt in 1790 for the merchant and banker Rudolf Schwartze, has pilaster strips with curious decorations between ground and first floor, and medallions over the doors showing portraits of the owner and his wife. The internal arrangement is of the traditional type, with offices on the ground floor and central ballroom on the first floor. **Haus Gössling** (1790), later Düttingsche Weinhandlung, is a Baroque house, given a classical façade with Louis XVI decorations. **Johannis Strasse 4** has the richest façade, with a central giant order of pilasters above a rusticated ground floor.

There are two outstanding examples of the Palladian phase, both by *Hollenberg*. The **Hirschapotheke** (1797–8) is a pharmacy ('at the sign of the stag') of palatial dimensions. The centre is marked by an applied Ionic portico; in the pediment and frieze and between the pilasters are Louis XVI swags, and in the centre between first- and second-floor windows is a relief incorporating a stag. **Haus Tenge** (*c.*1799) is similar to the pharmacy but with round-headed windows of which the central one is emphasized to indicate the ballroom behind. Other Palladian designs are the **Wesselsche Haus** (*c.*1800), **Langesche Haus**, **Löwenapotheke**, **Hotel Dütting**, and **Hakenstrasse 14**.

Notable buildings of the Schinkel-influenced period are the **Mohrenapotheke** (combining three houses designed by *Kemper c.*1830), and the **Haus Kamp** and **Grosse Strasse 80–81** (both *c.*1835).

Stuttgart

The capital of the Duchy of Württemberg since 1495, Stuttgart rose to prominence during the long reign of Duke Eugen (1744–93), although Ludwigsburg several times challenged its position. Like his predecessor Eberhard Ludwig, the creator of Ludwigsburg, Karl Eugen saw himself in the mould of Louis XIV and identified himself particularly with Frederick the Great, whose court he had attended in his youth. 'There was not another court like the one of Württemberg', wrote the amazed Baron Wimpfen in his memoirs, (1788): there 'one found the leading opera in all Europe, the leading orchestra, the most beautiful ballets, the best French comedy after that in Paris. And not only were there lavish shows almost every day which one could enjoy at no cost, but also there were many extraordinary festivities.'

Architecturally this magnificence found its expression in the grandiose Neues Schloss built in 1746–68 to the design of the Italian *Leopoldo Retti* (d.1751) and the Parisian *Philippe de la Guêpière* (*c.*1715–73). It was a decisive commitment to the French school and as such a first move towards progressive classicism in southern Germany. This transitional style was displayed in the many palaces built for Karl Eugen: the charming lakeside Monrepos (1760–64) by *Guêpière*; the Sanssouci-like Solitude (1763–*c.*1769) by *Guêpière* and *Johann Friedrich Weyhing* (1716–81); and the ambitious palace at Hohenheim (1785–96) by Guêpière's pupil *Reinhard Ferdinand Heinrich Fischer* (1746–1813), who succeeded his master as court architect in 1773.

Karl Eugen's successor, Friedrich I (1797–1816), was likewise a tyrannical and capricious ruler but less concerned with palace building. However, he had important parts of the palace interiors at Stuttgart, Ludwigsburg, Monrepos and Hohenheim remodelled or redecorated by the Paris-trained architect *Nicolaus Friedrich von Thouret* (1767–1845) in the new Neo-classical style. This was developed into an unusually lavish Empire Style after Friedrich had been created

226 A typical Osnabrück house of the 1780s or 90s, in Bierstrasse.

king of Württemberg by Napoleon in 1806. It was also at this time that the Friedrichsstadt was commissioned from Thouret to accommodate the expansion of Stuttgart.

Most of the public buildings were erected under King Wilhelm I (1816–64), a stern and responsible ruler, who reformed the administration and finances of the kingdom. Married to Queen Katharine, daughter of Tsar Paul I, he lived an unostentatious domestic life which was reflected in the design of his two new palaces, the town-house-like Wilhelmspalais and the severe summer palace of Rosenstein. It was during his cautious and conservative reign that Stuttgart turned from a gay and vivacious court town into a modern industrial city. The architects he employed were *Giovanni Salucci* (1769–1845), *Georg Gottlob Barth* (1777–1848), *Johann Michael Knapp* (1793–1861), *Karl Ludwig Wilhelm Zanth* (1796–1857), and *Christian Friedrich Leins* (1814–1892).

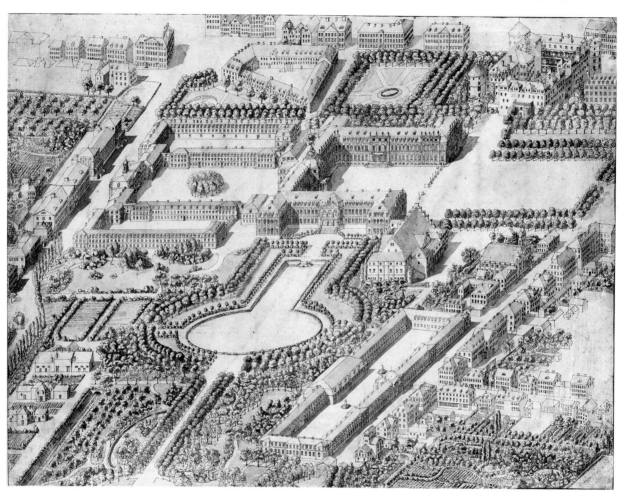

227 Nicolaus Friedrich von Thouret: bird's-eye view of the centre of Stuttgart showing the Altes Schloss (top right), the Neues Schloss (centre) and the Academy (top left), and Schlossgarten with mews in the foreground.

Neues Schloss (1746, 1748–51, *Retti*; 1751–8, *Guêpière*; *c*.1803–15 etc., *Thouret*) Designs were commissioned from Retti in 1746, and although other projects were then submitted by Johann Friedrich von Oettinger, Johann Christoph David von Leger, Mauritio Pedetti, Alessandro Galli da Bibiena and later by Balthasar Neumann, in 1748 work started on Retti's scheme. When he suddenly died in 1751 two-thirds of the L-shaped palace had been erected (*corps de logis* and garden wing), but only the foundations of the town wing had been laid. None of the interiors had been completed.

Guêpière was called in to finish the building, and the town wing was erected in 1751–6 in the classical style of his master, Blondel. Guêpière's building had a block-like centre pavilion, rectangular windows with simple architrave surrounds, and plain undecorated walls. By adding a portico to the south front of the *corps de logis* in 1758 he tried to minimize the earlier building's Baroque character. He also adapted the interior as far as possible to the new classical taste. The decoration of the oval entrance hall had a crisp flat clarity, and the staircase was modelled on French examples such as that of the

Hôtel Salé in Paris, while the Garde Saal had a more tranquil linear effect. The Great Marble Hall, the principal room in Retti's plan, was finally decorated in an extraordinary mixture of Baroque and classical motifs later critized by Goethe. This French early classicism naturally appeared at its purest in Guêpière's own town wing, in the Hall of Mirrors and above all in the White Hall.

The last major architect to be involved in the 360-room palace was *Thouret*, who created many interiors in the early 19c., such as the elegant and refined Blue Marble Hall, Throne Room, and Red Marble Hall or Summer Hall. Most of these rooms did not survive severe bombing in the war, and were rebuilt differently.

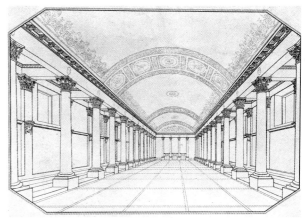

229 Nicolaus Friedrich von Thouret: Redoutensaal, Stuttgart, remodelled 1813.

228 Nicolaus Friedrich von Thouret: Blue Marble Hall of the Neues Schloss, Stuttgart, early 19th century.

Catholic church of St Eberhard (*c.*1770, *Fischer*) Originally built near Karl Eugen's Solitude, and re-erected in the Königsstrasse in 1808 by *Karl von Uber*, with interior by Thouret. Uber's façade was more cubic and massive, with a Corinthian portico supporting a block-like attic storey with a stepped gable, the whole surmounted by a spire. Rebuilt after the war with faint references to the original.

44 **Akademiesaal/Hall of the Carlsakademie** (1774–5, *Fischer*) A charming Pantheon-like rotunda with coupled Corinthian columns supporting a gallery and a shallow dome. The structure began life as part of a barracks building, first remodelled in 1740–45 by *Leger*, before Fischer's further modifications for the Carlsakademie (founded in 1770 at Solitude and dissolved in 1794). It was designed to serve as a dining hall for Karl Eugen and his wife when they visited the Academy; later King Friedrich used it for part of the court library. It was destroyed by bombing in 1941.

Redoutensaal (remodelled 1813, *Thouret*) A building designed for balls and concerts, with a magnificent hall surrounded by a Corinthian colonnade supporting a barrel vault with elegant Greek decoration.

'Halbmondsaal'/Chamber of Deputies (1817, *Barth*) The half-moon-shaped chamber, based on Gondoin's Ecole de Médecine, was surrounded by Corinthian columns, with a gallery for spectators between the columns at first-floor level.

230 Georg Gottlob Barth: 'Halbmondsaal' (Chamber of Deputies), Stuttgart, 1817.

Katharinenhospital (1820, *Thouret*) A plain exterior, with a rusticated ground floor and pedimented centrepiece.

257

Staatsarchiv und Naturhistorisches Museum/ State Archives and Natural History Museum (1821, *Barth*) One of the major public buildings erected in the Neckarstrasse (now Konrad Adenauer Strasse), this was a long two-storeyed structure with taller corner pavilions, each with a portico of unfluted Greek Doric columns, indicating its dual function. The design was rather academic, with rows of windows and an undistinguished use of the orders. A third storey was later added. Destroyed by bombing.

231 Georg Gottlob Barth: Staatsarchiv, Stuttgart, 1821.

149 **Schloss Rosenstein** (1822–30, *Salucci*) The extensive royal summer palace, attractively situated on the top of a hill, is a low structure – mainly single-storeyed – built in a restrained Greek Revival style around two interior courtyards. The entrance front is marked by a majestic Ionic portico in the centre and by end pavilions with Doric porticoes, and the elevations are sparingly decorated by remarkably fine carved ornament. This austere exterior contains a rich interior, decorated largely in Pompeian style. The colonnaded hall, expressed on the exterior by the central portico, has a distinctly Roman flavour, with an impressive encircling carved frieze of the four seasons by *Konrad Weitbrecht*. The palace was burnt in 1943 and restored to house the Natural History Museum.

232 Giovanni Salucci: Schloss Rosenstein, Stuttgart, 1824–9.

Reithaus/Riding School, Neckarstrasse (c.1830, *Salucci*) A well proportioned rectangular building with a rusticated ground floor, entrance doors and corner pilasters, and round-headed windows. Given a mansard roof in the late 19c. and demolished in 1958.

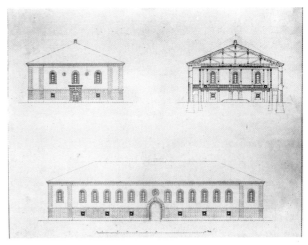

233 Giovanni Salucci: section, front and side elevations of the Reithaus, Stuttgart, c.1830.

Bazaar (1834–7, *Thouret*) A vast multi-storeyed building on a corner site, with an imposing arcade on unfluted Greek Doric columns at street level. Much altered, and then destroyed by bombing.

234 Nicolaus Friedrich von Thouret: Bazaar, Stuttgart, 1834–7.

Wilhelmspalais (1835–40, *Salucci*) Built for two 147 princesses of the house of Württemberg, in a dull Italianate classical style, but with a noble porte cochère. Now the town library.

Wilhelma Theatre, Neckartal-Pragstrasse (1838–40, *Zanth*) One of the first buildings erected in the complex which also included the **Villa Wilhelma** (1837–51), this was in marked contrast to the other structures' Moorish style, displaying a Palladian composition with Greek ornamental motifs.

148 **Museum der bildenden Künste** (now **Staatsgalerie**)/**Museum and Academy of Arts** (1838–42, *Barth* after *Thouret*) A palatial building with three ranges round a courtyard, in a Klenze-like style. The ends of the projecting wings are soberly adorned with reliefs representing the development of painting and sculpture.

Münze/Mint, Neckarstrasse (1842–4, *Gross*) In Renaissance style.

235 Gross: Mint, Stuttgart, 1842–4.

Jubilee Column, Schlossplatz (1842–8, *Knapp*)

Villa Berg (1845–53, *Leins*) A picturesque eclectic building combining Renaissance and Greek elements in the Italian villa manner expressed by Schinkel at Charlottenhof. Formerly the summer palace of Crown Prince Karl, the villa is now a radio station.

Kronprinzenpalais (1846–50, *Gaab*) Designed for the crown prince, with different classical motifs on each of the three storeys. The palace was not rebuilt after bombing, but part of the portico was preserved as a memorial in the Schlossplatz.

236 Gaab: Kronprinzenpalais, Stuttgart, 1846–50.

Königsbau (1856–60, *Knapp/Leins*) Designed by Knapp and modified by Leins, this complex including assembly rooms and shops is a late classical building of monumental strength and grandeur which anticipates the large-scale public buildings of the late 19c. Its imposing colonnade of twenty-six Ionic columns and its two Corinthian porticoes placed off centre proclaimed a challenge to the Neues Schloss on the opposite side of the square.

237 Johann Michael Knapp and Christian Friedrich Leins: Königsbau, Stuttgart, 1856–60.

Environs of Stuttgart

Monrepos (1760–64, *Guêpière*) A country retreat for 24 Duke Karl Eugen. The plan is still Rococo, but the elevations, with their flat surface treatment, rectangular windows, cornices, crisp swags and square-cut niches, bound together and firmly controlled by an architrave, are a decisive expression of classicism. The same is true of the interior. Only the entrance hall was entirely designed by Guêpière. The elegant central hall and other rooms were remodelled by *Thouret*, whose influence is seen particularly in the details. The sculptors involved in the 1760s were *Philipp Jakob Scheffauer* (entrance hall), *Pierre Lejeune* (some of the external sculpture), *Johann Gottlieb Friedrich* and *Wilhelm Ludwig Mack* (lions flanking the entrance steps). As in many of Karl Eugen's other palaces, there were frescoes by *Nicolas Guibal*.

Solitude (1763–*c.*1769, *Weyhing* and *Guêpière*) Originally planned as a simple hunting lodge for Karl Eugen, Solitude developed into a grandiose country house with extensive outbuildings, rooms for theatre and opera, and many famous garden follies. The house stands on an arcaded basement, as at Monrepos, but it is single-storeyed, with an oval rotunda dominating the wings. Also as at Monrepos, the influence of French classicism is apparent in the treatment of the elevations – here a firm and flat pilaster-architrave composition with rectangular windows filling the whole width of the bays.

The interior has an intricate plan, developed in response to Karl Eugen's continuing demands as he visited the site, taking an active part in the designing. Most of the rooms have Rococo decoration, but already set within a rectangular framework. Classicism is more apparent in the central Weisser Saal (White Hall), an oval saloon with an architrave supported on coupled Corinthian columns and largely monochrome colour scheme, and is most clearly displayed in the Marmorsalon (Marble Saloon), where a disciplined use of the order gives an effect of festive austerity.

Of the many garden structures none has survived. The famous stables for nearly 800 horses were dismantled and re-erected in Stuttgart. Most of the interiors of the Court buildings have been altered, but the splendid Catholic court chapel in the western part survives.

238 Johann Friedrich Weyhing: Solitude, near Stuttgart, 1763–79.

Schloss Hohenheim (1785–96, *Fischer*) The palace was commissioned by Karl Eugen for his much-loved mistress and later wife, Franziska von Hohenheim. Of the grand scheme drawn up by Fischer in 1782–3 only parts were realized, but they are in a striking style transitional between late Baroque and French classicism. The composition, with *corps de logis* and flanking wings, is still Baroque, but the elevations are much plainer, and accented only by horizontal rows of windows; the central pavilion alone is given an order. This centre also no longer projects, as in a Baroque design; instead, its geometrical qualities are stressed by a plain saucer dome and block-like Tuscan portico. Fischer's surviving interiors are the lower and upper vestibules with the staircase. A dining room and other

rooms are known from drawings. The entrance hall was conceived in the French manner, as an open vestibule of extraordinary purity, with two screens of coupled Tuscan columns supporting an architrave. The staircase and upper vestibule, though less restrained, are treated in the same controlled fashion with an emphasis on rectangular flat forms. In the upper vestibule Fischer created an elegant festive prelude to the enfilade of rooms blending Baroque and Neo-classical features, some of which anticipated Percier and Fontaine. Several of the rooms were later completed or redecorated by *Thouret*. Since the early 19c. the building has housed an agricultural college.

The garden was once famed as one of the leading German Picturesque parks, with an abundance of temples, grottoes, towers, an 'English Village', etc., which Goethe already considered too overpowering. Several of the now-lost buildings, such as the boudoir with its remarkable rotunda, or the Temple of Cybele, though opulently decorated, also displayed Fischer's transitional style.

239, 240 Reinhard Ferdinand Heinrich Fischer: two buildings from the 'English Village' of Schloss Hohenheim, near Stuttgart, 1785–6: the 'Rathaus' (above) and 'Temple of Cybele' (below).

Rotenberg: Grabkapelle/Mausoleum for Queen Katharine (1820–24, *Salucci*) For his wife King Wilhelm commissioned a mausoleum in the form of a rotunda with a crypt below, spectacularly sited on top of the Rotenberg hill overlooking vineyards. Designs were submitted by Knapp and Salucci, mostly classical but some Gothic. Salucci's design for a rotunda with Ionic porticoes facing the four cardinal directions was chosen. A monumental flight of steps lined by bronze candelabra leads first to a terrace and then to the entrance of the mausoleum, marked by the inscription 'And love will never end'. Its simple grandeur of design and refinement of detail – including reliefs by *J. H. Dannecker* and *Thorvaldsen* inside – make this one of the best Neoclassical buildings of Stuttgart.

241, 242 Giovanni Salucci: exterior and interior of the Mausoleum for Queen Katharine, Stuttgart, 1820–24.

Bad Canstatt: Kursaal/Pump Room (*c.*1825, *Thouret*) An elegant single-storeyed building resembling an orangery, built for this popular 19c. spa to the northeast of Stuttgart. A pedimented projecting centre block with a semi-circular unfluted Doric portico marks the entrance, which is a rather extraordinary monumental glazed arch in the manner of French Revolutionary architecture.

Weimar

It was a propitious moment for German intellectual life when in 1772 Wieland was invited by the dowager Grand Duchess Anna Amalia of Saxe-Weimar to educate her two sons, especially the Crown Prince Karl August (1757–1828). As grand duke, Karl August was a lover of the arts who drew to his court the most distinguished of the rising geniuses of the country – Goethe, Herder, Schiller and Jean Paul. Weimar became the centre from which German national literature evolved. The most popular of the German princes and known for his enlightened rule, Karl August raised his small state to a remarkable eminence considering its geographical remoteness – set on the small river Ilm in a flat and uninteresting landscape – and its political insignificance.

Architecturally, on the other hand, there were no ambitious urban schemes like those of Kassel, Karlsruhe or Brunswick, and until 1816, when *Clemens Wenzeslaus Coudray* (1775–1845) was appointed Oberbaudirektor, Weimar had no leading architects of its own. Goethe lamented that outside help had to be sought for the rebuilding of the Schloss after a fire in 1774, a project that he masterminded. Following Goethe's advice in architecture as in literature, the grand duke invited outstanding architects to submit designs for his palace. Proposals came from French architects, including *Clérisseau*, but, interestingly, Germans were preferred. The first of them was *Johann August Arens* (1757–1806), from Hamburg, who after training in Paris visited England and Italy, where he was discovered by Goethe. He was followed by architects borrowed from other German courts – *Nicolaus Friedrich von Thouret* (1767–1845) from Stuttgart, and *Heinrich Gentz* (1766–1811) from Berlin. Thanks to them, Weimar received a few superb examples of Neo-classicism, such as the Greek Revival palace interiors and the Römisches Haus. Public architecture only started to flourish modestly in the 1820s under *Coudray*. Although Weimar was devastated during the war, a substantial part of its classical architecture has been restored.

Schloss (1789–94 *Arens*, 1798–1800 *Thouret*, 1801–3 *Gentz;* west wing 1830–45, *Coudray*) The overall plan was established by *Arens*, using the old foundations and ruins. He stayed only until 1794, and was eventually replaced by *Thouret*. Difficulties over finance caused tension and Thouret resigned, which brought *Gentz* to Weimar in 1800. In spring 1801 the Landesstände (Estates) of Weimar, Jena and Eisenach met to grant financial support for the building of the palace, and from then on construction progressed rapidly, involving at times 325 workmen. In the summer of 1803 the ducal family moved in.

A rather severe exterior, relieved only by *Arens's* Tuscan colonnade on the river front, conceals delicate interiors by Thouret and Gentz. *Thouret* had prepared drawings for the decoration of five rooms, of which the Round Room (1798–1800), in a delicate Pompeian style, stands out as the most elegant. It was an ante-room

for Grand Duchess Louise (of Hesse-Darmstadt), and her name was boldly inscribed in a charming painted frieze running below the exquisitely decorated ceiling executed by Goethe's friend, the painter *Johann Heinrich*
56 *Meyer. Gentz's* interiors, especially the Festsaal or banqueting hall, great staircase and Falcon Gallery, are the touchstones of the Greek Revival in Germany. The double-height Festsaal (1802–3) is surrounded by an Ionic colonnade; the walls are bare except for a continuous classical frieze running below the ceiling, highlighting the room's chaste elegance. Some gilding was intended, but it was abandoned for the sake of economy. The two statues in niches, modelled on the popular actresses Karoline Jagemann and Friederike Muzelmann, are like the reliefs by *Christian Friedrich Tieck* (1776–1851), a pupil of Schadow and David d'Angers. Tieck also carved the sculptural decorations of the staircase hall in the east wing. The Falcon Gallery (1803) owed its shape to the shell of the old palace, but was ingeniously transformed by an impressive richly coffered vaulted ceiling. Beautifully inlaid wooden floors enhanced all the interiors.

In 1830–45 *Coudray* added a west wing, with rooms dedicated to Weimar's intellectual geniuses – Goethe, Schiller, Wieland and Herder. The walls of these shrines are decorated with remarkable frescoes depicting scenes from their writings, while busts represent the poets themselves. The Goethe Gallery was based on a design by *Schinkel*.

In 1913 a fourth range on the south was added, in a disturbing Neo-Baroque style. Since 1923 most of the palace has served as an art museum.

Hoftheater/Court Theatre The building of 1779–80 by *J.F.R. Steiner* was remodelled in 1798 by *Thouret*, on the pattern of Ledoux's theatre at Besançon. Thouret's creation, which was supervised by Goethe and drawn by Gilly, was destroyed by fire in 1825. Its replacement, by *Coudray*, was demolished in 1905.

57 **Römisches Haus/Roman House** (1791–7, *Arens*) The design, almost certainly influenced by Goethe, incorporates an Ionic portico at one end and at the other, leading to a crypto-porticus, stunted Paestum Doric columns carrying segmental arches. The interiors were designed by *Schuricht* after Arens's departure in 1794. In 1819 the pediment was adorned by a figure of a genius stretching out to allegories of art, science and agriculture, by *Johann Peter Kaufmann* (1764–1829).

Bertuch Häuser (1780–1800, architect unknown) Commissioned by Johann Justin Bertuch – author, publisher and entrepreneur and an important figure in Weimar – this combination of three houses is one of the town's most splendid private dwellings. It has a seven-bay three-storeyed façade in Palladian style with an applied tetrastyle Ionic portico. In a modernization of 1803 it was provided with a magnificent entrance hall in a severe Greek Doric style inspired by Gentz. Today it is the Museum of Local History.

243 Heinrich Gentz: Festsaal of the Schloss, Weimar, 1802–3.

244 Clemens Wenzeslaus Coudray: Goethegalerie in the Schloss, Weimar, 1830–45.

245 Bertuch Häuser, Weimar, 1780–1800.

Reithaus/Riding School (remodelled 1803–4, *Gentz*) The building of 1715–17 was re-cast by Gentz with prominent Greek key friezes, similar to those of the Vieweg House in Brunswick.

246 Heinrich Gentz: Reithaus, Weimar, remodelled 1803–4.

247 Clemens Wenzeslaus Coudray: Grand Ducal Mausoleum, Weimar, 1822–4.

Fürstengruft/Grand Ducal Mausoleum (1822–4, *Coudray*) Some years before his death Grand Duke Karl August commissioned a mausoleum for his family to be erected in the New Cemetery, opened in 1818. His forefathers were buried in it in 1824, and three years later he ordered Schiller's remains to be laid to rest there. In 1828 he himself was interred, followed in 1832 by Goethe. The main feature of the building is a portico of four unfluted Greek Doric columns leading to a centrally planned interior with an octagonal lantern of striking simplicity.

Bürgerschule/Municipal School (1822–5, *Coudray*) Coudray had designed several country schools before he drew up the plans for this, his largest public building. It contained 8 classrooms, 4 for boys and 4 for girls, said to hold up to 100 pupils each. A Lehrerseminar formed part of the school. Goethe, who took a keen interest in the project, praised the interior, believing it to have an elevating effect on the pupils. The chaste exterior still retains elements of the Franco-Prussian style of a generation earlier.

Other public works by *Coudray* show something of the Franco-Prussian style: the **Erfurter Tor** (1822–4), the **Wagenremise/Coach House** (1823) and the **Hauptwache/Main Guard House** (1834–8). He also enjoyed an extensive private practice, some of it on a scale similar to Nash's Regent's Park houses. Examples are in **Heinrich Heine Strasse** (1817, 1821), **Heinrich Hess Strasse**, and **Steubenstrasse 2–8** (1827).

Wiesbaden

From 1744 the seat of the court of Nassau-Usingen, and from 1806 capital of the newly created Duchy of Nassau, Wiesbaden was important in the 19c. as a spa. Second only in fame to Baden Baden, it attracted the fashionable crowds of Europe – 'from sovereigns, princes, and dukes down to the Frankfurt merchant', as an English visitor observed in 1842. The spa's success largely stemmed from the architectural setting created for it. The first to recognize the necessity of improvement and expansion was the Elector Friedrich Wilhelm, who in 1803, the year of his death, publicly invited private enterprise to back his project. Finally it was the Napoleonic bribe of making Wiesbaden the capital of a duchy that set the architectural scheme in motion. Only a year later the new duke, Friedrich August (1803–16), appointed *Johann Christian Zais* (1770–1820) as his architect and in a lengthy 'Publicandum' expounded the first important project, the Kurhaus. To revive and capitalize on the famous hot springs, new spa buildings, hotels and places of entertainment were needed. Under Friedrich August and even more under Duke Wilhelm (1816–39) new streets and squares were laid out, with the Wilhelmstrasse as the main street and monumental entrance to Wiesbaden leading in a straight line to a grand piazza formed by the palace-like composition of the Kurhaus to the right and the Theaterplatz with all the famous hotels to the left. The town grew rapidly, nearly doubling its inhabitants between 1799 and 1814 and increasing its buildings from 877 in 1840 to 1,620 in 1870. Unfortunately this second layer of development in the later 19c. destroyed many of the earlier schemes, but several survive and the grandeur of the overall composition was never lost.

Along with *Zais*, who was responsible for most of the spa buildings, the main architects working in Wiesbaden were *Carl Florian Götz* (1763–1829) and *Theodor Götz*, who specialized in domestic architecture, Baurat *Heinrich Jakob Zengerle*, and *Georg Moller* (1784–1852) from Darmstadt, who designed one major building, the Schloss.

Kurhaus/Assembly Rooms (1808–10, *Zais*) The assembly rooms and casino were built at the edge of town to avoid congestion and noise. This allowed a splendid setting of which the architect made clever use, designing the façade as a focal point when approached from the centre of town or from outside. A magnificent deep Ionic portico covered the main block thus marking the building's festive centre, its grand assembly hall. Lower Doric colonnades linked the centre to little terminal pavilions accentuated by Palladian windows. This spectacular town façade contrasted with a relatively simple and informal park front. The main and most magnificent feature of the interior was the Kursaal or assembly hall occupying the whole of the centre block and reaching its full height. Rows of Corinthian marble columns with gilded capitals line its long sides supporting a richly carved architrave surmounted by a deeply coffered coved ceiling. Great doors lead immediately into the gardens behind, which formed an important extension to the festive setting for the immense crowds coming here. Additions during the 19c. constantly adapted the building to the growing needs of the spa. In 1904–5 *Friedrich von Thiersch* totally remodelled and rebuilt the exterior, preserving vital parts of Zais's interior.

249 Johann Christian Zais: Kursaal, Wiesbaden, 1808–10.

Hotel Zais and **Hotel Nassauer Hof** The Hotel Zais, built in 1810 as a town house, with its twin the Hotel Nassauer Hof, formed the side of the Theaterplatz facing the Kurhaus. In the 1830s both received an additional storey to match the height of the adjacent Hotel Vierjahreszeiten, to which they related stylistically. Neither survives.

248 Johann Christian Zais: park front of the Kurhaus, Wiesbaden, 1808–10.

250 Johann Christian Zais: Prinzenpalais, Wiesbaden, 1812–18.

Prinzenpalais (1812–18, *Zais*) Built as a town palace for the ducal family, but transformed into a museum and library in 1821 and from 1824 seat of the Society of Antiquaries. Placed at the corner of Wilhelmstrasse and Friedrichstrasse, immensely long (seventeen bays) and three storeys high, it was a key building for the monumental layout of the Wilhelmstrasse. The composition is Nash-like, the centre emphasized by a raised tetrastyle portico of free-standing Ionic columns. The grandest interiors are the entrance hall, dignified by Doric columns, and the staircase hall. The building now houses the Industrie und Handelskammer.

Hotel Vierjahreszeiten (1817–18, *Zais*) Its position near the Kurhaus and occupying a complete side of the Theaterplatz proclaimed the building's status as the foremost hotel in Wiesbaden. Behind an elegant, dignified façade, it provided all the luxury and grandeur expected by a glamorous cosmopolitan clientèle. With 150 rooms and 44 baths it was one of the largest hotels in Germany, widely admired for its dining hall (seating 124) and banqueting hall adorned by a spectacular array of columns. Zais financed the project as well as designing it, and ensured its success by additional personal attendance. The building was remodelled in 1881, and destroyed during the last war.

Kurhausarkaden (north 1825, south 1839, *Zengerle*) Two colonnaded arcades of shops forming a sort of *cour d'honneur* to the Kurhaus, and echoing its own colonnaded wings. They contained 'pretty little shops forming a sort of bazaar in the open air' where 'the fantastic costume of the vendors, who were Savoyards, Tyrolese, and Swiss' gave 'to the whole scene the air of a fancy fair'.

Schauspielhaus/Theatre (1826, *Zengerle*) A modest structure which fitted well into the Neo-classical ensemble of the Theaterplatz, its porticoed porch approached by a broad flight of steps and supporting a balcony echoing that of the Hotel Zais across the square. No longer extant.

Catholic church of St Boniface (1829) Designed with a Corinthian portico flanked by twin campanile-like towers fronting a majestic cube with projecting short side wings, the church would have been a landmark in the Luisenstrasse. Construction began in 1829 but two years later, in 1831, the building collapsed before completion. A Neo-Gothic church was eventually built in 1845–9.

Münze/Mint (1829) A simple utilitarian structure two storeys high with a three-bay central projection.

Schloss (1837–41, *Moller*) The narrow complicated site of the old Renaissance palace, in the heart of town overlooking the market square and allowing no impressive setting or commanding vista, called for skilful planning. Moller ingeniously made use of the *parti* of his Kasino in Darmstadt, itself based on a design by Weinbrenner for the Karlsruhe Museum. Sensitively responding to the irregular market square, Moller placed the building at an angle, emphasizing the projecting corner by a tower with an elegant circular porch of Doric columns supporting a balustraded balcony. Heavy window heads marked the first floor, which was surmounted by a massive cornice linking elevations and tower. To the later 19c. the design of the 1830s appeared too chaste, and the elevations were enriched. The suite of rooms within, with a splendid circular domed Festsaal or banqueting hall, music room and dining room on the first floor, came as a surprise after the sober exterior. There were painted decorations by *Ludwig* and *Friedrich Pose* (1840) in the Pompeian and Empire styles and sculpture by *Schwanthaler*. An extensive programme of restoration, begun in 1961, has removed the late 19c. decoration and revived the former splendour of the palace, which is used as a chamber of deputies and seat of local government.

Taunusbahnhof/Railway Station (1839–42) One of the early group of stations built in a Neo-classical style; the entrance is marked by a higher centre section topped by a small Italianate tower. It is now used as a public hall and known as Rhein Main Halle.

The high standard of domestic architecture in Neo-classical Wiesbaden, which reflected the spa's wealth, can still be seen in houses like **Marktstrasse 1–3** (1803–4, *C.F. Götz*), **Friedrichstrasse 32** (1817) and **Luisenstrasse 12** (1825).

251 Heinrich Jakob Zengerle: Schauspielhaus, Wiesbaden, 1826.

On the outskirts

Schloss auf der Platte (1822–4, *Schrumpf*) A large hunting lodge some 6 km from Wiesbaden built for Duke Wilhelm. Its situation, on a hill commanding the countryside, gave it its name, which means 'the Schloss on the platform'. The plan and elevations provided by Baurat Schrumpf of Biebrich were of the Villa Rotunda type. Each of the four façades was marked by a pedimented portico (columns on the south front and pilasters elsewhere). Inside there were four principal rooms behind the porticoes and square cabinets in the corners, arranged around a circular domed centre. The latter housed an impressive two-armed staircase leading to a gallery with columns supporting the dome. Remarkable plaster ceilings and a marbled dining hall were special features of the interior, which had painted decorations by *Reuren* celebrating the hunt. The building was gutted during the war.

Wolfenbüttel see Brunswick

Würzburg

This exuberant Baroque town has very little Neo-classical architecture, but that little is of excellent quality. Würzburg was shaped by its history as a wealthy seat of prince-bishops, and for them from 1719 onwards Balthasar Neumann and others created the Residenz Schloss which still commands the town today. Under Napoleon's reorganization Würzburg was secularized in 1803 and came under Bavarian rule, interrupted only by a short interlude between 1806 and 1814 when, under the terms of the Treaty of Pressburg, Grand Duke Ferdinand III of Tuscany ruled as regent. It was then that Neo-classicism found a brief and brilliant expression, in the grand duke's redecoration of parts of the Residenz, and above all in the work of the remarkable *Peter Speeth* (1772–1831), whom Ferdinand had appointed with the French architect *Nicolas-Alexandre Salins de Montfort* (1753–1839) as his architectural director.

Residenz Schloss The shell of the building and the celebrated Rococo interiors were substantially complete when in the reign of Adam Friedrich von Seinsheim (1755–79) a change of taste towards early classicism took place. The three most northern rooms of the *corps de logis* (guest-room I 1764, guest-room II 1766–7, and the famous Green Varnished Room 1769–72) already show signs of the new style as interpreted by *Lodovico* and *Materno Bossi*. With their controlled framework, rectangular overdoors and, in the guest-rooms, white and gold decoration, they present a curious mixture of Würzburg Rococo and Louis XVI styles. A more severe version of the latter appears in the stuccoed staircase hall (1765–6) by *Lodovico Bossi*, though still with a hectic movement in the Corinthian pilasters. Finally a splendid pure Louis XVI enhances the Fürstensaal or banqueting hall

(1771–2) and the redecorated bishop's suite in the north wing, the Ingelheimer Zimmer (1776–81), both designed by *Materno Bossi* and *Johann Peter Wagner*.

Next, various rooms were remodelled for the grand duke of Tuscany between 1807 and 1810. The Toskanazimmer were commissioned by Ferdinand immediately after his accession in the fashionable Empire Style, to emphasize his emulation of the Napoleonic court. By then, too, the existing style of the Residenz appeared impossibly old-fashioned. As his architect he chose *Salins de Montfort*, who was then working in Frankfurt and was probably recommended by Karl Theodor von Dalberg. Twenty rooms were redecorated, divided into three separate apartments. Those in the north-eastern corner of the south wing were designed for state occasions; those in the south-western corner, extending along the southern garden front, were the grand duke's private apartments; and others in the north wing became the living quarters of his daughter Charlotte. Although Salins de Montfort was inspired in his designs by the Work of Percier and Fontaine, he had only taken up their style a few years earlier, having been trained in the Louis XVI tradition, and his manner is less ostentatious and more graceful than the full-blooded Napoleonic style. His interiors, entirely executed by craftsmen from Frankfurt, represent a distinctive contribution from Germany to Neo-classicism.

252 Materno Bossi and Johann Peter Wagner: Ingelheimer Zimmer in the Residenz Schloss, Würzburg, 1776–81.

253 Peter Speeth: drawing for the Gerichtsdienerhaus, Würzburg, 1811.

254 The same house as it now is, with altered fenestration.

The Residenz was severely bombed in the war. The 18c. rooms were restored in the 1970s, but the Toskanazimmer still await restoration.

Gerichtsdienerhaus/House of the Court Usher, Turmgasse 9 (1811–13, *Speeth*) The unconventional design of the façade shows Speeth's commitment to French Revolutionary architecture. A monumental effect is achieved by the contrast between massive forms and small apertures, and between a rusticated ground floor and smooth wall surfaces above. The composition is treated as two layers, an Egyptian pylon shape appearing like a shallow relief sculpture set against a larger block. It is hard to believe that the original arrangement of windows suited the needs of the rooms inside – a suspicion which seems confirmed by the later insertion of more windows, as well as other changes.

63 **St Burkhardt Prison** (1811, 1826–7, *Speeth*) Speeth's best-known and most remarkable work, built as guards barracks and converted into a prison. The building's authoritarian function is announced by its massive walls, its small windows placed high up and the threatening heavy rustication of the ground floor. The low arch with its small entrance, through which it appears one would almost have to crawl, recalls similar designs by Ledoux and Boullée.

Zeller Tor Wachthaus Zellerstrasse 45 (1813–15, completed 1824, *Speeth*) The reduction of the composition of this guard house to geometric forms, the solid character, the use of Greek Doric rather than the Tuscan order, and finally the concept of the building as a Propylaea-like structure, are all elements derived from French Revolutionary architecture, particularly as expressed in Ledoux's *barrières*. This is an impressive building, single-storeyed except for a raised central pavilion which has an open portico on the ground floor and Durand-like round-headed windows above, surmounted by a shallow dome. The heavy rustication wrapping it right up to the arched window tops immediately gives the impression of a stronghold.

House in Bohnesmühlgasse (*c.* 1820) A building with *Speeth*-like features, which has been attributed to him.

Bibliography

General

Andrews, Keith *The Nazarenes*, Oxford, 1964
Arnold, Christoph Friedrich *Practische Anleitung zur bürgerlichen Baukunst*, Karlsruhe and Freiburg, 1833
– *Projekte der bürgerlichen Baukunst*, Karlsruhe, 1831
Beenken, Hermann *Das allgemeine Gestaltungsproblem in der Baukunst des Klassizismus*, Munich, 1920
– 'Der Historismus in der Baukunst', in *Historische Zeitschrift*, 157, 1938
– *Das neunzehnte Jahrhundert in der deutschen Kunst*, Munich, 1944
– *Schöpferische Bauideen der Deutschen Romantik*, Mainz, 1952
Benevolo, L. *Storia dell'architettura moderna*, Bari, 1960 (*History of Modern Architecture*, Cambridge, Mass., 1971)
Benjamin, Walter *Der Begriff der Kunstkritik in der deutschen Romantik*, Frankfurt, 1973
Bertig, R. *Theaterbauten der Rheinprovinz in der ersten Hälfte des 19 Jahrhunderts.*
Bourier, K. *Bayerns Verdienste um Griechenland im 19. Jh. Bayerland*, Munich, 1932
Brinckmann, Albert Erich *Bauten des 17. and 18. Jahrhunderts in den romanischen Ländern.* (Handbuch der Kunstwissenshaft) Berlin 1915.
– *Deutsche Stadtbaukunst.* Frankfurt a. Main 1911.
– *Stadtbaukunst des 18. Jahrhunderts.* Berlin 1914.
Bringmann, Michael *Das 19. und 20. Jahrhundert, Land Baden-Württemberg*, Archivverwaltung, Stuttgart, 1974
Butler, Eliza Marian *The Tyranny of Greece over Germany*, Cambridge, 1935
Colombier, Pierre du *L'Architecture française en Allemagne au XVIIIᵉ siècle*, Paris, 1956
Corti, Egon Cäsar *Ludwig I. von Bayern*, 6th edn, Munich, 1960
Curtius, Ludwig *Die Wandmalerei Pompejis*, Berlin, 1972
Dehio, Ludwig *Friedrich Wilhelm IV. von Preussen, ein Baukünstler der Romantik*, Munich, 1961
Döhmer, Klaus *In welchem Stil sollen wir bauen? Architekturtheorie zwischen Klassizismus und Jugendstil.* Munich 1976
Dolgner, Dieter *Die Architektur des Klassizismus in Deutschland*, Dresden, 1971
– 'Der Rundbogenstil: Ein Versuch der architektonischen Erneuerung des 19 Jahrhunderts', in: *Wissenschaftliche Zeitschrift der Hochschule für Architektur und Bauwesen Weimar*, Heft 4. Weimar 1980.
Ebe, Gustav *Die Dekorationsformen des 19. Jahrhunderts*, Leipzig, 1900

Einem, Herbert von 'Die Wendung zu den Griechen in der deutschen Baukunst des Klassizismus', in *Festschrift für Franz Graf Wolff Metternich*, Neuss, 1973
Evers, Hans Gerhard 'Historismus', in L. Grote, ed., *Historismus und bildende Kunst*, Munich, 1965
– *Vom Historismus zum Funktionalismus*, Baden Baden, 1967
Fahrnbacher, Heinrich *Erinnerungen an Italien, Sicilien und Griechenland aus den Jahren 1826–1844*, Munich, 1851
Forssman, Eric *Dorisch, Ionisch, Korinthisch*, Uppsala, 1961
Friedell, Egon *Kulturgeschichte der Neuzeit*, Munich, 1929
Geller, Hans *Die Bildnisse der deutschen Künstler in Rom 1800–1830*, Berlin, 1952
Germann, Georg *Gothic Revival in Europe and Britain: Sources, Influences and Ideas*, London, 1972
Giedion, Sigfried *Spätbarocker und romantischer Klassizismus*, Munich, 1922
Grass, H.M. *Bibliotheksbauten des 19. Jahrhunderts in Deutschland.* Munich 1976.
Grimm, Emil Ludwig *Erinnerungen aus meinem Leben*, Leipzig, 1911
Grote, Ludwig, ed. *Historismus und bildende Kunst*, Munich, 1965
– *Die deutsche Stadt im 19. Jahrhundert*, Munich, 1974
Gruber, Karl *Die Gestalt der deutschen Stadt.* Munich 1952.
Gurlitt, C. *Geschichte des Klassizismus*, Stuttgart, 1889
– *Die deutsche Kunst des 19. Jahrhunderts*, Berlin, 1900 (reissued as *Zur Befreiung der Baukunst*, Berlin, 1968)
Hahn, August *Der Maximilianstil. Festschrift 100 Jahre Maximilianeum*, Munich, 1952
Hallbaum, Franz *Der Landschaftsgarten. Sein Entstehen und seine Einführung in Deutschland durch Friedrich Ludwig von Sckell, 1750–1823*, Munich, 1927
Hart, F. *Architektur und Ingenieurbau* (Deutsches Museum, Abhandlungen, 29, 3), Munich, 1961
Hatfield, H.C. *Winckelmann and his German Critics 1755–81*, New York, 1943
– *Aesthetic Paganism in German Literature from Winckelmann to the Death of Goethe*, Cambridge, Mass., 1964
Hederer, Edgar *Novalis*, Stuttgart, 1950
Hederer, Oswald *Klassizismus*, Munich, 1976
Heideloff, Carl Alexander *Architectonische Entwürfe und ausgeführte Bauten im Byzantinischen und Altdeutschen Styl*, Nuremberg, 1850 (I) and 1851 (II)
Heigel, K.T. von 'König Ludwig I. von Bayern. Denkwürdigkeiten des bayerischen Staatsrats G.L. von Maurer', in *Sitzungsberichte der Bayerischen Akad.*

der Wissenschaften Hist. Kl. 1903, Leipzig, 1872

Heise, Wolfgang 'Weltanschauliche Aspekte der Frühromantik', in: *Weimarer Beiträge. Zeitschrift für Literaturwissenschaft, Ästhetik und Kulturtheorie*. Berlin, Weimar 1978, Vol. 24, 4th series p. 21 fl.

Hempel, Eberhard *Baroque Art and Architecture in Central Europe*, Harmondsworth, 1963

Herrmann, Wolfgang *Laugier and Eighteenth-Century French Theory*, London, 1962

– *Deutsche Baukunst des 19 und 20 Jahrhunderts*. vol 1 1770–1840. Breslau 1932. (New ed. in Schriftenreihe des Instituts für Geschichte und Theorie der Architektur Zürich No 17., Basel Stuttgart 1977.)

Hildebrandt, Edmund *Friedrich Tieck. Ein Beitrag zur deutschen Kunstgeschichte im Zeitalter Goethes und der Romantik*, Leipzig, 1906

Hitchcock, Henry-Russell *Architecture Nineteenth and Twentieth Centuries*, Harmondsworth, 1958

Hojer, Gerhard 'Maximilianstrasse und Maximilianstil', in L. Grote, ed., *Die deutsche Stadt im 19. Jahrhundert*, Munich, 1974

Irwin, David, ed. *Winckelmann, Writings on Art*, London, 1972

Joseph, D 'Geschichte der Baukunst in 19. Jahrhundert', in: *Handbuch der Architektur* Vol 3, (after 1902).

Kalnein, Wend Graf and Levey, Michael *Art and Architecture of the Eighteenth Century in France*, Harmondsworth, 1972

Kauffman, Hans 'Das Florenzbild der Deutschen', in *Festschrift für Herbert von Einem*, Berlin, 1965

Kaufmann, Emil 'Architektonische Entwürfe aus der Zeit der französischen Revolution', in *Zeitschrift für bildende Kunst*, 63, 1929–30

– *Autonome Architektur*, Baden Baden, 1970

Kaufmann, F.A. *Roms ewiges Antlitz*, Berlin, 1940

Keller, Harald 'Goethe, Palladio und England', in: *Sitzungsberichte der bayrischen Akademie der Wissenschaften, philosophisch-historische Klasse*. Heft 6, 1971.

Kempen, Wilhelm van 'Die Baukunst des Klassizismus in Anhalt nach 1800', in: *Marburger Jahrbuch für Kunstwissenschaft*. Vol 4 p 1–87.

Kerssen, Ludger *Das Interesse am Mittelalter im deutschen Nationaldenkmal (Arbeiten zur Frühmittelalter-Forschung. Schriftenreihe des Institutes für Frühmittelalterforschung der Universität Münster, 8)*, Berlin and New York, 1975

Kiener, Hans *Die Baukunst des deutschen Klassizismus*, Munich, 1935

Klassizismus in Bayern, Schwaben und Franken, Architektur-Zeichnungen 1775–1825, Technische Universität, Munich, 1980

Die klassizistische Form im 19. Jahrhundert. Festschrift für H. Wölfflin, Munich, 1924

Klein, J.A. *Rheinreise von Strassburg bis Düsseldorf*, 1828, 2nd edn 1843

Klessmann, E. *Deutschland unter Napoleon in Augenzeugenberichten*. Düsseldorf 1965.

Klinkert, W. *Bemerkung zur Technik der pompejianischen Wanddekoration*, Berlin, 1972

Klopfer, Paul *Von Palladio bis Schinkel. Eine Charakteristik der Baukunst des Klassizismus (Geschichte der neueren Baukunst, IX)*, Esslingen, 1911

Koepf, Hans *Deutsche Baukunst*, Stuttgart, 1956

Koopmann, H. H. and Schmoll, J.A., eds., *Beiträge zur Theorie der Künste im 19. Jahrhundert (Studie zur Philosophie und Literatur des 19. Jahrhunderts*, XII, 2), Frankfurt, 1972

Kordt, Walter 'Klassizistische Baukunst am Niederrhein', in: *Jahrbuch der Rheinischen Denkmalpflege*, 1953 p 141–152

Kreisel, Heinrich *Die Beurteilung der Kunst der letzten hundert Jahre*, Munich, 1957

Krüger, Renate *Das Zeitalter der Empfindsamkeit. Kunst und Kultur des Späten 18. Jahrhunderts in Deutschland*. Leipzig 1972.

Kugler, Franz 'Kunstreise im Jahre 1845', in *Kleine Schriften und Studien zur Kunstgeschichte*, III, Stuttgart, 1854

Kuhn, Alfred *Peter Cornelius und die geistigen Strömungen seiner Zeit*, Berlin, 1921

Kunstdenkmäler von Bayern und Schwaben, Munich, 1954

Landsberger, Franz *Die Kunst der Goethezeit*, Leipzig, 1931

Lankheit, Klaus *Revolution und Restauration*, Baden Baden, 1965

Liebmann, Hilda (ed) *Bibliographie zur Kunstgeschichte des 19. Jahrhunderts*. Publikationen der Jahre 1940–66.

Macaulay, R. *Pleasure of Ruins*. London, 1964.

Macmillan Encyclopaedia of Architects, London and New York, 1982

Mann, A. *Die Neuromantik*, Cologne, 1966

Mann, Golo *Deutsche Geschichte des 19. und 20. Jahrhunderts*, 2nd edn, Frankfurt, 1959

Mebes, Paul *Um 1800, Architektur und Handwerk im letzten Jahrhundert ihrer traditionellen Entwicklung*, Munich, 1908

Metken, Günter *Utopien auf dem Papier*, Baden Baden, 1970

Milde, Kurt *Neorenaissance in der Deutschen Architektur des 19. Jahrhunderts*, Dresden, 1981

Mittig, Hans-Ernst and Plagemann, Volker *Denkmäler im 19. Jahrhundert, Deutung und Kritik*, Munich, 1972

Nerdinger, Winfried *Von Klassizismus zum Impressionismus, eine Kunstgeschichte des 19. Jahrhunderts in Einzelinterpretationen*. Munich 1980.

Neumayer, Alfred 'Monument to Genius in German Classicism', in *Journal of the Warburg and Courtauld Institutes*, II, London, 1938

Nipperday, Thomas 'Nationalidee und Nationaldenkmal in Deutschland', in *Historische Zeitschrift*, 206, 1968

Noack, Friedrich *Deutsches Leben in Rom 1700–1900*, Stuttgart and Berlin, 1907

– *Das deutsche Rom*, Rome, 1912

– *Das Deutschtum in Rom seit Ausgang des Mittelalters*, Berlin and Leipzig, 1927

Overbeck, Johann and Mau, August *Pompeji in seinen Gebäuden, Altertümern und Kunstwerken*, 4th edn, Leipzig, 1884

Paetel, W. *Zur Entwicklung des bepflanzten Stadtplatzes in Deutschland vom Beginn des 19. Jahrhunderts bis zum 1. Weltkrieg*. Diss. Hanover 1977.

Pecht, Friedrich *Deutsche Künstler des 19. Jahrhunderts*, IV, Nördlingen, 1885

Persius, Ludwig 'Das Tagebuch des Architekten Wilhelm IV. ed. by E. Börsch-Supan', in: *Kunstwissenschaftliche Studien* Vol 51. Deutscher Kunstverlag Munich 1980.

Petzet, Michael *König Ludwig II. und die Kunst*, exh. cat., Munich, 1968

Pevsner, Nikolaus *Some Architectural Writers of the Nineteenth Century*, Oxford, 1972

Pinder, W. *Der deutsche Park vornehmlich des 18. Jahrhunderts.* Königstein, Leipzig 1927.

Plagemann, Volker *Das deutsche Kunstmuseum 1790–1870*, Munich, 1967

Rave, Paul Ortwin *Gärten der Goethezeit*, Berlin, 1981
– 'Anfang preussischer Kunstpflege am Rhein', in: *Walraff-Richartz Jahrbuch* 9 (1936) p. 181–204.

Réau, Louis *L'Art français sur le Rhin au XVIIIᵉ siècle*, Paris, 1922

Reidelbach, Hans *König Ludwig I. von Bayern und seine Kunstschöpfungen*, Munich, 1888

Reinle, Adolf *Kunstgeschichte der Schweiz*, IV, *Die Kunst des 19. Jahrhunderts*, Frauenfeld, 1962

Revolutionsarchitektur. Boullée, Ledoux, Lequeu, exh. cat., Düsseldorf, 1971

Riegel, Alois *Der moderne Denkmalkultus, sein Wesen und seine Entstehung*, Vienna and Leipzig, 1903

Robson-Scott W.D. *The Literary Background of the Gothic Revival in Germany*, Oxford, 1965

Rome, Accademia Nazionale di San Luca *I desegni di architettura dell'Archivo storico dell'Accademia di San Luca*, ed, P. Marconi, A. Cipriani and E. Valeriani, Rome 1974

Ross L. *Erinnerungen aus Griechenland*, Berlin, 1863

Sauer, J. *Die kirchliche Kunst der ersten Hälfte des 19. Jahrhunderts in Baden*, Freiburg, 1933

Schefold, Karl *Pompejanische Malerei. Sinn und Ideengeschichte*, Basel, 1952

Schindler, Herbert *Grosse Bayerische Kunstgeschichte*, Munich, 1963

Schrade, Hubert *Das deutsche Nationaldenkmal. Idee, Geschichte, Aufgabe*, Munich, 1934

Schumacher, Fritz *Strömungen in der deutschen Baukunst seit 1800*, Leipzig, 1950

Sedlmayr, Hans *Der Tod des Lichts*, Salzburg, 1964

See, Klaus von *Deutsche Germanen-Ideologie. Vom Humanismus bis zur Gegenwart*

Spindler, Max *König Ludwig I. als Bauherr*, Munich, 1958

Thinesse-Demel, Jutta 'Vom Rokoko zum Klassizismus' Munich 1980. Diss. publ. in: *Miscellanea Bavarica Monacensia. Dissertationen zur Bayrischen Landes und Münchner Stadtgeschichte.*

Trier, Eduard and Weyres, Willy, eds. *Kunst des 19. Jahrhunderts im Rheinland*, I-II, *Architektur*, Düsseldorf 1980–81

Van Zanten, David *The Architectural Polychromy of the 1830's*, New York & London 1977

Vehse, Eduard *Geschichte der deutschen Höfe seit der Reformation.* 48 Vol. 1851–60.

Verbeek, Albert 'Preussen und die Kunstpflege in den Rheinländern', in: *Rheinische Heimatpflege* II 1965 p 86ff

Vogel, Hans *Deutsche Baukunst des Klassizismus*, Berlin, 1937

Vogt, Adolf Max *Revolutionsarchitektur und Naziklassizismus*, Cologne, 1970

Werner, Peter *Pompeji und die Wanddekoration der Goethezeit*, Munich, 1970

Weyres, Willy and Mann, Albrecht *Handbuch zur rheinischen Baukunst des 19. Jahrhunderts*, Cologne, 1968

Wietek, Gerhard *Goethes Verhältnis zur Architektur*. Diss. Kiel 1951.

Winkler, Wilhelm 'Der schriftliche Nachlass König Ludwigs von Bayern', in *Archivalische Zeitschrift*, III, Munich, 1926

Wittelsbach und Bayern. Krone und Verfassung, König Max I. Joseph und der neue Staat, exh. cat., Munich and Zurich, 1980

Wörner, Hans Jakob *Architektur des Frühklassizismus in Süddeutschland*, Munich and Zurich, 1979

Zahn, Wilhelm *Die schönsten Ornamente und merkwürdigsten Gemälde aus Pompeji, Herculaneum und Stabiae*, Berlin, 1828–52

Zeitler, Rudolf *Die Kunst des 19. Jahrhunderts* (Propyläen Kunstgeschichte, XI), Berlin, 1966

Zetzsche, Carl *Zopf und Empire in Mittel- und Norddeutschland.* 2 vol Leipzig 1909

Exhibition Catalogues

Borchers, Rudolf ed. *Preussische Baukunst in Westfalen in der ersten Hälfte des 19. Jahrhunderts*, exh. cat. Münster, 1933

The Age of Neo-classicism, exh. cat., Arts Council of Great Britain, London, 1972

Aufklärung und Klassizismus in Hessen-Kassel unter Landgraf Friedrich II. 1760–1785, exh. cat., Staatliche Kunstsammlungen, Kassel, 1979

Barock und Klassik, Kunstzentren des 18. Jahrhunderts in der DDR, exh. cat., Schallaburg, 1984

Fünf Architekten des Klassizismus in Deutschland, exh. cat., *Dortmunder Architekturhefte*, no. 4, Dortmund, 1977

Habel, Heinrich *Architektur des 19. und frühen 20. Jahrhunderts*, exh. cat., Munich, 1972

Vollrath, Wolfgang *Pompeji und die Deutschen*, exh. cat., Essen and Recklinghausen, 1973

Architekten der Fridericiana, Skizzen und Entwürfe seit Friedrich Weinbrenner, Staatliche Kunsthalle, Karlsruhe, 1975

Klassizismus in Bayern, Schwaben und Franken. Architekturzeichnungen 1775–1825. exh. cat. Stadtmuseum München, 1980

Preussische Bauten am Rhein ed. Institut für Landes- und Stadtentwicklungsforschung des Landes Nordrhein-Westfalen, Dortmund, 1983

Individual architects and artists

JOHANN AUGUST ARENS 1757–1806
J.A. Arens, ein Hamburger Architect des Klassizismus, exh. cat., Altonaer Museum, Hamburg 1972

GEORG GOTTLOB BARTH 1777–1848
Obituary by L. Fischer in *Schwäbische Chronik des Schwäbischen Merkurs*, 2nd ser. 1848, p. 694

MATTHÄUS BIERCHER 1797–1869
Brucher, Rudolf *Der Baumeister Matthäus Biercher*, diss. Aachen
Vogts, Hans 'Klassizistische Baukunst in Köln', in *Denkmalspflege und Heimatschutz*, 21 (1929) p. 32
Cölnische Abendzeitung 1833, No 39
JOHANN KONRAD BROMEIS 1788–1854
Hoffmeister 'Künstler und Handwerk in Hessen', in *Deutsche Bauzeitung*, 1908, p. 413 ff
AXEL BUNDSEN 1768–1832
Bau- und Kunstdenkmäler der Provinz Schleswig-Holstein, Vol. 1, p. 180, 279, 457
CARL FERDINAND BUSSE 1802–1868
Behrend, W.C. 'Carl Ferdinand Busse. Ein preussischer Baubeamter', in *Zentralblatt der Bauverwaltung*, 52 (1932) p. 628–36
Börsch-Supan, Eva *Berliner Baukunst nach Schinkel 1840–1870*, p. 560–563
ALEXIS DE CHATEAUNEUF 1799–1853
'The Career of Alexis de Chateauneuf', in *Architectural Review* Vol 45, 1919, p. 53–56
Schumacher, Fritz 'Die neuen Regungen des Hamburger Backsteinbaus in der Mitte des 19. Jahrhunderts', in *Zentralblatt der Bauverwaltung* Vol. 43, 1923, p. 61–65, 73–78, 85–86, 113–138
Speckter, Hans *Der Wiederaufbau Hamburgs nach dem Grossen Brande 1842*, Hamburg, 1952
Lange, Günther *Alexis de Chateauneuf: Ein Hamburger Baumeister (1799–1853)*, Hamburg, 1965
C.W. COUDRAY 1775–1845
Schneemann, Walther *C.W. Coudray, Goethes Baumeister*, Weimar, 1943
JOHANN PETER CREMER 1785–1863
Everling, Johannes *Die Architekten Franz Friedrich Leydel und Johann Peter Cremer und ihre Bedeutung für die Aachener Baugeschichte*, diss. Aachen, 1923
Cremer, Johann Peter 'Einige Nachrichten von dem neuen Schauspielhaus zu Aachen', in *Journal für die Baukunst*, Vol. 1, Berlin 1829, p. 68–72
 – 'Das neue Rathaus in Elberfeld', in *Zeitschrift für Bauwesen*, 1852, p. 81ff
PIERRE MICHEL D'IXNARD 1726–1798
D'Ixnard, Michel *Recueil d'architecture*, Strasbourg, 1790/91
Vossnack, L.L. *Pierre Michel d'Ixnard 1723–1795. Französischer Architekt in Südwestdeutschland*, diss., Frankfurt: Remscheid, 1938
Franz, E. *Pierre-Michel d'Ixnard 1723–1795. Leben und Werk* Weissenhorn, 1985
Klaiber, H. 'Der Stuttgarter Architektur-Sammelband von Pierre Michel Dixnard', in *Jahrbuch der Staatlichen Kunstsammlungen in Baden-Württemberg*, Vol. 6, Berlin, 1969 p. 161–188.
SIMON LOUIS DU RY 1726–1799
Gerland, Otto *Paul, Charles and Simon Louis du Ry. Eine Künstlerfamilie der Barockzeit*, Stuttgart, 1895
Boehlke, Hans Kurt *Simon Louis du Ry als Stadtbaumeister Landgraf Friedrichs II von Hessen Kassel*, Kassel, 1958; originally diss. Göttingen, 1953.
 – 'Die städtebauliche Entwicklung Kassels', in *Aufklärung und Klassizismus in Hessen Kassel unter Landgraf Friedrich II, 1760–85*, exh. cat. Kassel 1979,

p. 60–75, 204–5
 – *Simon Louis du Ry. Ein Wegbereiter klassizistischer Architektur in Deutschland*, sponsored by the Sparkasse Kassel with main contributions by H.K. Boehlke.
FRIEDRICH WILHELM VON ERDMANNSDORFF 1736–1800
Harken, Marie-Luise, *Erdmannsdorff und seine Bauten in Wörlitz*, Wörlitz, 1973
Riesenfeld, Erich Paul *Erdmannsdorff, der Baumeister des Herzogs Leopold Friedrich von Anhalt-Dessau*, Berlin, 1913
KARL VON FISCHER 1782–1820
Schindler, Herbert *Carl von Fischer (1782–1820), ein Architekt des Münchner Klassizismus*, diss., Munich, 1951
Hederer, Oswald *Karl von Fischer, Leben und Werk*, Munich, 1961
Dischinger, Gabriele 'Karl von Fischer als Lehrer und Gutachter', in *Klassizismus in Bayern, Schwaben und Franken*, exh. cat. Munich 1980, p. 21–29
Carl von Fischer 1782–1820, exh. cat., Neue Pinakothek, Munich, 1982
REINHARD FERDINAND HEINRICH FISCHER 1746–1813
Pfeiffer, B. *Herzog Carl Eugen von Württemberg und seine Zeit*, 1907
Widmann, O. *Reinhard Ferdinand Heinrich Fischer, 1746–1813. Ein Beitrag zur Geschichte des Louis XVI. in Württemberg*, Stuttgart, 1928
FRANZ GUSTAV JOACHIM FORSMANN 1795–1878
Grundmann, Günther, *Jenischpark und Jenischhaus, Hamburg*, Hamburg 1957
Hoffmann, Paul Theodor, *Die Elbchaussee, ihre Landsitze, Menschen und Schicksale*, Hamburg, 1966, 7th ed
Küster, Christian L. *Jenisch Haus*, Schnell Kunstführer, No 1322, Munich, Zürich, 1982
FRIEDRICH VON GÄRTNER 1792–1847
Moninger, Hans *Friedrich von Gärtner*, 1882
Willich, Hans *Friedrich Gärtner*, in Thieme-Becker, Leipzig 1937
Eggert, Klaus *Friedrich von Gärtner. Der Baumeister König Ludwig I*, (Neue Schriftreihe des Stadtarchivs München. Vol 15) Munich, 1963
Hederer, Oswald *Friedrich von Gärtner. 1792–1847, Leben, Werk und Schüler*, Munich, 1976
HEINRICH GENTZ 1766–1811
Doebber, Adolph *Das Schloss in Weimar*, Jena, 1911
 – *Heinrich Gentz, ein Berliner Baumeister um 1800*, Berlin, 1916
Schmitz, H. *Berliner Baumeister vom Ausgang des 18. Jahrhunderts*, Berlin, 1914
Schroth, I *Die Nachahmung des Griechischen durch die Berliner Baumeister der Goethezeit*, diss Freiburg 1938
Berlin und die Antike, ex. cat, Berlin 1979, article by W. Hoepfner p. 291, 343
Gentz, H. *Geometrisches und perspektivisches Zeichenbuch für Bauwerksleute . . .* Berlin 1803 publ. by Friedr. Unger with the accompanying vol. of illustrations: *Des Elementarzeichenwerks zum Gebrauch der Kunst- und Gewerkschulen der Preussischen Staaten, erstes Heft*
 – *Architektonisches Elementarbuch die Säulenordnungen enthaltend . . .* Berlin 1806 with the accompanying vol. of ill.: *Des Elementarzeichenwerkes zum Gebrauch der*

Kunst- und Gewerkschulen der Preussischen Staaten, zweites Heft
– *Beschreibung des neuen Königlichen Münzgebäudes. Rede des Baumeisters bei der Einweihung des Hauses*, in *Sammlung nützlicher Aufsätze und Nachrichten die Baukunst betreffend,* Vol, 1, Berlin 1800, p. 14 ff

ALBERT GEUTEBRÜCK 1800–1868
Nieper, *Leipzig und seine Bauten*, 1892
Füssler, Heinz *Leipziger Universitätsbauten*, Leipzig, 1961

DAVID GILLY 1748–1808
Gilly, David *Sammlung nützlicher Aufsätze und Nachrichten die Baukunst betreffend*, Berlin, 1798–1806
Lammert, Marlies *David Gilly, ein Baumeister des deutschen Klassizismus*, Berlin 1964 (Studien zur Architektur und Kunstwissenschaft, 3)
Gilly, David *Über Erfindung: Construction und Vortheile der Bohlen-Dächer*, Berlin, 1797
– *Handbuch der Landbaukunst*, 2 Vols, Berlin, 1797–1798
– *Praktische Anweisung zur Wasserbaukunst*, Berlin, 1809–1818

FRIEDRICH GILLY 1772–1800
Levesow, Konrad *Denkschrift auf Friedrich Gilly*, Berlin, 1801
Riemer, H. *Friedrich Gilly's Verhältnis zum Theaterbau* diss. Berlin, 1931
Oncken, Alste *Friedrich Gilly, 1772–1800* (Forschungen zur deutschen Kunstgeschichte, 5), Berlin, 1935
Neumeyer, Alfred 'Monuments to "Genius" in German Classicism', in *Journal of the Warburg and Courtauld Institutes*, Vol 2, 1938, p. 159–163
Rietdorf, A *Gilly, Wiedergeburt der Architektur*, Berlin 1940
Klinkott, Manfred 'Friedrich Gilly, 1772–1800' in *Fünf Architekten des Klassizismus in Deutschland*, Dortmunder Architekturhefte 4, 1977, p. 11–41
– *Friedrich Gilly, 1772–1800, und die Privatgesellschaft junger Architekten*, Berlin, 1984

PIERRE-LOUIS-PHILIPPE DE LA GUÊPIÈRE 1715–1753
Klaiber, Hans Andreas *Der Württembergische Oberbaudirektor Philippe de la Guêpière* (Forschungen der Kommission für geschichtliche Landeskunde in Baden-Württemberg, IX) Stuttgart 1959

GEORG HAGENAUER 1746–1835
Preysing, August Graf 'Schloss Freudenhain bei Passau', in *Der Zwiebelturm*, 5, 1950, p. 175–180
Habermann, S. 'Schloss und Garten Freudenhain bei Passau' in *Klassizismus in Bayern, Schwaben und Franken*, exh. cat., Münchner Stadtmuseum, Munich 1980, p. 309–312.

JOHANN CARL CHRISTOPH JOACHIM FREIHERR HALLER VON HALLERSTEIN 1774–1817
Heigel, K.T. von 'Briefe des Kronprinzen Ludwig von Bayern an Karl Haller von Hallerstein', in *Zeitschrift für Bildende Kunst*, XVIII, 1883
Kiener, Hans 'Hallers Entwürfe zur Glyptothek und Walhalla', in *Münchner Jahrbuch der bildenden Kunst*, 13, 1923
Frässle, Klaus *Karl Haller von Hallerstein (1774–1817)*, diss. Freiburg-im-Breisgau, 1971

CHRISTIAN FREDERIK HANSEN 1746–1845
Jakstein, W. 'C.F. Hansen in Hamburg', in *Architekten* 16 (1913/14) p. 45ff
– *Landesbaumeister Christian Friedrich Hansen, der Nordische Klassizist*, Neumünster, 1937
'C.F. Hansen und sein Landhaus Thornton', in *Bau Rundschau*, 1915, No. 18/19, p. 65 ff
'C.F. Hansen Landhaus Godeffroy', in *Bau-Rundschau*, 1917, No. 22/26 p. 57 ff
Christian Frederik Hansen 1756–1845, exh. cat. Altonaer Museum, Hamburg 1968
Wietek, Gerhard (ed) *C.F. Hansen 1756–1845 (und seine Bauten in Schleswig Holstein) (Kunst in Schleswig Holstein*, Vol. 23, Neumünster 1982)

KARL ALEXANDER VON HEIDELOFF 1789–1865
Boeck, *Karl Alexander Heideloff*, diss. Tübingen 1950

EMANUEL JOSEPH VON HERIGOYEN 1746–1817
Reidel, Hermann *Emanuel Joseph von Herigoyen*, Munich and Zurich, 1982

JAKOB IGNAZ HITTORFF 1792–1867
Hammer, K. *Jakob Ignaz Hittorff*, Stuttgart, 1967

PHILLIP HOFFMANN 1806–1889
Phillip Hoffmann 1806–1889. Ein nassauischer Baumeister, exh. cat. Nassauischer Kunstverein, Wiesbaden 1982/83

HEINRICH HÜBSCH 1795–1863
Hübsch, Heinrich *Die Architektur und ihr Verhältnis zur heutigen Malerei und Skulptur*, Stuttgart and Tübingen, 1847
Valdenaire, Arthur *Heinrich Hübsch*, Karlsruhe, 1926
Göricke, Joachim *Die Kirchenbauten des Architekten H. Hübsch*, Karlsruhe, 1974
Heinrich Hübsch 1795–1863, der grosse badische Baumeister der Romantik, exh. cat., Stadtarchiv, Karlsruhe, 1983

PIERRE MICHEL D'IXNARD (see above under D)

HEINRICH CHRISTOPH JUSSOW 1754–1825
Heinrich Christoph Jussow 1754–1825. Baumeister in Kassel und Wilhelmshöhe, exh. cat., Kassel, 1958
Klein, Jürgen 'Heinrich Christoph Jussow Erbauer der "Löwenburg" zu Kassel, und die englische Neugotik', in *Architectura, Zeitschrift für Geschichte der Baukunst*, Munich, 1975, Vol. 5, 2, pp 138

LEO VON KLENZE 1784–1864
Klenze, Leo von *Sammlung architektonischer Entwürfe*, Munich, 1830–50
– *Anweisung zur Architektur des christlichen Cultus*, Munich, 1834
– *Die Walhalla in artistischer und technischer Beziehung*, Munich, 1843
Kiener, Hans *Leo von Klenze, Architekt Ludwig I., 1784–1864*, 1. Hälfte, diss., Munich, 1921
Hederer, Oswald *Leo von Klenze*, Munich, 1964
– 'Das Bild der Antike in den Augen Leo von Klenzes', in *Koldeweg Gessellschaft, Bericht über die 23. Tagung der Koldeweg Gessellschaft in Hildesheim*, Kevelaer 1965
Ettlinger, Leopold 'Denkmal und Romantik. Bemerkungen zu Leo von Klenzes Walhalla', in *Festschrift für Herbert von Einem*, Berlin, 1965
Sczesny, Marina *Leo von Klenze 'Anweisungen zur Architektur des christlichen Cultus'*, diss., Munich, 1967
Lieb, Norbert, and Hufnagl, Florian *Leo von Klenze, Gemälde und Zeichnungen*, Munich, 1979
Schaefer, Veronika *Leo von Klenze. Möbel und Innenräume (Neue Schriftenreihe des Stadtarchivs München)*, Munich, 1980
Haltrich, Günther-Alexander *Leo von Klenze. Die*

Allerheiligenhofkirche in München (Neue Schriftenreihe des Stadtarchivs München), Munich, 1983

GEORG WENCESLAUS VON KNOBELSDORFF 1699–1753

Kadatz, Hans-Joachim, and Murza, Gerhard *George Wenzeslaus von Knobelsdorff, Baumeister Friedrichs II.*, Munich, 1983

PETER JOSEPH KRAHE 1758–1840

Claussen, Carl *P.J. Krahe – Ein Meister der Stadtbaukunst um 1800*, diss. Technische Hochschule Braunschweig 1919.

Stubbe, Wolf, *P.J. Krahe – Ein Meister proportionaler Baukörperfertigung im deutschen Klassizismus*, diss. Rostock 1933

Dorn, Reinhard *Peter Joseph Krahe*, Brunswick, 1969 and 1971

Bockius, F. 'P.J. Krahe. Das Koblenzer Wirken des vorbildlichen klassizistischen Architekten', in *Theater der Stadt Koblenz* 1971/72, Heft 19, Koblenz 1972

CARL GOTTHARD LANGHANS 1732–1808

Hinrichs, W.T. *Carl Gotthard Langhans, ein schlesischer Baumeister* Strasbourg, 1909

JOHANN CLAUDIUS VON LASSAULX 1781–1848

Feldbusch, H. *J.C. von Lassaulx – Ein Beitrag zu seinem Werk*, diss. 1939

Schwieger, F. *Johann Claudius von Lassaulx 1781–1848. Architekt und Denkmalpfleger in Koblenz*, Neuss, 1968

GEORG LUDWIG LAVES 1788–1864

Hoeltje, Georg *Georg Ludwig Laves*, Hanover, 1964

Weber, Helmut 'Georg Ludwig Friedrich Laves als Bauingenieur', in Hoeltje, op. cit.

Georg Ludwig Friedrich Laves 1864–1964, exh. cat., Niedersächsische Landtag, Hanover, 1964

JEAN-LAURENT LEGEAY C.1710–1786

Erouart, Gilbert *L'Architecture au pinceau, Jean-Laurent Legeay*, Milan and Paris, 1982

PETER JOSEF LENNÉ 1789–1866

Hinz, Gerhard *Peter Josef Lenné und seine bedeutendsten Schöpfungen in Berlin und Potsdam*, Berlin, 1937

WILHELM FERDINAND LIPPER 1733–1800

Bussmann, K. *W. F. Lipper*, Münster, 1972

Der münstersche Oberbaudirektor Wilhelm Ferdinand Lipper, 1733–1800, exh. cat. Westfälisches Landesmuseum Münster, 1981

J.B. MÉTIVIER 1781–1857

Rose, Hans 'J.B. Métivier. Der Erbauer des Braunen Hauses in München', in *Zeitschrift des Deutschen Vereins für Kunstwissenschaft*, Vol 1, 1934, pp 49

GEORG MOLLER 1784–1852

Sack, B. *Georg Moller*, Darmstadt, 1908

Fröhlich, Marie, and Sperlich, Hans-Günther *Georg Moller: Baumeister der Romantik*, Darmstadt, 1959

FERDINAND JAKOB NEBEL 1782–1860

Dauber, Reinhard *Ferdinand Jakob Nebel (1782–1860) Königlich Preussischer Landbauinspektor in Koblenz*, diss., Aachen, 1975

LUDWIG PERSIUS 1803–1845

Fleetwood-Hesketh, R. and P. 'Ludwig Persius of Potsdam' in: *Architects' Journal*, 68, 1928, pp 77–87, 113–120

Börsch-Supan, Eva *Ludwig Persius, das Tagebuch des Architekten Friedrich Wilhelms IV.*, Munich, 1980

FRANZ AND FERDINAND PETTRICH

Geller, Hans *Franz und Ferdinand Pettrich*, Dresden, 1955

A.F. PEYRE 1739–1823

Peyre, A.-F. (le Jeune), *Oeuvres d'architecture*, Paris, 1818

JOHANN CHRISTIAN REINHART

Feuchtmayr, Inge *Johann Christian Reinhart*, Munich, 1975

GIOVANNI SALUCCI 1769–1845

Speidel, Wilhelm 'Giovanni Salucci', in *Darstellungen aus der Württembergischen Geschichte*, XXVI, Stuttgart, 1936

KARL FRIEDRICH SCHINKEL 1781–1841

Schinkel, K.F. *Dekorationen auf den königlichen Hof-Theatern zu Berlin*, Berlin, 1819–24

– *Sammlung architektonischer Entwürfe*, Berlin, 1819–40

– and Beuth, Peter *Vorbilder für Fabrikanten und Handwerker*, Berlin, 1821-37

– *Werke der höheren Baukunst*, Potsdam, 1848–50

– *Reise nach England, Schottland und Paris im Jahre 1826*, ed. Gottfried Riemann, with introduction by David Bindman, Berlin, 1986

Wolzogen, Alfred Freiherr von, ed. *Aus Schinkel's Nachlass*, Berlin, 1862–4

Fiebiger, 'Schinkel in Dresden' in *Dresdener Geschichtsblätter*, 1910–13

Spiero, Sabine 'Schinkels Altes Museum in Berlin', in *Jahrbuch der preussischen Kunstsammlung*, LV, 1934, Beiheft 41–81

Karl Friedrich Schinkel Lebenswerk, ed. Paul Ortwin Rave (vols. 1–11) and Margarete Kühn (vol. 12 ff), Berlin, 1939 ff:

(1) *Potsdam. Staats- und Bürgerbauten* (Hans Kania, 1939)

(2) *Schlesien* (G. Grundmann, 1941)

(3) *Berlin, I: Bauten für die Kunst, Kirchen, Denkmalpflege* (P.O. Rave, 1941, reprinted 1981)

(4) *Bauten für den Prinzen Karl von Preussen* (Johannes Sievers, 1942)

(5) *Berlin, II: Stadtbaupläne, Brücken, Strassen, Tore, Plätze* (Rave, 1948)

(6) *Die Möbel* (Sievers, 1950)

(7) *Pommern* (Hans Vogel, 1952)

(8) *Bauten für die Prinzen August, Friedrich und Albrecht von Preussen. Ein Beitrag zur Geschichte der Wilhelmstrasse in Berlin* (Sievers, 1954)

(9) *Die Arbeiten von K.F. Schinkel für Prinz Wilhelm, späteren König von Preussen* (Sievers, 1955)

(10) *Mark Brandenburg* (Hans Kania and Hans Herbert Möller, 1960)

(11) *Berlin, III: Bauten für Wissenschaft, Verwaltung, Heer; Wohnbau und Denkmäler* (Rave, 1962)

(12) *Die Rheinlande, etc.* (Eva Brües, 1968)

(13) *Westfalen* (Ludwig Schreiner, 1969)

(14) *Das architektonische Lehrbuch* (Goerg Peschken, 1979)

Ettlinger, Leo 'A German Architect's Visit to England in 1826' in *Architectural Review*, 97, May 1945

Pevsner, Nikolaus 'Karl Friedrich Schinkel' in *Journal of the Royal Institute of British Architects*, 3rd ser. LIX, 1951–2 (reprinted in *Studies in Art, Architecture and Design*, I, London, 1968)

Lorck, Carl von *Schinkel, Reisen in Deutschland*, Essen, 1956

Kauffmann, Hans 'Zweckbau und Monument: Zu

Friedrich Schinkels Museum am Berliner Lustgarten', Gerhard Hess, ed., *Eine Freundesgabe der Wissenschaft für Ernst Hellmut Vits*, Frankfurt, 1963

– 'Friedrich Schinkel und seine Stellung in der Architekturgeschichte', in *Stil und Überlieferung in der Kunst des Abendlandes, Epochen Europäischer Kunst 1 (Akten des 21. Internationalen Kongresses für Kunstgeschichte in Bonn 1964)*, Berlin, 1967

Koch, Georg Friedrich 'Schinkels architektonischen Entwürfe im gotischen Stil 1810–1815', in *Zeitschrift fur Kunstgeschichte*, XXXII, 1969

Peschken, G. 'Technologische Ästhetik in Schinkels Architektur', in *Zeitschrift des deutschen Vereins für Kunst und Wissenschaft*, 1968, pp 25

Posener, Julius 'Schinkel's English Diary', in *From Schinkel to the Bauhaus*, New York, 1972

Pundt, Hermann *Schinkel's Berlin, a Study in Environmental Planning*, Cambridge, Mass., 1972

Knopp, N. 'Schinkels Theorie einer Stilsynthese', in *Beiträge zum Problem des deutschen Stilpluralismus. Studien zur Kunst des 19.Jh.*, Vol. 38, Munich, 1977, pp. 245

Carter, Rand 'Schinkel's Project for a Royal Palace on the Acropolis', in *Journal of the Society of Architectural Historians* (USA), XXXVIII, no. 1, 1979

Riemann, Gottfried *Karl Friedrich Schinkel, Reisen nach Italien*, Berlin, 1979

– 'Englische Einflüsse im architektonischen Spätwerk K.F. Schinkels', in *Forschungen und Berichte*, Vol. 15, Berlin-East 1973, p. 79–103

Watkin, David, 'Schinkel: Royal Patronage and the Picturesque', in *Architectural Design*, September 1979

Zadow, Mario *Karl Friedrich Schinkel*, Berlin, 1980

Waagen, G.F., *K.F. Schinkel als Mensch und als Künstler*. Reprint Berlin 1980

Hoepfner, W. 'Zwischen Klassik und Klassizismus. K.F. Schinkel und die antike Architektur', in *Bauwelt* 10, 1981, pp 338

Forssmann, Erik *Karl Friedrich Schinkel, Bauwerke und Baugedanken*, Munich and Zurich, 1981

Karl Friedrich Schinkel, exh. cat., Staatliche Museen zu Berlin/DDR, 1981

Karl Friedrich Schinkel, exh. cat., Verwaltung der Staatlichen Schlösser und Gärten, Schloss Charlottenburg, Berlin, 1981

Karl Friedrich Schinkel, Werke und Wirkungen, exh. cat., Martin-Gropius Bau, Berlin, 1981

Karl Friedrich Schinkel, Werke und Wirkungen in Polen, exh. cat., Martin-Gropius Bau, Berlin, 1981

1781–1841 Schinkel, l'architetto del principe, exh. cat., Comune di Venezia and Comune di Roma, 1982

Springer, Peter *Schinkels Schlossbrücke in Berlin, Zweckbau und Monument*, Frankfurt-am-Main, Berlin and Vienna, 1981

Wiederanders, Gerlinde *Die Kirchenbauten Karl Friedrich Schinkels*, Berlin, 1981

Gärtner, H., ed. *Schinkel-Studien*, Leipzig, 1984

LUDWIG MICHAEL SCHWANTHALER 1802–1848

Otten, Frank *Ludwig Michael Schwanthaler 1802–1848*, Munich, 1970

Eidlinger, Karl *Ludwig Michael von Schwanthaler*, exh. cat., Reichersberg, 1974

JOHANNES SEIZ d.1779

Lohmeyer, Karl *Johannes Seiz*, Heidelberg, 1914

GOTTFRIED SEMPER 1803–79

Manteuffel, C. Zoege von *Die Baukunst Gottfried Sempers*, diss. Freiburg, 1952

Fröhlich, Martin *Gottfried Semper*, Basel, 1974

AUGUST SOLLER 1805–53

Grundmann, Günther *August Soller 1805–1853. Ein Berliner Architekt im Geiste Schinkels*, Munich, 1973

PETER SPEETH 1772–1831

Haug, I. *Peter Speeth Architekt 1772–1831*, diss., Bonn, 1969

GOTTLOB FRIEDRICH THORMEYER 1757–1842

Schilde, G. *Gottlob Friedrich Thormeyer, ein spätklassizistischer Architekt Sachsens*, diss. (Technischen Hochschule, Dresden), Munich, 1922

NIKOLAUS FRIEDRICH VON THOURET 1767–1845

Faerber, Paul *Nikolaus Friedrich von Thouret, ein Baumeister des Klassizismus*, Stuttgart, 1949

ADOLPH VON VAGEDES 1777–1842

Kordt, Walther *Adolph von Vagedes. Ein rheinisch-westfälischer Baumeister der Goethezeit*, Ratingen, 1961

Zimmerman, Wolfgang *Adolph von Vagedes und seine Kirchenbauten*, Cologne, 1964

FRIEDRICH WEINBRENNER 1766–1826

Weinbrenner, Friedrich *Architektonisches Lehrbuch*, Tübingen, 1810–17

– *Ausgeführte und projektierte Gebäude*, Karlsruhe, 1822, 1835 (ed. H.A. Schreiber)

– *Entwürfe und Ergänzungen antiker Gabäude*, Karlsruhe and Baden, 1822 (I), 1839 (II)

– *Sammlung von Grundplänen . . . herausgegeben von mehreren seiner Schüler*, Frankfurt-am-Main, 1847

Schreiber, [H.] A. *Friedrich Weinbrenner. Ein Denkmal der Freundschaft*, Karlsruhe, 1826

– ed. *Friedrich Weinbrenner, Denkwürdigkeiten aus seinem Leben*, Heidelberg, 1829

Seneca, O. *Friedrich Weinbrenner*, Karlsruhe, 1907

Koebel, Max *Friedrich Weinbrenner*, Berlin, c.1920

Valdenaire, Arthur *Friedrich Weinbrenner – sein Leben und seine Bauten*, Karlsruhe, 1926, 2nd edn 1976

Lankheit, Klaus 'Friedrich Weinbrenner: Beitrage zu seinen Werk', in: *Fridiriciana, Zeitschrift der Universität Karlsruhe*, 19, 1976

– *Friedrich Weinbrenner und der Denkmalskult um 1800*, Basel, 1979

Schirmer, W. and Göricke, J. *Friedrich Weinbrenner, 1766–1826*, exh. cat., Staatliche Kunsthalle, Karlsruhe, 1977

Friedrich Weinbrenner, 1766–1826, exh. cat., Architectural Association, London, 1982

CARL LUDWIG WIMMEL 1786–1845

Hannmann, Eckhart *Carl Ludwig Wimmel 1786–1845, Hamburgs erster Baudirektor*, Munich, 1975

JOHANN CHRISTIAN ZAIS 1770–1820

'Johann Christian Zais 1770–1820', in *Nassauische Lebensbilder*, V, 1955

Places

The architecture of the major cities is generally described in two series:
Publications of the Architects and Engineer Associations *Veröffentlichungen der Architekten and Ingenieur Vereine* (Berlin, Munich, Hamburg, Danzig, Düsseldorf, Frankfurt, Cologne, Leipzig, Mannheim, Strassburg) *Kunstdenkmäler e.g. Die Kunstdenkmäler der Rheinprovinz*

AACHEN

Laurent, Pick and Schmidt-Burgh *Die Kunstdenkmäler der Rheinprovinz, Aachen*, II, *Profane Denkmäler*, Düsseldorf, 1924
Vollings, W. *Das Aachener Stadttheater*, diss., Aachen, 1964

ANSBACH

Fehring, G.P. *Stadt und Landkreis Ansbach* (Bayerische Kunstdenkmäler), Munich, 1958

ASCHAFFENBURG

Kunstdenkmäler Baden. Stadt Aschaffenburg, 1918
Kreisel, H. *Schloss Aschaffenburg und Pompejanum. Amtlicher Führer und Gemäldekatalog*, Munich, 1932
Coudenhove-Erthal, E. 'Die Kunst am Hofe der letzten Kurfürsten von Mainz' in *Wiener Jahrbuch für Kunstgeschichte*, X, 1935
Bachmann, E. *Schönbusch bei Aschaffenburg. Amtlicher Führer*, Munich, 1963

ATHENS

Russack, H. Hermann *Deutsche bauen in Athen*, Berlin, 1942
Demostenopoulou, Elpiniki *Öffentliche Bauten unter König Otto in Athen. Begegnung mit Griechenland. Auffassung und Auseinandersetzungen*, diss., Munich, 1970

AUGSBURG

Architektur des 19. Jahrhunderts in Augsburg, exh. cat. Augsburg 1979

AYBLING

Woerl, Leopold *Das Theresien-Monument bei Aybling*, Aybling, 1833

BAD BUCHAU

Klaiber, H. *Stift und Stiftskirche zu Buchau*, Augsburg, 1929

BADEN BADEN

Klüber, J.L. *Baden bei Rastatt*, 1807
Walz, J.L. *Notizen aus dem Bad in Baden*, Karlsruhe, 1807
Schreiber, H.A. *Baden-Baden. Neuer Führer für Reisende und Kurgäste in und um Baden*, Karlsruhe and Baden, 1839
– *Der Sagen-Cyclus zu Götzenbergers Wandgemälde in der neuen Trinkhalle von Baden Baden*, Baden Baden, 1849, 3rd edn 1904
Guinot, E. *Ein Sommer in Baden*, Leipzig, 1858
Anon. 'Baden Baden and its Environs', in *Illustrated Europe*, II, Zurich, 1880
Stürzenacker, A. 'Das Kurhaus in Baden Baden und dessen Neubau', in *Badische Heimat*, 4, 1917
– *Das Kurhaus und dessen Neubau 1912–17*, Karlsruhe, 1918

Berl, H. *Geschichtlicher Führer durch Baden Baden*, Baden Baden, 1936
Lacroix, E., ed. *Die Kunstdenkmäler Badens*, II, *Stadtkreis Baden Baden*, Karlsruhe, 1942

BAD DOBERAN

Thielke, Hans *Die Bauten des Seebades Doberan-Heiligendamm um 1800 und ihr Baumeister Severin*. Diss. Doberan, 1917.

BAD EMS

Luthmer, Ferdinand *Die Bau- und Kunstdenkmäler des Lahngebietes*, Frankfurt, 1907
Bach, Adolf *Die Emser Spielbank*, Bad Ems, 1924
Bach, Gertrud *Kleine Chronik von Bad Ems*, 2nd edn, Bad Ems, 1968
Custodis, Paul Georg 'Bad Ems', in *Rheinische Kunststätten*, VI, 1975

BAD HOFGEISMAR

Bott, Gerhard 'Landgraf Wilhelm IX. als Förderer des kurhessischen Badewesens. Die Bäder Hofgeismar, Wilhelmsbad und Nenndorf im ausgehenden 18. Jahrhundert', in: *Hessische Heimat*, Vol. 34, (Heft 2/3) 1984, p. 61
Baeumerth, Angelika 'Das Bad Hofgeismar im Jahre 1786', in *Hessische Heimat*, Vol. 34 (Heft 2/3), 1984, p. 49

BAD KISSINGEN

Krening, E. Günther *Bad Kissingen* (*Mainfränkische Hefte*, 41). Würzburg, 1970

BAD LAUCHSTÄDT

Ehrlich, Willi *Bad Lauchstädt. Historische Kuranlagen und Goethe-Theater*. Ed. Nationale Forschungs- und Gedenkstätten der klassischen deutschen Literatur in Weimar, Weimar, 1968
Maak, *Das Goethetheater in Lauchstädt*, Lauchstädt, 1905

BAD NAUHEIM

Lohr, Siegfried 'Bad Nauheim und der Kasseler Baumeister Julius Eugen Ruhl (1796–1871)', in *Hessische Heimat*, Vol. 34 (Heft 2/3) 1984, p. 79

BAD NENNDORF see BAD HOFGEISMAR

BAMBERG

Reitzenstein, A. von *Bamberg*, Munich, 1972

BAYREUTH

Habermann, Sylvia *Bayreuther Gartenkunst*, Worms, 1982

BERLIN

Osborn, Max *Berlin*, Leipzig, 1909. Vol 43 of *Berühmte Kunststätten*
Peschken, Goerd *Schinkels Bauakademie in Berlin. Ein Aufruf zu ihrer Rettung*, Berlin, 1961
Kauffmann, Hans 'Zweckbau und Monument. Zu. F. Schinkels Museum am Berliner Lustgarten', in *Eine Freundesgabe für Ernst Hellmut Vits*, Frankfurt a. M. 1963, p. 135–166
Gaus, Joachim 'Schinkels Entwurf zum Luisen-

mausoleum', in *Aachener Kunstblätter*, Vol. 41, 1971, p. 254–63 (Festschrift für Wolfgang Krönig)

Hoffman, Hans *Schloss Charlottenhof und die Römischen Bäder*, Potsdam 1971 (Guidebook)

Börsch-Supan, Helmut *Der Schinkel-Pavillon im Schlossgarten zu Charlottenburg*, Berlin 1976 (Guidebook 2nd ed.)

– *Das Mausoleum im Charlottenburger Schlossgarten*, Berlin, 1976 (Guidebook)

Mielke, Friedrich and Jutta v. Simson *Das Berliner Denkmal für Friedrich den Grossen*, Berlin, 1976

Sperlich, Martin and Michael Seiler 'Schloss und Park zu Glienicke', in *Zehlendorfer Chronik*, Heft 2, 1977

Segers-Glocke, Christiane 'Zur Wiederherstellung der Grossen Neugierde im Schlosspark zu Klein-Glienicke', in *Schlösser, Gärten, Berlin, Festschrift für Martin Sperlich*, Tübingen, 1980, p. 131–152

Merckle, Kurt *Das Denkmal König Friedrichs des Grossen in Berlin*, Berlin, 1894

Schmitz, Hermann *Berliner Baumeister vom Ausgang des 18. Jahrhunderts*, Berlin, 1914

Schroth, Ingeborg *Die Nachahmung des Griechischen durch die Berliner Baumeister der Goethezeit*, diss., Freiburg-im-Breisgau, 1944

Rodenwald, Gerhard *Griechisches und Römisches in Berliner Bauten des Klassizismus*, Berlin, 1956

Bauch, Kurt *Das Brandenburger Tor*, Cologne, 1966

Die Bauwerke und Kunstdenkmäler von Berlin, ed. Senator für Bau- und Wohnungswesen - Landeskonservator, Berlin, 1970–

Berlin und seine Bauten edited by the Architekten -Verein zu Berlin and Vereinigung Berliner Architekten. Berlin 1877 2nd ed. in two Vols Berlin, 1896.

Berlin und seine Bauten, Berlin and Düsseldorf, 1970–

Bloch, Peter and Grzimek, Waldemar *Das klassische Berlin. Die Berliner Bildhauerschule im neunzehnten Jahrhundert*, Frankfurt, Berlin and Vienna, 1978

Reuther, Hans, *Die Museumsinsel in Berlin*. Frankfurt 1978.

Berlin und die Antike ed. W. Arenhövel. exh. cat., Deutsches Archäologisches Institut und Staatliche Museen Preussischer Kulturbesitz, Schloss Charlottenburg, Berlin, 1979.

Klünner, Hans-Werner and Peschken, Goerd, eds. *Das Berliner Stadtschloss*, Frankfurt, Vienna and Berlin, 1982

Die Bau- und Kunstdenkmäler in der DDR, I, *Hauptstadt Berlin*, I, Berlin, 1983

BONN

Hundeshagen, Bernhard *Die Stadt und Universität Bonn am Rhein mit ihren Umgebungen*, Bonn, 1832

Geschichte der Rhein. Friedr. Wilhelms Universität zu Bonn, II, *Institute und Seminare 1818–1933*, Bonn, 1934

Küstner, F. 'Die Bonner Sternwarte', in *General Anzeiger für Bonn*, 4 Oct. 1934

BREMEN

Wegener, H. ed. *Schönes altes Bremen in Stichen und Lithographien*, n.d.

Stein, Rudolf *Klassizismus und Romantik in der Baukunst Bremens*, I, *Das Gebiet der Altstadt und der Alten Neustadt.*

Der Wall und die Contrescarpe, Bremen, 1964; II, *Die Vorstädte und die Stadt-Landgüter Vegesack und Bremerhafen*, Bremen, 1965

BRUNSWICK

Heusinger, E. *Geschichte der Residenzstadt Braunschweig von 1806–1831*, Brunswick, 1861

Doerins, Oskar *Braunschweig*, Leipzig, 1905

Meier, P.J. and Steinacker, K. *Die Bau- und Kunstdenkmäler der Stadt Braunschweig*, rev. edns, Brunswick, 1926, 1931

Meier, P.J. *Braunschweig*, Berlin, 1929

Stelzer, Otto *Braunschweig*, Brunswick, 1952

Dorn, Reinhard, 'Die Villa Salve Hospes in Braunschweig', in *Grosse Baudenkmäler*, 235, Munich and Berlin, 1969

Brunswiek 1031–Braunschweig 1981, exh. cat., Städtisches Museum, Brunswick, 1981

Rauterberg, Claus *Bauwesen und Bauten im Herzogtum Braunschweig zur Zeit Carl Wilhelm Ferdinands 1780–1806* (Diss. Brunswick 1970)

Romero, Rolf *Die Toranlagen P.J. Krahes in Braunschweig als Ausdruck klassizistischen Zeitgeistes*. Diss, Brunswick, 1949.

Banse, Ewald 'Die Entwicklung der Wallanlagen der Stadt Braunschweig aus der alten Befestigung', in *Braunschweigisches Jahrbuch*, Vol 1, 1940, p. 5–28.

Böhlke, Arno *Das freistehende Einfamilienhaus in Braunschweig in der Zeit von 1800–1870*. Brunswick, Berlin, Hamburg 1929, Diss TH. Braunschweig 1925.

COBURG

Teufel, R. *Bau- und Kunstdenkmäler in Coburg*, Coburg, 1956

Brunner, H. and Fischer, M.F. *Coburg Schloss Ehrenburg*, Munich, 1972

COLOGNE

Cölnische Zeitung, 1829, Beiblatt 2 & 4 (on the Theatre)

Füssli, W. *Die wichtigsten Städte am Mittel- und Niederrhein*, 1843

Köln und seine Bauten (Architekten- und Ingenieurverein, Cologne), 1888

Vogts, H. 'Klassizistische Baukunst in Köln', in *Denkmalpflege und Heimatschutz*, XXXI, 1929

Clemen, Paul, ed. *Die Kunstdenkmäler der Stadt Köln*, II, *Profane Denkmäler*, Düsseldorf, 1930

DARMSTADT

Koch, A. and Zobel, V. *Darmstadt*, 1915

Haupt, Georg *Die Bau- und Kunstdenkmäler der Stadt Darmstadt*, Darmstadt, 1952–4

Die St. Ludwigskirche in Darmstadt, *Wilhelminenplatz*, Munich and Zurich, 1961

Zimmermann, Georg *Das Darmstädter Schloss und seine Baugeschichte*, Darmstadt, 1978

DESSAU

Harksen, Marie Luise *Die Stadt Dessau*, (Die Kunstdenkmale des Landes Anhalt, ed. H. Giesau, Vol. 1), Berg-Magdeburg, 1937

DRESDEN

Becker, Wilhelm Gottlob *Das Seifersdorfer Tal*, Leipzig and Dresden, 1792

Haug, Heinrich 'Die Demolition der Dresdener Festungswerke', in *Dresdener Geschichtsblätter*, 1898

Richter, Otto *Dresden sonst und jetzt*, Dresden, 1905

Barth, Alfred *Zur Baugeschichte der Dresdener Kreuzkirche*, Dresden, 1907

Fiebiger, 'Schinkel in Dresden', in *Dresdener Geschichtsblätter*, 1910–13

Kluge, H.J. *Dresdener Friedhöfe und Grabdenkmäler in der Zeit der Freiheitskriege und der Romantik*, Dresden, 1937

Löffler, Fritz *Das Alte Dresden*, Dresden, 1955

DÜSSELDORF

Süttenfuss, Paul 'Das neue Düsseldorf nach Schleifung der Wälle', in *Zeitschrift des rheinischen Vereins für Denkmalpflege und Heimatschutz*, 1924, p. 48 ff

Riemann, Karl 'Der Düsseldorfer Stadtbauplan vom Jahre 1831', in *Düsseldorfer Heimatblätter (Das Tor)*, IX 1940

Pfeffer, Klaus 'Spätklassizismus in Düsseldorf', in *Düsseldorfer Jahrbuch*, 51, 1963

Zebisch, Günther, *Die städtebauliche Entwicklung der Königsallee in Düsseldorf*, diss Aachen s.d. 1968?

Pfeffer, Klaus, 'Düsseldorf Anlagen und Bauten des 19. Jahrhunderts', in *Rheinische Kunststätten*, Vol. 8, 1973

EDENKOBEN/VILLA LUDWIGSHÖHE

Bornheim gen. Schilling, Werner, (ed) *Schloss 'Villa Ludwigshöhe'* (guidebook No. 13 of Führer der Verwaltung der staatlichen Schlösser Rheinland-Pfalz), Mainz, 1981

ELBERFELD

Busse, C.F. 'Das Landgerichtsgebäude in Elberfeld', in *Zeitschrift für Bauwesen*, II, 1852

Klapheck, R. 'Das klassizistische Elberfeld', in *Rheinische Kunststätten*, XII, no. 1, 1935

FRANKFURT

Jung, R. 'Die Niederlegung der Festungswerke in Frankfurt am Main 1802–1807', in *Archiv für Frankfurts Geschichte und Kunst*, 3rd Series, 1913, Vol. 2, p. 157 ff.

Vogt, Günther *Frankfurter Bürgerhäuser des Neunzehnten Jahrhunderts, ein Stadtbild des Klassizismus*, Frankfurt, n.d.

Merten, Klaus and Mohr, C. *Das Frankfurter Westend*, Munich, 1974

Klassizistische Architektur in Frankfurt am Main, Frankfurt am Main, 1985

FULDA

Schloss Fasanerie bei Fulda, guidebook of Schnell Kunstführer no. 973 Munich/Zürich 1974, 2nd ed 1981.

HAMBURG

Dammann, W. 'Die Anfänge des Klassizismus im Hamburgischen Bauwesen', in *Bau-Rundschau*, 1918, No. 10/13 p. 43 ff.

Volckens, W. 'Die Landhäuser der Flottbecker Chaussee auf Othmarscher und Övelgönner Gebiet im 19. Jahrhundert', in *Mitteilungen des Vereins für Hamburgische Geschichte* 13 (1917–19) p. 119 ff.

Jakstein, W. 'C.F. Harsdorff und seine Bedeutung für Altona', in *Amtsblatt der Stadt Altona*, 1929, No. 3.

Becker, H. *Das Landhaus Hamburgs um die Zeit von 1800*; diss. Brunswick 1931

Elingius, Erich and Werner Jackstein *Die Palmaille in Altona, ein Kulturdokument des Klassizismus*, Hamburg, 1938

Brauer, H., W. Scheffler and H. Weber *Die Kunstdenkmäler der Provinz Schleswig-Holstein. Kreis Pinneberg*, Berlin, 1939

Grundmann, Günther *Jenischpark und Jenischhaus*, Hamburg, 1957

Gobert, R.K. *Die Bau- und Kunstdenkmale der Freien und Hansestadt Hamburg. 2 Vols, Vol 1 Bergedorf-Vierlande-Marschlande. (1953) Vol 2 Altona-Elbvororte. (Hamburg 1959)*

Hoffman, Paul Theodor *Die Elbchaussee, ihre Landsitze, Menschen und Schicksale*, Hamburg, 1966, 7th ed

Knupp, Chr. *Die Profanarchitektur des Frühklassizismus in Hamburg*, MA thesis, Hamburg, 1967

Kopenhagen-Hamburg-Altona: eine künstlerische Beziehung 1750–1850. exh. cat. Hamburg Altonaer Museum 1968

Ruhmor, v. H. *Schlösser und Herrenhäuser im Herzogtum Schleswig*, Frankfurt, 1968

– *Schlösser und Herrenhäuser in Ostholstein*, Frankfurt, 1973.

– *Schlösser und Herrenhäuser im nördlichen und westlichen Holstein*, Frankfurt, 1981.

Hirschfeld, P. *Herrenhäuser und Schlösser in Schleswig-Holstein.* Munich, Berlin, 1980 5th ed.

HANOVER

Hoeltje, G. *Hannover*, Berlin, 1931

– 'Pläne zum Umbau des hannoverschen Leineschlosses aus dem Jahre 1816 von H. Chr. Jussow und G.L.F. Laves', in *Niederdeutsche Beiträge zur Kunstgeschichte*, III, Berlin and Munich, 1964

Zur Eröffnung nach dem Wiederaufbau im Jahre 1950, exh. cat., Opera House, Hanover, 1950

Deckert, Hermann and Roggenkamp, Hans *Das Alte Hannover*, Berlin, 1952

Schnath, Georg *Das Leineschloss*, Hanover, 1962

Alvensleben, Udo von and Reuther, Hans *Herrenhausen. Die Sommerresidenz der Welfen*, Hanover, 1966

Dörries, Bernhard and Piath, Helmut *Alt-Hannover. Die Geschichte einer Stadt in zeitgenössischen Bildern 1500–1900*, Hanover, 1967

HOMBURG VOR DER HÖHE

Biehn, Heinz *Schloss Homburg vor der Höhe*, 1976

INGOLSTADT

Müller, Theodor *Ingolstadt*, Munich, 1963

Reitzenstein, A. von *Die Festung Ingolstadt König Ludwigs I.*, Ingolstadt, 1974

KARLSRUHE

Die Residenzstadt, ihre Geschichte und Beschreibung, Karlsruhe, 1858

Fecht, K.G. *Geschichte der Haupt- und Residenzstadt Karlsruhe*, Karlsruhe, 1887

Ehrenberg, Kurt *Baugeschichte von Karlsruhe 1715–1820, Bau-und Bodenpolitik. Eine Studie zur Geschichte des Städtebaus*, diss. Karlsruhe, 1908

– *Baugeschichte von Karlsruhe 1715–1870*, Karlsruhe, 1909

Gutmann, E. *Das Grossherzogliche Residenzschloss zu Karlsruhe*, Heidelberg, 1911

Delenheinz, L. 'Alt-Karlsruhe und Friedrich Weinbrenner', in *Zeitschrift für Bauwesen*, X-XII, 1913

Rott, H. *Kunst und Künstler am Baden-Durlacher Hof*, Karlsruhe, 1917

Lacroix, Emil 'Zur Baugeschichte des Karlsruher Marktplatzes. Ein Beitrag zur Geschichte des Städtebaus im 19. Jh.' in *Zeitschrift für die Geschichte des Oberrheins*, n.s., XLVII, 1934

Huber, Walter *Die Stephaniestrasse; Ein Stück Bau- und Kulturgeschichte aus Karlsruhe*, Karlsruhe, 1954

Göricke, J. *Bauten in Karlsruhe*, Karlsruhe, 1971

Schirmer, Wolf and Göricke, J. *Architekten der Fridericiana, Skizzen und Entwürfe seit Friedrich Weinbrenner* (exh., Staatliche Kunsthalle Karlsruhe), cat. in *Fridericiana, Zeitschrift der Universitäts Karlsruhe*, XVIII, 1975

Goldschmidt, R. *Die Stadt Karlsruhe 1715–1915*

Grosch, O. *Das Rathaus zu Karlsruhe.*

KASSEL

Günterrode *Briefe eines Reisenden über den gegenwärtigen Zustand von Cassel*, Frankfurt and Leipzig, 1781

Holtmeyer, A. 'Alt Cassel (mit Stadtplan, 96 Tafeln und 75 Textbildern)', in *Beiträge zur Kunstgeschichtlichen Heimatkunde*, Marburg, 1913

– *Die Bau- und Kunstdenkmäler im Regierungsbezirk Kassel*, VI, *Kassel Stadt*, Marburg, 1923

Boehlke, Hans Kurt *S. L. du Ry als Stadtbaumeister Landgrafs Friedrichs II. von Hessen-Kassel*, diss., Göttingen, 1953, 1958

Vogel, H. 'Englische Kultureinflüsse am Kasseler Hof des späten 18. Jh.', in *Hessisches Jahrbuch für Landesgeschichte*, VI, 1956

Kaltwasser, K., ed. *Paul Heidelbach: Kassel ein Jahrtausend Hessischer Stadtkultur*, Kassel and Basel, 1959, reprint Heidelbach 1920

Aufklärung und Klassizismus in Hessen-Kassel unter Landgraf Friedrich 1760–85, exh. cat., Kassel, 1979

Diettscheid, H.C. 'Charles de Wailly in den Diensten des Landgrafen Friedrich II. von Hessen-Kassel', in *Kunst in Hessen und Mittelrhein*, XX, 1981

Schweitzhart, G., ed. 'Stadtplanung und Stadtentwicklung in Kassel im 18 Jh.', in *Kasseler Hefte für Kunstwissenschaft und Kunstpädagogik*, V, 1983

KASSEL WILHELMSHÖHE

Krieger, Joh.Chr. *Geschichte und Beschreibung des kurfürstlich-hessischen Lustschlosses Wilhelmshöhe und seiner Anlagen von erster Enstehung an, bis auf gegenwärtige Zeiten*, Marburg, 1805.

Heidelbach, P. *Die Geschichte der Wilhelmshöhe*, Leipzig, 1909

Hübner, P.G. *Wilhelmshöhe*, Berlin, 1927

Paetow, Karl *Klassizismus und Romantik auf Wilhelmshöhe*, Kassel, 1929

Kramm, W. 'Kassel, Wilhelmshöhe, Wilhelmsthal', Berlin 1931, in *Deutsche Kunst*, ed. B. Meier

Vogel, Ewald 'Die Löwenburg bei Kassel und ihre Romantik', in *Heimat und Bild, Beilage zum Giessener Anzeiger (Giessen)* 11.1.1940

Kaltwasser, K. *Wilhelmshöhe und Schloss Wilhelmsthal*, Königstein, 1955.

Schenk zu Schweinsberg, E. Freiherr von 'Zur Wiederherstellung des Weissensteiner Flügels', in *Hessische Heimat*, No 6, 1956/57, Heft 2, p. 77 ff.

– 'Die wiedereingerichtete Löwenburg', in *Hessische Heimat* No. 11, 1961, Heft 2/3

Lometsch, Fr. *Wilhelmshöhe*. Kassel 1961

Guidebooks all ed. by 'Verwaltung der Staatlichen Schlösser und Gärten in Hessen', Bad Homburg v.d. Höhe

Schloss Wilhelmshöhe, ed. Biehn, Heinz 1968, rev. 1974 by W. Einsigbach and Karl-Heinz Rohde

Park Wilhelmshöhe, ed. Alfred Hoffmann, s.d. (after 1961)

Dittscheid, Christopher, Wolfgang, Einsigbach and Adolf Fink *Kassel, Löwenburg im Bergpark Wilhelmshöhe*, Bad Homburg v.d. Höhe, 1976

KELHEIM

Fischer, Manfred F. *Befreiungshalle in Kelheim*, Munich, 1971

KOBLENZ

Klein, J.A. *Rheinreise von Strassburg bis Düsseldorf*, 1828, 1843

Domenicus, A. *Coblenz und der letzte Kurfürst von Trier. 1768–94*, Koblenz, 1869

Eltester, L. von *Das königliche Schloss zu Koblenz*, 1872

Lehfeld, P. *Die Bau- und Kunstdenkmäler des Reg.-Bez. Koblenz*, 1886

Reimer, H. *Das königliche Schloss zu Coblenz*, 2nd edn. 1907

Weichelt, W.W. *Casino Koblenz 1808–1908*, Koblenz, 1908

Becker, W.J. *Forschungen zum Theaterwesen von Koblenz*, diss., Giessen, Bonn, 1915

Bär, M. *Aus der Geschichte der Stadt Koblenz, 1814–1914*, Koblenz, 1922

Hager, Ernst *Die Koblenzer Residenz, ein Schlossbau des Klassizismus*, 1927

Werkhäuser, F.R., ed. *150 Jahre Theater der Stadt Koblenz*, Koblenz, 1937

Michel, Fritz *Die Kunstdenkmäler der Rheinprovinz, Koblenz Vororte und profane Bauten*, Düsseldorf, 1954

– *Die Kunstdenkmäler der Stadt Koblenz*, Munich, 1954

Bockius, F., ed. *175 Jahre Theater der Stadt Koblenz*, Koblenz, 1962

Theater der Stadt Koblenz, Generalinstandsetzung 1984/85, ed. Stadt Koblenz, Presse und Informationsamt, Dokumentation der Stadt Koblenz, Koblenz 1985

Dollen, Busso von der, 'Raumplanung für die

Erweiterung einer rheinischen Residenz im 18. Jahrhundert und ihre Auswirkung auf die moderne Stadttopographie am Beispiel Koblenz', in *Die Stadt in der europäischen Geschichte* (Festschrift Edith Ennen), 1972.

Bornheim, gen. Schilling, W. 'Das Koblenzer Residenzschloss und der Klassizismus', in *Jahrbuch für Geschichte und Kunst des Mittelrheins* No 8/9, 1956/57 p. 78–93.

Koblenz, Schloss und Neustadt, exh. cat. Koblenz, 1975

Dollen, Busso von der *Die Koblenzer Neustadt. Planung und Ausführung einer Stadterweiterung des 18. Jh.*, 1979

KREFELD
Brües, E. *Die Denkmäler des Rheinlandes, Krefeld*, Düsseldorf, 1967

LAHR
Beck, W. *Die Stadt Lahr im 18. und 19. Jahrhundert*, Lahr, 1913

LEIPZIG
Blümner *Geschichte des Theaters in Leipzig*, Leipzig, 1818

'Über den Bau des Dr. Härtel'schen Hausses in Leipzig', in *Allgemeine Bauzeitung Wien*, 1836, p. 144

Vogel, Julius, *Das römische Haus in Leipzig. Ein Beitrag zur Kunstgeschichte des 19. Jahrhunderts*, Leipzig, 1903

Sydow, Eckhart von 'Schinkels Anteil am Bau des Leipziger Augusteums', in *Kunstchronik und Kunstmarkt*, NF. No. 31 1919/20, p. 901–906 and No. 32 1920/21 p. 170–173

Füssler, Heinz *Leipziger Universitätsbauten*, Leipzig, 1961

Rudolff-Hille, Gertrud *Das Theater auf der Ranstädter Bastei-Leipzig 1766*, Leipzig, 1969

LINDAU
Wolfart, K. *Geschichte der Stadt Lindau im Bodensee*, Leipzig, 1909

– *Das gesellige Leben in Lindau während des 19 Jahrhunderts. Neujahrsblatt des Museumsvereins*, Lindau, 1911

Gruber, B. *Lindenhof*, Leipzig, 1938

Die Kunstdenkmäler von Bayern und Schwaben, IV, *Stadt- und Landkreis Lindau Bodensee*, Munich, 1954

Thorbecke, Jan, ed. *Friedrich Gruber. Ein Lindauer Kaufmann nach Briefen und Tagenbüchern*

MANNHEIM
Pichler, A. *Chronik des grossherzoglichen Hof- und Nationaltheaters in Mannheim*, Mannheim, 1879

Walter, F. *Aus der Geschichte des Mannheimer Nationaltheaters*

Huth, Hans *Die Kunstdenkmäler des Stadtkreises Mannheim*, 1982

Buss, Hermann Eris 'Mannheim', in *Badische Heimat*, Karlsruhe, 1927

MUNICH
Woltmann, Alfred *Die Münchner Architektur dieses Jahrhunderts*, Munich, 1863

Bulle, H. 'Zur Geschichte des Münchner Königsplatz', in *Helbings Monatsberichte für Kunstwissenschaft und Kunsthandel*, Munich, 1902

Stieler, Eugen von *Die königliche Akademie der bildenden Künste zu München*; I, *1808–1858* (*Festschrift zur Hundertjahrfeier*), Munich, 1909

Wiedenhofer, Josef *Die bauliche Entwicklung Münchens*, Munich, 1916

Rose, Hans *München als Organismus*, Munich, 1928

Dombart, Theodor *München, Das Werden und Wachsen des Stadtbildes*, Munich, 1931

– *Der Englische Garten zu München*, Munich, 1972

Karlinger, Hans *München und die Kunst des 19. Jahrhunderts*, Munich, 1933

Pölnitz, Winfried von *Münchner Kunst und Münchner Kunstkämpfe*, Munich, 1936

Hederer, Oswald *Die Ludwigstrasse in München*, Munich, 1942

– *Bauten und Plätze in München. Ein Architekturführer*, Munich, 1979

Lieb, Norbert *München – Lebensbild einer Stadtkultur*, Munich, 1952/1972

Habel, Heinrich *Das Odeon in München und die Frühzeit des öffentlichen Konzertsaalbaus* (*In Neue Münchner Beiträge zur Kunstgeschichte*, VIII), Berlin, 1967

Dirrigel, Michael *Residenz der Museen*, Munich, 1970

Wanetschek, M. *Die Grünanlagen in der Stadtplanung Münchens von 1790–1860*, Munich, 1971

Zimmermann, Florian *Klenzes Kriegsministerium*. MA Thesis, Munich, 1977

Gallas, Klaus *München*. Dumont Kunst-Reiseführer, Köln, 1979

Friedrichs, Carola *Die politische Selbstdarstellung der bayrischen Monarchie beziehungsweise des bayrischen Staates in der Architektur des 19. Jh*. Munich, 1980 (Heft 97 of Miscellanea Bavarica Monacensia, Dissertationen zur Bayerischen Landes- und Münchner Stadtgeschichte)

Wasem, Eva Maria, *Die Münchner Residenz unter Ludwig I, Bildprogramme und Bildausstattungen in den Neubauten*, Munich, 1981. (Heft 101 of Miscellanea Bavarica Monacensia . . .)

Bosl, Karl *München*, Munich, 1971

Habel, Heinrich *Der Münchner Kirchenbau im 19. und frühen 20. Jahrhundert*, Munich, 1971

Hollweck, Ludwig *München. Liebling der Musen*, Vienna, 1971

Böttger, Peter *Die Alte Pinakothek in München. Architektur, Ausstattung und museales Programm*, Munich, 1972

Schattenhofer, Michael *Das alte Rathaus in München*, Munich, 1972

Lieb-Sauermost, N. *Die Kirchen in München*, Munich, 1973

Schwahn, Britta -R. *Die Glyptothek in München – Baugeschichte und Ikonologie*, diss., Munich, 1976 (Heft 83 of Miscellanea Bavarica Monacensia, Dissertationen zur Bayerischen Landes – und Münchener Stadtgeschichte, 1979)

Glyptothek München 1830–1980, exh. cat., Glyptothek, Munich, 1980

MUSKAU
Arnim, Hermann Graf von *Ein Fürst unter den Gärtnern, Pückler als Landschaftskünstler und der Muskauer Park*, Frankfurt, Berlin and Vienna, 1981

OLDENBURG

Pleinter, E. *Oldenburg im 19. Jahrhundert*, Oldenburg, 1900

Lübbing, Hermann *Oldenburg. Ein norddeutsches Stadtbild im Wandel der Zeiten*, Oldenburg, 1975

Gilly, Wilhelm *Biedermeierliche Blätter aus Oldenburg*, Oldenburg, 1976

Braun, Hermann and Neumann, Michael *Die Oldenburger Neustadtquartiere Dobben und Haarenesch*, Oldenburg, 1978

Herzog Peter Friedrich Ludwig von Oldenburg (1755–1829), exh. cat., Oldenburg, 1979

PILLNITZ

Hartmann, Hans-Günther *Pillnitz, Schloss, Park und Dorf*, Weimar, 1981

POTSDAM

Kurth, W. *Sanssouci. Seine Schlössen und Gärten*, Berlin, 1959

Mielke, Friedrich *Potsdamer Baukunst, Das klassische Potsdam*, Frankfurt, Berlin and Vienna, 1981

REGENSBURG

Schulz, P. 'Das Kepler-Denkmal in Regensburg', in *Kepler-Festschrift*, part 1, 1930, p. 116

Die Kunstdenkmäler von Bayern, Oberpfalz 22, Stadt Regensburg III, Munich, 1933

Boll, W., *Das Thon-Dittmer-Palais*. Festschrift zur Eröffnung der Niederlassung Regensburg der Bank für Gemeinwirtschaft A.G. Regensburg. s.d. (1970)

Piendl, M., 'Die fürstliche Residenz in Regensburg im 18. und beginnenden 19. Jahrhundert', in *Thurn und Taxis Studien* 3, 1963, p. 85–87

– 'Der fürstliche Marstall in Regensburg', in *Thurn und Taxis Studien* 4, Kallmünz, 1966

– 'Ein Jahrhundert Schlossbaugeschichte Regensburg 1812–1912', in *Thurn und Taxis Studien* 11, Kallmünz, 1979.

Reidel, H. 'Die bürgerliche Architektur in Regensburg von 1650–1910', in R. Strobel (ed) *Regensburg. Die Altstadt als Denkmal*. Munich, 1978

– 'Die Villenbauten Emanuel Joseph von Herigoyens in Regensburg', in *Verhandlungen des Historischen Vereins für Oberpfalz und Regensburg*, Vol 118, 1978, p. 112–127

SCHWETZINGEN

Die Kunstdenkmäler Badens, X, Vol. 2, *Schwetzingen* by Kurt Martin, Karlsruhe, 1933

Sillib, Rudolf *Schloss und Garten in Schwetzingen*, Heidelberg, 1907

Carl Theodor und Elisabeth Auguste, Höfische Kunst und Kultur in der Kurpfalz, exh. cat. Heidelberg, 1979, ed. by Jörn Bahns

STUTTGART

Hartmann, Julius *Chronik der Stadt Stuttgart*, Stuttgart, 1886

Leins, C.F. von *Die Hoflager und Landsitze des württembergischen Regentenhauses*, Stuttgart, 1889

Schmidt, Richard *Schloss Solitude bei Stuttgart*, Gerlingen, 1931

Wais, Gustav *Alt-Stuttgarts Bauten im Bild*, Stuttgart, 1951

Klaiber, Hans Andreas 'Die Entstehung der Fassade des Neuen Schlosses', in *Schwäbische Heimat*, 1956, 2

– *Schloss Solitude*, Stuttgart, 1961

– and Kilian H. *Stuttgart*, Constance, 1961

– 'Der Wiederaufbau des Neuen Schlosses zu Stuttgart', in *Deutsche Kunst und Denkmalpflege*, 1966

– *Kunstwanderungen in Württemberg*

Kleemann, G. *Schloss Solitude bei Stuttgart, Aufbau, Glanzzeit, Niedergang (Veröffentlichungen des Archivs der Stadt Stuttgart)*, Stuttgart, 1966

Weber, Wilhelm *Villa Ludwigshöhe – Ein Schlossbau des Spätklassizismus*, Kaiserslautern, 1969

Kleemann, G. *Schloss Solitude und seine Geschichte*, 2nd edn 1972

Schümann, Carl Wolfgang 'Olga wohnt himmlisch. Studien zur Villa Berg in Stuttgart', in *Jahrbuch der Staatlichen Kunstsammlungen in Baden Württemberg*, X, 1973

Bach, Max *Stuttgarter Kunst 1794–1860*, Stuttgart, 1900.

Baum, *Württembergische Fürstensitze*, 1913

Siegler, Karl George *Stuttgart*, Munich, Berlin, 1968

Konkathedrale St. Eberhard. Diözese Rottenburg-Stuttgart, ed. Dompfarramt St. Eberhard, Stuttgart, 1978

St. Eberhard in Stuttgart. ed Paul Mai, Schnell Kunstführer No 1443, 1984

Iffert, Heike and Falk, Jaeger *100 Bauwerke in Stuttgart*, Zürich, 1984

STUTTGART HOHENHEIM

Nau, Elisabeth *Hohenheim Schloss und Garten*, Constance/Stuttgart, 1967

WALHALLA

Ludwig I, King of Bavaria *Walhalla's Genossen, geschildert durch König Ludwig den Ersten von Bayern, dem Gründer der Walhalla*, Munich, 1842

Stoltz, Ruprecht *Die Walhalla. Ein Beitrag zum Denkmalgedanken in 19. Jh.*, diss. Cologne, 1977

Traeger, Jörg, ed. *Die Walhalla, Idee, Architektur, Landschaft*, Regensburg, 1980

WEIMAR

Doebber, Adolph 'Das Schloss in Weimar. Seine Geschichte vom Brande 1774 bis zur Wiederherstellung 1804', in *Zeitschrift des Vereins für Thüringische Geschichte* (3rd paper), Jena, 1911

– 'Schinkel in Weimar', in *Jahrbuch der Goethe-Gesellschaft*, Vol. 10, 1924, p. 103–130

Piana, Theo *Weimar. Stätte lebendiger Tradition*, Berlin and Weimar, 1969

Jericke, Alfred and Dolgner, Dieter *Der Klassizismus in der Baugeschichte Weimars*, Weimar, 1975

WIESBADEN

Schaller, C. *Flüchtige Bemerkungen auf einer Reise von Nürnberg über Würzburg, Frankfurt, Mainz und Koblenz . . . im Jahre 1825*, Nuremburg, 1826

Zimmermann, J.P. *Wiesbaden mit seinen Ungebungen*, Wiesbaden, 1826

Spielmann, C. *Das Kurhaus zu Wiesbaden 1808–1904*, Wiesbaden, 1904

Luthmer, Ferdinand, ed. *Die Bau- und Kunstdenkmäler der Kreise Unter-Westerwald . . . und Wiesbaden Stadt und Land*, Frankfurt, 1914

Henrichsen, Hermann *Der Klassizismus der Stadt Wiesbaden in seiner städtebaulichen Entwicklung und seinen wesentlichen Bauwerken*, diss., Darmstadt, 1925

Hildner, Heinz *Wiesbadener Wohnbauten der klassizistischen Zeit*, Wiesbaden, 1931

Weiler, Clemens 'Romantische Baukunst in Nassau', in *Nassauische Annalen*, LXIII, 1952

Fink, Otto E. *Wiesbaden – so wie es war*, Düsseldorf, 1976

Kleineberg, Günther 'Morgensterns und Bleulers Ansichten vom "Cur-Saal",' in *Wiesbadener Leben*, May 1978

– 'Wiesbaden in Ansichten des 19. Jahrhunderts', in *Fünfzehn historische Wiesbadener Stadtansichten*, Mainz, 1978

– 'Der "Cur-Saal" zu Wiesbaden und sein Publikum (1810–1904); in *Hessische Heimat* Vol 34 (Heft 2/3) 1984, p. 61-66

Volmer, Eva Christina *Das Schloss in Wiesbaden*, Wiesbaden, 1983

WORLITZ

Lein, Kurt *Führer durch den Landschaftspark Wörlitz. Geschichte und Beschreibung*, ed. Staatliche Schlösser und Gärten Wörlitz, Oranienbaum und Luisium.

Rode, August v. *Das Gothische Haus zu Wörlitz nebst anderen Ergänzungen der Beschreibung des Herzoglichen Landhauses und Gartens zu Wörlitz*, Dessau, 1818

WÜPPERTALL see ELBERFELD

WURZBURG

Miller, Albrecht *Die Residenz in Würzburg*, Königsstein-in-Taunus, n.d.

Sedlmaier, Richard and Pfister, Rudolf *Die fürst-bischöfliche Residenz zu Würzburg*, Munich, 1923

Feulner, a. 'Die Toskana Zimmer der Würzburger Residenz', in *Zeitschrift für Kunstgeschichte*, III, 1934

Helmrich, I. 'Die Toskanazimmer der Würzburger Residenz', in *Klassizismus in Bayern, Schwaben und Franken. Architekturzeichnungen 1775–1825*, exh. cat., Munich, 1980

Nerdinger, W. 'Gerichtsdiener-Wohnhaus Turmgasse 9 in Würzburg', and 'Das Wachthaus am Zeller Tor in Würzburg', in *Klassizismus in Bayern*, cit.

Roda, Burkard von *Adam Friedrich von Seinsheim, Auftraggeber zwischen Rokoko und Klassizismus (Quellen und Darstellungen zur fränkischen Kunstgeschichte, VI)*, Neustadt/Aisch, 1980

Bachmann, Erich, ed. *Residenz Würzburg und Hofgarten*, 6th edn, Munich, 1981

Photographic Acknowledgments

Architektursammlung der Technischen Universität, München: 115, 126
Bayerische Verwaltung der staatlichen Schlösser, Gärten und Seen Museumabteilung: V
Bildarchiv Foto Marburg 2, 3, 4, 5, 6, 7, 8, 9, 10, 11, 12, 14, 16, 17, 18, 19, 20, 21, 22, 23, 28, 29, 30, 31, 32, 33, 34, 35, 37, 38, 40, 41, 42, 43, 45, 47, 55, 56, 63, 72, 73, 75, 76, 77, 79, 80, 82, 87, 88, 89, 97, 100, 101, 105, 113, 123, 124, 131, 143, 152, 153, 154, 156, 157, 158, 159, 163, 164, 165, 167, 168, 185, 186, 204, 207, 209, 210, 211, 212, 213, 215, 216, 217, 224, 225, 226, 238, 242, 243, 244, 245, 246, 247, 252
Deutscher Kunstverlag, München: 132
Foto Wolf, Koblenz: 220, 221
Gemälde und Skulpturenphotographie Jörg P. Anders: I
A.F. Kersting: 117, 118, 122
Landesamt für Denkmalpflege Schleswig-Holstein: 112
Landesbildstelle Baden: 134, 135, 136, 137, 138, 139, 140, 141, 160, 200, 201, 202, 203, 204, 205, 206
Landesbildstelle Berlin: 13, 54, 67, 78, 85
Landesbildstelle Rheinland: 91, 92, 93, 94, 163, 185, 188, 189, 190, 191, 222, 223
Landesbildstelle Württemberg: 24, 44, 58, 59, 60, 61, 148, 149, 150, 151, 226, 227, 228, 229, 230, 231, 232, 233, 234, 235, 236, 237, 241, 242
Emily Lane: IX, 129
Museum für Hamburgische Geschichte: 107
Niedersächsisches Landesverwaltungsamt: 39, 61, 62, 95, 96, 98, 99, 166, 170, 171, 172, 173, 174, 175, 176, 177, 192, 193, 194, 195, 196, 197, 198
A. Oncken: 53, 83
Rheinisches Bildarchiv: 90, 178, 179, 180, 181, 248, 251
Schinkel Museum, Nationalgalerie Berlin: II, 65, 68
Staatliche Graphische Sammlung, München: 1, 114, 116, 130, VIII
Staatliche Landesbildstelle Hamburg: 102, 103, 104, 106, 108, 109, 110, 111
Staatliche Landesbildstelle Hessen: 133, 142, 144, 182
Stadtmuseum München: VI
Dr. Franz Stoedtner: 70, 71, 121, 127

Index of Places

Numbers in italic refer to illustrations, Roman numbers to colour plates.

Index of People